Straight and devious
pathways from
childhood to adulthood

Straight and devious pathways from childhood to adulthood

Edited by
LEE N. ROBINS
Washington University School of Medicine

and

MICHAEL RUTTER
MRC Child Psychiatry Unit
Institute of Psychiatry, London

CAMBRIDGE
UNIVERSITY PRESS

Published by the Press Syndicate of the University of Cambridge
The Pitt Building, Trumpington Street, Cambridge CB2 1RP
40 West 20th Street, New York, NY 10011-4211, USA
10 Stamford Road, Oakleigh, Melbourne 3166, Australia

© Cambridge University Press 1990

First published 1990
First paperback edition 1991
Reprinted 1993, 1995

Printed in the United States of America

Library of Congress Cataloging-in-Publication Data is available.

A catalogue record for this book is available from the British Library.

ISBN 0-521-36408-6 hardback
ISBN 0-521-42739-8 paperback

Contents

Contributors

Anne S. Bassett, M.D.
*Queen Street Mental
  Health Centre
Toronto, Ontario*

Nazli Baydar, Ph.D.
*Department of Psychiatry
Columbia University*

Peter M. Bentler, Ph.D.
*Department of Psychology
University of California,
  Los Angeles*

L.R. Bergman, Ph.D.
*Department of Psychology
University of Stockholm*

Judith S. Brook, Ed.D.
*Department of Psychiatry
Mt. Sinai School of Medicine,
  New York*

Remi J. Cadoret, M.D.
*Department of Psychiatry
University of Iowa*

Tyrone D. Cannon, M.A.
*Social Science Research Institute
University of Southern California*

Avshalom Caspi, Ph.D.
*Department of Psychology
University of Wisconsin, Madison*

Stella Chess, M.D.
*Department of Psychiatry
New York University School of
  Medicine*

Jacob Cohen, Ph.D.
*Department of Psychology
New York University*

Patricia Cohen, Ph.D.
*School of Public Health
Department of Epidemiology
Columbia University
New York State Psychiatric Institute*

Barbara A. Cornblatt, Ph.D.
*Department of Medical Genetics
New York State Psychiatric Institute*

Mark Davies, M.P.H.
*Department of Psychiatry
College of Physicians & Surgeons
Columbia University
New York State Psychiatric Institute*

Glen H. Elder Jr., Ph.D.
*Department of Sociology
University of North Carolina,
  Chapel Hill*

L. Erlenmeyer–Kimling, Ph.D.
*Department of Medical Genetics
New York State Psychiatric Institute*

David P. Farrington, Ph.D.
*Institute of Criminology
University of Cambridge*

Marc Garcia, M.S.
New York State Psychiatric Institute

Tina Louise Giampino, B.A.
*Children's Behavior Disorder Clinic
Research Department
Long Island Jewish Medical Center
Department of Clinical Psychology
New York State Psychiatric Institute*

Madelyn S. Gould, Ph.D., M.P.H.
*Department of Psychiatry
School of Public Health
College of Physicians & Surgeons
Columbia University
New York State Psychiatric Institute*

Lesley Gulliver, B.A.
MRC Child Psychiatry Unit
Institute of Psychiatry, London

Ellen S. Herbener, Ph.D. candidate
Department of Psychology
Harvard University

Jonathan Hill, M.D.
University Department of
  Psychiatry
Child and Adolescent
  Psychiatry and Psychology
Royal Liverpool Children's
  Hospital

Ulla Hilldoff-Adamo, M.A.
Department of Medical Genetics
New York State Psychiatric
  Institute

Merja Kaleva, M.D.
Department of Psychiatry
University of Oulu, Finland

Denise Kandel, Ph.D.
Department of Psychiatry
Columbia University

Rachel Gittelman Klein, Ph.D.
Children's Behavior Disorders Clinic
Research Department
Long Island Jewish Medical Center
Department of Clinical Psychology
New York State Psychiatric
  Institute

Paula Horowitz Konig, B.A.
Children's Behavior Disorders Clinic
Research Department
Long Island Jewish Medical Canter
Department of Clinical Psychology
New York State Psychiatric Institute

Ilpo Lahti, M.D.
Turku, Finland

Marc LeBlanc, Ph.D.
School of Psycho-Education
University of Montreal

Rolf Loeber, Ph.D.
Western Psychiatric Institute
  and Clinic
School of Medicine
University of Pittsburgh

David Magnusson, Ph.D.
Department of Psychology
University of Stockholm

Salvatore Mannuzza, Ph.D.
Children's Behavior Disorders Clinic
Research Department
Long Island Jewish Medical Center
Department of Clinical Psychology
New York State Psychiatric Institute

Barbara Maughan, M.S.
MRC Child Psychiatry Unit
Institute of Psychiatry, London

Joan McCord, Ph.D.
Department of Criminal Justice
Temple University

Lawrence McEvoy, B.A.
Department of Psychiatry
Washington University Medical School

Sarnoff A. Mednick, Ph.D.
Social Science Research Institute
University of Southern California

Linda Moreno Merchant, M.D.
Department of Psychiatry
University of Iowa

Steven O. Moldin, Ph.D.
Department of Psychiatry
Washington University
Jewish Hospital of St. Louis

Juha Moring, M.D.
Department of Psychiatry
University of Oulu, Finland

Mikko Naarala, M.D.
Department of Psychiatry
University of Oulu, Finland

Michael D. Newcomb, Ph.D.
Department of Counseling
University of Southern California

Josef Parnas , M.D.
Psychology Institute
Department of Psychiatry
Kommunehospitalet, Copenhagen

Andrew Pickles, Ph.D.
MRC Child Psychiatry Unit
Institute of Psychiatry, London

David Quinton, Ph.D.
MRC Child Psychiatry Unit
Institute of Psychiatry, London

Simone Roberts, B.S.
Department of Medical Genetics
New York State Psychiatric
Institute

Lee N. Robins, Ph.D.
Department of Psychiatry
Washington University Medical School

Bryan Rodgers, M.A., M.S.
MRC National Survey of Health and
Development
University College London and
The Middlesex Hospital Medical
School
Department of Community Medicine

Michael Rutter, M.D., F.R.S.
MRC Child Psychiatry Unit
Institute of Psychiatry, London

David Shaffer, M.D.
Department of Psychiatry
College of Physicians & Surgeons
Columbia University
New York State Psychiatric Institute

Anneli Sorri, M.D.
Department of Psychiatry
University of Oulu, Finland

Alexander Thomas, M.D.
Department of Psychiatry
New York University School of
Medicine

Pekka Tienari, M.D.
Department of Psychiatry
University of Oulu, Finland

Edward Troughton, B.A.
Department of Psychiatry
University of Iowa

Welmoet B. Van Kammen, Ph.D.
Western Psychiatric Institute and Clinic
School of Medicine
University of Pittsburgh

C. Noemi Velez, Ph.D.
Department of Epidemiology
University of Puerto Rico

Karl-Erik Wahlberg, Ph.D.
Department of Psychiatry
University of Oulu, Finland

Allan Whitters, M.D.
Medical Director
Abbey Center
Cedar Rapids, Iowa

Lyman C. Wynne, M.D., Ph.D.
Department of Psychiatry
University of Rochester
School of Medicine

Introduction

This volume is a series of chapters largely based on invited papers presented at the Life History Research Society in October 1987. This Society has as its theme longitudinal studies in psychopathology. The current volume centers on particularly long-term studies of this kind, those that begin in childhood and end in adulthood. The theme of the book is both continuities and discontinuities. The goal of these papers is not merely to note the frequency with which childhood factors predict adult outcomes, but to observe under what conditions the predicted links occur, and what prevents them from occurring. In addition, these papers ask how consistent is the pathway between childhood and adult life: Is it straight and narrow, or full of detours and unexpected reversals? Appearing in this volume are the initiators and torchbearers of many distinguished studies. Their results are exceptionally consistent, replicating across time and nations despite their use of varied methodologies. These leaders have been creative in answering increasingly difficult questions by inventing and borrowing new methodologies with which to answer them.

Longitudinal studies that begin with children and follow them into adult life have had two major thrusts: to learn whether personality traits have long-term stability and to identify early predictors of adverse outcomes. Deciding whether personality traits are stable has been problematic, because the same trait may be expressed differently at different ages. Nor does continuity of behavior necessarily mean continuity of personality traits, because the meaning of a behavior varies with age.

On the other hand, the second goal, finding predictors in childhood of adult outcomes, has been clearly met for one set of adult problems. A syndrome of adverse outcomes, including crime, low occupational achievement, substance abuse, and marital instability, is clearly predicted by a child's antisocial, noncooperative, or confrontive behavior combined with pathology in the family of rearing, as indicated by parents' psychiatric illness, crime, and violent or erratic child-rearing practices. Childhood behavior problems are virtually necessary to the display in adulthood of a general failure to conform to adult norms, although on rare occasions no warning signs appear until middle or late adolescence. The role of the family pathology in adult nonconformity is almost as clear. In the current volume, Cohen and co-workers in a new study allow family characteristics to compete with peer relationships and neighborhood quality in predicting adult nonconformity, and they reaffirm the family as the dominant contributor. However, they suggest that substance abuse may not be simply a part of the predicted adult constellation, since its occurrence is much more dependent on neighborhood characteristics. The neighborhood lived in presumably determines how readily drugs are available. Newcomb and Bentler support substance abuse as a syndrome separable from other types of nonconformity by showing that earlier drug history is the best childhood predictor of later drug use. They also show that substance abuse is itself a true syndrome, because it is not easy to distinguish predictors of use of specific substances such as cocaine from predictors of use of other drugs.

Each study that has shown the virtual necessity of childhood behavior problems to adult nonconformity has also recognized that behavior problems are by no means sufficient to create this outcome. Recovery from behavior problems before reaching adulthood is common. Many difficult children become less difficult with age, and a minority of very difficult children become apparently normal adults. The natural histories of children who turn out to be normal adults despite the serious behavioral problems that generally predict adult difficulty are of great interest because they may reveal environmental interventions or concurrent personality traits and skills that seem to counterbalance the bad prognosis associated with this behavior. If such benevolent environments can be intentionally created for youngsters who would not encounter them naturally and if protective traits and skills can be taught or cultivated, they could constitute the basis for interventions particularly likely to succeed. Environments that have been implicated in increasing the risk of nonconformity in adulthood for antisocial children are broken homes, institutionalization, bad neighborhoods, deviant peers, and easy availability of psychoactive substances.

Trying to separate behavior-disordered children into those who will and those who will not recover has proved difficult. Authors of several chapters in this volume are looking for combinations of childhood behaviors and family characteristics that together greatly increase the risk. They also seek elements of the typical childhood configuration of predictors that are essential to continuity into adulthood, so that their absence would vitiate the predictive powers of others. Magnusson and Bergman find that aggression does not predict alcoholism or crime in adult life unless it appears as part of a syndrome of severe behavior problems. Robins finds that conduct problems are virtually necessary for the development of substance abuse, but that risks are greatly increased when the child with conduct disorder is exposed to alcohol or drugs before the age of 15, and greatly decreased when exposure is deferred past age 18. McCord shows that broken homes predict crime only when the parents are incompetent or the father is alcoholic or criminal. These studies also consider the possibility that *adult* events may be necessary to the continuity of adversity from childhood. Rutter, Quinton, and Hill find that lack of a good marriage may be an essential factor for the adverse effects of institutional rearing and childhood behavior problems to continue into adulthood. Marriage, like choice of friends, is a problematic variable, because wisdom in selecting a mate may show that a shift from a deviant pathway has already occurred. Kandel, Davies, and Baydar discuss the difficulty of assigning causal power to friendships and matings. They believe that the best model is a reciprocal one; like chooses like, and the pair become even more alike on the basis of their association. But the tendency to choose someone like oneself (homophily) seems itself to be a personal predisposition that varies across individuals. Lack of homophily may be protective for a youngster with behavior problems.

The predictive power of childhood problems other than antisocial and confrontive behavior for adult life has not been as well substantiated. Some of the childhood behaviors that have been investigated are strongly correlated with conduct problems, for example, attention deficit, hyperactivity, substance abuse, and temper tantrums. For those behaviors, it is difficult to know whether they are themselves predictive, independent of the accompanying conduct problems. Two chapters, one by Mannuzza and co-workers and the other by Farrington and coworkers, address this problem by looking separately at hyperactive children with and without conduct problems to decide whether hyperactivity itself has predictive power. Their results seem to suggest that hyperactivity is a form of the broader spectrum of behavior problems, because hyperactive children without conduct problems have adult problems of the same type as do antisocial children. Indeed, Mannuzza and co-workers report no differences in diagnostic outcome whether antisocial behavior is absent or present. Farrington, Loeber, and van Kammen similarly find hyperactivity predicts crime in the absence of conduct problems, but also point to its unique effect on the timing of criminal offenses. Since hyperactivity begins very early in childhood, it may not be surprising that it is associated with particularly early convictions. Caspi, Elder, and Herbener's look at the consequences of temper tantrums suggests that they also belong to the conduct problem syndrome. Children who had temper tantrums between ages 8 and 10 grew up to have poor achievement educationally, in the military, and in jobs, similar to children with more serious behavior problems.

For the purely emotional difficulties of childhood, studies of their predictive power have been uncertain or even negative. In the 1950s a remarkable follow-up of patients of a children's clinic thought to be at risk of schizophrenia because of excessive shyness found no such connection, but it did find continuity in their shyness: they became psychiatrically normal but shy adults (Michael, Morris, Soroker, 1957). Since then, there has been considerable argument about whether over-inhibited, worrying, nervous children have only transient problems limited to childhood, or whether they have the beginnings of a long-term deficit that has not been clearly described. More definitive results are now possible because of the availability of very large epidemiological studies, such as that reported by Rodgers. Interestingly he has shown that adult stressors must occur in order for childhood neurotic symptoms to be associated with an excess of adult psychiatric symptoms. This suggests that one of the reasons for variable results in past studies is that they ignored effects of the current environment on the expression of a "neurotic" predisposition dating from childhood. Or, the error may have been their treatment of emotional problems of childhood as a single syndrome. Caspi, Elder, and Herbener find that shyness and over-dependence in childhood have quite different adult consequences, the first negative and the second positive. Previous studies may have compared samples containing different mixes of more than one syndrome, thus yielding inconsistent results. Quinton, Rutter, and Gulliver, following children of psychiatric patients, found that those with emotional problems had as high a level of continuity into adulthood as did those with childhood conduct problems. And, as had been found for adult nonconformity, they found a virtual absence of adult problems in those offspring with no serious problems in childhood or adolescence.

The view that all human behavioral problems require both a genetic liability and an environmental trigger is as well accepted nowadays as the finding that adult antisocial behavior virtually requires a history of child behavior problems and poor parenting. But it was not long ago when there were violent battles between the hereditarians and the environmentalists. Adoption studies were designed to discriminate the genetic from the environmental contributions of the family. Since the offspring followed as adults had not been in contact with their biological parents since birth, the biological parents contributed only a genetic liability. When the children were found to have an increased risk for the biological parents' disorders while adopted children of unaffected parents did not, the role of a genetic factor was confirmed. But modern adoption studies like those of Tienari et al. and Cadoret et al. have contributed to a reconciliation of the genetic and environmental views by showing that whether or not the parents' disorder is actually expressed in their offspring depends both on the early experiences associated with the adoption process itself (length of initial institutionalization or placement in foster care and age at adoption) and the quality of the adoptive home. Mednick and coworkers played a vital role in fostering the study of environmental factors within the high-risk design, in which

children presumed at genetic risk because of having affected parents were studied over time. They studied intrauterine and perinatal trauma as environmental factors that influenced both whether the parental illness would be expressed, and how. Cannon, Mednick, and Parnas propose that perinatal insult is detectable in tests of psychophysiological responsiveness. The tests plus teacher observations predict the form in which the offspring of schizophrenics will express the disorder, with predominantly negative or predominantly positive symptoms.

Most of these long-term studies have spent much effort on discriminating which forms of the child's behavior are predictive. Yet Erlenmeyer-Kimling and co-workers, using the high-risk design, find considerable overlap in outcomes for children of parents with schizophrenia and major affective disorders. Further, adjustment during follow-up is not continuous. One can infer from their results that cross-sectional follow-ups would greatly underestimate the number of offspring who will develop a disorder, since many of those well at the time of follow-up will have had previous episodes of poor adjustment. Maughan and Pickles have similar results when investigating the outcome of adopted illegitimate children compared with a control group of legitimate children. The adoptees' disadvantage was most marked at age 11; thereafter, they began more closely to resemble the legitimate control group.

All of these studies contrast status in childhood with adult status. In some cases, this is done through prospective follow-ups, beginning with evaluations in childhood and later reassessing the same subjects as adults, with varying frequency of assessments in the interval between. Prospective studies linking childhood to adulthood can take a very long time. Some studies in this book were begun by their authors when they were very young, and it is a tribute to their perseverance and to the prescience of their original design for data collection that their studies are still ongoing and are useful for answering the more complex questions that are now being put to them. Investigators Chess and Thomas recognized the potential of longitudinal studies for answering questions about the interactions of predisposition and environment from the very beginning. They were among the first to argue that personality is a product of both what one is born with and how one's parents react to that initial package, a viewpoint that few would disagree with now but that was somewhat heretical when they began their study more than 30 years ago. Their long case histories based on multiple observation points demonstrate how insight into predispositions detectable in early childhood can help adults manage their lives successfully, particularly if they were reared in supportive and understanding families.

Authors who did not undertake follow-up studies early in their own careers have been able to accomplish long-term follow-ups by inheriting populations of children assembled by their seniors, and they have added the

dedication needed to keep the follow-up going into their subjects' early and middle adulthood, often well beyond the period when their originators expected the study to terminate. Joan McCord, for example, has so fostered the Cambridge-Somerville study that her name is now better known in connection with it than are the names of Witmer and Powers, who first wrote about its results. Similarly, Glen Elder inherited the Berkeley Guidance Study and has made it his own; he has now found a third generation to take it over in Avshalom Caspi. Elder, like Farrington, who inherited West's study of 8-year-old boys in working-class London, has enriched the original design as well as extended its duration. Heirs of exceptionally large samples include Bryan Rodgers, a third-generation investigator after James Douglas and Michael Wadsworth, and Barbara Maughan, who inherited work from Butler and others. They are following two of Britain's three mammoth birth cohorts of children born in a single week 12 years apart. Neither study began with a primarily psychological focus; yet both authors have carved studies of psychological and behavioral problems from them.

An alternative to inheritance as a way to conduct a child-to-adult longitudinal study is to build a longitudinal extension onto a platform of existing old administrative records (as have Rutter, et al., LeBlanc, Cadoret, et al. and Tienari et al.) or onto old protocols of cross-sectional or short-term longitudinal research (Cohen et al., Quinton et al.). The old records serve as the initial assessment, allowing the researcher to begin his or her work after the subjects are already adult, thus saving the long wait. A judicious selection of record sources is needed to acquire systematically collected childhood data that cover the vital predictors of outcome. One report (Robins and McEvoy) in the current volume has trusted the recall of childhood behavior by adults, thus making a cross-sectional study serve to connect child and adult measures in lieu of long-term follow-up. Trusting recall is a dangerous enterprise, since it will be imperfect and, more seriously, may be biased by the subsequent adult history. However, the topics covered in their report—childhood behavior problems and substance use and abuse—are ones that have been extensively tested for reliability, and recall for them has been found to remain surprisingly intact over time.

A few studies reported here took none of these short-cuts (Magnusson and Bergman, Chess and Thomas, Erlenmeyer-Kimling et al., Cannon et al., Mannuzza et al., Kandel et al., Newcomb and Bentler), but the investigators began the studies themselves and continue to follow the subjects over time. When these initiators are still reasonably young, their studies can qualify for inclusion in a volume linking child to adult statuses only if the subjects are children in or near adolescence, so that the interval from childhood to early adulthood is brief. And even so we must admit to an occasional stretching of the definition of adult to include papers by authors who have developed

powerful tools for studying predictors of change over time (a troublesome analytic problem still), tools that will be of great use to their colleagues struggling to disentangle risk from protective factors. Perhaps it is just as well to have a few results for adolescents as well as adults, since Gould, Shaffer, and Davies point to adolescent death as a factor that will limit the proportion of initial samples who will survive to be followed as adults. They show that suicides increase with each year of life, and particularly diminish samples of antisocial and substance-abusing white males.

Lee Robins, Ph.D.
Michael Rutter, M.D.

Reference

Michael, C.M., Morris, D.P., & Soroker, E. (1957). Follow-up studies of shy, withdrawn children. II: Relative incidents of schizophrenia. *The American Journal of Orthopsychiatry, 27,* 331–337.

**Straight and devious
pathways from
childhood to adulthood**

I   Survival to follow-up

1 Truncated pathways from childhood to adulthood: Attrition in follow-up studies due to death

MADELYN S. GOULD, DAVID SHAFFER, AND MARK DAVIES

Most of the studies in the current volume concern transitions from adolescence to adulthood. One of the major problems for such longitudinal studies is attrition due to failure to recover a large proportion of the sample. Attrition may be differentially related to exposure and outcome status and can produce biases in the estimates of measures of association (Kelsey et al., 1986). Researchers, therefore, spend tremendous energy in urging respondents to remain in the study.

Longitudinal investigations have employed a number of procedures to stem losses due to the well-recognized problems of high family mobility and lack of continuing interest by study participants. At the initial assessment, study participants are usually asked to provide the name and address of an individual who would be likely to know the participant's whereabouts in case of a change of address. If the study participant cannot be located at follow-up, then an informant can be contacted. Other means of tracing participants have been through state departments of motor vehicles. Information on recent changes of address can be requested of the postal service. Birth records, social security numbers, and credit bureaus have been employed for linkage for longitudinal research. Interim newsletters and other correspondence are sent to keep the participants engaged and interested, and monetary reimbursements have often been a means for increasing compliance.

But one source of loss which cannot be avoided no matter how ingenious the researcher is death. This problem is relatively small if the time span of the study is adolescence to young adulthood, because this is a period during which natural deaths are very uncommon. Nonetheless, there are adolescents who will not survive until follow-up assessment, even if the interval is only 10 years or so. It is useful to know the likelihood and causes of death among adolescents in order to estimate what proportion of a childhood sample can be expected to be available for follow-up as adults and how representative the survivors will be of the original population. The use of a case-control design to make these estimates and to identify these risk factors is the focus of the present paper. We will look at the frequency of

3

truncated pathways from childhood to adulthood, their causes, and, while focusing on death by suicide, we will consider what parts of a sample are most at risk of mortality before follow-up.

Prevalence of adolescent death

The death rate from all causes in youths ages 15 to 24 was 96.8 per 100,000 in 1984. For white males in this age range it was 138.8 and for black males in this age range it was 163.9 per 100,000 (National Center for Health Statistics, 1986). In other words, in any group of 1,000 young people, one individual would be expected to die within the year. Therefore, in a 10-year follow-up from ages 15 to 25, 1% of the sample is likely to be lost by death. Among black males, the expected death rate would be closer to 2%.

Accidents, suicide, and homicide are the three leading causes of death among youths ages 15 to 24 in the United States. There is a differential ranking of these causes of death for white and black youth. Motor vehicle accidents are the leading cause of death among white males (59.1 deaths per 100,000), followed by suicide (22.0 per 100,000) and homicide (11.1 per 100,000). Whereas, homicide is the most common cause of death among black males (61.5 per 100,000), followed by motor vehicle accidents (31.9 per 100,000) and suicide (11.2 per 100,000) (National Center for Health Statistics 1986).

Estimation of risk rates for adolescent death

In predicting availability to follow-up it is possible to take into account predictors of adolescent and young adult death other than the race and sex categories provided routinely on death certificates. Two basic longitudinal strategies can be used to explore the correlates of specific causes of mortality: the follow-up of a general population or of a high-risk population. Longitudinal designs have the advantage over case-control studies of sound baseline information, and they permit direct calculation of the magnitude of outcomes for persons with and without hypothesized risk factors. One way of expressing this excess is the *relative risk*, the ratio of the incidence rate of those with the risk factor to the incidence rate of those without the risk factor (Mausner & Bahn, 1974).

However, when an outcome is as rare as is adolescent death, the sample size needed from the general population to yield enough cases to be useful is daunting. Instead, samples stratified to overrepresent high-risk groups would be a recommended strategy if the risk factors had been previously identified; however, when the risk factors are not known ahead of time, stratification may not improve the rate of outcomes of interest. In this situation, a case-control study is preferable, because it allows exploring a wide variety of possible risk factors.

In a case-control study, the proportion of cases and controls with the risk factor can be readily estimated and employed to estimate the relative risk in the population if (1) the outcome is rare, (2) the cases are representative of all cases, and (3) the controls are representative of the general population. If these assumptions are satisfied, the *odds ratio* is a good estimate of the relative risk (Mausner & Bahn, 1974). In addition to the relative risk, one would like to be able to estimate what proportion of people in the population with a particular pattern of risk factors will die per year. For this, one needs to know the risk of death in the total population and the proportion of the population with the risk factor, as well as the association between the risk factor and death. The overall incidence of deaths is available in published death statistics, and rates of specific risk factors can be estimated from the control group if the controls are "general population" controls, rather than being matched to the cases on variables that are correlated with the risk. The odds ratio provides the needed measure of the association between the risk factors and death.

Suicide research as an illustration

Our ongoing case-control study of youth suicide can both illustrate how deaths and risk factors can be estimated, and provide information on the risk factors for adolescent suicide.

This case-control study was designed to obtain a detailed psychiatric profile of a consecutive series of completed adolescent suicides through the use of the psychological autopsy technique. The term *psychological autopsy* was coined to describe a procedure that involves "reconstruction of the life-style and circumstances of the victim, together with details of behaviors and events that led to the deaths of that individual" (Farberow & Neuringer, 1971). The psychological autopsy method is a retrospective inquiry from a surviving informant(s) or from contemporary records. It has the potential for obtaining representative, albeit incomplete, information. Psychological autopsy studies of consecutive reported suicides within a predefined geographical area can be assumed to be representative because suicides are subject to reporting requirements, and there is no evidence to suggest that suicides missed are themselves so unrepresentative as to make the identified remainder unrepresentative (Shaffer & Fisher, 1981). The psychological autopsy is an inherently incomplete method because inquiries about the victim's state of mind or early experiences will be confined to the knowledge of the informant(s) and what is in records. Record studies always raise questions about whether missing information is truly absent or simply not noted. Despite these limitations, the psychological autopsy is a useful approach to studying causes of suicide because it covers a more representative sample than do follow-up studies of such rare events, which are necessarily confined to studies of high-risk groups (Shaffer et al., 1988). In addition, prospective studies will not have collected data close to the time of the suicide, so that immediate provoking events will be missed.

Compilation of risk factors. Our current study conducts psychological autopsies of a consecutive series of 173 suicides by persons under age 20 within a 2-year period in the New York/Tri-State metropolitan region, including New York City and 28 surrounding counties. This design is likely to yield representative cases of suicide, a necessity for estimating relative risks. The study includes two control groups: an age-, ethnic-, and sex-matched comparison group of suicide attempters identified from a wide variety of different hospitals within the region, and a stratified random sample of young people of the study region, stratified on the sex, age, and ethnic distribution of the completed suicide cases. This second control group is representative of the population that is demographically similar to the suicide completers; however, it is not representative of the general population in the age range studied because, given the sex, age, and ethnic distribution of suicide completers, the sample overrepresents older ages, whites, and males. However, by weighting cases to make these demographic characteristics like those of the total youth population in this area, the normal controls can provide estimates of the prevalence of risk factors in the general population.

The fact that age, sex, and race distributions of the suicides are not the same as for the general population shows that age, sex, and race are important risk factors for suicide. The fact that suicides are concentrated in older teenagers means that in a follow-up study beginning with adolescents, the risk will not be evenly distributed over the follow-up period, but rather will increase with each additional year of follow-up. Indeed, suicide is extremely rare before age 12. Because suicide is about four times as common in adolescent boys as girls, and rare in blacks as compared with whites, death will lead to more attrition in follow-up studies that have predominantly white male samples.

In addition to these demographic risk factors ascertainable from death records, preliminary data based on 114 "psychological autopsies" reveal the following:

> Approximately a quarter of the victims had made a previous suicide attempt, and more girls than boys had a history of previous attempts.
> Approximately half of the suicide completers had previously consulted a mental health professional. This is in line with studies in the United States that were not restricted to adolescents and to those in other countries (Robins et al., 1959; Barraclough et al., 1974; Shaffer, 1974).

Symptoms of major depressive disorder were found in approximately a quarter of the youngsters, a much lower rate than among suicides from the full age range.

A history of aggressive and antisocial behavior was present in just under half of the victims, a much higher rate than in studies of the full age range.

Drug and alcohol abuse alone or in combination with depression or antisocial behavior were found in approximately a third of the suicide completers, about the same as for adult suicides.

Uncomplicated depression without associated behavior problems was found predominantly among girls. However, unlike adults, manic-depressive disorder and schizophrenic psychosis accounted for only a small proportion of teenage suicides, although Brent et al. (1988) and Shaffi et al. (1985) found that bipolar symptoms were common in the suicide victims they studied.

Over a third of the suicide completers had a first- or second-degree relative who had previously attempted or committed suicide.

Computation of odds ratios. Once these associations with risk factors are determined in a case-control study, odds ratios can be computed, from which relative risks in the population are estimated. In our study, the odds ratio for committing suicide for boys with a previous suicide attempt is 22.5. This odds ratio was calculated on the basis of the proportion of the boys in the general population control group with a history of a previous suicide attempt (i.e., exposed). From death records, it is known that the annual mortality rate from suicide among boys ages 15 to 19 is approximately 15 per 100,000. These data allow estimating the incidence among non-attempters as follows:

$$\frac{15 \text{ per } 100,000}{[(.012) \times (22.5)] + (.988)} = 11.9 \text{ per } 100,000 \text{ per year for non-attempters}$$

The estimate of the suicide rate among boys with a history of previous suicide attempts is then $(11.9) \times (22.5)$ or 268 per 100,000. If a longitudinal study is made of a group likely to contain a large number of suicide attempters (e.g., a follow-up of drug abusers), deaths from suicide by follow-up can be expected to be over 2%, since the group will be largely male, will be aging, and will contain many attempters.

Applying these procedures to additional risk factors yields the following estimated risks of suicide: 40/100,000 and 8/100,000 for boys and girls with antisocial behavior, respectively; 70/100,000 and 3/100,000 for boys and girls abusing drugs and/or alcohol; 100/100,000 and 80/100,000 for boys and girls with a major depressive disorder; 270/100,000 and 20/100,000 for boys and girls who have made a previous suicide attempt; and 35/100,000 and 6/100,000 for boys and girls with family members who have either committed or attempted suicide (Table 1). Because only preliminary data are

Table 1. *Risk factors for suicide in teenagers*

Risk factor	Normals	Suicides	Approximate odds ratio	Approximate suicide rate/100,000
		Males		
	(N = 65)	(N = 97)		
Prior attempt	1.2%	21%	22.5	270
Major depression	2%	21%	8.6	100
Substance abuse	7%	37%	7.1	70
Antisocial behavior	17%	67%	4.4	40
Family history of suicide or attempt	17%	41%	3.0	35
(General population)				15
		Females		
	(N = 20)	(N = 17)		
Prior attempt	6%	33%	8.6	20
Major depression	2%	50%	49.0	80
Substance abuse	7%	5%	0.8	3
Antisocial behavior	12%	30%	3.2	8
Family history of suicide or attempt	13%	33%	2.7	6
(General population)				3.3

currently available, these estimates are not precise. Moreover, the prevalence of risk factors in the control group is unweighted and, therefore, relative risks are probably underestimated as compared with results after weighting to account for stratification by age and race. Although the presence of multiple risk factors undoubtedly increases the risk of suicide, estimates for samples with multiple risks are not simple sums of risk rates, because these risk factors tend to be intercorrelated. So far only univariate analyses have been conducted with these data; multivariate analyses will show how powerful combinations of risk factors are. Nevertheless, the estimates have provided an approximate relative ranking of potential high-risk groups for suicide.

Conclusion

Case-control studies are useful for estimating expected attrition in longitudinal studies due to death, incarceration, and other relatively rare events that are difficult to study prospectively. They can provide annual risks by age group, making it possible to estimate risks for various lengths of follow-up with cohorts of varying ages. In our study, it appears that previous suicide attempts, depression, substance abuse, antisocial behavior, and suicidal behavior in the family increase the likelihood of suicide among teenagers.

Some of the samples that are the focus of longitudinal investigations presented in other chapters in this volume have high rates of these risk factors and, therefore, measurable loss by suicide can be anticipated. When their samples are appropriately large and representative, these longitudinal studies can provide estimates of the incidence of risk factors by age and sex groups, which could be used to make accurate estimates of risk-specific outcomes based on case-control studies. Thus, these two study designs complement each other in providing estimates of rare outcomes that cannot otherwise be studied.

Acknowledgments

This work for this paper was partially supported by research grant # R01-MH-38198 from the National Institute of Mental Health and a Faculty Scholars Award 84-0954-84 from the William T. Grant Foundation.

References

Barraclough, B. M., Bunch, J., Nelson, B., & Sainbury, P. (1974). A hundred cases of suicide: Clinical aspects. *British Journal of Psychiatry, 125,* 355–373.

Brent, D. A., Perper, J. A., Goldstein, C. E., Kolko, D. J., Allan, M. J., Allman, C. J., & Zelenak, J. P. (1988). Risk factors for adolescent suicide: A comparison of adolescent suicide victims with suicidal inpatients. *Archives of General Psychiatry, 45,* 581–588.

Farberow, N. L., & Neuringer, C. (1971). The social scientist as coroner's deputy. *Journal of Forensic Sciences, 16,* 15–39.

Kelsey, J. L., Thompson, W. D., & Evans, A. S. (1986). *Methods in observational epidemiology.* New York: Oxford University Press.

Mausner, J. S., & Bahn, A. K. (1974). *Epidemiology: An introductory text.* Philadelphia: W. B. Saunders.

National Centre for Health Statistics (1986). *Health, United States, 1986.* DHHS Pub. No. (PHS) 87–1232. Public Health Service, December. Washington, DC: U.S. Government Printing Office.

Robins E., Gassner, S., Kayes, J., Wilkinson, R. H. Jr., & Murphy, G. E. (1959). The communication of suicide intent: A study of 134 consecutive cases of successful (completed) suicide. *American Journal of Psychiatry, 115,* 724–733.

Shaffer, D. (1974). Suicide in childhood and early adolescence. *Journal of Child Psychology and Psychiatry, 15,* 275–291.

Shaffer, D., & Fisher, P. (1981). The epidemiology of suicide in children and young adolescents. *Journal of the American Academy of Child Psychiatry, 20,* 545–565.

Shaffer, D., Garland, A., Gould, M., & Fisher, P. (1988). Preventing teenage suicide: A critical review. *Journal of the American Academy of Child and Adolescent Psychiatry, 27*(6), 671–687.

Shaffi, M., Carrigan, S., Whittinghill, J. R., & Derrick, A. (1985). Psychological autopsy of completed suicide in children and adolescents. *American Journal of Psychiatry, 142,* 1061–1064.

II Adult outcomes

2 Childhood personality and the prediction of life-course patterns

AVSHALOM CASPI, GLEN H. ELDER, JR., AND
ELLEN S. HERBENER

The central question addressed in life-span developmental research concerns the links between early behavior and circumstances of life and later behaviors. Does childhood personality anticipate the nature and course of adult development and aging? Any satisfactory answer to this question must draw on the growing body of evidence from longitudinal studies.

Most developmental research approaches the longitudinal task by focusing on regularities over time in the same characteristic (Moss & Susman, 1980). The search for homotypic continuities and phenotypic persistence has exerted a strong influence on how longitudinal researchers analyze their data and on how their critics evaluate the results. Indeed, Livson and Peskin (1980) suggest that developmental research has been fundamentally handicapped by an exclusive focus on the individual-difference stability of personality characteristics over time. The difficulty is not whether there exists a convincing body of data pointing to regularities in the persistence of specific traits, but whether it is possible to tie this evidence to any full-blown theory of personality development.

A second approach representative of much longitudinal developmental research involves the prediction of an individual's later outcome on the basis of earlier attributes (e.g., Cornblatt & Erlenmeyer-Kimling, 1984; West & Farrington, 1977). Studies of this type typically sample a broad range of childhood variables in the hopes of finding a small subset that are highly predictive of specific outcomes in later years (e.g., school drop-out, delinquency and criminality, adult psychopathology).

Other creative ways of investigating pathways from childhood to adulthood include Block's (1971) typological approach, yielding evidence for distinct personality trajectories marked by either continuity or discontinuity, and Kandel's application of event-history analysis to the description of sequential developmental patterns leading to different psychopathological syndromes (e.g., Yamaguchi & Kandel, 1984a, 1984b). Approaches of this kind have produced fresh thinking about continuity and change in life-span development.

Our research on pathways from childhood to adulthood adopts yet a

13

different approach. We focus on the coherence of interactional styles across social transformations in the age-graded life course; on how individuals meet developmental challenges, adapt to new settings, and the long-term consequences of these adaptational strategies. We have attempted to accomplish this by combining the longitudinal assessment of persons with the longitudinal assessment of situations in order to show how early personality shapes achievements and relationships in diverse circumstances at different ages. In short, we have attempted to account for individual differences in life-course patterns.

A perspective on life-course continuity

Our search for continuity thus defined has two important implications. First, phenotypic regularities provide only a selected view of connectedness across the life span. Indeed, a formulation of psychological structures that is isomorphic with behavior is misleading (Hinde & Bateson, 1984). This point is best appreciated by considering contextual influences. For example, preschoolers classified as dependent on the basis of maternal interviews tend to control and to initiate joint activities with their mothers during home observations. In school, however, dependent girls tend to be rather passive and play interactively less than their nondependent peers (Hinde et al., 1985). Invariant behavior patterns do not emerge in these findings. Instead, we see a coherent way of relating to the environment in different social settings.

Qualities of behavior are often maintained despite changing forms and, although behavioral manifestations may differ across time and circumstance, they do so in predictable ways (Sroufe, 1979). Thus, a greater appreciation of situational factors in behavioral continuity suggests that prospective studies must attend to qualitative similarities in behavior patterns rather than simply to behavioral constancies. To do so requires knowledge not only of the constructs underlying behavioral organization, but also of the relevant settings in which they may be expressed.

A second issue concerns the tendency to infer discontinuity or change in behavior on the basis of nonsignificant correlations between two points in time (Hinde & Bateson, 1984). Behavioral continuities are much more complex than those revealed by simple test–retest correlations. For example, earlier behaviors or circumstances may affect later behavior by an indirect route. Although the direct correlation between the two may be weak, it may still be possible to trace an effect through intervening steps. For example, Quinton and Rutter (1984) have shown that the effects of institutional rearing on women's parental styles persist largely because institution-reared women are significantly more likely to marry men with psychosocial problems.

Such findings suggest that behavioral continuities are unlikely to occur in all developmental domains independent of intervening mechanisms. The inadequacy of previous developmental predictions may have been due not to the absence of lawful relations but to the inability to locate the critical links between antecedents and consequences. For this reason, an adequate account of personality continuity also requires a social theory identifying roles and developmental tasks in the life course that are critical for the organization of behavior and that may elicit earlier established interactional styles (Caspi, 1987).

We conceive of the life course as a sequence of culturally defined age-graded roles and social transitions that are enacted over time. Every culture features a set of roles that must be filled by individuals. Some are quite specific, but others such as work, marriage, and parenthood are assumed by a large segment of the population. These age-stratified roles represent socially recognized divisions that constitute a basis for self-definition. In addition to age-stratified roles, each culture values certain competencies and specifies appropriate behaviors to be mastered by its members. Some of the skills required for fulfilling these roles contribute to survival in a direct sense, whereas others allow a social system to function smoothly.

Personality differences should have lawful implications for how individuals confront and adapt to these age-graded roles, and we expect to see this in how experience is registered, how environments are selected, and how the stages of life are negotiated. Moreover, we believe that meaningful continuities are likely to be observed by focusing on people's characteristic ways of approaching and responding to their social world and on their stylistic method of exercising control in and over their environments. We thus concur with Wachtel (1977) and others before him (Cottrell, 1969; Sullivan, 1953) that the personality variables most suitable for understanding people in the life course—across time and in diverse circumstances—are interactional styles that evoke supporting, maintaining, and validating responses from others.

In our work we have sought to explore the emergence and unfolding of life-course trajectories by using archival data to study the continuities and consequences of three interactional styles in late childhood. *Ill-temperedness* refers to an interactional style characterized by explosive temper tantrums in reaction to frustration and authority. *Shyness* refers to an interactional style characterized by emotional inhibition and discomfort in social settings. *Dependency* refers to an interactional style characterized by the tendency to seek attention, company, approval, and help. These interactional styles are of interest because they index individual differences that may shape the influence of environments on individuals as well as the influence of individuals on their own environments (Bronson, 1966). Indeed, interactional styles of this kind may persist across the life course by eliciting similar reactions from different people in diverse circumstances and by selecting individuals into environments that further sustain and support their behavior patterns (Caspi et al., 1987, 1988, 1989).

The Study

Subjects

Data for our research were obtained from the archives of the Institute of Human Development at the University of California, Berkeley. The subjects are members of the Berkeley Guidance Study (Eichorn, 1981), an ongoing study initiated in 1928–1929 with every third birth in the city of Berkeley over 18 months. Most of the 214 subjects in the original sample came from white, Protestant, native-born families. Slightly more than 60% were born into middle-class homes.

This chapter focuses on the life-course patterns of males. The original sample contained 102 males, of which a maximum of 87 have been followed up into adulthood. There are no significant differences between those who were followed up and those who were not across the three childhood interactional styles ($t's<1$), adolescent measures of intelligence ($t<1$), or family social class at the time of their births ($t = 1.23$, ns). Respondents were slightly better educated than nonrespondents, however ($t = 1.77$, $p = .08$).

Childhood data

Childhood data on the Berkeley subjects were obtained from clinical interviews with their mothers and subsequently organized into ratings on 5-point behavior scales by Macfarlane (1938; Macfarlane et al., 1954). Ill-temperedness is assessed by two scales: the severity and the frequency of temper tantrums. The severity scale ranges from 1, "anger reactions practically nonexistent," to 5, severe tantrums involving "biting, kicking, striking, and throwing things" as well as verbal explosions such as "swearing, screaming, and shouting accompanied by marked emotional reactions." Tantrum frequency ranges from one per month to several times a day. For our analyses, we combined these two ratings into a single 5-point scale and averaged the scale scores across the annual assessments at ages 8, 9, and 10 (1936–1938). The reliability (α) of this scale is .74. For some of our analyses we have designated any child with a score greater than 3 on the 5-point scale as having had a history of childhood ill-temperedness. In all, 38% of the boys were so classified.

Shyness is assessed by two scales: shyness and excessive reserve. The shyness scale ranges from 1, "exceptionally easy and quick social contacts, enjoys meeting new people," to 5, "acute discomfort to the point of panic in social situations." The reserved scale ranges from 1, "spontaneous and uninhibited expression of integrated feelings," to 5, emotional inhibition that "produces feelings of strain and awkwardness in others." For our analyses, we combined these two ratings into a single 5-point scale and averaged the scale scores across the annual assessments at ages 8, 9, and 10 (1936–1938). The reliability (α) of this scale is .91. For analytic purposes we have designated any child with a score greater than 3 as having had a history of childhood shyness. In all, 28% of the boys were so classified.

Childhood dependency is also assessed by two scales: dependency and attention demanding. The dependency scale ranges from 1, "easy attachments" to others and "not possessive, accepts parents as persons and not facets of own personality," to 5, "intense attachments" in which "parents' approval dominates the child's interests and values." The attention-demanding scale ranges from 1, "self-reliant," to 5, "constant demanding of attention; insecure and anxious without the attention of others." Again, we combined these two ratings into a single 5-point scale and averaged the scale scores across the annual assessments at ages 8, 9, and 10 (1936–1938). The reliability (α) of this scale is .71. For analytical purposes, we designated any child with a score greater than 3 as having had a history of childhood dependency. In all, 33% of the boys were so classified.

The correlations between the childhood interactional styles are shown in Table 1. The low and nonsignificant correlations suggest that each of the three measures may capture a unique childhood interactional style. In addition, the correlations between the childhood interactional styles and adolescent IQ are also low and not significant. These results suggest that the long-term consequences of each interactional style are unlikely to be accounted for by differences in intellectual capacities.

Adulthood data

Personality assessments. Adult personality information on the Berkeley subjects is coded in the form of Q-sort items. At least two professional clinicians read each interview from the age 30 (1960) follow-up and provided a description of the subject using the 100-item California Q set (Block, 1971). The interjudge reliability of the Q-sort assessment is .74.

Life records. Detailed information on each subject's education, work, marriage, and parenthood patterns is based on interviews with them when they were about 30 years of age (1960) and again when they were about 40 (1968–1971).

Our analyses of life-course patterns are organized around two themes: the transition to adulthood and subsequent aspects of work and family life. In our exploration of personality in the life course we have thus obtained

Table 1. *Correlations between interactional styles in late childhood and IQ*

	Ill-Temperedness	Shyness	Dependency	IQ
Ill-temperedness	—	.08	.19	− .05
Shyness		—	− .02	− .08
Dependency			—	.10
IQ				—

measures of adjustment to age-graded events and roles by sampling behavior from the life-record domain, that is, actual records of the person's behavior in society (Cattell, 1957). Childhood interactional styles should relate importantly to L-data, to observations that are made in situ and that are embedded in the group culture pattern. There are sound methodological grounds for this claim. Rather than measure behavior at a given moment, L-observation is usually spread over longer periods of time, rendering the data relatively free of unreliability (e.g., Block, 1977). In addition, as Cattell suggested, there are equally compelling theoretical reasons for emphasizing L-data. Insofar as life-span development involves interaction with institutions, mores, and the general culture pattern, the natural history mapping of behavior as expressed in L-data is most promising, because L-data are ultimately concerned with inclination and volition, with how, whether, and when a person chooses to perform.

Life-course patterns of ill-tempered children

The need to delay gratification, control impulses, and modulate emotional expression is the earliest and most ubiquitous demand that society places upon the developing child. Some children, however, fail to achieve mastery of such ego control and continue to react to frustration and adult authority with explosive tantrums.

Temper tantrums are an especially vivid and disruptive expression of self-will that includes elements of defiance, control seeking, and social aggression (Achenbach & Edelbrock, 1978). Their value as a means of achieving personal control and for securing gratification can be learned as a way of dealing with new and frustrating situations (Patterson, 1982). In addition, temperamental differences in reactivity and self-regulation may lead some children more than others to react to frustration in such a manner (Chess & Thomas, 1987). Would children who become highly skilled and effective in using temper tantrums to alter their environment continue with similar efforts in later settings?

Phenotypic persistence

Q-sort data can provide a rich clinical portrait of a group of individuals if the significantly correlated items cluster in a theoretically coherent way. But because many individual correlations are computed we will here emphasize global trends more than single correlations and item variations. With this caveat, then, we can venture into the clinical thicket of Q-items that are significantly correlated with childhood ill-temperedness (Table 2).

As Table 2 reveals, childhood ill-temperedness is coherently correlated with personality attributes across the life span. Ill-tempered boys are described 20 years later as undercontrolled, irritable, and moody. In addition, they are described as less productive, ambitious, and dependable than their even-tempered peers.

Life-course patterns

Some of the implications of this childhood interactional style can be seen in Tables 3–5, which provide educational and occupational data for men with and without a history of temper tantrums stratified by their social class of origin. The most striking finding across the three time periods reflected in these tables is the progressive deterioration of socioeconomic status for ill-tempered boys from the middle class. Table 3 shows that ill-tempered boys are somewhat more likely to lose out in formal education than are their even-tempered peers [$F(1,86) = 3.24$, $p = .07$]. By the time they enter the labor force (Table 4), their childhood tantrums are as strong a predictor of occupational status as are their social class origins [$F(1,81) = 11.07$, $p < .05$ and $F(1,81) = 11.24$, $p < .05$, respectively]. By midlife (Table 5), those who were ill-tempered as boys from the middle class have become indistinguishable from their working class counterparts, as reflected by the significant interaction between childhood tantrums and class origins [$F(1,75) = 5.99$, $p < .05$]. The downward mobility of these ill-tempered boys from the middle class is further confirmed by a comparison of their occupational status at age 40 with that of their father at a comparable age (1938–1939). A majority of them (53%) experienced downward mobility compared to only 28% of their even-tempered, middle-class peers ($p < .01$).

What accounts for the far-reaching effects of such childhood behavior? The pathway from childhood tantrums to adult occupational status is illustrated in Figure 1. Apparently, middle-class boys with a history of childhood tantrums arrive at lower occupational status at midlife because they cut short their formal education. A history of childhood tantrums is as good a predictor of educational attainment as is IQ ($\beta = -.34$ and $.32$, p's $< .05$, respectively). In turn, educational attainment strongly predicts occupational status ($\beta = .59$, $p < .001$). There is, however, no significant

Table 2. *Q-sort correlates in adulthood of childhood ill-temperedness*

Q-sort item	Correlation
Tends toward under-control of needs and impulses; unable to delay gratification	.45***
Tends to perceive many different contexts in sexual terms; eroticizes situations	.36***
Characteristically pushes and tries to stretch limits; sees what he can get away with	.36***
Is self-dramatizing; histrionic	.33***
Overreactive to minor frustrations; is irritable	.32**
Is guileful, deceitful, manipulative, and opportunistic	.31**
Has fluctuating moods	.29**
Is a talkative individual	.27**
Is self-indulgent	.27**
Emphasizes being with others; gregarious	.26**
Is self-pitying	.26**
Initiates humor	.26**
Is basically anxious	.25*
Responds to humor	.24*
Is self-defeating	.23*
Is unpredictable and changeable in behavior and attitudes	.22*
Tends toward over-control of needs and impulses; binds tension excessively; delays gratification unnecessarily	− .46***
Behaves in an ethically consistent manner; is consistent with own personal standards	− .43***
Is a genuinely dependable and responsible person	− .38***
Is productive; gets things done	− .36***
Is calm, relaxed in manner	− .34***
Has high aspiration level for self	− .33***
Is fastidious	− .32**
Behaves in masculine style and manner	− .31**
Is turned to for advice and reassurance	− .29**
Is emotionally bland; has flattened affect	− .28**
Prides self on being "objective," rational	− .26**

*p<.10
**p<.05
***p<.01

direct effect of temper tantrums on occupational status ($\beta = -.10$).

But what about the ill-tempered working class boys? Because of the strong and structurally constraining effect of social class no additional debilitating effects of temper tantrums could be discerned for them in our analysis of occupational attainment. As it happens, however, history performed a natural experiment for us by assigning nearly 70% of the Berkeley men to military service, mostly during the Korean War. The

Table 3. *Educational attainment of male subjects by childhood temper tantrums and social class origins*[a]

	Class origins		
Temper tantrums	Middle class	Working class	Mean
Low	7.03	5.43	6.35
High	6.38	5.07	5.83
Mean	6.77	5.29	

[a]1 = less than 7th grade; 5 = high school diploma; 8 = professional degree

Tantrums	$F(1,86) = 3.24$, $p < .07$
Class	$F(1,86) = 25.61$, $p < .001$
Tantrums × class	$F(1,86) < 1$

Table 4. *Occupational status of first job of male subjects following completion of education by childhood temper tantrums and social class origins*[a]

	Class origins		
Temper tantrums	Middle class	Working class	Mean
Low	5.48	3.95	4.84
High	3.95	3.00	3.54
Mean	4.86	3.56	

[a]1 = unskilled employee; 7 = higher executive

Tantrums	$F(1,81) = 11.07$, $p < .001$
Class	$F(1,81) = 11.24$, $p < .001$
Tantrums × class	$F(1,81) < 1$

results show that, in this setting, childhood tantrums were equally good predictors of performance among men from both social classes. In particular, men with a childhood history of tantrums achieved significantly lower military rank at the time of their discharge than their even-tempered peers ($r = -.33$, $p < .05$), a relationship that obtains for men from both middle class and working class backgrounds and remains unaltered when controlled for adolescent IQ.

Military service is also of conceptual interest in this case because it

Table 5. *Midlife (age 40) occupational status of male subjects by childhood temper tantrums and social class origins[a]*

Temper tantrums	Class origins		Mean
	Middle class	Working class	
Low	5.96	4.40	5.31
High	4.94	4.92	4.93
Mean	5.59	4.59	

[a] $1 =$ unskilled employee; $7 =$ higher executive

Tantrums	$F(1,75) = 1.43$, $p < .24$
Class	$F(1,75) = 10.64$, $p < .01$
Tantrums × class	$F(1,75) = 5.99$, $p < .05$

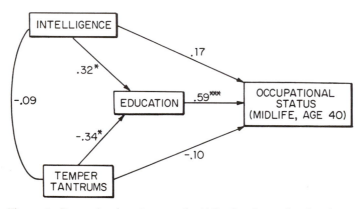

Figure 1. Occupational attainment of middle class boys, showing the cumulative effects of childhood ill-temperedness. *$p < .05$, ***$p < .001$.

imposes the kind of frustration and controlling authority that probably provoked tantrums in the childhood years. And like military service, most low-status jobs are characterized by a low degree of autonomy and a high degree of supervision by authority (Kohn & Schooler, 1983), suggesting that the occupational consequences of an ill-tempered interactional style should be especially marked for men in such jobs (Robins, 1966).

We sought evidence for this hypothesis by first examining each subject's work history from ages 18 to 40, calculating the number of months he was unemployed, the number of jobs held, the number of employers served, and the number of career switches between functionally unrelated lines of work. These were converted to z scores and averaged into a single index of erratic work history. The sample was then divided into men holding high-status jobs (I and II on the Hollingshead index) and those holding low-status jobs (III–V).

The results show a significant effect of childhood tantrums and a near-significant effect of job status on the erratic quality of men's work histories [$F(1,70) = 16.97$, $p < .001$ and $F(1,70) = 3.67$, $p = .06$, respectively]. But most importantly, there is a significant interaction effect between these variables [$F(1,70) = 4.47$, $p < .05$]. Men who had a history of childhood temper tantrums and who held low-status jobs were more prone to erratic worklives than the remaining groups ($t = 4.64$, $p < .001$). Moreover, regression analyses reveal that both the main effect of temper tantrums and the interaction effect between tantrums and job status remain significant when controlled for class origin, educational level, and adolescent IQ.

A history of childhood tantrums also affects the domestic sphere. Men with such a history were significantly less likely to have an intact first marriage at midlife (age 40) by better than a 2:1 margin; almost half (46.4%) of these men divorced or separated, compared with only 22.2% of the men without such a history ($p = .02$).

Surprisingly, a history of childhood ill-temperedness does not predict punitive or arbitrary parenting among men. Information on parenting was obtained from both spouses and children who were asked independently in 1970 to assess the subjects' parental anger and loss of control. Neither the spouse nor child index reveals a significant direct effect of childhood tantrums on parenting behavior. As we have seen, however, nearly half of the men with a history of childhood tantrums were no longer in their first marriage at the time of these interviews. It may be that their parenting is not harsh or ill-tempered, but remote or virtually nonexistent.

Life-course patterns of shy children

In a society that emphasizes action and initiative a shy interactional style may preclude the ability to effectively handle those tasks and crises that are inevitable in the course of assuming new roles and entering new relationships. The developmental literature suggests that shy children may not experience many of the role and rule negotiations that are important to the growth of social knowledge and social skills (Putallaz & Gottman, 1981). They may thus become increasingly unlikely to initiate or to respond appropriately to social overtures, thereby selecting themselves into further isolation. In addition, their lack of assertiveness in ongoing social interactions may cause them to be ignored, overlooked, or mistreated by their peers, the result being that shy children are likely to undergo aversive conditioning when they occasionally hazard social interactions (Rubin, 1982, 1986). Moreover, research on adults suggests that shy people begin to worry when they have to perform in unfamilar situations; they are the object of attention and critical evaluation by others (Pilkonis, 1977).

In tracing the life-course consequences of childhood shyness we thus focused on the passage from youth to young adulthood when our subjects would have to abandon familiar roles and enter new and unfamiliar social settings. Because shy individuals seem particularly disadvantaged when they are thrust into unfamiliar settings in which the interpersonal or role requirements are new and ambiguous (Jones & Carpenter, 1986), we expected men with a history of childhood shyness to encounter difficulties when called upon by society to initiate those actions and social contacts required for assuming the adult roles of marriage, parenthood, and career.

Phenotypic persistence

As we saw earlier, men who were ill-tempered as children were described in adulthood as undercontrolled, irritable, and moody. Table 6 shows that similar continuity can be discerned in the description of men who were rated as shy and reserved in late childhood. Although only a few adult Q-sort items are correlated with the childhood measure, shyness nevertheless appears to be related to a coherent cluster of personality attributes across 20 years. Men with a history of childhood shyness are described in adulthood as bothered by demands, withdrawing when frustrated, and showing a reluctance to act. They are also less assertive and insightful, all traits that could imply difficulties in making transitions into new roles and life settings.

Life-course patterns

Our most striking discovery about men who were shy and reserved as children is their delay in marrying, becoming fathers, and establishing stable careers. Men with a history of childhood shyness are significantly older than others in their cohort when they marry [25.5 vs. 22.5 years, $t(75) = 3.80$, $p < .001$], when they first become fathers [28.2 vs. 24.1 years, $t(67) = 3.25$, $p < .003$], and when they first enter a stable career, that is, a career in which they hold a functionally related job for at least 6 years [28.2 vs. 25.3 years, $t(75) = 2.35$, $p < .02$] (Elder & Rockwell, 1979). Moreover, regression analysis shows that childhood *shyness* remains a significant predictor of these several role-transition ages even with statistical controls for class origin, educational level, age at completion of formal education, age at entry into the labor market, military service, and physical attractiveness.

In all, men who were reluctant to enter social settings as children were likely to repeat this pattern of behavior in the new and unfamiliar settings required by the adult transitions into marriage, parenthood, and career.

Table 6. *Q-sort correlates in adulthood of childhood shyness*

Q-sort item	Correlation
Has a brittle ego-defense system; has a small reserve of integration; would be disorganized and maladaptive when under stress or trauma	.31**
Withdraws when frustrated	.28**
Reluctant to commit self to any definite course of action; tends to delay or avoid action	.23*
Is bothered by anything that can be construed as a demand	.22*
Behaves in an assertive fashion in interpersonal situations	−.26**
Has insight into own motives and behavior	−.22*

*$p<.10$
**$p<.05$
***$p<.01$

Although the available data do not permit a detailed examination of the behavioral processes entailed in the transition to adulthood, shy children appear to exert different selection efforts and respond differently to social demands than their more outgoing counterparts. Indeed, it is known that in the domain of heterosexual relations, shy men often find it difficult to initiate courtship (Curran, 1977), an interactional barrier that could itself delay the transition into marriage and parenthood. In the domain of work, shyness may also preclude the American ideal of male self-assertion and conspire to delay men's transition into stable career lines (cf. Super, 1957).

In sociological terms, men with a history of childhood shyness can be said to be normatively "off-time" in their transitions to age-graded roles (Elder, 1985; LeVine, 1980; Neugarten, 1979). If we define off-time as at least a year above the median age for the cohort as a whole, then 44% of these men are off-time in marrying compared to only 17% of the other men in the cohort; 60% are off-time in becoming fathers compared to only 30% of other men; and 54% are off-time in entering a stable career compared to 30% of other men.

From a sociological perspective, the timing of role transitions represents an important contingency in the life course that has implications for achievements and subsequent behavior (Hogan, 1980). In particular, delays in social transitions often produce conflicting obligations and options that enhance later difficulties, in part because individuals who are off-time must cope with the demands of their multiple roles without the benefit of those social structures that support and smooth the way for persons who are "on-time" (Elder, 1975; Goode, 1960). As we shall see, evidence for this progressive accumulation of consequences is provided by an examination of the occupational careers of men with a childhood history of shyness.

In tracing the continuities and consequences of childhood shyness, we used the same indices of occupational status and instability that we used in tracing the course of ill-temperedness, as well as an additional index of adult achievement. Follow-up studies of children identified as extremely shy/withdrawn suggest that, by adolescence, these children consistently underestimate their performance and exaggerate their poor achievement (Moskowitz & Schwartzman, 1988). It is thus possible that low expectancies for achievement may inhibit shy children from pursuing opportunities in the labor market and from attaining the accomplishments of which they are capable.

For this analysis, then, we also constructed an ipsatized index of occupational achievement. For subjects who had completed some college but not gone on to postgraduate work, we regressed occupational status at midlife on educational level, adolescent IQ, senior high grade point average (GPA), and a measure of adolescent career aspirations (see Elder & Rockwell, 1979). Subjects were classified as low achievers if they fell below their predicted occupational status by 1.0 or more on the 7-point occupational status scale; all others were defined as high achievers. To obtain greater discriminability at the lower and upper ends of the educational spectrum, two judges classified subjects who had either less than a college education or had gone on to postgraduate work into achievement categories on the basis of detailed life-history records. (Interjudge agreement = .80.)

As shown in Figure 2, childhood shyness has significant effects on two of these three indices, occupational stability and occupational achievement. Shyness predicts delayed entry into a career line ($\beta = .27$, $p < .05$), which, in turn, predicts less stability ($\beta = -.30$, $p < .05$). In addition, Figure 2 shows that childhood shyness does not directly predict low achievement. Instead, men with a history of childhood shyness achieve less than they "should have" by age 40 because they were late in entering a stable career ($\beta = -.29$, $p < .05$). It appears that by entering an occupational career at an older age, men with a childhood history of shyness may have forgone

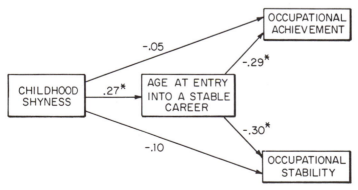

Figure 2. Occupational stability and achievement in adulthood as a function of shyness in late childhood. *$p < .05$.

investments in skills and benefits and thus increased their vulnerability to career disruption and sacrificed higher achievements.

We saw earlier that childhood ill-temperedness predicted marital instability. Overall, this is not the case for childhood shyness. This childhood interactional style is not correlated with marital instability nor with indices of marital satisfaction at midlife. And finally, we found no distinctive effects of childhood shyness on men's later parenting. It may be that shyness produces anxious inhibition in novel situations but not in more familiar, on-going settings and relationships (Buss, 1980).

Life-course patterns of dependent children

A child's dependency on parents and other significant persons has been considered an important source of influence in both psychodynamic and social learning theories of personality development (Bandura & Walters, 1963; Bowlby, 1975; Freud, 1921; Hirschi, 1969). The fact that children and adults value the attention and approval of significant others and fear their loss is a powerful motive for imitation, identification, internalization of behavior controls, and conformity to societal norms and expectations.

Dependency as an individual interactional style may be self-perpetuating because dependent individuals are motivated to select and construct environments that sustain and nourish their need for company, approval, and help. Moreover, children who come to rely on dependency as their primary technique for controlling their environment may become increasingly skilled in evoking attending responses from others. Indeed, experimental studies of dependent persons suggest that they are significantly more responsive to social reinforcement and are likely to strive for social reinforcers by engaging in behaviors that elicit approval from authority figures and significant others (Cairns, 1961).

Phenotypic persistence

Do dependent boys become dependent men? The answer is complex. Men who were rated as dependent in late childhood emerge in adulthood with a quite distinctive catalog of impressive attributes. As shown in Table 7, they are judged as calm, warm, giving, sympathetic, insightful, undefensive, incisive, consistent across roles, comfortable with ambiguity and uncertainty, and socially poised. Moreover, they tend to arouse nurturance and are turned to for advice by others.

Life-course patterns

As we have already seen, interactional styles in late childhood affect the pattern of transitions into adulthood. For example, childhood ill-

Table 7. *Q-sort correlates in adulthood of childhood dependency*

Q-sort item	Correlation
Behaves in a giving way toward others	.35***
Has warmth; is compassionate	.32**
Enjoys sensuous experiences	.32**
Does not vary roles; relates to everyone in the same way	.32**
Is calm, relaxed in manner	.30**
Evaluates the motivation of others in interpreting situations	.30**
Behaves in a sympathetic or considerate manner	.29**
Has insight into own motives and behavior	.26**
Seeks reassurance from others	.23*
Arouses nurturant feelings in others	.23*
Is turned to for advice and reassurance	.23*
Tends to arouse liking and acceptance in people	.22*
Is protective of those close to him	.22*
Appears straightforward, forthright, candid in dealing with others	.22*
Responds to humor	.22*
Is thin-skinned; vulnerable to anything that can be construed as criticism or an interpersonal slight	−.45***
Has hostility toward others	−.36***
Is uncomfortable with uncertainty and complexities	−.33***
Is power-oriented; values power in self or others	−.32**
Has a brittle ego-defense system; has a small reserve of integration; would be disorganized and maladaptive when under stress or trauma	−.29**
Tends to be self-defensive	−.26**
Extrapunitive; tends to transfer or project blame	−.23*
Is bothered by anything that can be construed as a demand	−.23*
Handles anxiety and conflicts by, in effect, refusing to recognize their presence; repressive or dissociative tendencies	−.22*

*p < .10
**p < .05
***p < .01

temperedness predicts an early exit from formal schooling. Likewise, childhood shyness predicts delayed entry into family and work roles. In sociological terms, both ill-tempered and shy children are "off-time" in their transition to adulthood, albeit in different ways. How do children characterized by dependency in late childhood negotiate the transition to adulthood and their subsequent work and family roles?

On the one hand, it seems possible that childhood dependency would also delay the transition to adulthood because dependent individuals might be too attached to their families of origin to initiate careers and families of procreation. On the other hand, their dependent styles might facilitate establishing new relationships. Moreover, if dependency is the forerunner of conformity to societal norms and expectations, as developmental theories assert, then dependent individuals might be even more likely than others to march "on-time" through the normative sequence of age-graded roles and to select themselves into settings and to engage in behaviors that meet the standards of their reference group. The data are most consistent with the latter suggestion. Men with a history of childhood dependency were likely to be on-time in their transition to adulthood; for example, 80% of them married within two years of the median age for the cohort as a whole, compared to only 59% of the other men ($p<.05$); similarly, 78% became fathers on-time compared to 49% of other men ($p<.01$).

In addition to normative timing, there is also a normative sequence of role transitions (Foner & Kertzer, 1978). For example, in our society one should finish school before getting married, and one should get married before having children. Indeed, demographic studies suggest that marriage following the completion of other transitions associated with the passage from youth to adulthood lessens the chances of career disruptions and marital instability among American males (Hogan, 1981).

Our follow-up analyses of childhood dependency suggest that this interactional style also predicts adherence to a normative sequence of life-course transitions. As shown in Figure 3, men with a childhood history of dependency were significantly more likely to follow the normative sequence of completing school before assuming a career or getting married (p's$<.05$). In addition, they were somewhat more likely to assume an occupational career before marriage ($p = .16$). Whether these patterns reflect their ease in establishing new interpersonal relationships or greater conformity to societal norms generally is difficult to say. It does appear, however, that individual differences in childhood personality influence in important ways intracohort variations in the timing and sequence of life-course transitions.

Despite their orderly passage from youth to adulthood, the worklives of men with a childhood history of dependency are not particularly distinctive. In general, there are no significant associations between the measure of childhood dependency and our midlife measures of occupational status, achievement, or stability. It may be that childhood dependency fosters the internalization of societal norms about reliability and competence in the workplace, but it does not provide an extra push toward achievement.

Not unexpectedly, the warm, nurturant adult style of men with a history of childhood dependency confers its most obvious advantage in the domestic sphere. Men with such a history were significantly more likely to have an intact first marriage at midlife (age 40) by better than a 2:1 margin. Only 17.4% of these men divorced or separated, whereas 38% of the other men did so ($p = .05$). Additional information on marital relations, obtained from the 1970 interviews with their spouses, shows that wives of men with a

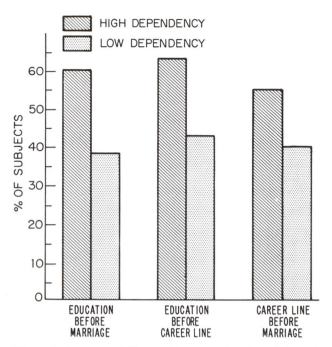

Figure 3. Sequence of life transitions as a function of dependency in late childhood.

history of childhood dependency were significantly more satisfied with their marriages ($r = .30$, $p < .05$). Finally, the harmony suggested by these findings is further confirmed by reports of parental congruence with regard to child-rearing practices. Information on areas of parental congruence was obtained from the 1970 interviews with both subjects and spouses who were asked to indicate independently their agreement on 5-point scales. The marriages of men with a childhood history of dependency are characterized by significantly greater interparental consistency with regard to the discipline ($r = .37$, $p < .01$), affection ($r = .32$, $p < .05$), and attention ($r = .32$, $p < .05$) given to their children.

In summary, the phenotypic interactional style of childhood dependency is not simply carried forward through the life course. Rather, men in this cohort seem to have transformed their childhood dependency into a mature, nurturant style in adulthood that serves them particularly well in the intimate world of home and family.

Conclusion

In the introduction we noted that personality differences should have lawful implications for how individuals meet developmental challenges and adapt to new settings. We also suggested that the most striking differences between people are to be found not by studying their responses to the same social episode, but by analyzing their construction of new situations and roles. Indeed, the influence of dispositional factors on behavior is most pronounced in settings that require individuals to master new demands and tasks, as well as in relatively unstructured situations that force individuals to rely primarily on their own internal traits and dispositions as a behavioral guide (Monson et al., 1982; Snyder & Ickes, 1985). Life-course continuities in behavior are thus most likely to be observed when people assume new roles and enter new relationships, for in these circumstances individuals bring their unique characteristics to bear on the interpretation and enactment of roles they are required to play.

Transitions and adjustments to new roles and relationships are the core social-developmental tasks people face across the life course. Accordingly, we have charted the course of development as a series of behavioral reorganizations around age-graded transitions and roles, and have sought to examine the emergence and unfolding of life-course patterns by first identifying people who differ along fundamental behavioral dimensions and then tracing their lives through a succession of social changes. Our empirical strategy thus entailed casting features of the individual in the role of the independent variable and casting features of the environment in the role of the dependent variable, exploring how people select their environments and choose their social experiences in the age-graded life course.

The findings summarized here suggest that childhood interactional styles do, in fact, have lawful implications for adaptation and adjustment across the age-graded life course—across time and diverse circumstances, in work and family patterns.

Our analysis of ill-temperedness pointed to the discriminatives of this childhood interactional style across many of life's tasks, from patterns of early adult achievement to marital patterns. Thus men who reacted with temper tantrums to frustration and adult authority as children encountered difficulties when they again faced frustration and controlling authority (as in school, the armed services, and low-level jobs) or were immersed in life situations requiring the frequent management of interpersonal conflicts (as in marriage).

Our analysis of shyness showed that this interactional style is evoked again in life situations in which people are called upon to make critical choices and decisions about family and career formation. In particular, a shy interactional style affected men's transition to adulthood and proved somewhat problematic in their efforts to negotiate traditional masculine roles involving mate selection and vocational decision making. A large percentage of men who were shy and reserved as children were normatively off-time in their transitions to these age-graded roles, and these delayed transitions served as the mediating link between childhood shyness and subsequent outcomes in their worklives.

Finally, our analysis of dependency implicated this childhood interactional style in the formation and maintenance of work and family roles. Men with this childhood history adhered to conventional roles across the life course. For example, a large percentage of them were normatively on-time in their transition to adulthood. They were also less likely to spend time in non-normative combinations of activities and adhered to an orderly sequence of age-graded events. Moreover, expressions of childhood dependency were observed in their family patterns distinguished by stability and harmony.

In general, it appears that life-course patterns depend, importantly and coherently, on the individual's patterns of approach and response. Elsewhere we have proposed that interactional styles established earlier in life may persist across time because they directly provoke the environment to respond to the individual in characteristic ways, thereby setting up reciprocal person-environment interactions that may be replicated in new situations. Moreover, because individuals selectively seek out situations that are compatible with their dispositions, they may thereby construct skewed environments that sustain and support their orientation to the world (Caspi, et al., in press; Caspi & Elder, 1988). More fine-grained analyses are obviously required to document and substantiate the operation of such continuity-promoting processes in development. Before hypotheses about mediating mechanisms can be put to a test, however, we need to describe development as it transpires in its naturalistic context.

Our effort here, then, has been aimed at providing a longitudinal survey of the environmental landscape as it is influenced by dispositional factors and at documenting the manifestations of childhood behavior in the timing, sequence, and content of social roles across the life course. Of course, the specific results must be viewed in cultural and historical perspective. Particular life-course patterns depend not only on the individual's distinctive interactional styles, but also on the structure of the environment in any given historical period. But while social change may alter role structures and produce change in particular manifestations of a disposition, the enduring qualities of personality in the life course may still be abstracted by investigating individual differences in the assumption of socially defined roles.

Acknowledgments

We are indebted to the Institute of Human Development, University of California, Berkeley, for permission to use archival data from the Berkeley Guidance Study. This research was supported in part by a grant from the National Institute of Mental Health (MH-41827). Glen H. Elder, Jr., was supported by a Senior Scientist Research Award from NIMH (MH-00567).

References

Achenbach, T. M., & Edelbrock, C. S. (1978). The classification of child psychopathology: A review and analysis of empirical efforts. *Psychological Bulletin, 85,* 1275–1301.

Bandura, A., & Walters, R. H. (1963). *Social learning and personality development.* New York: Holt, Rinehart & Winston.

Block, J. (1971). *Lives through time.* Berkeley: Bancroft.

Block, J. (1977). Advancing the psychology of personality: Paradigmatic shift or improving the quality of research. In D. Magnusson & N. S. Endler (Eds.)., *Personality at the crossroads: Current issues in interactional psychology.* Hillsdale, NJ: Erlbaum.

Bowlby, J. (1975). Attachment theory, separation, anxiety and mourning. In S. Arieti (Ed.), *American handbook of psychiatry.* New York: Basic Books.

Bronson, W. C. (1966). Central orientations: A study of behavior organization from childhood to adolescence. *Child Development, 37,* 125–155.

Buss, A. H. (1980). *Self-consciousness and social anxiety.* San Francisco: Freeman.

Cairns, R. B. (1961). The influence of dependency inhibition on the effectiveness of social reinforcement. *Journal of Personality, 29,* 466–488.

Caspi., A. (1987). Personality in the life couse, *Journal of Personality and Social Psychology, 53,* 1203–1213.

Caspi, A., Bem, D. J., & Elder, G. H., Jr. (1989). Continuities and consequences of interactional styles across the life course. *Journal of Personality, 57,* 375–406.

Caspi, A., & Elder, G. H., Jr. (1988). Emergent family patterns: The intergenerational construction of problem behavior and relationships. In R. A. Hinde & J. Stevenson-Hinde (Eds.)., *Relationships within families.* New York: Oxford University Press.

Caspi, A., Elder, G. H. Jr., & Bem. D. J. (1987). Moving against the world: Life-course patterns of explosive children. *Developmental Psychology, 23,* 308–313.

Caspi, A., Elder, G. H. Jr., & Bem. D. J. (1988). Moving away from the world: Life-course patterns of shy children. *Developmental Psychology, 24,* 824–831.

Caspi, A., Elder, G. H. Jr., & Bem. D. J. (1989). Moving toward the world: Life-course patterns of dependent children. Unpublished manuscript, Harvard University.

Cattell, R. B. (1957). *Personality and motivation structure and measurement.* New York: World Book.

Chess, S., & Thomas, A. (1987). *Origins and evolution of behavior disorders: From infancy to early adult life.* Cambridge, MA: Harvard University Press.

Cornblatt, B., & Erlenmeyer-Kimling, L. (1984). Early attentional predictors of adolescent behavioral disturbances in children at risk for schizophrenia. In N. Watt, E. J. Anthony, L. C. Wynne, & J. Rolf (Eds.), *Children at risk for schizophrenia: A longitudinal perspective.* New York: Cambridge University Press.

Cottrell, L. S. (1969). Interpersonal interaction and the development of the self. In D. A. Goslin (Ed.), *Handbook of socialization theory and research.* Chicago: Rand McNally.

Curran, J. P. (1977). Skills training as an approach to the treatment of heterosexual–social anxiety: A review. *Psychological Bulletin, 84,* 140–157.

Eichorn, D. H. (1981). Samples and procedures. In D. H. Eichorn, J. A. Clausen,

N. Haan, M. P. Honzik, & P. H. Mussen (Eds.), *Present and past in middle life*. New York: Academic Press.

Elder, G. H., Jr. (1974). *Children of the Great Depression*. Chicago: University of Chicago Press.

Elder, G. H., Jr. (1975). Age differentiation and the life course. *Annual Review of Scoiology* (Vol. 1). Palo Alto: Annual Reviews.

Elder, G. H., Jr. (1985). Perspectives on the life course. In G. H. Elder, Jr. (Ed.), *Life course dymamics: Transitions and trajectories*. Ithaca, NY: Cornell University Press.

Elder, G. H., Jr., & Rockwell, R. C. (1979). Economic depression and postwar opportunity in men's lives: A study of life patterns and health. In R. G. Simmons (Ed.), *Research in community and mental health*. Greenwich, CT: JAI Press.

Foner, A., & Kertzer, D. I. (1978). Transitions over the life course: Lessons from age-set societies. *American Journal of Sociology, 83*, 1081–1104.

Freud, S. (1921). *Group psychology and the analysis of the ego*. New York: Norton.

Goode, W. J. (1960). A theory of role strain. *American Sociological Review, 25*, 483–496.

Hinde, R. A., & Bateson, P. (1984). Discontinuities and continuities in behavioural development and the neglect of process. *International Journal of Behavioural Development, 7*, 129–143.

Hinde, R. A., Stevenson-Hinde, J., & Tamplin, A. (1985). Characteristics of 3-4-year-olds assessed at home and their interactions in preschool. *Developmental Psychology, 21*, 130–140.

Hirschi, T. (1969). *Causes of delinquency*. Berkeley: University of California Press.

Hogan, D. P. (1980). The transition to adulthood as a career contingency. *American Sociological Review, 45*, 261–276.

Hogan, D. P. (1981). *Transitions and social change*. New York: Academic Press.

Jones, W. H., & Carpenter, B. N. (1986). Shyness, social behavior, and relationships. In W. H. Jones, J. M. Cheek, & S. R. Briggs (Eds.), *Shyness: Perspectives on research and treatment*. New York: Plenum.

Kohn, M. L., & Schooler, C. (1983). *Work and personality: An inquiry into social stratification*. Norwood, NJ: Ablex.

LeVine, R. A. (1980). Adulthood among the Gusii of Kenya. In N. J. Smelser & E. Erikson (Eds.) *Themes of work and love in adulthood*. Cambridge: Harvard University Press.

Livson, N., & Peskin, N. (1980). Perspectives on adolescence from longitudinal research. In J. Adelson (Ed.), *Handbook of adolescent psychology*. New York: Wiley.

Macfarlane, J. W. (1938). Studies in child guidance I: Methodology of data collection and organization. *Monographs of the Society for Research in Child Development, 3*, Serial No. 6.

Macfarlane, J. W., Allen, L., & Honzik, M. P. (1954). *A developmental study of the behavioral problems of children between twenty-one months and fourteen years*. Berkeley: University of California Press.

Monson, T. C., Hesley, J. W., & Chernick, L. (1982). Specifying when personality traits can and cannot predict behavior: An alternative to abandoning the attempt to predict single-act criteria. *Journal of Personality and Social Psychology, 43*, 385–399.

Moskowitz, D. A., & Schwartzman, A. E. (1988). *Painting group portraits: Assessing life outcomes for aggressive and withdrawn children*. Manuscript submitted for publication.

Moss, H. A., & Susman, E. J. (1980). Longitudinal study of personality development. In O. G. Brim, Jr., & J. Kagan (Eds.), *Constancy and change in human development*. Cambridge: Harvard University Press.

Neugarten, B. (1979). Time, age, and the life cycle. *American Journal of Psychiatry, 136,* 887–894.

Parker, J. G., & Asher, S. R. (1987). Peer relations and later personal adjustment: Are low-accepted children at risk? *Psychological Bulletin, 102,* 357–389.

Patterson, G. R. (1982). *Coercive family process*. Eugene, OR: Castalia.

Pilkonis, P. A. (1977). Shyness, public and private, and its relationship to other measures of social behavior. *Journal of Personality, 45,* 585–595.

Putallaz, M., & Gottman, J. M. (1981). Social skills and group acceptance. In S. R. Asher & J. M. Gottman (Eds.), *The development of children's friendships*. New York: Cambridge University Press.

Quinton, D., & Rutter, M. (1984). Parenting behavior of mothers raised 'in care'. In R. Nicol (Ed.), *Longitudinal studies in child psychology and psychiatry: Practical lessons from research experience*. Chichester: Wiley.

Robins, L. N. (1966). *Deviant children grown up*. Baltimore: Williams & Wilkins.

Rubin, K. H. (1982). Social and social-cognitive developmental characteristics of young isolate, normal, and sociable children. In K. H. Rubin & H. S. Ross (Eds.), *Peer relationships and social skills in childhood*. New York: Springer.

Rubin, K. H. (1986). Socially withdrawn children: An "at risk" population? In B. Schneider, K. H. Rubin, & J. E. Ledingham (Eds.), *Peer relationships and social skills in childhood* (Vol. 2). *Issues in assessment and training*. New York: Springer.

Snyder, M., & Ickes, W. (1985). Personality and social behavior. In E. Aronson & G. Lindzey (Eds.), *Handbook of social psychology* (Vol. 2). New York: Random House.

Sroufe, L. A. (1979). The coherence of individual development. *American Psychologist, 34,* 834–841.

Sullivan, H. S. (1953). *The interpersonal theory of psychiatry*. New York: Norton.

Super, D. E. (1957). *The psychology of careers*. New York: Harper.

Wachtel, P. L. (1977). *Psychoanalysis and behavior therapy*. New York: Basic Books.

West, D. J., & Farrington, D. P. (1977). *Who becomes delinquent?* London: Heinemann.

Yamaguchi, K., & Kandel, D. B. (1984a). Patterns of drug use from adolescence to early adulthood-II. Sequences of progression. *American Journal of Public Health, 74,* 668–672.

Yamaguchi, K., & Kandel, D. B. (1984b). Patterns of drug use from adolescence to early adulthood-III. Predictors of progression. *American Journal of Public Health, 74,* 673–681.

3 Adopted and illegitimate children growing up

BARBARA MAUGHAN AND ANDREW PICKLES

Adoption studies, in addition to their relevance for social policy, constitute valuable natural experiments for assessing the interplay of genetic and environmental influences on development. Other contributions to this volume attest to the power of genetically oriented strategies by examining outcomes for adoptees at risk because of known parental psychopathology (see Chapters 16 and 20). Our aim in this chapter is a different one: to trace the progress of a representative sample of adoptees as they moved from childhood into adulthood, and to contrast their development with a group from similar birth circumstances but brought up by their natural parents.

We still know relatively little about the long-term implications of adoptive placement, which is usually into relatively favored social circumstances for children whose life course might have been different had they stayed in their families of origin. How far can adoption offset the risks such children might otherwise have faced? How far does it carry its own stresses, made evident in different ways? Are particular steps on the path from childhood to adulthood likely to be especially difficult or vulnerable ones for adoptees? These are the questions we will address.

Existing research

Adoption has been proposed as perhaps the most effective 'preventive' strategy for reducing the risks of poor adjustment for illegitimate children born into unpromising circumstances. It is also recognized that the special nature of the adoptive experience may in itself increase vulnerability, whether by virtue of threats to secure attachment in infancy, "genealogical bewilderment" in childhood and beyond, or as a result of the role handicaps experienced by adoptive parents. Existing research presents a somewhat inconsistent picture of how far these concerns are borne out.

Studies of clinical populations include a number of reports of higher than expected rates of referral to specialist agencies among adopted children (Mech, 1973; Schechter, 1960). There are well recognized methodological problems in studies of this kind (Shaw, 1984). When these are handled satisfactorily, the overrepresentation of adoptees is generally reduced, though not entirely eliminated; it is, of course, still questionable how far we can generalize from findings on clinical samples to conclusions about the adjustment of adoptees as a group.

Studies of nonclinical samples have been of two main kinds. The first involves cross-sectional comparisons of adoptees with non-adopted individuals. The findings are conflicting. A number of studies report no differences in behavioral or psychological adjustment between adopted and non-adopted children (see e.g., Norvell & Guy, 1977; Elonen & Schwartz, 1969), while others find higher rates of problems among adoptees. Lindholm and Touliatos (1980), for example, using teacher ratings, reported higher levels of conduct disturbance among adopted elementary school children, increasing rates of difficulty across the elementary grades, and more marked sex differences in adopted than non-adopted groups. Brodzinsky et al. (1984), in a larger sample of 6- to 11-year-olds, also found adoptees rated higher than matched controls, but failed to confirm any major developmental trends in rates or types of difficulty. Both these reports note that although problem levels were elevated in the adopted samples, their scores were nevertheless well within the normal range and carried no implications of severe pathology. Similar conclusions were reached by Hoopes (1982).

The third source of evidence comes from a small group of longitudinal studies, which have extended this type of design in two ways: first, by providing further evidence on possible developmental trends, and second, by including as additional comparison groups not only non-adopted individuals, but also other groups sharing some aspects of adoptees' experience, such as similar birth circumstances or separations from parents, but not adoption per se. Findings of this kind are currently available from two of the prospective British birth cohort studies up to late childhood. In analyses of the National Child Development Study (NCDS) (the 1958 cohort, which we will be reporting on further), illegitimately born adoptees have been compared with other children who were also illegitimately born but brought up by their natural parents. Results at age 7 showed generally satisfactory adjustment for adoptees. Their behavior appeared to deteriorate over the next four years, however, and was closer to that of other illegitimate children at the time of the 11-year follow-up (Lambert & Streather, 1980). At both ages, the illegitimate group appeared particularly at risk of developing behavioral problems. A not dissimilar change in the behavior ratings of adoptees between ages 5 and 10 has emerged from reports on the 1970 cohort (St. Claire & Osborn, 1987).

Taking the picture forward to adolescene, Hodges and Tizard (1989, *a* and *b*) have reported on the progress of a rather special group of children, all of whom spent their early years in residential care, but who were then either adopted or restored to their natural parents before age 7. By age 16, the adoptees showed an attenuation of the restless, distractible pattern that had characterized their behavior at age 8, but they continued to have difficulties in peer relationships. In addition, they differed from "restored" adolescents in showing various behaviors indicative of anxiety, a pattern that had not been evident earlier.

To date, only one prospective study has provided evidence into early adulthood. Bohman (1970) traced the adjustment of a group of Swedish children all of whose mothers initially contacted adoption agencies, but who subsequently received a variety of placements. Assessments at age 11 showed the adopted boys to have significantly higher rates of nervous and behavioral disturbance than classroom controls; by age 15, however, there were no differences in adjustment and much lower rates of difficulty overall. For adopted girls, the slight excess in behavior difficulties at age 11 was also reduced by age 15. Record searches of registrations for criminality and alcohol abuse at age 23 found no differences between adoptees and controls (Bohman & Sigvardsson, 1985). Children restored to their biological mothers showed considerably poorer outcomes than controls at both ages 11 and 15, but no differences in criminality or alcohol registrations at age 23. The authors comment that although their classifications of "problem children" at age 11 had fairly low predictive power across the sample as a whole, discontinuities between one age period and another were most marked for adoptees.

It would obviously be unwise to draw any but the most tentative conclusions on developmental trends from these few, relatively diverse, studies. The picture they suggest is an interesting one, however, and raises a number of questions. Much theoretical writing on adoption would suggest adolescence as a time of heightened risk for emotional or behavioral difficulties, as issues of identity come to the fore. The studies cited point to a rather different pattern, with any excess in adjustment problems for adoptees most likely in middle and late childhood, and much less evident in either adolescence or—on the measures studied so far—early adulthood. A rather similar picture is suggested in a retrospective study of young adult adoptees (Raynor, 1980).

More generally, existing research suggests that adopted boys may be more vulnerable than girls, and that, with the possible exception of the late childhood period, adoptees show much lower rates of difficulty than other children from similar birth circumstances. Their generally more advantaged social and material circumstances may be of particular importance. Finally, there are suggestions that particular patterns of adjustment problems may be characteristic of adoptees at certain ages. Our aim in this chapter is to take up a number of these issues, using data from the more recent phases of NCDS.

The National Child Development Study

NCDS is a prospective study of all children in Britain born in the week of March 3–9, 1958; some 17,000 in all. The children were originally studied as part of the Perinatal Mortality Survey (Butler & Bonham, 1963). Since then, there have been four main follow-ups: at age 7 (Davie et al., 1972), at 11 (Wedge, 1969), at 16 (Fogelman, 1983), and most recently when cohort members were 23. An additional sub-study of adoptees was undertaken when the children were ages 8 and 9 (Seglow et al., 1972). In each of the main childhood sweeps of the study, information was collected from a number of different sources: the children's parents or guardians, their teachers, school medical officers, and the children themselves, who completed attainment tests at each school-age sweep, and an additional questionnaire at age 16. At age 23, data collection was by means of interviews with the cohort members.

The study is especially valuable in providing three related groups for comparison: illegitimately born children who were subsequently adopted, other illegitimate children who remained with their natural parents, and the large majority of legitimate children in the cohort. With a design of this kind, it becomes possible to pursue two related sets of questions: first, how far adoptive placement can reduce the risks associated with illegitimate birth; and second, how far it may nevertheless be associated with some increased vulnerability to problems of adjustment when comparisons are made with non-adopted children in similar social and economic circumstances. Our prime interest is to extend the existing picture of the adjustment of these three groups (Lambert & Streather, 1980) into adolescence and early adulthood; we begin with a brief sketch of their circumstances up to this point.

Family circumstances of the children studied

In the Britain of the late 1950s, illegitimacy was relatively rare; only 3.6% ($N = 543$) of the total NCDS cohort traced at the first follow-up (at age 7) had been born illegitimate. One third of these children ($N = 180$) had been adopted by age 7, while the remainder (to be referred to as the "illegitimate" group) had stayed with one or both of their natural parents. These two groups form the starting point for the comparisons. For reasons of computational ease, we have restricted the non-adopted, legitimately born comparison in this study group to a 10% random sample of all legitimate children in the cohort ($N = 1,435$).

Illegitimacy was associated with a number of other potential risk factors at the time of the children's birth. The mothers of all illegitimately born children—both those who were subsequently adopted and others—were younger than married mothers, and had received considerably poorer antenatal care. As a group, the illegitimate babies were also of lower birthweight than babies born to married mothers. At this point, they clearly constituted a potentially vulnerable group.

Two thirds of these unmarried mothers chose to bring up their children themselves. By no means all, however, did so alone; about a fifth were cohabiting at the time of the child's birth (Crellin et al., 1971), and at each of the subsequent childhood contacts some 40% of the children were living with both their natural parents, and a further 20% to 25% were in two-parent families including a step-parent or cohabitee. The remaining 30% to 35% were in single-parent families. As we shall see, family disruption was much more frequent for illegitimate children, and their living conditions were often extremely poor. Many of the mothers had experienced downward social mobility since the birth of their child, and they were much more likely than other mothers to have worked, often on a full-time basis, before their children started school. The illegitimate children were, as a consequence, more likely to have experienced substitute care of one sort or another in the preschool period.

The adoptees, by contrast, had generally entered more favored social circumstances at the time of their placements. Adoption can take place in a variety of circumstances: the group selected for our study excludes adoptions by own or step-parents, and with only occasional exceptions (such as one child adopted by grandparents) focuses primarily on adoption by nonrelatives. The great majority of the children were adopted as infants; over 75% were placed with their adoptive parents at or before 12 weeks of age, and only a handful at 12 months or older.

As might be expected, the social and material circumstances of these two groups differed widely throughout their childhoods. Table 1 illustrates these differences with measures from the 16-year contact. As at each earlier study sweep, the illegitimate children were the most likely to be in families receiving state benefits and to be in housing conditions which were either crowded or lacked basic amenities, or both. Although the adoptees were by no means all in middle class homes, few had faced acute economic or housing difficulties of this kind. Adopted children were the most likely to have grown up in small families, while the illegitimate group were overrepresented in both the smallest and the largest family-size groupings.

The final section of Table 1 gives some indication of the continuity of parenting experienced by children in each group. If we classify as a change in parenting either the loss of a parent from death, divorce, or separation, or the arrival of a new parent figure in a family, nearly one third of the illegitimate children had faced at least one such change between the ages of 7 and 16, and almost 10% had experienced two. In their teens, the adoptees also experienced higher than average rates of family change, though the

Table 1. *Family circumstances at age 16 (percentage)*

	Illegitimate	Adopted	Legitimate
Class/economic background			
Nonmanual	9.7	56.6	32.9
Free school meals	25.3	3.8	9.4
Housing			
Owner-occupied	22.2	64.2	43.9
Lacking amenities	16.4	2.4	7.7
Family size			
1–2 children	16.9	29.7	10.8
5 or more children	37.8	11.0	29.7
Changes in parental care			
Between ages 7–11	17.8	5.5	4.5
Between ages 11–16	26.3	17.2	6.7
Between ages 7–16	29.5	20.7	9.4

reasons in this case were markedly different. For the illegitimate group, family instability was largely the result of parental separations and divorce (with their attendant likelihood of earlier discord), together with the start of newly constituted families. Both these sets of experiences are well known to carry increased risks of behavioral and emotional difficulties for children. For adoptees, the pattern was a very different one; in the great majority of cases, the changes resulted from the death of an adoptive parent. Since adoptive parents are in general older than natural parents, a pattern of this kind should not be unexpected; it does, however, serve to highlight a further source of potential vulnerability for at least some groups of adoptees. Finally, illegitimate children were by far the most likely to have been separated completely from their families and to have spent some time in public care.

This brief outline gives some flavor of how the childhoods of the illegitimate and adopted groups, born in broadly similar circumstances, differed both from each other and from those of the majority of the legitimate members of the cohort. For many of the illegitimate children who had remained with their mothers, the picture is one of continuing material disadvantage and an increased likelihood of family instability. For those who were adopted, later family and material circumstances were generally much more favorable, but the adoptive situation itself doubtless created its own particular demands, less easily captured by survey measures such as these. Our concern is to explore how these various factors were reflected in the young people's patterns of adjustment in adolescence and early adulthood.

Patterns of adjustment

Some methodological considerations. The NCDS data set has both advantages and limitations for a study of this kind. Its strengths lie in the unselected nature of the sample of adoptees, the availability of both legitimate and other illegitimately born children as comparisons, and the long time span of the data collection. Few other studies have prospective data covering a comparable age range, which means that NCDS is particularly valuable for exploring developmental trends from childhood to adulthood.

Set against these assets are certain inherent limitations. With the exception of the additional study of adoptees at age 8 (Seglow et al., 1972), the study was not specifically planned to explore the effects of illegitimacy or adoption; although the parental interviews at each stage provide measures of the children's social and material circumstances, they give very little insight into the nature of family relationships, or the particular stresses or difficulties that might be faced in families such as these. There are thus clear restrictions on the range of explanatory factors or processes that can be explored. In addition, the most recent follow-up (at age 23) was undertaken when many of the young people were still in the process of establishing themselves in the world of work and only beginning to marry and build families. The measures at this point largely concentrate on their functioning in these areas. Young men and women from different social backgrounds differed quite markedly in the extent to which they had begun to make these transitions to adult roles, and these variations inevitably complicate comparisons between the groups of particular interest to us. The 23-year data should thus best be seen as providing pointers to early adult adjustment, which require further confirmation in later years.

Finally, our initial analyses suggested that nonresponse (which showed an interesting pattern of variation between the groups) could raise particular difficulties in these samples. This problem, and the imputation and weighting procedures used to overcome it, are discussed further in the Appendix. In brief, the 16-year analyses were conducted on the 1,188 cases (213 illegitimate, 82 adopted and 893 legitimate) with complete behavioral data at each childhood sweep; occasional missing data on independent variables were imputed, and the sample re-weighted to take account of possible sample selection bias. Since we wished in each analysis to make multiple paired comparisons between the groups, contrasting the scores of the illegitimate with the legitimate, and the adoptees with each in turn, we have throughout used the approach of Gabriel (1966) to reduce the risk of inflating significance levels. In this instance, this involved obtaining p values for the χ^2 test statistics from a χ^2 distribution with two rather than one degree of freedom.

Our analyses build directly on the picture of these groups' first steps on the path to adulthood as detailed in earlier publications (Crellin et al., 1971; Lambert & Streather, 1980). These had shown that illegitimate children remaining with their natural parents showed the highest levels of behavior problems at both age 7 and 11, even after taking account of their disadvantaged social circumstances. Adoptees differed little from legitimate children at age 7, but by 11, especially when their more favored social situation had been taken into account, their adjustment appeared to have deteriorated and was closer to that of the illegitimate than the legitimate group.

We begin by adding findings on their adjustment in adolescence to this existing picture to assess developmental trends across the full range of the school years and to explore the extent of continuities in behavior problems from one study contact to the next. We then consider the measures of functioning available in early adulthood and the further trends that these suggest. The outcomes in this case largely consist of binary measures. It is well known that measurement error in binary response data often attenuates the estimated effects of explanatory variables; it has also been found (Rutter & Quinton, 1984) that between-group differences on measures of behavioral adjustment can be detected more easily among those with difficulties that are persistent over time. To take account of both these factors, we turn finally to a rather different aspect of continuity: the extent to which individuals showed persistent difficulties across all four study sweeps, and how far, if at all, the legitimacy status groups differed in this respect.

Behavioral adjustment in adolescence. As in earlier sweeps, both parent and teacher ratings of behavior were available from the 16-year contact. We focused on the teacher ratings made using the Rutter B(2) questionnaire (Rutter, 1967), a 26-item scale tapping a range of both behavioral and emotional difficulties. This scale has been widely used in epidemiological research and has been shown to correlate highly ($r = .92$; Yule, 1968) with scores on the Bristol Social Adjustment Guides (Stott, 1969), the measures used in earlier NCDS sweeps. We explored the 16-year data in two ways: first, using total scores to assess overall levels of behavioral difficulty at this point, and second, focusing on selected groups of questionnaire items to examine how far *types* of adjustment problems in adolescence might differ between the groups.

Overall levels of adjustment. Simple between-group comparisons of mean behavior scores at age 16 again showed illegitimate adolescents having the highest rates of difficulty overall, and the adopted group falling between the legitimate and illegitimate. Regression analyses were used to assess how far these differences could be accounted for by variations in social and family circumstances and to examine scores at age 16 in the light of similar assessments at age 11. Table 2 shows the results of these analyses.

Table 2. *Total behavior scores at age 16 (N = 1,188)*

	Simple means		Including weightings and background co-variates		Including weightings, background co-variates and behavior at age 11	
Legitimacy status	(a)	(b)	(a)	(b)	(a)	(b)
Illegitimate	2.280	(0.092)	1.671	(0.131)	0.852	(0.144)
Adopted	−0.580	(0.174)	−0.237	(0.168)	−0.253	(0.159)
Legitimate	−0.765	(0.102)	−0.528	(0.104)	−0.415	(0.099)
Sex						
Girls			−0.233	(0.075)	−0.071	(0.073)
Housing tenure and conditions						
Owner-occupied			0.331	(0.134)	0.347	(0.128)
Council tenant			0.421	(0.095)	0.414	(0.090)
Other tenure			0.598	(0.130)	0.530	(0.124)
Lacking amenities						
Economic status						
Nonmanual			0.248	(0.092)	0.159	(0.087)
Manual			0.254	(0.212)	0.180	(0.202)
No male head			0.694	(0.146)	0.489	(0.139)
Receiving benefits						
Family size			0.164	(0.086)	0.066	(0.083)
Behavior at age 11			—		0.289	(0.026)
Between-group contrasts			χ_2^2	p	χ_2^2	p
Illegitimate vs. legitimate			25.73	0.000	17.45	0.000
Illegitimate vs. adopted			1.99	0.370	2.54	0.281
Adopted vs. legitimate			4.15	0.126	1.40	0.497

Note: (a) Regression parameter estimates; (b) standard errors

Across the sample as a whole, sex effects at age 16 were less marked than at younger ages, though still important, and the indicators of social class and economic circumstances, housing conditions, and family size all showed associations with behavioral adjustment. There were no significant interactions between any of these factors and legitimacy status. Behavior scores were not significantly different for adolescents in single- or two-parent families, nor according to natural mother's class of origin, once these other factors had been taken into account. Within the group of adoptees, age at placement showed no association with behavioral difficulties at age 16. Including all significant co-variates in the analyses, the illegitimate group's scores were still significantly poorer than those of the legitimate group, and the adoptees fell midway between the other groups, significantly different from neither. Figure 1 displays the initial comparisons of simple mean and estimates of group differences taking account of background factors, taking scores for legitimate adolescents as the reference group and showing estimates for the other groups as departures from these. To set the 16-year results in context, we have repeated comparable analyses at ages 7 and 11, and these are also displayed in Figure 1.

To provide some assessment of continuities since late childhood,

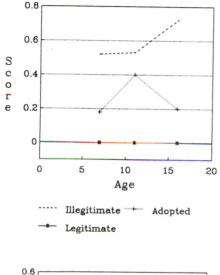

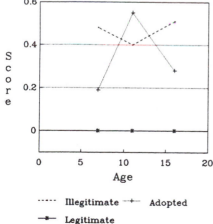

Figure 1. Behavioral adjustment over time of illegitimate and adopted groups as compared to legitimate adolescents. Top: simple group means; bottom: adjusted for background factors.

11-year-old behavior scrores were then added to the analysis. As Table 2 shows, the between-group comparisons remained essentially as before. Illegitimate adolescents showed poorer adjustment than the legitimate group even after taking account of their earlier, poorer scores, while the adoptees retained their position between the other two groups. Correlations between behavior ratings of this kind at different ages are in general relatively low; they were in this case .40 across the sample as a whole for scores at ages 11 and 16. Because of the low expectations of stability on these measures, it is difficult to interpret the findings for adoptees in any straightforward way as indicating "improvement" since age 11; the results do nevertheless suggest that the apparent deterioration in their adjustment between ages 7 and 11 did not continue into adolescence.

Perhaps the most interesting features of these findings are the differing age trends in adjustment problems suggested for the two illegitimately born groups. Illegitimate children who remained with their natural parents had shown the highest rates of behavioral difficulties from the first follow-up at age 7, and the gap between them and the legitimate group remained wide in their teens. Scores for the adoptees, by comparison, reflected some increased vulnerability to problems of adjustment throughout, but this had clearly peaked around the time of the 11-year contact and was much less marked in adolescence.

These differing profiles remained after fairly major differences in social and material circumstances had been taken into account. We were not able to include a second potentially important set of co-variates—those reflecting changes in parent figures and family disruption—in the main analyses, because of problems of missing data, which could not be adequately addressed by simple imputation procedures. We have, however, made tests of their effects on the smaller subset of cases with complete data from all the childhood sweeps. These revealed a complex pattern of effects, varying both by sex of child and by type of family change, whether disruption of an existing unit or constitution of a new one. Effects of this kind have been explored in detail in studies of children in step-families within NCDS (Ferri, 1984). Like Ferri, we found that the implications of family change were quite marked for some subgroups of children and adolescents (e.g., girls between ages 11 and 16 in families with a new parent figure) but less so for others. Within legitimacy status groups, these effects frequently operated in different directions; it was thus unlikely that they could play any major role in accounting for the overall pattern of differences between the legitimacy status groups at this stage.

Subsets of behavior problems. High overall scores on behavior ratings may reflect a variety of different types of problem behavior. To assess these, we went on to compare the groups on four more specific subsets of items from the 16-year-old teacher questionnaires: tapping, restless, overactive behavior; antisocial or conduct problems; emotional difficulties; and problems in relationships with peers. The distributions of scores on these subsets of items demanded a somewhat different approach to the analyses. In each case, a majority of the sample had zero scores, and the remainder formed a long tail. There is no sensible way of transforming such distributions to normality, so these subsets of items were analyzed using Poisson regression and quasi-likelihood. The Poisson distribution is able to deal with a dominance of zero scores, but requires the additional variance that quasi-likelihood can provide to cope with the long tail or overdispersion (McCullogh & Nelder, 1983).

There were significant sex differences in each area and significant effects for all the social and family background factors considered previously. Taking these into account, and weighting the scores as appropriate, the illegitimate group showed higher rates of difficulty than the legitimate group on all but the emotional item subset. Their high overall behavior scores appeared to reflect a wide spectrum of difficulties in adolescence, not confined to any particular problem category. For adoptees, however, the pattern was much more specific; they did not differ from legitimate adolescents on either the restless or the antisocial items, but they had the highest scores on items reflecting unhappy, anxious behavior, and, like the illegitimate group, were rated as showing significantly greater problems in their relationships with peers (Table 3). For adoptees, this combination of anxiety and peer relationship difficulties closely echoes the adolescent findings for later-placed adoptees reported by Hodges and Tizard (1989a and b).

Patterns in early adulthood. We now examine how far these patterns persisted beyond adolescence, as the young people began making the transition to the very different demands of adult roles and independent living. The interviews at age 23 focused on a wide range of aspects of their early adult lives. As a measure of possible mental health difficulties, respondents completed the Malaise Inventory (Rutter et al., 1070), a 24-item questionnaire tapping affective disturbance, which has been widely used in community surveys as an indicator of nonclinical depression. In other areas, however, the interviews were not specifically designed to focus on disorder or on problems in psychosocial functioning. We have thus used the more general measures collected at this stage to derive a number of indicators, mainly in the areas of marriage, family formation, and work, which might provide pointers to patterns of poor adaptation in each group.

As noted earlier, the results must be approached with some caution. Poor social functioning in these areas might be evident in two rather different ways: taking the example of marriage and cohabitation, in a somewhat older sample we might consider both failure to engage in relationships and

Table 3. *Subscores at age 16*

Questionnaire item subscores $(N = 1,109)^a$

	Restless		Antisocial		Emotional		Peer problems	
	(a)		(a)		(a)		(a)	
Illegitimate	− 0.59	0.00	− 0.29	0.00	− 0.51	0.00	− 0.21	0.00
Adopted		− 0.32		− 0.25		0.18		0.08
Legitimate		− 0.44		− 0.60		− 0.19		− 0.50

Between-group contrasts

	χ^2	p	χ^2	p	χ^2	p	χ^2	p
Illegitimate vs. legitimate	9.92	0.007	13.80	0.001	3.11	0.211	15.54	0.000
Illegitimate vs. adoped	1.63	0.443	0.78	0.677	1.05	0.592	0.17	0.919
Adopted vs. legitimate	0.23	0.891	1.53	0.465	5.50	0.064	9.47	0.009

Note: (a) Logit parameter estimates
^{a} Controlling for housing and economic circumstances at 16, family size, and sex of child at age 16.

experience of relationship breakdowns as indicators of difficulties in social functioning. In a sample of 23-year-olds, it would clearly be inappropriate to consider the first of these as in any sense problematical. Our measures thus generally reflect only one of these two possible poles of difficulty— patterns indicative of instability, and perhaps discord, in social functioning. In each area, cohort members who had not yet entered the relevant adult arena are by definition excluded from the analyses. The particular focus, and inevitable limitations, of these measures must be borne in mind throughout.

Analyses of the early adult measures are further complicated by systematic variations between the sexes and between groups from differing social backgrounds in the stages they had reached in their working lives, their likelihood of marriage, and so forth. While the majority of women had married or cohabited by age 23, for example, less than half the men had done so. To take account of sex differences of this kind, we present all the early adult findings separately for women and men. Social background differences raised more complex problems, because adoptees and illegitimate young people in particular differed so widely in this respect. We have made every effort to account for these variations in making the comparisons, but some caution may be appropriate until more complete assessments can be obtained in later adulthood.

Response rates were rather higher in all groups at age 23 than at age 16, but there were nevertheless some further losses from the groups studied thus far. To maintain the longitudinal focus of the analyses, we have based the comparisons at this point on cases with both behavioral data and family background measures from the 16-year sweep. This approach, which provided a total of 864 cases for analysis, ensured continuity in the groups studied at each stage, and enabled us to continue weighting the samples as before, to take account of cumulative sample selection bias at 11, 16 and 23 years. The form of the analysis at age 23 was also as before; we began by looking at simple between-group comparisons, and then included relevant social and family background indicators from the 16-year sweep; finally we tested how far poor adjustment at age 23 represented continuities with behavior at age 16. In addition, we introduced one new variable into the analyses at this stage: the educational qualifications achieved by the young people by age 23. This variable seemed likely to have direct implications for functioning in employment, and, as might be anticipated, the groups differed markedly in the levels of qualifications they had attained. Adoptees had achieved well both educationally and vocationally; over 80% had some formal qualifications by age 23, by comparison with just over 75% of the legitimate group. The illegitimate young people, and especially the women, had fared much less well; just under 30% of the men and over half of the women had no formal educational or vocational qualifications at all by this stage. An indirect effect of these differences was that the adoptees, as a corollary of their more extended education, were somewhat less likely to have entered other adult arenas by their early twenties.

Malaise Inventory scores. Very few of the measures at age 23 showed the clear pattern of statistically significant group differences found in adolescence, though broadly consistent trends emerged. The most direct assessment of possible mental health problems in early adulthood is the Malaise Inventory. High scores on this inventory are generally accepted as indicating an increased risk of depression. As we would anticipate in samples of this age, there were marked sex differences in the pattern of responses, with roughly twice as many women as men in the high-scoring groups. In addition, continuities with behavior scores at age 16 also differed between the sexes, with a significant association for women ($\chi^2_1 = 5.43$), doubtless reflecting continuities from earlier emotional problems, but not for men $\chi^2_1 = .20$). Among men, there were no differences between legitimacy status groups in tendencies to depressive symptomatology. For women, the illegitimate group showed the greatest vulnerability to depressed affect, although the contrasts between all three legitimacy status groups failed to reach statistical significance. Figure 2 illustrates these comparisons along with four other outcome variables, and Table 4 summarizes results of the analyses.

Relationship breakdowns. By age 23, almost 70% of women and 45% of

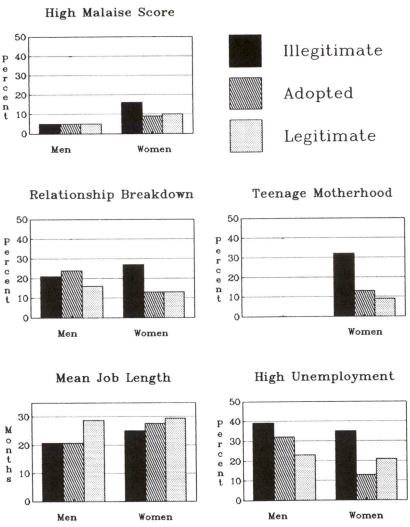

Figure 2. Group differences at age 23.

men in the sample had either married or had had a cohabitation lasting 6 months or longer. For both sexes, around 15% had already experienced a breakdown in these relationships. For women, simple probabilities of breakdown were highest in the illegitimate group, though the group differences failed to reach statistical significance; among men, adoptees were the most likely to have been involved in broken cohabitations, although, again, between-group comparisons were nonsignificant. Relationship breakdowns at this early adult stage showed no connection to any of the family or social background co-variates, and were the only 23-year-old indicators to

Table 4. *Age 23 measures*

	Simple comparisons		Between-group contrasts (χ^2)		
	Constant	Dummy variable	Single comparisons	Including 16-year background	Including 16-year background and behavior
			p	*p*	*p*
		Men			
Malaise scores					
Illegitimate	−2.96	0.00	I vs. L		
Adoped		−0.18	A vs. I		
Legitimate		0.03	A vs. L		
Separations					
Illegitimate	−1.30	0.00	I vs. L		
Adopted		0.13	A vs. I		
Legitimate		−0.51	A vs. L		
Mean job length					
Illegitimate	−3.03	0.00	I vs. L 0.001	0.008	0.01
Adopted		0.00	A vs. I NS	NS	NS
Legitimate		−0.33	A vs. L 0.015	0.006	0.004
High unemployment					
Illegitimate	−0.44	0.00	I vs. L 0.17		
Adopted		−0.30	A vs. I NS		
Legitimate		−0.79	A vs. L NS		
		Women			
Malaise scores					
Illegitimate	−1.66	0.00	I vs. L		
Adopted		−0.62	A vs. I		
Legitimate		−0.54	A vs. L		
Separations					
Illegitimate	−1.01	0.00	I vs. L		
Adopted		−0.87	A vs. I		
Legitimate		−0.90	A vs. L		
Teenage motherhood					
Illegitimate	−0.74	0.00	I vs. L 0.001	0.034	0.09
Adopted		−1.15	A vs. I NS	NS	NS
Legitimate		−1.62	A vs. L NS	NS	NS
Mean job length					
Illegitimate	−3.22	0.00	I vs. L		
Adopted		−0.10	A vs. I		
Legitimate		−0.16	A vs. L		
High unemployment					
Illegitimate	−0.63	0.00	I vs. L		
Adopted		−1.30	A vs. I		
Legitimate		−0.71	A vs. L		

Note: Between-group contrasts are reported for all comparisons in which $p<.2$.
NS = Not significant.

show no associations with behavior ratings at age 16 for either sex.

Teenage pregnancies. Only a minority of sample members had begun to have children by age 23, just over a third of women and a fifth of the men. Both men and women in the illegitimate group were more likely than others to have become parents by this age. The most marked group differences, however, occurred in relation to teenage pregnancies. We have focused on results for the women only, since the consequences of teenage parenthood were likely to be so much more serious for them (Kiernan, 1980). As Figure 2 illustrates, illegitimate women were by far the most likely to have had children in their teens, while the adopted and legitimate groups had similar, and low, rates of teenage births.

These between-group differences were reduced, but not eliminated, by the inclusion of social and family background co-variates. Behavior scores at age 16 also showed significant associations with the likelihood of teenage pregnancy ($\chi_1^2 = 6.21$); when these were added as further co-variates in the analyses, differences between the illegitimate women and other groups were again reduced (Table 4). Though we cannot be sure how these associations were mediated, it was clear that behavior problems toward the end of schooling either indicated or led to increased vulnerability to teenage pregnancy, which in its turn seemed likely to be a marker for later problems.

Job stability and unemployment. In the area of work, we have focused on two measures of potential employment problems: frequent job changes and lengthy periods of unemployment. At the time of the interviews at age 23, cohort members were at very different stages of their labor market experience; some, especially those who had gone on to further or higher education, had been working for relatively brief periods, while others were already well established in their chosen careers. Among the women, many had already stopped work to have children. To reduce some of this variability, and to avoid comparisons based on limited time periods, we restricted the analyses of employment indicators to both men and women who had spent at least 5 years in the labor market.

Within this group, there was a considerable range in terms of job stability and change. To illustrate this, Figure 2 shows the mean length of jobs at this point for men and women in each group. For women, job instability was associated with age-16 behavior scores ($\chi_1^2 = 12.26$), but not with educational qualifications. Comparisons between the legitimacy status groups were all nonsignificant, both with and without family background co-variates. For men, both earlier behavior ratings and educational qualifications added significantly to the analysis, though the latter appeared to be colinear with the indicators of 16-year-old housing conditions and tenure, and family size. Simple between-group comparisons showed both illegitimate and adopted men to have had considerably higher rates of job change than legitimate men; these contrasts remained significant once social background, behavior ratings at age 16, and qualification levels had all been included in the analyses.

Extensive unemployment, defined as 6 months or more for those 5 years or longer in the labor market, showed less marked group differences. Once again, earlier behavior ratings and qualification levels were important for men but not women, but none of the between-group comparisons showed significant differences for either sex.

Persistent difficulties in adjustment

Our final set of analyses was designed to focus on the issue of persistent, rather than more time-limited, difficulties in adjustment. We have already noted that the correlations between measures at the three childhood sweeps were only modest, in the order of .3 to .4 for the sample as a whole for adjacent measures. This confirms the picture from other studies that for many children, problems during the school years are likely to be relatively transitory, being perhaps the response to particular stressors. For some, however, more serious difficulties will persist. Our aim at this point was to test how far adopted or illegitimate children might differ in their likelihoods of showing more persistent problems of this kind. Combining both childhood and early adult indicators in such tests might also enable us to overcome difficulties concerned with measurement error and power.

The previous results from the early adult data were intriguing, but only occasionally statistically significant. As mentioned earlier, a more powerful test of group differences might be obtained from a simultaneous analysis of several outcome indicators, perhaps along the lines of the Analysis of Covariance Structures (ACOVS) model of Joreskog et al. (1971), which was recently applied to ratings of children's behavior by Ferguson and Horwood (1987) using Linear Structural Relationships (LISREL) (Joreskog & Sorbum, 1981). However, a model of this kind was not entirely suited to our own investigation. Although our interest in persistent difficulties could be easily addressed by appropriate restrictions on the parameters of the LISREL model, what was harder to encompass was our concern with a relatively severe level of behavioral disturbance at each point. This essentially required categorical outcome measures, for which LISREL is ill suited. In a clinical-based or high-risk sample, such levels of disturbance may be sufficiently common to make it possible to use simple cross-tabulation methods to identify "persisters" (Rutter & Quinton, 1984). In samples more representative of the ordinary population, even quite large ones as here, such an approach would identify so few individuals with persistent problems that it would possess little power (Ghodsian et al., 1980).

We therefore undertook a more unusual analysis, one that essentially corresponds to a categorical version of the ACOVS model. The outcome indicators were all expressed in a categorical form, and each was related by means of logistic regression to a set of relevant explanatory variables describing family and economic background, and also to a latent-class variable common to all regressions. The latent class defined just two categories, individuals with persistent disturbance and those without. The model calculates a posterior probability of belonging to the latent class for each individual, taking into account that his or her family and social background also contribute to the observed outcomes. It should be emphasized that we used the model as a framework for the statistical testing of intercorrelated outcome measures. There are numerous other possible specifications for the form of the latent variable and its continuity over time; without a more detailed testing of the specification of the estimated model and comparison with results from at least some of these alternatives, we are unwilling to place any direct interpretation on class membership probabilities.

For the men, five outcome measures were included: the behavior ratings from each of the childhood sweeps, together with the two early adult employment indicators, unemployment and job instability. Each measure was dichotomized to identify relatively high scorers at each point. Any cut-off of this kind is inevitably arbitrary. For the behavior ratings, we focused on the top 13% of the range, a figure broadly comparable with epidemiological findings for "deviant" scores on the Rutter scale (Rutter et al., 1975), and within the range classified as "maladjusted" on the 7- and 11-year ratings. On the employment measures (which again included only those men who had been in the labor market for at least 5 years), relatively severe problem levels had already been chosen. Nonresponse weights were not included, in order to simplify the E-M estimation method (Dempster et al., 1977), which required iterative weights of its own. Since any individuals with at least one of these outcome measures and a corresponding set of explanatory variables (housing conditions, economic circumstances, and family size), could be included in this analysis (giving 142 illegitimate, 88 adopted, and 726 legitimate men), our previous concerns over nonresponse bias were reduced. The prior probability of individuals in each of the two latent classes was allowed to vary across legitimacy groups, and the overall proportion in the persistent class was constrained to equal 0.1. Again, this figure was necessarily arbitrary; our aim was to focus on relatively high scores but without any implication of pathology. The computation, using an expanded data method (Hinde, 1982) within (Generalized Linear Interactive Model) GLIM (Baker & Nelder, 1978), was slow.

The fitting of a model with just co-variates is equivalent to treating each of the outcome variables as (conditionally) independent of the other four. The addition of the latent class, still restricting the proportion in this class in order to be equal across the legitimacy status groups, gave a substantial improvement in the fit of the model: $\chi_5^2 = 49.64$.[1] A further substantial improvement ($\chi_2^2 = 19.47$) was obtained if the prior probabilities of the legitimacy status groups were allowed to vary. The significance of these differences appeared to derive for the most part from the contrast between adopted and legitimate men: of the total χ^2 difference of 19.47, this contrast accounted for 14.06, while the adopted–illegitimate comparison accounted for only .41. Given their relatively advantaged social backgrounds, it appeared that adopted men were indeed substantially more likely than their legitimate peers to show continuing difficulties over time.

For women (192 illegitimate, 67 adopted, and 667 legitimate) the outcome measures again included the childhood and adolescent behavior ratings (using the same cut-offs as for men) and two adult measures (teenage pregnancy and Malaise scores). The addition of the latent class with equal prior probabilities across groups gave a substantial improvement in the fit of the model ($\chi_5^2 = 59.03$), with a further improvement if the prior probabilities could vary ($\chi_2^2 = 20.41$). Here, almost all the improvement was due to even poorer outcomes among the illegitimate girls than their relative measured social disadvantage would have predicted; neither of the contrasts involving adopted women proved significant (χ_1^2 of 1.42 and 0.57). As all of the earlier findings might have led us to expect, the illegitimate women were at by far the greatest risk of showing persistent adjustment problems.

Concluding remarks

We set out on our analyses with three central questions: how far adoption could be seen to offset the risks associated with illegitimate birth; how far it might nevertheless carry its own vulnerabilities; and how far particular patterns of problem behavior, or difficulties at particular developmental stages, might be especially characteristic of adoptees. The findings are not entirely unequivocal, but do provide some interesting pointers on each issue.

In general, the comparisons at each age point suggested relatively high levels of behavioral and adaptive problems in the illegitimate group. Illegitimate birth, when compounded with the later social and material problems that faced children who remained with their natural parents, not unexpectedly signaled difficulties in a range of areas. These did not seem entirely explicable in terms of contemporary social disadvantage, at least on the measures available here, so we must assume that other factors, constitutional or experiential, also played some part.

In many respects, the adoptees did indeed appear to have avoided this broad spectrum of risk; few of the comparisons showed significant differences from the legitimate group, even when account was taken of expectations for their relatively advantaged social circumstances. There were nevertheless some important qualifying aspects to this general picture.

Perhaps the most interesting of these becomes obvious when our findings are compared to those from earlier sweeps. As Figure 1 illustrated, the adoptees' scores were not entirely comparable with those of legitimate individuals at any point. The disparity was by far the greatest, however, and only reached statistical significance, at the 11-year assessment. This increase in problems in late childhood was clearly particular to, and also quite generally displayed by, adoptees; within the adopted group, it occurred for both boys and girls, and for children adopted into both working class and middle class homes.

We can only speculate on the factors that might underlie this increase in problems, including perhaps reactions to the changes in schooling that would have occurred for many of these children at around this age. For both of the illegitimately born groups, the relationships between school attainment and behavioral adjustment would seem well worth researching, and we hope to explore these in future analyses.

One further possibility however is that the findings may reflect more directly on reactions to the adoptive experience per se. It has generally been assumed that adolescence would constitute a period of increased vulnerability for adoptees, with its concerns over issues of identity. The higher rates of anxiety and emotional problems among adoptees at age 16 would be consistent with this view. Insofar as their poorer behavior ratings do reflect stresses associated with coming to terms with adoptive status, however, the findings suggest that this process may have begun considerably earlier. There are possible parallels in a study of children's beliefs about adoption (Singer et al., 1982). Adopted children were found to hold more positive attributions about adoption in the early school years, but to have moved to more negative positions by late childhood and early adolescence. More detailed studies of the links between such cognitive appraisals and patterns of behavioral difficulties in adoptees at different ages would be of considerable interest.

In early adulthood, we found suggestions of the sex differences reported by a number of earlier writers and noted in more limited ways in previous NCDS sweeps. Adopted women appeared to be faring well; their scores were almost exactly comparable with those of legitimate women in all of the areas we have been able to examine, and there were no indications of any elevated rates of difficulties in functioning. The picture was a less positive one for adopted men, with some indications that the transition to adulthood may have been less smooth for them. These indications were clearest in the area of job stability and change. We must bear in mind that men who had been in the labor market for less than 5 years, usually as a result of extended education, were excluded from these analyses, so that later assessments may modify the current picture; by age 23, those adopted men who had entered the labor force early had clearly experienced some difficulties in arriving at a settled pattern of employment. They also had the highest overall probability of relationship breakdowns, although group differences were small and not statistically significant. Once again, we must await later assessments to gauge whether these results reflected transitory reactions at this particular phase of the life span, or were the start of more persisting patterns of difficulty in adulthood. Our final analyses, focusing on more persistent difficulties up to this point, suggested that adopted men might well show increased vulnerabilities in this respect, in ways not shared by women adoptees. The possible reasons for these sex differences clearly warrant further attention.

As is so often the case in studies of this kind, the analyses raise quite as many questions as they answer. This is in many ways quite proper: large-scale prospective studies such as NCDS provide invaluable opportunities to explore the broad outlines of developmental patterns, to test out some initial hypotheses, and, equally importantly, to generate others. As we have indicated, some of the unresolved issues from our analyses may be answered in later sweeps, when patterns of adult development can be more clearly discerned. Others require different, but complementary, approaches, designed to tease out in greater detail the processes that underlie the trends now emerging. Important among these will be the task of incorporating the perceptions of adoptees and their families: their reactions to, and understandings of, this very particular form of life experience. We have been able to chart something of their progress on the path to adulthood from an external perspective; but a richer appreciation of that pathway, and in particular its more difficult stages, must also include the opinions of those most intimately involved.

Appendix

Nonresponse and missing data

Although response rates have been high within NCDS at each individual sweep, a considerable loss of "complete data" cases occurs where data from several instruments and several sweeps are required. For many analyses of the complete cohort this loss can be sustained without ill effect (Hutchison, 1986). However, we began with three subgroups, two of which were small and in addition showed rather different patterns of response. At the 16-year follow-up, members of the illegitimate group proved somewhat harder than others to trace, and at both the 11- and 16-year follow-ups, adoptive families had high rates of refusal (13.3% and 20.0% respectively, by comparison with 5.5% and 7.0% in the legitimate sample). There was thus a real risk of sample selection bias and of a reduction to such small numbers that even substantial differences between the groups might appear insignificant.

We chose a simple and inoffensive method for imputing the occasional missing values on independent variables, such as class and economic status, for cases with almost complete data, based on their responses on comparable items from previous sweeps. We could not, of course, use this approach to impute measures of stability or change in parent figures, because the prime interest here was in discontinuities from one sweep to the next. Restricting the analyses to samples with full data on these indicators would have resulted in considerable losses; we thus decided not to include them in the main analyses, but made separate tests of their likely effects. Since we did not wish to impute values for missing dependent variables (measures of behavior and adjustment) this still left us with 729 out of 1,917 cases that were nonresponders by age 16. We explored various procedures to compensate for potential sample selection bias (Heckman, 1979; Marini et al., 1979), and found that the estimation of case weights based upon the inverse of the estimated response probability appeared the most robust, simple, and flexible.

During these analyses, a clear and interesting pattern of nonresponse emerged. Among illegitimate adolescents, there was a trend for nonresponders at both ages 11 and 16 (including all cases without behavioral data, whether as a result of parental refusals, failures in tracing, or other factors) to include higher proportions of children with poor adjustment scores at younger ages. Since tracing difficulties were highest in the illegitimate group, and untraced cases frequently include high proportions of "deviant" individuals in all types of social research, this was not an unexpected pattern. A similar, but less marked, trend occurred in the legitimate group. For the adopted sample, however, the position was reversed; those children with previously poor scores were *more* likely to have remained in the study throughout, and the losses at age 16 were disproportionately among adolescents showing adequate and good adjustment at earlier sweeps. These effects are illustrated in Figure A1 for the children at age 16.

We can only speculate on the reasons for this somewhat unusual pattern. One at least plausible explanation would seem to lie in an extension of the suggestions put forward to explain the somewhat lower response rates across the sample as a whole at age 16. In that case, it appeared that some parents had wished to protect their children from the possible additional stress of testing at an important stage in their school careers. In a similar way, we might suppose that a number of adoptive parents, where placements were working out well, might be anxious to avoid any possibly disturbing effects from participation in the research. Whatever the reasons for these varying response patterns, it was clear that they were likely to lead to at least some degree of bias in estimates of between-group differences at age 16.

Accounting for weighting in the calculation of standard errors and test statistics can be complex in all but simple linear models. Weights were determined as the inverse of the product of the estimated response probabilities at each assessment, normalized so that the sum of the squares of the weights

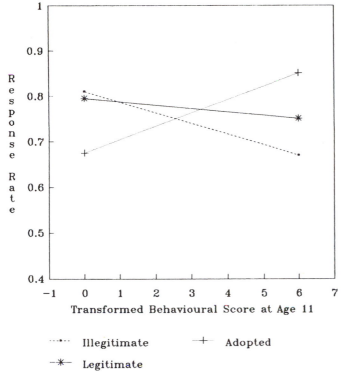

Figure A1. Patterns of response at age 16 for those with data at ages 7 and 11.

equaled the actual sample size. The response probabilities themselves were estimated using a logit model, with the terms of the three-way interaction of sex, legitimacy status, and previous behavioral score as explanatory variables.

Note

1 The χ^2 values cited derive from likelihood ratio tests. The exact distribution of such tests are not fully understood when used with latent class models of this sort, owing to a problem of testing on a boundary of the parameter space. However, in this application the values were either so large or so small that the inferential decisions made would remain the same even if the test statistic departed very considerably from the true χ^2 distribution.

Acknowledgments

This study is based on secondary analyses of NCDS data. The data set was prepared for us by staff at the National Children's Bureau. The study was completed in collaboration and discussion with Mr. Ken Fogelman and Ms. Lydia Lambert, both of whom have long associations with NCDS. We are grateful for their helpful suggestions and encouragement throughout.

References

Baker, R. J., & Nelder, J. A. (1978). *GLIM Release 3: Generalized linear interactive models*. Oxford: Numerical Algorithms Group.

Bohman, M. (1970). *Adopted children and their families*. Stockholm: Proprius.

Bohman, M., & Sigvardsson, S. (1985). A prospective longitudinal study of adoption. In A. R. Nicol (Ed.), *Longitudinal studies in child psychology and psychiatry*. Chichester: John Wiley.

Brodzinsky, D. M., Schechter, D. E., Braff, A. M., & Singer, L. M. (1984). Psychological and academic adjustment in adopted children. *Journal of Consulting and Clinical Psychology, 52*(4), 582–591.

Butler, N. R., & Bonham, D. G. (1963). *Perinatal mortality*. Edinburgh: Livingstone.

Crellin, E., Pringle, M. L. K., & West, P. (1971). *Born illegitimate*. Windsor: NFER.

Davie, R., Butler, N. R., & Goldstein, H. (1972). *From birth to seven*. London: Longman, in association with NCB.

Dempster, A. P., Laird, N. M., & Rubin, D. B. (1977). Maximum likelihood from incomplete data via the EM algorithm. *Journal of the Royal Statistical Society,* 39 B, 1–38.

Elonen, A. S., & Schwartz, E. M. (1969). A longitudinal study of emotional, social and academic functioning of adopted children. *Child Welfare, 48,* 72–78.

Ferguson, D. M., & Horwood, L. J. (1987). The trait and method components of ratings of conduct disorder—Part II. Factors related to the trait component of conduct scores. *Journal of Child Psychology and Psychiatry, 28,* 261–272.

Ferri, E. (1984). *Stepchildren*. Windsor: NFER-Nelson.

Fogelman, K. (1983). *Growing up in Great Britain*. London: Macmillan.

Gabriel, K. R. (1966). Simultaneous test procedures for multiple comparisons on categorical data. *Journal of the American Statistical Association, 61,* 1081–1096.

Ghodsian, M., Fogelman, K., Lambert, L., Tibbenham, A. (1980) Changes in behaviour ratings of a national sample of children. *British Journal of Social and Clinical Psychology, 19,* 247–256.

Heckman, J. J. (1979). Sample selection bias as a specification error. *Econometrica, 47,* 153–161.

Hinde, J. (1982). Compound Poisson regression models. In R. Gilchrist (Ed.), *GLIM82*. New York: Springer-Verlag.

Hodges, J., & Tizard, B. (1989*a*). IQ and behavioural adjustment of ex-institutional adolescents. *Journal of Child Psychology and Psychiatry, 30,* 53–75.

Hodges, J., & Tizard, B. (1989*b*). Social and family relationships of ex-institutional adolescents. *Journal of Child Psychology and Psychiatry, 30,* 77–97.

Hoopes, J. L. (1982). *Prediction in child development*. New York: Child Welfare League of America.

Hutchison, D. (1986). Response to a national longitudinal study: policy and academic implications for the study of change. *National Child Development Study User Support Group Working Paper Series No. 13.*

Joreskog, K. G., Gruvaeus, G. T. & Van Thillo, M. (1971). ACOVS: A general computer program for analysis of covariance structures including generalized MANOVA. *Educational Testing Service Research Bulletin,* 70–113.

Joreskog, K. G., & Sorbum, D. (1981). LISREL V: Analysis of linear structural relationships by maximum likelihood and least squares methods. *Research Reports 81–88.* University of Uppsala, Sweden, Department of Statistics.

Kiernan, K. (1980). Teenage motherhood—associated factors and consequences—

The experience of a British birth cohort. *Journal of Biosocial Science, 12,* 393–405.

Lambert, L., & Streather, J. (1980). *Children in changing families.* London: National Children's Bureau.

Lindholm, B. W., & Touliatos, J. (1980). Psychological adjustment of adopted and non-adopted children. *Psychological Reports, 46,* 307–310.

Marini, M. M., Olsen, A. R., & Rubin, D. B. (1979). Maximum likelihood estimation in panel studies with missing data. *In* K. F. Schnessler (Ed.), *Sociological methodology.* San Francisco: Jossey-Bass.

McCullogh, P., & Nelder, J. A. (1983). *Generalized linear models.* London: Chapman and Hall.

Mech, E. V. (1973). Adoption: A policy perspective. In B. Caldwell & H. Riciutti (Eds.), *Review of child development research* (Vol. 3, pp. 467–507). Chicago, IL: University of Chicago Press.

Norvell, M., & Guy, R. F. (1977). A comparison of self-concept in adopted and non-adopted adolescents. *Adolescence, 12,* 443–448.

Raynor, L. (1980). *The adopted child comes of age.* London: Allen and Unwin.

Rutter, M. (1967). A children's behaviour questionnaire for completion by teachers: Preliminary findings. *Journal of Child Psychology and Psychiatry, 8,* 1–11.

Rutter, M., Cox, A., Tupling, C., Berger, M., Yule, W. (1975). Attainment and adjustment in two geographical areas: I The prevalence of psychiatric disorder. *British Journal of Psychiatry, 126,* 493–509.

Rutter, M., & Quinton, D. (1984). Parental psychiatric disorder: effects on children. *Psychological Medicine, 14,* 853–880.

Rutter, M., Tizard, J., & Whitmore, K. (1970). *Education, health and behaviour.* London: Longman (reprinted 1980, Melbourne, Florida: Krieger).

St. Claire, L., & Osborn, A. F. (1987). The ability and behavior of children who have been "in-care" or separated from their parents. *Early Child Development and Care, 28,* 3.

Schechter, M. D. (1960). Observations on adopted children. *Archives of General Psychiatry, 3,* 21–32.

Seglow, J., Pringle, M. K., & Wedge, P. (1972). *Growing up adopted.* Windsor: NFER.

Shaw, M. (1984). Growing up adopted. In P. Bean (Ed.), *Adoption: Essays in social policy, law and sociology.* London: Tavistock.

Singer, L. M., Brodzinsky, D. M., & Braff, A. M. (1982). Children's beliefs about adoption: A developmental study. *Journal of Applied Developmental Psychology, 3,* 285–294.

Stott, D. H. (1969). *The social adjustment of children. Manual to the Bristol social adjustment guides* (3rd ed.). London: University of London.

Wedge, P. (1969). The second follow-up of the National Child Development Study. *Concern, 3,* 34–39.

Yule, W. (1968). Identifying maladjusted children. In *The Child and the Outside World.* Coventry: 29th Biennial Conference of the Association for Special Education.

4 Long-term criminal outcomes of hyperactivity–impulsivity–attention deficit and conduct problems in childhood

DAVID P. FARRINGTON, ROLF LOEBER, AND WELMOET B. VAN KAMMEN

This paper is concerned primarily with the later delinquent and criminal outcomes of boys characterized by hyperactivity–impulsivity–attention deficit problems (HIA). As Wallander and Hubert (1985) pointed out, "Few child disorders have undergone the definitional changes that ADD/H [Attention Deficit Disorder with Hyperactivity] has." The Hyperkinetic Reaction of Childhood in DSM-II (American Psychiatric Association, 1968) became Attention Deficit Disorder with or without Hyperactivity in DSM-III (American Psychiatric Association, 1980), focusing on the three core symptoms of hyperactivity, impulsivity, and attention deficit (Pelham, 1982).

The latest version of the Diagnostic and Statistical Manual, DSM-IIIR (American Psychiatric Association, 1987), defines attention-deficit hyperactivity disorder as having the three key components of "developmentally inappropriate degrees of inattention, impulsiveness and hyperactivity." Inattention is evident when children are easily distracted by extraneous stimuli and shift from one uncompleted activity to another. Examples of impulsiveness are working carelessly or messily, engaging in potentially dangerous activities without considering the possible consequences, and failing to heed directions fully before beginning to respond to assignments. Hyperactivity refers to difficulties in remaining seated, fidgeting, restlessness, and excessive "jumping about." Loeber (1988a) referred to this constellation of factors as "HIA" and we will follow this nomenclature in this paper. Interestingly, Douglas and Peters (1979) proposed that hyperactivity should be called "attention-impulsivity-hyperactivity disorder," and their work had a considerable influence on DSM-III (Carlson, 1986).

One of the most important current controversies centers on the extent to which HIA overlaps with or differs from conduct problems (CP) such as stealing, lying, destructiveness, defiance, truancy, disobedience, running away, threatening, fighting, and temper tantrums. According to several reviewers (Herbert, 1982; Shaffer & Greenhill, 1979; Taylor, 1986a), HIA and CP are highly intercorrelated, are associated with similar etiological factors, and have similar prognoses. Hence, it might be argued that they should be merged into a single behavior disorder category, possibly also including learning disabilities (Prior & Sanson, 1986).

It is true that HIA and CP measures are often highly correlated (at the level of 0.6 or 0.7), especially when they are derived from parent or teacher rating scales (Goyette et al., 1978; Lahey et al., 1980; Sandberg et al., 1978; Sandberg et al., 1980; Taylor et al., 1986*b*). However, part of this overlap is artefactual, because HIA and CP scales derived from factor analyses often contain overlapping items.

For example, in one of the largest studies, of over 9,000 Ottawa children ages 4 to 12, 6 of the 17 items loading highest on an HIA factor were also among the 14 items loading highest on a CP factor (Trites & LaPrade, 1983). Perhaps not surprisingly, the HIA and CP scales correlated 0.84 in this research. However, the items with the highest loadings of all did not overlap (restlessness, fidgeting, inattention, disturbing other children, implusiveness on HIA; stealing, lying, destructiveness, defiance on CP). Also, as Werry et al. (1987) pointed out, many of these studies are based on clinical samples, and children with both HIA and CP are more likely to be referred for treatment than those with only one set of symptoms, thereby artefactually increasing the apparent overlap.

Many of the factor analytic studies do yield distinct HIA and CP factors (Hinshaw, 1987; Quay, 1986). However, in determining whether HIA and CP are different syndromes, the most important issue is the extent to which they have different early background precursors or correlates and different later behavioral outcomes. Another possible criterion is the extent to which HIA and CP children show differential response to treatment. Although this question has rarely been addressed, Taylor et al. (1986*a*) reported that HIA boys were more responsive to stimulant medication than were CP boys.

Existing research

There have been many prospective longitudinal studies of the later out-comes of CP children, which have shown the extent to which they develop into juvenile delinquents or adult criminals (Farrington, 1987; Loeber & Dishion, 1983). However, there have been few longitudinal studies of the later outcomes of HIA children. Like cross-sectional studies of HIA children (Offord et al., 1979), prospective longitudinal studies have found that HIA children have relatively high rates of antisocial, delinquent, and criminal behavior in later life.

In a long-term follow-up of a large sample of over 2,000 child guidance cases in Stockholm, from ages 9 to 29, on average, Nylander (1979) discovered that one third of the hyperactive boys were officially registered for criminal acts. However, there was no control group in this study. Weiss and Hechtman (1986) followed up an original sample of 104 HIA children in

Montreal, from ages 9 to 25 on average, and reported that 23% of the HIA children had adult antisocial personality disorder, in comparison with 2% of a control group. Satterfield (1987) tracked 110 HIA and 88 matched control boys in Los Angeles from ages 9 to 17 and showed that six times as many of the HIA boys on average were arrested for serious offenses. Gittelman et al. (1985) followed up 100 HIA boys and 100 controls in New York from ages 9 to 18, and found that 20% of the HIA boys were arrested, in comparison with 8% of the controls.

Many of the children in these and other longitudinal studies (Huessy & Howell, 1985) displayed not only HIA but CP as well. In order to study the precursors and sequelae of HIA and CP separately, it is desirable to investigate four groups of children: those with both HIA and CP, those with HIA but no CP, those with CP but no HIA, and those with neither HIA nor CP (Campbell & Werry, 1986). These kinds of analyses have been carried out with aggressive behavior, recognizing that CP is a heterogeneous category that includes both aggression and dishonesty.

In studies of the early precursors or correlates of HIA and aggression, Loney and Milich (1982) found that aggression was linked to early environmental factors such as low socioeconomic status and parental rejection, whereas HIA was linked to poor cognitive and academic functioning. In an impressive longitudinal survey of over 900 New Zealand children between the ages of 5 and 9, McGee et al. (1984a, 1985) showed that aggressive boys tended to have been separated from their parents and to have come from single-parent families, whereas HIA boys had cognitive handicaps (in reading and intelligence). In a later survey of the same children between ages 11 and 13, Moffitt et al. (1987) reported that self-reported delinquency was related to family adversity, while HIA was related to cognitive handicaps. In several studies, children who were both HIA and aggressive were the most extreme on factors such as the number of behavior problems, age of onset of problems, intelligence, and reading ability (McGee et al., 1984b; Stewart et al., 1981).

Turning to studies of the later outcomes of HIA and aggressive children, Loney et al. (1982), in a follow-up of 135 HIA boys in Iowa from ages 9 to 14, concluded that child aggression predicted adolescent aggression and delinquency, whereas child hyperactivity predicted adolescent academic achievement. Loeber (1988a), in a 5-year follow-up of 210 Oregon boys ages 10 to 16, and Magnusson (1984), in a follow-up of 1,000 Swedish children from ages 10 to 28, found that both HIA and aggression led to an increase in the rate of offending. The results suggest that HIA and aggression might have independent effects on later outcomes.

The prospective studies are superior to previous retrospective ones, but they have some limitations. Attrition rates are often high; for example, Weiss and Hechtman (1986) could follow up only 63 out of an original sample of 104 HIA children. In some studies (Loney et al., 1982; Satterfield, 1987; Weiss & Hechtman, 1986), the HIA children received drug treatment, which made it difficult to know what their outcomes would have been in the absence of such treatment. Follow-up interviewers were often not blind to the original categorization of the children as HIA or controls; and control groups and numbers of subjects were often inadequate.

Most disturbingly, the existing studies rarely discuss possible causal links between early background factors, HIA, CP, and later outcomes such as offending. If HIA or CP causes offending, the nature of this link needs to be specified. For example, perhaps impulsive people pay less attention to the possible consequences of offending, and so are more likely to commit offenses; or perhaps children with poor concentration are likely to fail in school, and perhaps school failure leads to offending through some causal chain. Alternatively, HIA, CP, and offending may be linked because they all measure the same underlying theoretical construct of antisocial behavior. Another possibility is that HIA and CP in some sense act as stepping stones in a developmental sequence that leads to offending (Farrington, 1986).

In line with the developmental conceptualization of antisocial behavior formulated by Loeber (1988*b*), the negative outcome of CP may be aggravated by co-occurrence of HIA. It is possible that combined HIA-CP youngsters are more likely to become chronic delinquents than youngsters with only either HIA or CP, are also more precocious as shown by an earlier age of committing crime, and have a lower likelihood of initiating a delinquent career as late as adulthood. In contrast, the risk of delinquency in CP youngsters without HIA is likely to be less than that for HIA-CP youngsters, and least for HIA youngsters without CP.

The current research

In attempting to verify these hypotheses and resolve the issues, it is important to establish how far HIA and CP predict offending independently of each other and independently of other possible causal factors, and to what extent HIA and CP are themselves related to early background factors. These are the main aims of the present research, which investigates not only offending in general, but juvenile versus adult offending, official versus self-reported offending, early versus late offending, and chronic recidivism versus occasional offending.

One important implication of previous studies is that HIA and CP need to be measured using several different sources such as parents, teachers, and children themselves. Correlations between sources of HIA or CP are often lower than correlations between HIA and CP derived from the same source (McGee et al., 1985; Sandberg et al., 1980). This can mean either that children behave differently in different settings or that different sources have different response biases. In either case, the most valid measures of HIA and CP are likely to be obtained by combining measures from different sources, and this was done in the present research.

This research uses data collected in the Cambridge Study in Delinquent Development, a prospective longitudinal survey of 411 males.[1] When they were first contacted at age 8 or 9 in 1961–1962, the vast majority were on the registers of six state primary schools within a one-mile radius of our research office in a working class area of London, England. The boys were overwhelmingly white, working class, and of British origin. More details of this survey can be found in four books (West, 1969, 1982; West & Farrington, 1973, 1977), and a concise summary is also available (Farrington & West, 1981).

The aim in this survey was to measure as many factors as possible that were alleged to be causes or correlates of offending in investigating the development of juvenile delinquency and adult crime. Most information was derived from face to face contacts with subjects. The males were tested by psychologists employed by this study in their schools when they were about ages 8, 10, and 14, and they were interviewed in a research office at about ages 16, 18, and 21. The tests in schools measured intelligence, attainment, personality, and psychomotor coordination, while information was collected in the interviews about such factors as living circumstances, employment histories, relationships with females, leisure activities such as drinking and fighting, and offending behaviors.

The boys' parents were also interviewed, by psychiatric social workers employed by the study, about once a year from when the boy was age 8 until when he was age 14 or 15 and in his last year of compulsory schooling. The primary informant was the mother, although many fathers were also seen. The parents provided details about such matters as family income, family size, their employment histories, their child-rearing practices (including attitudes, discipline and parental agreement), their degree of supervision of the boy, and his temporary or permanent separations from them.

The boys' teachers completed questionnaires when the boys were about ages 8, 10, 12, and 14. These provided information about the boys' troublesome and aggressive school behavior, their school attainments, and their truancy. Ratings were also obtained from the boys' peers when they were in their primary schools, about such topics as their daring, dishonesty, troublesomeness, and popularity.

Measures of hyperactivity–impulsivity–attention deficit (HIA)

Three measures of HIA were obtained by combining information collected when the boys were ages 8 and 10.

Hyperactivity-attention deficit (teacher). At both ages, the teachers filled in a questionnaire about the boys that included the following item: Does he lack concentration or is he restless in a way that seriously hinders his learning? At age 8, 135 boys were thus identified by their teachers, and 145 were similarly identified at age 10. The combined rating at ages 8 and 10 contrasted 82 boys identified at both ages with the remaining 328 known.[2]

Risk taking–daring (mother, peer). At age 8, 75 boys were identified by their mothers as taking many risks, such as in climbing, traffic, and exploring. At age 10, 100 boys were rated by their peers as the most daring. At each age, all boys were scored 1 (cautious), 2 (average), or 3 (daring) points, and the scores at the two ages were added. The 121 boys who had a combined score of 5 or 6 were identified as the most daring (West & Farrington, 1973, pp. 104–105).

Psychomotor impulsivity (boy). At ages 8 and 10, the boys were given three tests of psychomotor performance, the Porteus maze, the spiral maze, and the tapping test (West & Farrington, 1973, p. 110). High scores on these tests reflected careless, clumsy, or impulsive behavior. A combined rating of psychomotor impulsivity was derived for each boy by averaging his percentile scores on the three tests at the two ages. The 104 most impulsive boys were then contrasted with the remaining 307.

Measures of conduct problems (CP)

Three measures of CP were also obtained by combining information collected when the boys were ages 8 and 10.

Naughtiness (teacher). At age 8 and 10, as already mentioned, the boy's teachers filled in questionnaires about their school behavior. At each age, the boys were divided into three groups, according to whether their total scores fell into the worst quarter (most naughty), the middle half, or the best quarter (least naughty) of their school class (West & Farrington, 1973, p. 108). The final combined rating was obtained by adding up the scores (3, 2, or 1) at each age, and the naughtiest 134 boys were those scoring 5 or 6.

Bad behavior (mother). At age 8, the psychiatric social workers identified 60 boys as badly behaved on the basis of their mothers' reports of lying, stealing, destructiveness, quarrelsomeness, and defiance. Similarly, 72 boys were identified at age 10 on the basis of their mothers' reports of stealing, truancy, fighting, disobedience, and other problem behaviors. The boys were scored 1, 2, or 3 at each age, and the scores were added, leading to the identification of 122 boys as the worst behaved at ages 8 and 10 combined.

Troublesomeness (peer). At age 10, as part of a peer rating test, the boys rated those of their classmates who "got into trouble most" (West & Farrington, 1973, pp. 100–101). As with the teacher ratings, the boys were divided into three groups, according to whether their total scores fell into the worst quarter (most troublesome), the middle half, or the best quarter (least troublesome) of their school class. The most troublesome group comprised 80 boys.

Measures of offending

Searches were carried out in the central Criminal Record Office in London to try to locate convictions of the boys (and of their parents and siblings). Convictions were counted only if they were for offenses normally recorded in the Criminal Record Office, thereby excluding minor crimes such as traffic offenses and drunkenness. The most common offenses included were thefts, burglaries, and unauthorized takings of motor vehicles. Eighty-four boys were convicted as juveniles (between the 10th and the 17th birthdays). Of the remaining 317 at risk up to the 25th birthday (not dead or emigrated), 52 were convicted as adults.

Altogether, 136 boys were convicted as juveniles or adults. Of these, 35 were convicted at the unusually early age of 10 to 13; 101 boys were convicted later. Of the 132 convicted boys at risk up to the 25th birthday, 83 became recidivists and 49 had only one conviction. Only 23 boys accounted for half of all the convictions (Farrington, 1983). These boys, who each had six or more convictions, were termed the "chronic offenders."

The conviction measures were supplemented by self-reports of offending obtained from age 14 onwards. At ages 14 and 16, the boys were asked to say whether they had committed each of 38 delinquent or fringe-delinquent acts (West & Farrington, 1973). The 80 boys who admitted 21 or more of these acts at one or both of these ages were identified as the "self-reported delinquents." Half of these boys (41) were convicted as juveniles.

Methods of analysis

In this analysis, each variable has been dichotomized, as far as possible, into the "worst" quarter (e.g., on HIA or CP measures) versus the remaining three-quarters of the sample. Variables are then related to each other in 2×2 tables, and χ^2 is used to test the statistical significance of each relationship. All χ^2 values reported in this paper are corrected for continuity and have one degree of freedom. One-tailed tests are used throughout in the light of the clear directional predictions (e.g., that HIA, CP, and offending are positively related).

With the usual kinds of social science variables (not intervally scaled and not normally distributed), product–moment correlations and associated parametric statistics, strictly speaking, should not be used. However, an advantage of using dichotomous variables is that ϕ correlations can be used as valid measures of strength of association. ϕ is simply related to uncorrected χ^2 values, since $\phi^2 = \chi^2/N$. Also, ϕ has a simple intuitive meaning, since ϕ^2 is the product of the difference of the row percentages and the difference of the column percentages. For example, in a 2×2 table in which (a) 40% of predicted youth and 10% of nonpredicted youth became delinquents, and (b) 40% of delinquents and 10% of nondelinquents were predicted, ϕ would be .30 (Farrington & Loeber, in press).

The maximum possible value of ϕ can be much less than 1 if the marginal frequencies in a 2×2 table differ. Hence, a low value of ϕ^2, interpretable as a low percentage of variance explained, does not necessarily correspond to a poor prediction or a weak relationship. In the interests of setting the maximum possible value of ϕ to 1, we had a consistent one-quarter/three-quarters split on all variables, since we expected that about one-quarter of the sample would be convicted as juveniles. Another advantage of the consistent split is that all variables are measured with comparable sensitivity, and an advantage of dichotomizing is that it makes the presentation of results easily understandable.

In investigating whether one variable is related to another independently of a third variable, partial ϕ correlations are used. In general, they give very similar results to loglinear analyses (Farrington et al., 1982), except when significant interaction effects occur. In many cases, loglinear analyses have also been carried out.

Interrelation of HIA and CP

Table 1 summarizes the interrelations of the three measures of HIA and the three measures of CP. This table shows χ^2 values and ϕ correlations. For example, hyperactivity was significantly related to daring ($\chi^2 = 10.22$ with Yates' correction for continuity, 1 df, $p < .001$, one-tailed; $\phi = .17$). In fact, 45% of 80 hyperactive boys were rated daring, in comparison with 26% of the remaining 327 known on both.

Table 1 shows that hyperactivity was also significantly intercorrelated with impulsivity. Daring and impulsivity were almost significantly intercorrelated: 30.6% of the 121 daring boys were also impulsive, in comparison with 22.6% of the remaining 287 known on both ($\chi^2 = 2.45$, $p = .059$, $\phi = .08$). The degree of overlap between these three measures was considered sufficient to justify combining them into a single index of HIA. In obtaining a combined score, each constituent measure was scored 1 to 3, and the major contrast was between 93 boys scoring 7 to 9 on HIA and the remaining 318. The combined HIA score reflected hyperactivity more than

Table 1. *HIA versus CP at ages 8–10*

	Daring (M, P)	Impulsivity (B)	Naughtiness (T)	Bad behavior (M)	Troublesomeness (P)
Hyperactivity (T)	10.22** (.17)	17.40** (.21)	93.32** (.48)	30.83** (.29)	19.27** (.24)
Daring (M, P)		2.45 (.08)	24.48** (.25)	37.47** (.32)	91.44** (.52)
Impulsivity (B)			20.25** (.23)	9.92** (.17)	7.54* (.15)
Naughtiness (T)				36.68** (.31)	39.36** (.34)
Bad behavior (M)					13.72** (.21)

Note: The table shows values of χ^2 obtained in a 2×2 table relating two variables. ϕ correlations are in parentheses.
Abbreviations: HIA = hyperactivity-impulsivity-attention deficit
CP = conduct problems, T = teacher, M = mother, P = peer, B = boy
*p<.05
**p<.001

the other two variables; 66 of the 82 hyperactives were among the 93 highest on HIA. Hence, HIA reflectes persistent hyperactivity, since the 82 hyperactives were identified at both ages 8 and 10.

Table 1 also shows that all three measures of CP were significantly intercorrelated. Consequently, they were combined into a single index on the same basis as HIA. The major contrast was between 99 boys scoring 7 to 9 on CP and the remaining 312. The combined CP score reflected naughtiness and bad behavior especially; 84 of the 99 CP boys were rated naughty by their teachers, and 78 were rated as badly behaved by their mothers. Again, CP reflects persistent bad behavior at ages 8 and 10.

Each measure of HIA was significantly related to each measure of CP. However, the highest values of χ^2 occurred when two measures were derived from the same source. For example, the χ^2 for the association between the teacher ratings of hyperactivity and naughtiness was 93.32.[3] The mother-peer rating of daring yielded a χ^2 of 91.44 when compared with the peer rating of troublesomeness and a χ^2 of 37.47 when compared with the mother rating of bad behavior.

The combined measure of HIA was significantly related to the combined measure of CP, and the degree of overlap was surprisingly high. Of the 93 boys who were worst on HIA, 63.4% were among the worst on CP, in comparison with only 12.6% of the remaining 318 ($\chi^2 = 99.04$, $p < .001$, $\phi = .50$). Conversely, 59.6% of the 99 boys with the worst CP manifested the worst HIA, in comparison with only 10.9% of the remaining 312. The degree of overlap raises the serious issue of whether HIA and CP are measuring the same or different underlying theoretical constructs. One way of investigating this is to divide the sample into the following four groups:

HIA and CP ($N = 59$)
HIA, but no CP ($N = 34$)

No HIA, but CP $(N = 40)$
No HIA and no CP $(N = 278)$

If HIA and CP are accurate measures of the same underlying theoretical construct, the 34 boys with HIA but no CP should be similar to the 40 boys with CP but no HIA, in relation to early background variables and later criminal outcomes. On the other hand, if CP and HIA are measuring different underlying constructs, these two groups of boys should be different.

Predicting juvenile convictions

Table 2 shows that all the measures of HIA and CP at ages 8 to 10 significantly predicted juvenile convictions (between ages 10 and 16). The fact that all the measures were significantly predictive, independently of their source (teacher, mother, peer, or boy), suggests that the theoretical constructs underlying HIA and CP are related in some way to the theoretical construct underlying juvenile convictions.

Focusing on the combined measure of HIA as probably the most valid, 37.6% of the 93 boys with the highest scores were convicted, in comparison with 15.4% of the 318 boys with lower scores ($\chi^2 = 20.51$, $p < .001$, $\phi = .23$). Similarly, 41.4% of 99 boys with the highest scores on CP were convicted, in comparison with 13.6% of the 312 boys with lower scores ($\chi^2 = 33.61$, $p < .001$, $\phi = .29$).

For purposes of comparison, Table 2 also shows the ability of other key variables measured in the survey at ages 8 and 10 to predict juvenile convictions: low family income, large family size, poor housing, separations from parents for reasons other than death or hospitalization, poor parental child-rearing practices (harsh or erratic attitude and discipline), poor parental supervision, low nonverbal intelligence (on the Progressive Matrices test), convicted parents, and delinquent older brothers. These factors have been discussed in more detail by West and Farrington (1973). In general, HIA predicted juvenile convictions as well as or better than all these background variables. Only convicted parents had a comparable degree of predictability.

Disentangling the effect of HIA and CP on later offending

Table 3 relates the four categories of boys described earlier, classified according to presence or absence of both HIA and CP, to measures of delinquency and crime. This table shows, for example, that 12.6% of 278 non-HIA/non-CP boys were convicted as juveniles, in comparison with 35% of 40 non-HIA/CP boys, 23.5% of 34 HIA/non-CP boys, and 45.8% of 59 HIA/CP boys. These percentages indicate that HIA and CP were both

Table 2. *Predicting juvenile convictions*[a]

	Low		High			
Measures at ages 8–10	(%) JC	N	(%) JC	N	χ^2	ϕ
Hyperactivity (T)	17.4	328	32.9	82	8.80**	.15
Daring (M, P)	12.9	287	38.8	121	33.49**	.29
Impulsivity (B)	16.6	307	31.7	104	10.01**	.16
HIA	15.4	318	37.6	93	20.51**	.23
Naughtiness (T)	11.9	277	38.1	134	36.38**	.30
Bad behavior (M)	14.4	263	32.0	122	14.91**	.20
Troublesomeness (P)	13.9	273	37.5	80	20.63**	.25
CP	13.6	312	41.4	99	33.61**	.29
Low income (M)	16.7	318	33.3	93	11.29**	.17
Large family size (M, R)	16.7	312	32.3	99	10.39**	.17
Poor housing (O)	16.9	260	26.5	151	4.80*	.11
Separations (M)	17.1	321	32.2	90	8.94**	.15
Poor parenting (M)	15.3	300	32.3	96	12.29**	.18
Poor supervision (M)	16.5	309	31.1	74	7.23*	.15
Low intelligence (B)	16.9	308	31.1	103	8.70**	.15
Criminal parent (R)	15.0	307	36.5	104	20.89**	.23
Delinquent brother (R)	18.1	365	39.1	46	9.87**	.16

Abbreviations: % JC = % with juvenile conviction,
  HIA = hyperactivity-impulsivity-attention deficit,
  CP = conduct problems, T = teacher, M = mother, B = boy, P = peer, R = records, O = observation
[a] Juvenile convictions are defined as convictions between ages 10 and 16 inclusive.
*$p < .05$
**$p < .001$

independently predictive of juvenile convictions, and that they had additive effects. Comparing non-HIA with HIA boys, holding CP status constant, the percentage convicted increased by about 11%. Comparing non-CP with CP boys, holding HIA status constant, the percentage convicted increased by about 22%. CP, therefore, was the better predictor.

The contributions of HIA to juvenile convictions independently of CP, and of CP to juvenile convictions independently of HIA, were investigated using loglinear analyses and partial ϕ correlations. Each loglinear analyses investigated the increased goodness of fit of a model that assumed that both HIA and CP contributed independently to juvenile convictions in comparison with a model that assumed that only one of them contributed. The measure of increased fit was G^2 (or deviance), the likelihood-ratio goodness of fit statistic. G^2 is distributed approximately as χ^2 with one degree of freedom. Table 3 shows that, according to both G^2 and the partial ϕ, HIA and CP were both independently predictive of juvenile convictions, although CP had the greater effect. There was no evidence of an interaction between HIA and CP.

Table 3. *HIA and CP as predictors of offending*

	Juvenile convictions (%)	Juvenile self-reported delinquency (%)	Adult convictions (%)
Non-H, non-C (*N* = 278)	12.6	13.3	14.3
Non-H, C (*N* = 40)	35.0	35.9	25.0
H, non-C (*N* = 34)	23.5	23.5	8.0
H, C (*N* = 59)	45.8	36.2	32.3
Loglinear G^2			
Contribution of H	3.55*	1.08	0.04
Contribution of C	15.52**	11.13**	5.77*
Interaction H × C	0.25	1.19	1.18
Partial φ			
Contribution of H	.102*	.056	−.018
Contribution of C	.211**	.177**	.145*

Abbreviations: H = HIA, C = CP
* = *p* < .05
** = *p* < 001

The relation between the four categories and juvenile self-reported delinquency was quite similar to the relation with juvenile convictions (see Table 3), suggesting that HIA and CP are related to delinquent behavior rather than to selection for official processing. However, there was very little difference between the non-HIA/CP and HIA/CP groups in the percentage who were self-reported delinquents. Consequently, HIA was not significantly related to self-reported delinquency independently of CP. Table 3 also shows that CP predicted first convictions as an adult independently of HIA, but that HIA did not predict these independently of CP. Very few of the HIA/non-CP boys began a criminal career in adulthood.

Table 4 shows to what extent HIA and CP predicted within the 136 convicted boys. Because of the smaller numbers in Table 4 (136) than in Table 3 (411), a much stronger relationship was required to achieve a statistically significant result. Table 4 shows that convictions at an unusually early age (10–13) were predicted better by HIA than by CP. The partial φ for HIA was on the borderline of statistical significance, while the G^2 for HIA was not far off significance. Conversely, the recidivists among the offenders were better predicted by CP than by HIA.

Perhaps the most interesting result is obtained in predicting the chronic offenders—those who amassed six or more convictions by their 25th birthday. The partial φ correlations show that chronic offenders were independently predicted just as well by HIA as by CP (see Table 4). The loglinear analyses show that the independent contributions of HIA and CP were reasonably comparable (2.28 and 2.71, respectively), but that there was

Table 4. *HIA and CP as predictors within the offenders*

	Convicted early (%)	Recidivists (%)	Chronics (%)
Non-H, non-C ($N = 69$)	15.9	51.5	5.9
Non-H, C ($N = 20$)	30.0	78.9	26.3
H, non-C ($N = 10$)	40.0	77.8	33.3
H, C ($N = 37$)	37.8	72.2	30.6
Loglinear G^2			
Contribution of H	2.23	0.36	2.28
Contribution of C	0.93	2.71*	2.71*
Interaction H × C	0.91	2.30	2.86*
Partial φ			
Contribution of H	.139*	.064	.155*
Contribution of C	.092	.148*	.156*

Abbreviations: H = HIA, C = CP
  * = $p < 0.5$
  ** = $p < .001$

a significant HIA – CP interaction ($G^2 = 2.86$, $p < .05$). The figures indicate that the effect of HIA was greater when CP was absent than when CP was present (or conversely, that the effect of CP was greater when HIA was absent than when HIA was present). The offenders with neither HIA nor CP were particularly unlikely to become chronics. These results suggest that HIA and CP may both assist in predicting the extent of a future criminal career at the time of the first conviction.

Differential relationships of HIA and CP with background factors

Since the major thrust of this paper is on the later outcomes of HIA and CP boys, it does not include an extensive analysis of background factors. However, Table 5 shows the relationship between the four (HIA, CP) groups and the major background factors mentioned earlier. For example, 37.3% of 59 HIA/CP boys came from low-income families. It can be seen that HIA and CP had very different patterns of relationships. HIA was particularly related to low intelligence, criminal parents, large family size, poor housing, and delinquent brothers; CP was particularly related to poor parenting, poor supervision, low income, and separations from parents.

With one exception, the ability of HIA and CP to predict offending held independently of all the major background factors. The exception was that HIA did not quite predict juvenile convictions independently of CP and of criminal parents (partial φ = .068, $p = .09$).

It might perhaps be argued that HIA is an earlier manifestation and CP a

Table 5. *The relationship between background variables, HIA, and CP*

Measures at ages 8–10	Non-H, non-C (%)	Non-H, C (%)	H, non-C (%)	H, C (%)	Partial ϕ	
					H	C
Low income	16.5	35.0	32.4	37.3	.087*	.120*
Large family size	19.8	22.5	41.2	35.6	.151**	−.004
Poor housing	29.9	42.5	50.0	57.6	.137*	.084*
Separations	19.4	27.5	11.8	35.6	−.006	.127*
Poor parenting	19.1	42.1	15.2	43.4	−.019	.216**
Poor supervision	12.5	34.2	15.2	46.9	.055	.241**
Low intelligence	17.6	30.0	41.2	47.5	.178**	.089*
Criminal parent	18.3	27.5	44.1	45.8	.190**	.055
Delinquent brother	7.9	12.5	17.6	22.0	.112*	.054

Abbreviations: H = HIA, C = CP
* = $p < .05$
** = $p < .001$

later manifestation of the same general disorder. Hence, the different relationships of HIA and CP with background factors seen in Table 5 might reflect differences in age of onset rather than between HIA and CP. If so, parental criminality and low intelligence might be more closely related to HIA only because they are associated with an earlier manifestation, whereas poor supervision and poor parenting might be more closely related to CP only because they are associated with a later manifestation.

These arguments were tested in two ways. First of all, the age of manifestation of the disorder was controlled more closely than it was in Table 5 (based on HIA and CP at ages 8 and 10) by dividing the boys into four (HIA, CP) groups on the basis of whether they scored high on HIA and CP at age 8 only. The pattern of partial ϕ correlations between HIA and CP and the nine background factors was found to be very similar to that shown in Table 5. Eleven of the 12 significant relationships in Table 5 were still significant of age 8 (all except between HIA and poor housing), while 4 of the 6 nonsignificant relationships were still nonsignificant at age 8 (the exceptions being between HIA and poor supervision, which was still weaker than between CP and poor supervision; and between CP and delinquent brothers, which was still weaker than between HIA and delinquent brothers).

Second, on the assumption that HIA and CP reflect the same underlying disorder and are interchangeable, the boys were divided into the following four groups, differing in the age of manifestation of the disorder (8 or 10):

HIA and/or CP at both 8 and 10 ($N = 76$)
HIA and/or CP at 8, but not at 10 ($N = 45$)
HIA and/or CP at 10, but not at 8 ($N = 64$)
No HIA and no CP at both 8 and 10 ($N = 226$)

If relationships involving HIA and CP merely reflect earlier versus later manifestation, the age 8 manifestation (HIA and/or CP) might be associated particularly with parental criminality and low intelligence, while the onset of the manifestation at age 10 might be associated particularly with poor supervision and poor parenting. However, these results were not obtained. All nine background factors were significantly related to the age-8 manifestation and were less closely related to the age-10 onset.

These results provide no support for the hypothesis that the different pattern of relationships between HIA and CP and background factors reflect differences in age of onset, although these tests are limited by the short age span (8–10) and by the fact that the temporal priority of HIA over CP may have occurred earlier than age 8. The results are consistent with the hypothesis that HIA and CP are distinctly different disorders.

Conclusions of the study

This study has a number of limitations. Because it is based on a lower-class, inner-city English sample, the results may not be generalizable to other populations. The HIA and CP boys investigated here are less extreme cases than those included in clinical samples. The HIA and CP measures were not specifically designed with modern criteria in mind; and the numbers of boys are quite small. The strengths of the study are that it has a prospective longitudinal design, attrition was very low, and several sources of data were obtained.

Three measures of HIA derived from different sources at two ages (8 and 10) were studied, together with three similarly derived measures of CP. There was a considerable overlap between HIA and CP, since about 60% of boys with one of these problems also had the other.

All measures of HIA and CP significantly predicted juvenile convictions (between ages 10 and 16). Furthermore, HIA predicted juvenile convictions independently of CP, and vice versa, and these two factors had additive effects. However, HIA did not predict juvenile convictions independently of CP and of criminal parents. Hence, criminal parents, HIA, and juvenile convictions may be part of the same causal or developmental sequence.

HIA and CP had a quite different pattern of relationships to major background factors. HIA was particularly related to criminal parents, low intelligence, and large family size, while CP was particularly related to poor supervision and poor parenting. The agreement between our results and those of Loney and Milich (1982) in the United States and McGee et al. (1985) in New Zealand is quite impressive. These studies and our research suggest that HIA, while controlling for conduct problems or aggression, is associated with cognitive handicaps. In contrast, conduct problems and delinquency, while controlling for HIA, appear more associated with inadequate child-rearing practices and disruptions in family functioning. Along that line, Loeber and Stouthamer-Loeber (1986) in their meta-analysis also found that parent-child socialization variables—involvement, rejection, and supervision—predicted later conduct problems and delinquency better than such factors as parental criminality.

HIA was particularly predictive of early convictions, while CP was more predictive of self-reported delinquency, adult convictions, and recidivism. In this project, a first conviction at an unusually early age foreshadowed later chronic offending (Farrington, 1983). HIA and CP also significantly predicted, out of all convicted youths, those who went on to become chronic offenders. Both were independently predictive of chronic offending. They had interactive effects, since chronic offending was especially low when neither HIA nor CP were present. Furthermore, the ability of HIA and CP to predict chronic offending held independently of other important predictors of offending investigated in this project.

The fact that HIA is helpful especially in predicting chronic offenders may possibly have practical implications. If such offenders could be identified at an early age, and if effective preventive action could be taken, this could lead to a significant reduction in crime (Blumstein et al., 1985). HIA has a remarkably early age of onset: before 5 in 95% of cases (Barkley, 1982), and an average of 2.9 in one study (Stewart & Behar, 1983). Taylor (1986b) concluded that most hyperactive children had been described as difficult from their first two years of life. Hence, HIA offers an earlier opportunity to intervene than CP of other behavioral precursors of offending.

The fact that HIA and CP are differently related to early background factors and to later criminal outcomes suggests that they are not merely measuring the same theoretical construct and they are not stepping stones on the same developmental sequence leading to delinquency and crime. HIA and CP could be part of different causal chains or different developmental sequences leading to offending. Equally, individual behaviors such as hyperactivity, impulsivity, attention deficit, stealing, lying, destructiveness, and fighting could be part of different chains or sequences. The key challenge facing researchers is to elucidate these chains or sequences; only then will it be possible to draw confident conclusions about prevention and treatment.

Notes

1 These analyses were carried out in Pittsburgh using the public-use data tape from this study held in the Criminal Justice Archive, Institute of Social Research, University of Michigan.
2 When a boy was "not known" on one variable, his score on the other was prorated in calculating a combined score. Usually, the proportion of "not knowns" on any one variable was less than 5%.
3 These measures were not independent, since hyperactivity was one of nine items constituting the naughtiness score. However, this small overlap between hyperactivity and naughtiness could not have accounted for much of the relationship.

References

American Psychiatric Association (1968). *Diagnostic and statistical manual of mental disorders* (2nd ed.). Washington, DC: Author.

American Psychiatric Association (1980). *Diagnostic and statistical manual of mental disorders* (3rd ed.). Washington, DC: Author.

American Psychiatric Association (1987). *Diagnostic and statistical manual of mental disorders* (3rd ed. rev.). Washington, DC: Author.

Barkley, R. A. (1982). Guidelines for defining hyperactivity in children: Attention deficit disorder with hyperactivity. In B. B. Lahey & A. E. Kazdin (Eds.), *Advances in clinical child psychology* (Vol. 5, pp. 137–180). New York: Plenum.

Blumstein, A., Farrington, D. P., & Moitra, S. (1985). Delinquent careers: Innocents, desisters, and persisters. In M. Tonry & N. Morris (Eds.), *Crime and justice* (Vol. 6, pp. 187–219). Chicago: University of Chicago Press.

Campbell, S. B., & Werry, J. S. (1986). Attention deficit disorder (hyperactivity). In H. C. Quay & J. S. Werry (Eds.), *Psychopathological disorders of childhood* (3rd ed) (pp. 111–155). New York: Wiley.

Carlson, C. L. (1986). Attention deficit disorder without hyperactivity: A review of preliminary experimental evidence. In B. B. Lahey & A. E. Kazdin (Eds.), *Advances in clinical child psychology* (Vol. 9, pp. 153–175). New York: Plenum.

Douglas, V. I., & Peters, K. G. (1979). Toward a clearer definition of the attentional deficit of hyperactive children. In G. A. Hale & M. Lewis (Eds.), *Attention and cognitive development* (pp. 173–247). New York: Plenum.

Farrington, D. P. (1983). Offending from 10 to 25 years of age. In K. T. Van Dusen & S. A. Mednick (Eds.), *Prospective studies of crime and delinquency* (pp. 17–37). Boston: Kluwer-Nijhoff.

Farrington, D. P. (1986). Stepping stones to adult criminal careers. In D. Olweus, J. Block, & M. R. Yarrow (Eds.), *Development of antisocial and prosocial behavior* (pp. 359–384). New York: Academic Press.

Farrington, D. P. (1987). Early precursors of frequent offending. In J. Q. Wilson & G. C. Loury (Eds.), *From children to citizens* (Vol. 3, pp. 27–50). New York: Springer-Verlag.

Farrington, D. P., Biron, L., & LeBlanc, M. (1982). Personality and delinquency in London and Montreal. In J. Gunn & D. P. Farrington (Eds.), *Abnormal offenders, delinquency, and the criminal justice system* (pp. 153–201). Chichester: Wiley.

Farrington, D. P., & Loeber, R. (in press), RIOC and phi as measures of predictive efficiency and strength of association in 2 × 2 tables, *Journal of Quantitative Criminology, 5.*

Farrington, D. P., & West, D. J. (1981). The Cambridge study in delinquent development. In S. A. Mednick & A. E. Baert (Eds.), *Prospective longitudinal research* (pp. 137–145). Oxford: Oxford University Press.

Gittelman, R., Mannuzza, S., Shenker, R., & Bonagura, N. (1985). Hyperactive boys almost grown up. *Archives of General psychiatry, 42,* 937–947.

Goyette, C. H., Conners, C. K., & Ulrich, R. F. (1978). Normative data on revised Conners parent and Teacher Rating Scales. *Journal of Abnormal Child Psychology, 6,* 221–236.

Herbert, M. (1982). Conduct disorders. In B. B. Lahey & A. E. Kazdin (Eds.), *Advances in clinical child psychology* (Vol. 5, pp. 95–136). New York: Plenum.

Hinshaw, S. P. (1987). On the distinction between attentional deficits/hyperactivity and conduct problems/aggression in child psychopathology. *Psychological Bulletin, 101,* 443–463.

Huessy, H. R., & Howell, D. C. (1985). Relationships between adult and childhood behavior disorders. *Psychiatric Journal of the University of Ottawa, 10,* 114–119.

Lahey, B. B., Green, K. D., & Forehand, R. (1980). On the independence of ratings of hyperactivity, conduct problems, and attention deficits in children: A multiple regression analysis. *Journal of Consulting and Clinical Psychology, 48,* 566–574.

Loeber, R. (1988*a*). Behavioral precursors and accelerators of delinquency. In W. Buikhuisen & S. A. Mednick (Eds.), *Explaining criminal behavior* (pp. 51–67). Leiden: Brill.

Loeber, R. (1988*b*). Natural histories of juvenile conduct problems, delinquency, and associated substance use: Evidence for developmental progressions. In B. B. Lahey & A. E. Kazdin (Eds.), *Advances in clinical child psychology* (Vol. 10, pp. 73–124). New York: Plenum.

Loeber, R., & Dishion, T. (1983). Early predictors of male delinquency: A review. *Psychological Bulletin, 94,* 68–99.

Loeber, R., & Stouthamer-Loeber, M. (1986). Family factors as correlates and predictors of juvenile conduct problems and delinquency. In M. Tonry & N. Morris (Eds.), *Crime and justice* (Vol. 7, pp. 29–149). Chicago: Chicago University Press.

Loney, J., Kramer, J., & Milich, R. S. (1982). The hyperactive child grows up: Predictors of symptoms, delinquency, and achievement at follow-up. In K. D. Gadow & J. Loney (Eds.), *Psychosocial aspects of drug treatment of hyperactivity* (pp. 381–415). Boulder, CO: Westview Press.

Loney, J., & Milich, R. (1982). Hyperactivity, inattention, and aggression in clinical practice. In M. Wolraich & D. K. Routh (Eds.), *Advances in behavioral pediatrics* (Vol. 3, pp. 113–147). Greenwich, CT: JAI Press.

Magnusson, D. (1984). *Early conduct and biological factors in the developmental background of adult delinquency.* Paper presented at the Henry Tajfel Memorial Lecture, Oxford, September.

McGee, R., Williams, S., & Silva, P. A. (1984*a*). Background characteristics of aggressive, hyperactive, and aggressive-hyperactive boys. *Journal of the American Academy of Child Psychiatry, 23,* 280–284.

McGee, R., Williams, S., & Silva, P. A. (1984*b*). Behavioral and developmental characteristics of aggressive, hyperactive, and aggressive-hyperactive boys. *Journal of the American Academy of Child Psychiatry, 23,* 270–279.

McGee, R., Williams, S., & Silva, P. A. (1985). Factor structure and correlates of ratings of inattention, hyperactivity, and antisocial behavior in a large sample of 9-year-old children from the general population. *Journal of Consulting and Clinical Psychology, 53,* 480–490.

Moffitt, T. E., McGee, R., & Silva, P. A. (1987). *Self-reported delinquency, neuropsychological deficit, and history of attention deficit disorder.* Paper presented at the Society for Life History Research meeting, St. Louis, Missouri, October.

Nylander, I. (1979). A 20-year prospective follow-up study of 2,164 cases at the child guidance clinics in Stockholm. *Acta Paediatrica Scandinavica,* supplement 276.

Offord, D. R., Sullivan, K., Allen, N., & Abrams, N. (1979). Delinquency and hyperactivity. *Journal of Nervous and Mental Disease, 167,* 734–741.

Pelham, W. E. (1982). Childhood hyperactivity: Diagnosis, etiology, nature and treatment. In R. Gatchel, A. Baum, & J. Singer (Eds.), *Behavioral medicine and clinical psychology: Overlapping disciplines* (pp. 261–327). Hillsdale, NJ: Erlbaum.

Prior, M., & Sanson, A. (1986). Attention deficit disorder with hyperactivity: A critique. *Journal of Child Psychology and Psychiatry, 27,* 307–319.

Quay, H. C. (1986). Classification. In H. C. Quay & J. S. Werry (Eds.), *Psychopathological disorders of childhood* (3rd ed.) (pp. 1–34). New York: Wiley.

Sandberg, S. T., Rutter, M., & Taylor, E. (1978). Hyperkinetic disorder in psychiatric clinic attenders. *Developmental Medicine and Child Neurology, 20,* 279–299.

Sandberg, S. T., Wieselberg, M., & Shaffer, D. (1980). Hyperkinetic and conduct problem children in a primary school population: Some epidemiological considerations. *Journal of Child Psychology and Psychiatry, 21,* 293–311.

Satterfield, J. H. (1987). Childhood diagnostic and neurophysiological predictors of teenage arrest rates: An 8-year prospective study. In S. A. Mednick, T. E. Moffitt, & S. A. Stack (Eds.), *The causes of crime* (pp. 146–167). Cambridge, England: Cambridge University Press.

Shaffer, D., & Greenhill, L. (1979). A critical note on the predictive validity of "the hyperkinetic syndrome." *Journal of Child Psychology and Psychiatry, 20,* 61–72.

Stewart, M. A. & Behar, D. (1983). Subtypes of aggressive conduct disorder. *Acta Psychiatrica Scandinavica, 68,* 178–185.

Stewart, M. A., Cummings, C., Singer, S., & DeBlois, C. S. (1981). The overlap between hyperactive and unsocialized aggressive children. *Journal of Child Psychology and Psychiatry, 22,* 35–45.

Taylor, E. A. (1986a). Childhood hyperactivity. *British Journal of Psychiatry, 149,* 562–573.

Taylor, E. A. (1986b). *The overactive child.* Oxford, England: Blackwell.

Taylor, E., Everitt, B., Thorley, G., Schachar, R., Rutter, M., & Wieselberg, M. (1986a). Conduct disorder and hyperactivity: II. A cluster analytic approach to the identification of a behavioral syndrome. *British Journal of Psychiatry, 149,* 768–777.

Taylor, E., Schachar, R., Thorley, G., & Wieselberg, M. (1986b). Conduct disorder and hyperactivity: I. Separation of hyperactivity and antisocial conduct in British child psychiatric patients. *British Journal of Psychiatry, 149,* 760–767.

Trites, R. L., & LaPrade, K. (1983). Evidence for an independent syndrome of hyperactivity. *Journal of Child Psychology and Psychiatry, 24,* 573–586.

Wallander, J. L., & Hubert, N. C. (1985). Long-term prognosis for children with attention deficit disorder with hyperactivity (ADD/H). In B. B. Lahey & A. E. Kazdin (Eds.), *Advances in clinical child psychology* (Vol. 5, pp. 113–147). New York: Plenum.

Weiss, G., & Hechtman, L. T. (1986). *Hyperactive children grown up.* New York: Guilford Press.

Werry, J. S., Reeves, J. C., & Elkind, G. S. (1987). Attention deficit, conduct, oppositional, and anxiety disorders in children: I. A review of research on differentiating characteristics. *Journal of the American Academy of Child Psychiatry, 26,* 133–143.

West, D. J. (1969). *Present conduct and future delinquency.* London: Heinemann.

West, D. J. (1982). *Delinquency: Its roots, careers, and prospects.* London: Heinemann.

West, D. J., & Farrington, D. P. (1973). *Who becomes delinquent?* London: Heinemann.

West, D. J., & Farrington, D. P. (1977). *The delinquent way of life.* London: Heinemann.

5 Two processes of the development of persistent offending: Activation and escalation

MARC LE BLANC

Up to now criminologists have approached offending using synthetic, unidimensional characteristics. We will call them descriptive and developmental parameters of offending. (A list of the most often used parameters is given in Table 1). What we want to illustrate in this chapter is how these characteristics combine to constitute processes that support the development of persistent offending. Over the past 15 years, since the research of Wolfgang et al. (1972, 1987), longitudinal studies, have furnished data on the relationship between several of the parameters of offending, while syntheses such as those of Loeber (1982, 1987), Blumstein et al. (1986), and Fréchette and Le Blanc (1987) have led to the clarification of the conceptualization of certain processes. All this work, however, is intuitive because it is not based on a well thought out procedure for reconstructing the natural dynamics of the development of offending.

We have proposed (Le Blanc & Fréchette, 1989) to define the processes that constitute the development of persistent offending as being the result of the relationship between two or more of the descriptive and developmental parameters listed in Table 1. The advantage of this procedure is that it offers clarity concerning the elements of offending used in the theoretical definition of concepts such as escalation. By applying this procedure, we can demonstrate the existence of two basic processes that support the development of persistent offending: activation and escalation (see definitions in Table 1). These two are perhaps not the only processes, but they may be the most significant ones.

Little is known about the first, activation; there are very few references to it in the literature surveyed by Loeber. He conceptualizes it as the variety hypothesis (1982) and later as the rate of progression or innovation rate (1987). The second, escalation, is the subject of numerous controversies in the criminological literature as shown in the surveys done by Loeber (1985, 1987) and Blumstein et al. (1986) on progression in offending. Let us define these processes.

The *activation process* refers to the way the development of persistent

Table 1. *Parameters and mechanisms of offending*

Parameters

Descriptive
   Participation
   Frequency
   Variety
   Seriousness
   Nature (types of crime)
   Crime mix (combinatory structure)

Developmental
   Onset
   Duration
   Age of termination
   Transfer (from juvenile to adult crime)

Mechanisms

Activation
   Acceleration (onset and frequency)
   Diversification (onset and variety)
   Stabilization (onset and duration)

Escalation (age, nature of crime, onset, duration, seriousness, age of termination)
   Gradation of offenses
   Progression through crimes

---

offending is stimulated as soon as it has begun and to the way its persistence is assured. Once this process has begun, the result is delinquent activities marked by a high level of frequency, duration, and variety. We find that the process of activation is based on three separate but closely interrelated mechanisms. *Acceleration* refers to the relationship between early onset and frequency; *diversification* is measured by the degree of variety of offending, taking onset into account, while *stabilization* refers to the relationship between onset and duration. This means that if delinquency starts early, it will more probably be abundant, lasting, and varied.

The *process of escalation* is fiercely debated in criminological circles. Blumstein et al. (1986) make a clear distinction between escalation, "the tendency for offenders to move to more serious offense types as offending continues" (p. 84) and specialization, "the tendency to repeat the same offense type on successive arrests" (p. 81). In terms of the descriptive and developmental parameters, we propose the following definition of escalation: the existence of a sequence in the appearance of diverse forms of delinquent activities, which go from minor infractions to the most serious crime against the person as the subject increase in age. This sequence represents a more or less standard pattern of development through which subjects pass who are heading for significant delinquency experience. The parameters such as nature of crimes, seriousness, age of onset, duration, and age of termination are obviously contributing factors in that process.

The study of these processes enables us to verify the extent to which the development of offending obeys the well known orthogenetic principle of developmental psychology, that is, it evolves from a state of relative globality marked by the absence of differentiation to a state of greater differentiation with articulation and hierarchic integration (Werner, 1957). If we see the processes of activation and escalation brought to an end among a significant group of individuals, then we can conclude that the orthogenetic principle applies to offending as well.

Methods

We used for our sample 470 French-speaking boys from the Island of Montreal, all wards of the court. Because we are concerned with processes in offending, activation and escalation, a representative sample of the population would have been inappropriate because of the low base rate of serious delinquency and, particularly, because of the low frequency for most crimes. For these reasons, we selected a sample at high risk of chronic criminality. In so doing, we followed the recommendation of Cernkovich et al. (1985), who showed that serious delinquents are too often absent from delinquency research because it is habitually based on representative samples of the population.

The sample consists of boys ages 14 (29.2%) to 16 (28.9%) who had been convicted and given a sentence other than a fine or a compensatory measure, community work, restitution, and so on. (For a detailed description of this sample, see Fréchette, 1980, and Lagier, 1983, 1988.) The 470 individuals were recruited between 1973 and 1976. All of them appeared in court under the Young Delinquent Act (67.6%) or under the Youth Protection Act (32.4%), and all were declared wards of the court following that appearance. For some it was their first appearance in court, while others had had other appearances or were again in contact because of action by the social services. At an initial interview some were on probation (43.6%), others in detention (27.7%) or in an open institution (28.7%). As we will see later on, some had not yet been convicted of a crime and did not declare any self-reported crime during the first interview, but every one of them had been placed under the authority of the court at the time of recruitment at an average age of 15 and all by follow-up had declared crimes or were convicted of crimes. This group is essentially a consecutive series of the most serious cases as defined by their sentence, probation, or placement in an institution. A few subjects were ineligible because they were mentally ill or feeble minded, and 6 boys refused to cooperate with us. These serious cases represent approximately 12% of adolescents arrested by police (Le Blanc, 1977).

Two years later, between 1975 and 1978, 396 of the 470 subjects were reinterviewed concerning that 2-year interval. Their average age was then 17. Six subjects died during that interval, and of the remaining subjects, 63 could not be located or no personal contact could be made with them (13.58%). Of the 401 subjects contacted, only 5 refused reinterview. In sum, 84% of the original wards of the court, 85% of the ones that were still living, and 99% of the subjects contacted were reinterviewed. A comparison of the original 470 with these 396 showed no significant differences between the two groups on a broad range of variables (Fréchette, 1980).

Five years later, in 1981–1982, we interviewed 219 subjects. The reduction in number was largely due to budget constraints in the context of an economic recession. An additional 8 subjects had died since the second interview, bringing the total deaths to 14 (3%). To make sure that the reduced sample would be representative of the original sample, the following strategy described by Lagier (1988) was applied. The original sample was divided into eight levels of persistency in delinquency according to their earlier interviews, and we calculated the proportion that each level formed of the original sample. Quotas were set for each level of persistency in delinquency to preserve these proportions in our target group. Then subjects were randomly interviewed, whether at liberty or incarcerated, up to the quotas for each level of persistency in delinquency and in the same time sequence as the first round of interviews.

The result was 219 interviews about offending since the last interview. These 219 subjects had, with a margin of less than 1.5%, the same frequency distribution of the eight levels of persistency in delinquency as the original sample (Lagier, 1988). Their average age was 24 at this time and their age distribution was the following: 22 (26.9%), 23 (29.2%), 24 (29.2%), and 25 (14.6%).

In this chapter, we will concentrate on the history of self-reported delinquency as reconstituted from the three semistructured interviews on 190 of these subjects. These 190 were selected so that the time intervals between interviews were the same for all and the age range was reduced to only 3 years.

The ward of the court was asked to recall the offenses he had committed. The interviewer started with the first crime, using a set of 14 precisely defined categories of crimes (petty theft, larceny, shoplifting, common theft, burglary, car theft, aggravated theft, vandalism, public mischief, personal attack, sex crime, drug trafficking, homicide, and fraud). For each crime, or set of crimes, he had a list of questions to cover: when the crime was first and last performed, the period during which there was any series of this type of crime, the frequency, and how the crime was carried out (planning, instrument, violence, accomplices, and so on). During the interview a report sheet was completed, which ordered all crimes and series of crimes with the appropriate information on each. With this type of data, it was possible to study precisely the development of persistent offending.

Our results for the 190 subjects on whom we have self-reported data from onset to the last interview at an average age of 24 are unadjusted for age or length of risk period. We restricted ourselves to unadjusted data for two reasons: first, the age range of the sample is very narrow, 3 years. The second reason is empirical; we have calculated adjusted data defining the risk period in various way [using age or legal age, the active period between onset and termination (Le Blanc & Beaumont, 1986), street time (Fréchette, 1980; Lagier, 1988), annual frequencies (Le Blanc & Fréchette, 1989); Lagier, 1988)], and the results are always the same. Finding no effect for adjustment is contrary to common scientific wisdom, but it can be explained in two ways: the narrow age range of the sample and the short incarcerations (in both the juvenile justice and adult justice systems). There are numerous incarcerations and some long sentences (more than 2 years for adults and, on occasion, more than one year for juveniles under 18), but very few subjects have experienced an effective sentence of longer than 6 months in prison because of "good time" and of parole. For these empirical reasons, we have opted to present only unadjusted data on the processes of activation and escalation in persistent offending.

Results

It is pertinent to present some descriptions of the patterns of delinquency in order to understand the degree of persistence of offending in our sample of wards of the court. A thorough description of self-reported and official offending is available in Le Blanc and Fréchette (1989). During adolescence, the *self-reported* delinquency of the 396 subjects was as follows: The overall median frequency was 33.17, the annual median frequency was 8.27, and subjects participated in a median of 3.07 categories of crimes. Forty percent were engaged in violent offenses, with a median of 4.35 offenses. They began their delinquent behavior at the median age of 10.83 and were active for 5 years (the median interval between the first and the last crime).

Total official delinquency, from onset to the end of 1984, had a median frequency of 8.68 and an annual frequency of 2; 48% were convicted of violent crimes and the median frequency was 2.53 violent offenses; they were convicted for the first time at the median age of 14.56 and they were active for a median of 4.84 years until the mid-20s.

If we restrict ourselves to the 190 cases for whom there were three interviews, the self-reported criminal activity (Table 2) started at age 11 (a mean of 11.18 and a median of 11.7). The age distribution for onset approximates a normal curve with a peak at age 12. The active period (duration) lasted for about 8 years (a mean of 8.11 and a median of 7.92, a bimodal distribution with peaks at ages 8 and 11). The typical pattern was diversified, including 4 of the 14 types of crimes (a mean of 4.71 and a median of 4.31), and the frequency was high, with a yearly average of about 10 crimes. Table 2 also shows that the distribution of the ages of onset is not random (χ^2 of 54.05, df = 13, and $p < .00001$).

Activation

Activation refers to the stimulating effect of precocity on frequency, duration, and variety of offending. Precocity, in these relationships, is a true independent variable; it is an antecedent condition because it occurs necessarily before the three other parameters of offending. Because of this sequence in time, we can expect precocity to be a necessary condition for acceleration, stabilization, and diversification.

Acceleration. The surveys on onset of offending (Loeber, 1982; Blumstein et al., 1986; Farrington et al., 1986) all point to the fact that the earlier the illicit activity begins, the greater the probability that it will continue and become chronic delinquency. The perpetration of crimes at an early age would be a sort of behavioral matrix necessary for the appearance of an intense subsequent commitment to offending. With acceleration, it is the influence of precocity on the number of offenses subsequently committed that is in question. Table 2 shows that there is such connection, since the Spearman correlation of $-.31$ is statistically significant at $p < .001$ (we used Spearman's rather than Pearson's r because our frequency distributions are biased by a limited number of subjects with very high frequencies). This relationship is also attested to by the one sample runs test ($n_1 = 7$, $n_2 = 12$, $r = 4$, $p = .05$), which tells us that the distribution of the medians of frequency across ages of onset is not random.

Table 2 furnishes some additional information on the mechanism of acceleration (the medians are given, since there is often a considerable gap between the mean and the median for each age of onset because of a few subjects with a very high frequency of offenses). First, we confirm the few existing studies (Hampariam, et al., 1978; Farrington, 1983; Loeber, 1982; Fréchette & Le Blanc, 1979; and Tolan & Lorion, 1988) that are limited to the period before age 17. Our data show a decreasing frequency of criminal acts with an increase of the starting age, and this decrease is particularly evident if childhood is compared with adolescence and adulthood.

Secondly, if we examine the distribution of the median frequencies between age 4 and the early 20s, we see that there are five starting periods

Table 2. *Activation: Age of onset in relation to frequency, duration, and variety (medians and descriptive statistics, n = 190)*

Age of onset (yr.)	Number of cases	Number of crimes, frequency	Number of types, variety	Interval first to last duration (yrs.)
4	3	1884	5	18
5	5	797	2	15
6	13	852	3	12.75
7	12	114	3.75	9
8	13	430	7.67	11.75
9	13	81	4.25	8.63
10	22	94	7.08	10.67
11	8	243	3.5	6
12	30	75.5	5.83	7.5
13	22	21.5	3.5	4.25
14	20	23.5	4.75	6
15	13	50	2.83	6
16	8	80.5	4.5	2.5
17	4	35	2.5	2.5
18	1	14	1	5
19	1	76	5	3
20	0	0	0	0
21	1	2	2	1
22	1	1	1	1
Mean	11.18	1093.31	4.71	8.11
Median	11.7	93	4.31	7.92
Mode	12	6	1	11
St. dev.	3.42	2200.42	2.88	4.24
Range	18	10054	11	19
Min	4	1	1	1
Max	22	10055	12	20
Kurtosis	−0.18	6.09	−1.13	−0.42
Skewness	0.06	2.57	0.31	0.27

	Chi square	*runs test*	*runs test*	*runs test*
	54.05	$n_1 = 7$, $n_2 = 12$	$n_1 = 7$, $n_2 = 12$	$n_1 = 7$, $n_2 = 12$
df	13	$r = 4$	$r = 14$	$r = 2$
p	.00001	.05	.1	.05

that have a different stimulating effect on subsequent illicit activities. Subjects who begin in the first period, before age 9, show the greatest frequency of offending later on, a median of about 800 offenses. Those starting in the second period, between ages 9 and 12, show the disturbing impact of puberty, with a median of around 90 crimes. The third period in order of predicting high rates is midadolescence, ages 15 and 16, with a median of about 65 offenses. The fourth period (ages 13–14) is a period associated with much lower frequencies than the preceding periods, with a median of 22 crimes. Finally, when the starting age is after 20, very little offending ensues.

Thus, there are two main periods that trigger high rates of offending, early childhood (ages 4–8) and latency or late childhood (ages 9–12). These two periods illustrate the theory of precocity. The third period, midadolescence, may be related to the disturbing influence of the end of obligatory schooling. The 15th birthday in Quebec is the time when the great majority of the subjects of our sample leave school if they have not done so before (Fréchette & Le Blanc, 1987). These data support our proposition that there exists a mechanism of acceleration by which certain ages of onset produce a higher frequency of offenses. And precocity appears a necessary condition for abundant offending.

Stabilization. Since offending lasts 8 years on average, the question is whether or not onset might be the principal source of this stabilization in the life of the wards of the court. Table 2 clearly shows that the earlier they begin, the longer they tend to continue. On the one hand, the Spearman correlation–.61, is the highest, and it is statistically significant at $p < .0001$; on the other hand, the median duration gradually diminishes as the starting age increases. The one sample runs test ($n_1 = 7$, $n_2 = 12$, $r = 2$, $p = .05$) also indicates that the distribution of the medians is not random across ages of onset.

According to our data, the early practice of criminal activities fosters their stabilization. Some may argue that our results are an artefact of the longer period at risk with early onset, but this is not highly probable for three reasons. First, 98% of the sample had started before age 18 and 63% before age 12. Thus, virtually all cases had at least a 6-year risk period during adulthood. If there were another adult onset period that triggered high rates of offending, it would affect only a very limited number of cases. Second, the latecomers to crime, those beginning after age 18, have medians of frequency, variety, and duration that are very low as compared to the central tendencies of the whole group and even as compared to official delinquency (see descriptive data reported by Le Blanc & Fréchette, 1989). This means that there is virtually no chance that the late starters will show acceleration or stabilization. Third, a recent follow-up of the official delinquency of this sample between 1984 and 1988 shows that with one exception, none of the latecomers have recidivated.

What is remarkable in the distribution of the medians of duration reported in Table 2 is their generally monotonic decrease when compared with the medians of frequency, which indicated five periods of acceleration. Childhood, then, is a crucial period of acceleration and stabilization, whereas midadolescence can be a period of acceleration but not one of greater stabilization. Midadolescence may be the time for an explosion of criminal activity, but the explosion will generally be of shorter duration than if it had started during childhood. It should also be noted that the mechanism of stabilization is much more robust than the mechanism of acceleration; the correlation between onset and duration ($-.61$) is double the correlation between onset and frequency ($-.31$).

Diversification. Whereas acceleration and stabilization seem to be important mechanisms in the development of offending, are they sustained by diversification? *Diversification* measures the variety of the crimes, the number of categories of offenses committed (see Table 2).

An examination of Table 2 shows that there is a slight tendency that the earlier illicit activity begins, the greater its variety later on; with onset during childhood, the median types of crime is 4.25, while it is 3.5 when onset is during adolescence. However, the relationship here is less impressive than with acceleration and stabilization; in fact, the Spearman correlation ($-.04$) is not statistically significant, and the distributions of the medians (the median number of crime categories of offenses) fluctuates. This observation is confirmed by the one sample runs test ($n_1 = 7$, $n_2 = 12$, $r = 14$), which shows that the distribution of the medians for crime variety is nearly random.

Although we have shown elsewhere (Le Blanc & Fréchette, 1989) that diversification is striking during the period of adolescence, contrary to the hypothesis of Loeber (1982), the difference in the level of variety between early and late starters is not great. Therefore, diversification is not the mechanism through which age of onset affects acceleration or stabilization.

The effect of activation. The data analyzed so far support the fact that the earlier a person starts his criminal activities, the more numerous and the more lasting they will be. The mechanisms of acceleration, stabilization, and diversification, then, tell us how criminal activities develop. We have postulated that these mechanisms are autonomous, but also closely interrelated, and that their combination is necessary if offending is to persist. To confirm this, we did an analysis of the correlations between onset, frequency, duration, and variety (again using the Spearman correlations because there are very few subjects who have scrores that differ enormously from the general tendency). The simple and partial correlations displayed in Figure 1 will assist us in discussing the process of activation.

It must be pointed out that onset is by definition an antecedent variable and the other three parameters are necessarily consequents; furthermore, the variables of duration, frequency, and variety are necessarily concurrent characteristics of offending. The one-directional light arrows in Figure 1 show the antecedent relations, whereas the two-directional arrows

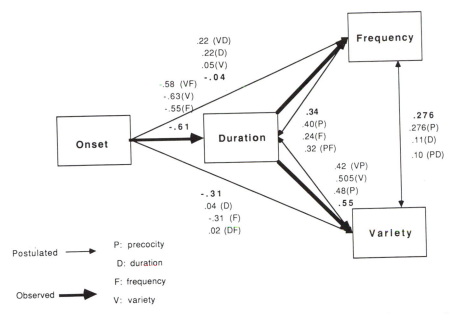

Figure 1. The correlations between onset, duration, frequency, and variety in the process of activation.

show the concurrent variables which are mutually influential. The correlation between onset and duration is much higher (− .61) than that between onset and variety (− .31), or frequency (− .04).

The major effect of onset age (precocity) appears to be on persistence (duration), a mechanism of stabilization seemingly more fundamental to persistent offending than is acceleration or diversification. This conclusion is confirmed by the partial correlations. The partial correlation between precocity and duration does not change significantly if frequency, variety, or both variables are controlled, moving only from − .61 to − .58. However, the partial correlations between onset and variety and onset and frequency are drastically changed if duration is controlled; even the signs change.

The correlation between variety and frequency is spurious because it disappears when duration is controlled, while the correlations between duration and variety and duration and frequency are not significantly modified if the other two variables are controlled. As shown in Figure 1 with the large arrows, the effect of precocity is first in terms of duration; it then manifests itself in variety and frequency. The effect of activation depends on the stabilization of offending in the behavioral pattern of the subject, and it is then amplified through acceleration and diversification.

In short, stabilization must be conceived as the direct effect of precocity on duration, while acceleration and diversification have to be redefined as the indirect effects of precocity on frequency and variety through duration. Offending must last before it will become abundant and varied. The process of activation has a number of effects, the first being stabilization. Precocity is proven to be a strong source of duration; the illicit activities are continuous but not necessarily abundant or varied. The second effect is acceleration. When criminal behavior is reiterated over time, this leads to a high frequency; the offenses are then numerous and lasting but not necessarily varied. The third effect is diversification, with precocity fostering duration rather than a large degree of diversity; the criminal activities are then lasting and heterogeneous but not necessarily abundant. Finally, the fourth effect, the most criminogenic of all, is inferred from the interaction between duration, frequency, and variety on a foundation of precocity. Offending, that starts early is long-lasting, and later becomes abundant and varied due to the dynamic effect of these three mechanisms.

Escalation

The study of escalation will be carried out based on two conceptual frameworks (Table 3). The first, which is centered on the illicit acts themselves, tries to discover a specific sequence of crimes in the development of offending. The second, focused on the individuals, attempts to show a gradual mode of involvement in offending. As we have demonstrated elsewhere (Le Blanc & Fréchette, 1989), a good part of the confusion in the criminological literature is due to the lack of differentiation between these two complementary perspectives on escalation.

To verify that the development of offending conforms to a particular model of evolution, it must be shown that the sequence of delinquent acts is marked by a constant increase in the seriousness of the acts. What we expect to observe is a string of crimes that becomes more and more serious as time goes on. The progression from minor crimes to major ones, as the subject's age increases, will enable us to state that the development of criminal activities is not due to chance and that it is organized according to the principle of predictability, which could even imply an invariant sequence over time. Robins and Wish (1977) clarified this principle by showing that the maximum exactitude in predicting problem behaviors can only be attained on the condition that they are constantly adjacent to one another in the course of development.

To support the fact that people who are involved in delinquency go through specific stages of development is to suggest a particular pattern of criminalization. This pattern obviously implies an increasing capacity to commit crimes, and if the evolution of offending conforms to a developmental pattern, we think it is in the form of a hierarchical model rather than an embryonic model, according to the distinction made by Loevinger (1968).

Table 3. *Development of offending:*
escalation

Acts: gradation
Limited predictability
Retention
Stages
    emergence
    exploration
    explosion
    conflagration
    outburst

Individuals: progression through the stages
Progression
Stability
Regression

The hierarchical model does not imply that all individuals go through the same stages and arrive at serious delinquency but rather that most start or stop at different stages, and only a certain number go through all the stages of offending. The embryonic model, on the other hand, states that all individuals go through the same stages in the same manner.

In criminology, as Blumstein et al. (1986) state, "a belief in escalation is probably the most widely held view of the pattern of criminal careers" (p. 84). In fact, Worstly more than a century ago described the progression "from petty delinquencies to greater and more heinous crimes" (1849, p. 12; cited by Morris & Giller, 1987). In spite of all the similar assertions since this distant era and even with numerous empirical studies, criminologists are far from being unanimous on this question, as evidenced in the recent surveys of Cohen (1986) and Loeber (1987).

The gradation of criminal activities. Our descriptive analysis of the parameters of offending shows that types of crime could be graded according to the starting age, the age when they stopped, the duration, the types of crimes committed (including crime mixes), the frequency, and the seriousness of the illicit activities. We found that the latter three categories change as the subject increases in age (Fréchette & Le Blanc, 1979, 1987). To better illustrate the gradation, taking into account the possible interactions among these aspects of the offense, we constructed Figure 2 as an adaptation from Le Blanc and Fréchette (1989). The abscissa of this figure represents the age of the individuals. On the ordinate, the types of crimes are ordered according to the average age at which each type of crime began. The figure in parentheses is the average degree of seriousness for each category of crime

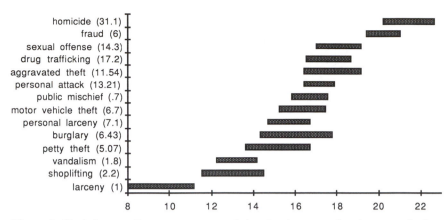

Figure 2. Gradation, median age at onset, and duration by age and seriousness of crime. From M. Le Blanc and M. Fréchette, 1989, *Male criminal activity from childhood to youth,* New York: Springer-Verlag.

based on the scale designed by Sellin and Wolfgang. Each bar begins with the average age of onset and ends with the average age of stopping. The obvious conclusion from an examination of this graph is that a specific sequence of crimes exists in the development of offending.

Three other conclusions are also evident. The first concerns the spectacular increase in the variety of crimes, especially after age 12 and up to about age 14, as if the polymorphous nature of the activities was intensified at this time to culminate in a diversity of acts. The second conclusion refers to the early discarding of a number of minor infractions (petty larceny, shoplifting) and the concentration on more serious crimes in midadolescence. The third conclusion is that not only are all forms of crime, from the most benign to the most serious, typically set in motion by age 14, but they tend to decline by about age 16. Thus it is clear, on the basis of these three conclusions, that delinquency is primarily a problem of the first part of adolescence; it tends to have only a limited duration, and up to midadolescence appears to be essentially heterogeneous. This means that each age level has one or several particular forms of offending, but at the same time, it is clear that from one level to another, there is a constant increase of the seriousness of the acts and a retention of other forms of crime.

Reading these data once again, we find that there are five stages in the development of offending and that they form a sequence. They are, in order, emergence, exploration, explosion, conflagration, and out-burst. As first, usually between ages 8 and 10, the delinquent activities are homogeneous and benign, almost always expressed in the form of petty larceny; this is the stage of *emergence*. This period is followed, generally between ages 10 and 12, by a diversification and escalation of the offenses, essentially comprising shoplifting and vandalism; this stage is one of *exploration*. Later, at about age 13, there is a substantial increase in the variety and seriousness of the crimes, and four new types of crime develop—common theft, public disorder, burglary, and personal theft; this is the stage of *explosion*, with burglary constituting the major component of this expansion, as indicated by its greater average duration (2.29 years). Around age 15, variety and seriousness increase further as four more types of crime are added—drug trafficking, motor vehicle theft, armed robbery, and personal attack; this is the stage of *conflagration*. Thus, by midadolescence the entire gamut of crimes has been experienced, with the exception of homicidal acts and fraud. Figure 2 also shows a fifth stage which occurs only during adulthood; it is a progression toward more sophisticated or more violent forms of criminal behavior; it is called *outburst*.

In addition, the overlapping of the durations clearly shows an important retention; the same crimes are committed from one stage to another, particularly in the shift from exploration to explosion and explosion to conflagration. Moreover, the hypothesis of predictability, advanced by Robins and Wish (1977) concerning the sequence of childhood behavior problems, appears to apply to the gradation of crimes, namely, that the behavior involving a less serious category of crime is the best predictor of the next most serious category of crime; for example, that petty larceny better predicts its neighbor, aggression or vandalism, than it does armed robbery.

Our demonstration of a gradation of the categories of offenses has been based solely on the main tendency with regard to seriousness, duration, and precocity. According to the scalogram technique of Guttman, a cumulative scale can be constructed with items whose degree of difficulty keeps increasing. A scale of this type implied the embryonic model of development, which means that every individual goes through the same stages in the same order. There is a predictability that extends to all the stages, even the more distant ones. Wohlwill (1973) proposes the use of Guttman scaling as one of the techniques for the construction of developmental scales. We have used it to show that the development of criminal activities does not follow an embryonic model but rather a hierarchical model (Le Blanc & Fréchette, 1989).

We found that over the period from childhood to the mid-20s, the coefficient of reproducibility was only .56. The correlations between the stages showed that each stage predicted the next stage but not the later ones, meaning that the appropriate model was hierarchical. When we limited the period covered to childhood and adolescence, and conducted the Guttman analysis of 396 delinquents with reference to the four stages that seem to characterize the development of offending during this period, the results were both disappointing and convincing. They were disappointing because although precocity seems to be the driving force activating delinquency, the stage of emergence, in which petty larceny was dominant between ages 8 and 11, did not trigger escalation. In fact, the coefficients from the application of the Guttman technique are as low as those previously reported for the five stages. Only if we limit the analysis to the three middle stages—exploration, explosion, and conflagration—do we achieve a coefficient of reproducibility close to the acceptable threshold, .75. Because of those results we can conclude that the development of offending is a hierarchical process, and this is confirmed by the coefficients of association between adjacent stages (Yule's Q is .52 between exploration and explosion and .47 between explosion and conflagration, but much less (.09) between exploration and conflagration.)

These results lead to two conclusions. The first is that the gradation of crime categories should not be conceived as a certain ordering of all specific crimes, but rather as a progression across three groups of crimes. The first group in the sequence would be composed of shoplifting and vandalism between ages 11 and 14; the second of four other types of theft—common theft, burglary, personal larceny, and automobile theft—between ages 14 and 17, and the third of personal attack, armed robbery, and drug trafficking between ages 16 and 19. In this perspective, the crimes at the two extremes of the continuum of seriousness, petty larceny at the lower end and fraud and homicidal conduct at the upper end, would have an unspecified role in determining the development of offending.

The second conclusion is that, even though precocity has emerged as the driving force activating offending, only the progression of the crimes found in the three middle stages constitute the true process of escalation. Hence, once precocity has activated offending (aided by stabilization, diversification, and acceleration), offending develops with increasing seriousness during adolescence, according to a single hierarchical sequence beginning with exploration, then explosion, and finally conflagration.

Progression through stages. In order to complete this analysis, we must learn how delinquents go through the different stages of development in their delinquent activity. First, do a significant proportion of subjects, during their evolution, progress from minor crimes to very serious crimes? This way of dealing with the question of progression seems to be rare among all the studies surveyed by Cohen (1986), which generally focused on crime switching and on the gradation in types of crime. Only studies on behavior problems, such as that by Robins and Wish (1977), have addressed such questions.

Le Blanc et al. (1988) have developed a strategy of analysis that makes it possible to calculate what proportion of delinquents progressed, regressed, or remained stable over time. Over a 2-year period, the respective percentages were 32, 31, and 29 for a sample of the population of adolescents living in Montreal. Looking at the data gathered from the interviews with this group of delinquents and the stages of progression in offending, we observe a progression in 92.1% of the cases when the five stages are taken into account (30.9% of stage one, 42.7% of two, 24.9% of three, and 2.8% of four). If we limit ourselves to the three fundamental stages that foster the process of escalation, it is interesting to note that 71% of delinquents change their level of offending over time, whereas 29.3% limit themselves to a single stage of offending (6% at the exploration stage, 22% at the explosion state, and the rest at the conflagration stage). Among the subjects who change the level of their illicit activities, 77.6% do so according to the hierarchical model described before, whereas 22.4% deviate from this model, 61% of them going from exploration to explosion and 39% from exploration to explosion and conflagration.

To sum up, for the large majority of our wards of the court their illicit activities progress from minor crimes to more serious ones. Not only do they progress, the majority do so in sequence, many going from exploration to explosion, many from exploration to explosion, and then to conflagration. Although about a quarter of the subjects limit themselves to the crimes common to a single stage, and in this case usually the stage of explosion, which is mainly due to their preference for burglary, the others, in keeping with the rules of the hierarchical model, go through several stages. They do not all start with the same one nor end with the same one, and their transition from one to the other is not always standard, but they do follow the evolutional direction stipulated by the sequential progression of the stages.

Appendix: Definitions of different types of offenses

Petty larceny: Category including acts of minor gravity similar to the "childhood offenses" committed principally during pre-puberty, but capable of appearing at adolescence as well. These are of an impulsive and/or hedonistic nature marked by the theft of sweets, cigarettes, toys, small amounts of money, school supplies, or shoplifting (at the corner store, for example).

Shoplifting: Category comprising more serious offenses than the preceding one because committed either at a more advanced age (with knowledge of the illegality of the act) and with a coefficient of greater risk (in department stores, for instance) or carried out in a well planned and organized way.

Petty theft: Category covering a precise group of thefts excluding those involving breaking and entering, personal robbery; it comprises a great diversity of offenses, from the theft of various objects, including bicycles and sums of money to receiving stolen merchandise.

Burglary: Category containing all kinds of illegal entry, breaking and entering for purposes of theft, whether successful or not; this means that intention and attempt are included, as well as theft inside a motor vehicle and possession of tools for purposes of burglary.

Personal larceny: Crime depriving the victim of a possession by means of physical attack; the principal offenses here are theft with violence, aggravated theft, theft from a delivery person, purse-snatching, pickpocketing, etc. The perpetration of these crimes implies the use of force in any form, but on condition that it is against one or several private individuals.

Theft of motor vehicles: Homogeneous category concerning the theft of any motorized vehicle, from motorcycles and heavy trucks to trains, aeroplanes, and boats, and so on.

Aggravated theft: Fairly limited category comprising thefts of a more criminal nature; the principal offenses are business or bank hold-ups, the theft of arms, mail, and so on.

Vandalism: Category of crimes whose intention is the destruction or deterioration of private or public property, such as misdemeanors, damage to property, fires, breakages, and so on.

Personal attack: A specific criminal activity defined as a physical attack against a person without element of theft; the main manifestations are assault, assault and battery, grievous bodily harm, mugging and attempts...; by extension, this category can also include threats and suicide attempts as well as possession of arms (with intent to threaten or attack someone).

Public mischief: A heterogeneous category of activities more deviant than delinquent, comprising acts such as disturbing the peace, illicit presence, vagrancy, running away (if officially charged), infractions of highway code, possession of forbidden objects, sounding a false alarm, and so on.

Drugs: A category which is composed of possession and trafficking.

Sexual offenses: A specific category of crimes including indecency, indecent exposure, soliciting, rape, attempted rape, and so on.

Fraud: A fairly homogeneous category of crimes including appropriation by means of trickery, such as fabrication of false documents or forged money, the use of forged checks or stolen credit cards, false representation, bank or business frauds, and so on.

Homicide: All types of homicide and attempts.

Acknowledgments

This research was supported by Canada Council, the Ministry of the Solicitor General of Canada, la Fondation Richelieu, and l'Université de Montréal.

References

Blumstein, A., Cohen, J., Roth, J. A., & Visher, C. A. (1986). *Criminal careers and career criminals* (Vols. I and II). Washington DC: National Academic Press.

Cernkovich, S. A., Giordano, P. C., & Pugh, M. D. (1985). Chronic offenders: The missing cases in self-reported delinquency research. *The Journal of Criminal Law and Criminology, 76*, 705–732.

Cohen, J. (1986). Research on criminal careers: Individual frequency rates and offense seriousness. In A, Blumstein, J. Cohen, J. A., Roth, & C. A. Visher (Eds), *Criminal careers and career criminals* Vol. I, pp. 292–418. Washington, DC: National Academic Press.

Farrington, D. (1983). Offending from 10 to 25 years of age. In K. T. Van Deusen & S. A. Mednick (Eds.), *Antisocial and prosocial behavior*. Boston: Kleuwer-Nijhoff.

Farrington, D., Ohlin, L. E., & Wilson, J. Q. (1986). *Understanding and controlling crime: Toward a new research strategy*. New York: Springer-Verlag.

Fréchette, M. (1980). Portrait de la délinquance. Groupe de recherche sur l'inadaptation juvénile. Université de Montréal.

Fréchette, M., & Le Blanc, M. (1979). *La délinquance à l'adolescence*. Cahier 1, Inadaptation Juvénile. Group de recherche sur l'inadaptation juvénile. Université de Montréal.

Fréchette, M., & Le Blanc, M. (1987). *Délinquances et délinquants*. Chicoutimi: Gaétan Morin.

Hampariam, D. M., Schuster, R., Dinitz, S., & Conrad, J. P. (1978). *Violent few: A study of dangerous juvenile offenders*. Lexington, MA: D. C. Heath.

Lagier, P.-M. (1983). Programme de recherche Myosotis IV: diagnostic et pronostic de la criminalité vraie chez les jeunes adultes. Rapport d'étape 1981–1982. Université de Montréal, Centre international de criminologie comparée.

Lagier, P.-M. (1988). La production criminelle et la vie quotidienne des ex-pupilles du tribunal des mineurs. Université de Montréal, Centre international de criminologie comparée.

Le Blanc, M. (1977). *La délinquance juvénile au Québec*. Québec: Ministère des affaires sociales.

Le Blanc, M., & Beaumont, H. (1986). De la délinquance à la criminalité. Université de Montréal, Centre international de criminologie comparée,

Le Blanc, M., & Fréchette, M. (1989). *Male criminal activity from childhood through youth:* Multilevel and development perspectives. New York: Springer-Verlag.

Le Blanc, M., Loeber, R., & Coté, G. (1988). Temporal paths in delinquency: Stability, regression and progression analysed with panel data from an adolescent and delinquent male sample. Manuscript submitted for publication.

Loeber, R. (1982). The stability of antisocial and delinquent child behavior: a review. *Child Development, 53*, 1431–1446.

Loeber, R. (1985). Les débuts précoces et la progression de la carrière des jeunes délinquants. In M. Le Blanc (Ed.), *Conduites délinquantes et personnalités criminelles*. Cahier 20. Université de Montréal, École de criminologie.

Loeber, R. (1987). Natural histories of conduct problems. delinquency and associated substance use: Evidence for developmental progressions. In B.B. Lahey & A. E. Kazdin (Eds.), *Advances in clinical child psychology* (Vol. 10). New York: Plenum.

Loevinger, J. (1968). The meaning and measurement of ego development. *American Psychologist, 21*, 195–206.

Morris, A., & Giller, H. (1987). *Understanding juvenile justice.* London: Croom Helm.

Robins, L. N., & Wish, E. (1977). Childhood deviance as a developmental process: A study of 233 urban black men from birth to 18. *Social Forces, 56*, 448–483.

Tolan, P. H., & Lorion, R. P. (1988). Multivariate models of delinquent behavior in males. *American Journal of Community Psychology.*

Werner, H. (1957). The concept of development from a comparative and organismic point of view. In D. B. Harris (Ed.), *The concept of development.* Minneapolis: University of Minnesota Press.

Wolfgang, M. E., Figlio, R. M., & Sellin, T. E. (1972). *Delinquency in a birth cohort.* Chicago: University of Chicago Press.

Wolfgang, M. E., Thornberry, T. P., & Figlio, R. M. (1987). *From boy to man, from delinquency to crime.* Chicago: University of Chicago Press.

Wohlwill, J. F. (1973). *The study of behavioral development.* New York: Academic Press.

6   A pattern approach to the study of pathways from childhood to adulthood

DAVID MAGNUSSON AND L. R. BERGMAN

One main characteristic of traditional developmental research is that it is *variable oriented*. This implies that it is the variable per se that is the main unit of analysis and the main object of interest. This orientation can be seen in almost all main areas of developmental research: in the study of stability and consistency of single aspects of individual functioning, in the investigation of interrelations among single aspects of individual functioning, and in research on the relation between aspects of the environment and aspects of individual functioning. Commonly used methods for pursuing such research include comparisons between means, correlation, and regression analysis, and structural equation modeling. Thus, a main characteristic of variable-oriented research is that it is directed toward analyses of variables and expresses the results in terms of some kind of weights indicating the relative role of these variables in processes and in outcomes.

Variable-oriented research is, of course, important and necessary for understanding the developmental process underlying molar individual functioning. However, especially when seen from an interactional perspective, it raises a series of theoretical, methodological, and research strategy problems. Therefore, variable-oriented research has to be complemented with *person-oriented* research, that is, with research in which the person is the main unit of analysis and the main object of interest (Bergman & Magnusson, 1987; Block, 1971; Cairns, 1986; Magnusson, 1985, 1988; Magnusson, & Bergman, 1984, 1988). As a general idea the person orientation is a very old notion. The present purpose is to combine this thinking, within an interactional paradigm, with a study of individual differences using objective, quantitative methods to permit generalizations and the cumulative building of knowledge.

The person-oriented paradigm can be operationalized in different ways in empirical research. We will discuss only one obvious such approach, namely the study of patterns or configurations of relevant person characteristics in a developmental perspective. This has important implications with regard to methodology and research strategy, with the main point being that it is essential to consider the information about each individual as a whole, using appropriate methods. Such methods are those that focus on studying individuals by analyzing patterns, such as cluster analysis. In this kind of methodology each subject's complete profile of available data is considered and individuals are grouped together on the basis of similarities in these profiles. Discussions of methods and research strategies in this field are given by Bergman (1988 *a*), Bergman & Magnusson (1983, 1984 *a*, 1984 *b*, 1987), and Block (1971).

The distinction between a variable-oriented and a person-oriented approach to the study of developmental issues concerns both concepts and research strategy. As such neither need be and cannot be proved right or wrong by statistical tests. For example, even if a variable-oriented approach provided a stronger prediction of adult behavior from certain measures of childhood behavior than that provided by a person-oriented approach, the latter might still give us a greater understanding of the processes of individual development.

A critical discussion of traditional variable-oriented methods for studying developmental issues and a presentation of an alternative person-oriented approach is beyond the scope of this chapter. The aim is not to discuss all the theoretical and methodological problems connected with the two approaches. Rather it is to draw attention to what we regard as an important research strategy issue with far reaching implications and to illustrate the merits of a person approach, not as a substitute but as a complement to variable-oriented developmental research.

An illustration to a pattern approach

The empirical illustration that will be presented here is concerned with the implications of overt adjustment problems among boys at an early age for the development of adult maladjustment in terms of criminality, alcohol problems, and psychiatric problems. Over the years, there have been many studies showing how each of a number of single aspects of individual functioning—aggressiveness, hyperactivity, low school motivation, poor peer relations—is significantly related to various aspects of adult maladjustment (Kirkegaard-Sörensen & Mednick, 1977; Loeber & Dishion, 1983; McCord, 1983; Robins, 1966; Roff & Wirt, 1984; Rutter & Giller, 1983; West & Farrington, 1973). Applying the pattern approach to this research area, the focus instead becomes: what typical patterns or configurations of adjustment problems of this kind actually exist in childhood; how are major adjustment problem areas in adult age interconnected; and what are the relations between typical problem patterns in childhood and typical problem patterns in adulthood.

The data to be considered here come from a longitudinal project, Individual Development and Adjustment (IDA), conducted in Stockholm by the first author since the mid-1960s. The group studied consists of all boys who attended grade 6 in the school system in one community in Sweden in 1968 ($N = 545$). The majority of these boys were at that time age 13. Since almost all children in Sweden attend the general school system, it can be assumed for most purposes that the studied group is representative of the corresponding age cohort in that community. The only boys not included in the study are those who were severely retarded or were in mental hospitals (about 1% of the cohort). This implies that the sample represents the whole range of basic upbringing factors (Magnusson, 1988; Magnusson & Duner, 1981; Magnusson et al., 1975).

The data used in the study presented here are data for behavior problems at age 13 and data from official records for criminal offences, alcohol problems, and psychiatric care during the age period before age 18 and from ages 18 through 23. The drop-out at age 13 was negligible (only 5 boys), and the data from official records were complete, except for 2 boys who had died. For 32 boys, one of six values at age 13 was initially missing and had to be imputed, using for this purpose information about the values in the other indicators (Bergman & Magnusson, 1984a).

Patterns of conduct problems at age 13

At the age of 13 the boys were grouped on the basis of their specific patterns for six aspects of overt adjustment problems:

Aggressiveness
Motor restlessness
Lack of concentration
Lack of motivation
Underachievement
Poor peer relations

Data for the first four of these variables were obtained as teachers' ratings. The teachers had known their pupils for about 3 years and had had the opportunity of observing them in a variety of situations in the school yard and in the classroom. The ratings were performed on 7-point scales. Data for "underachievement" were obtained for each boy as the difference between actual achievement in terms of grades and achievement predicted from intelligence scores. "Poor peer relations" was measured by peer ratings of popularity in classroom situations and in the school yard.

Ideally, a pattern analysis in the present connection should be based on absolute measures of the variables under consideration (Magnusson & Bergman, 1984). Such data are rarely available in psychological research. In order to meet the requirement as far as possible, the raw data for each variable were transformed into a 4-point quasi-absolute scale with the following definition of the value codes:

0: no adjustment problem
1: the adjustment is not good, but no clear problem
2: an adjustment problem
3: a pronounced adjustment problem

These data constituted the basis for six scales; the main purposes were to achieve a multivariate scaling, in the sense that all variables were scaled within the same frame of reference, and to achieve a scaling that reflected the fact that different problems may have different prevalence. The scoring was thus made on the basis of considerations of the presence of the various levels of problems for an adjustment variable, independent of the relative frequency of its occurrence.

One implication of this approach is that distinctions on the "positive" side of the distribution of adjustment scores are neglected in this specific analysis, since the interest is devoted to maladjustment. For instance, with regard to the teachers' ratings, which were made on 7-point scales, the values 1 to 4 were coded 0, 5 was coded 1, 6 was coded 2, and 7 was coded 3. The reasons for the quasi-absolute scaling are discussed by Bergman and Magnusson (1983, 1987). In the 1983 reference, a more detailed presentation of the underlying theoretical background and taxonomy is given. The indicators are described in more detail in Bergman and Magnusson (1984b, 1987).

The scaled values in the six indicators formed the basis for grouping the individuals on the basis of their patterns, using cluster analysis in two steps. First, individuals were grouped according to a hierarchical method (Ward, 1963) to obtain 12 clusters. Second, the result of this classification was taken as the input for a relocation cluster analysis, in which each subject was relocated to the cluster leading to the smallest error sum of squares. The two most similar clusters were then fused and the relocation process repeated. A special feature was that a residue was formed of "unclassified" subjects, those who did not fit into any cluster; for this procedure there are both theoretical and technical reasons (see Bergman, 1988a). The complete analysis is called RESCLUS (Bergman & Magnusson, 1987); the CLUSTAN statistical package was used for the calculations (Wishart, 1982). A solution with eight clusters was chosen based on the notable increase in both the total error sum of squares and the size of the residue when the number of clusters was reduced to seven.

The eight-cluster solution of the cluster analysis is presented in Table 1. A number of observations can be made by inspection of this table. First, as expected, one large cluster (no. 1, $N = 296$) is characterized by the absence of problems; the mean in all six indicators is less than 1. Second, none of

Table 1. *Clusters of boys at age 13 based on data for overt adjustment problems*

		Cluster means						
Cluster no.	Size	Average coefficient[a]	Aggressiveness	Motor restlessness	Lack of concentration	Low school motivation	Underachievement	Poor peer relations
1	296	.12	—[b]	—	—	—	—	—
2	23	.30	—	—	—	—	—	2.4
3	40	.28	—	—	—	—	2.6	—
4	61	.39	1.3	1.4	—	—	—	—
5	41	.39	—	1.5	2.3	1.9	—	—
6	12	.56	1.7	1.8	2.3	1.9	2.6	—
7	37	.37	2.3	2.3	1.9	1.3	—	—
8	22	.48	2.2	2.7	2.6	2.4	—	1.9
Residue	8		1.5	1.4	1.3	1.3	1.3	2.3

[a] Average coefficient means average error sum of squares within the cluster.
[b] Indicates that the cluster mean of a variable is less than 1 in the 4-point scale coded 0, 1, 2, 3.

four variables, "aggressiveness," "motor restlessness," "lack of concentration," and "low school motivation," all of which have been shown to be related to adult adjustment problems, appears as a single characteristic of any group. Only "underachievement" and "poor peer relations" are characteristics of single-problem clusters (no. 3, $N = 40$, and no. 2, $N = 23$, respectively). These two adjustment problems have also been shown in earlier studies in our program to be characteristic of single-problem clusters at age 10 (Bergman & Magnusson, 1987). Third, conduct problems in their strong manifestations appear to occur together in multi-problem syndromes with or without the simultaneous occurrence of "underachievement" and "poor peer relations." Fourth, only 8 boys did not fit any cluster and were left unclassified and placed in the residue. [For more details, see Bergman and Magnusson (1984*b*)].

An important issue when interpreting the significance of the outcome of these analyses is the reliability and validity of the grouping of individuals as presented in Table 1. The stability of the RESCLUS method with regard to sampling variation was studied on approximately the same boys when they reached age 10. For this purpose the sample was split into random halves and for each half a RESCLUS analysis was performed. The two solutions obtained were similar with respect to the clusters that emerged (Bergman & Magnusson, 1984*a*). The individual stability or reliability of the clustering has recently been studied using test-retest data based on pupils' questionnaires for the rather similar RESIDAN method. For this type of data, which have a substantially lower reliability and a less clear cluster structure than is the case for the data analyzed here, a significant individual stability was found between the classification based on the questionnaire data from occasion 1 and the classification based on the questionnaire data from occasion 2. The individual stability was studied by first forming the most similar pairs of clusters between the two occasions and then counting the number of subjects belonging to these pairs. It was then found that 40.2% of the subjects were thus characterized as compared to 13.6% as expected by chance ($p < .001$; it should be observed that the upper limit in this connection is lower than 100%).

In spite of these results, the clusters should not be over-interpreted. Undoubtedly, if somewhat different variables and a different method of cluster analysis were used, the grouping would be slightly different on an individual level and, presumably, fairly similar but not identical clusters would emerge. Here especially the choice of variables appears to be very important (Milligan, 1981). Thus, one must be cautious about generalizing the results to situations in which other variables are used if these variables tap different latent dimensions of adjustment problems than were measured here.

Both laboratory and field research have demonstrated a negative relation between social adjustment and autonomic activity–reactivity in terms of adrenaline excretion (Johansson et al., 1973; Olweus, 1985). Among other things, results from IDA have shown that those who were found in official records during the age period of 18 to 26 for criminal offences had already at age 13 demonstrated a significantly and conspicuously lower level of adrenaline excretion in two independent situations as compared to a control group (Magnusson, 1988). Given this relationship, one indication of the validity of the present grouping would be that those individuals belonging to the cluster characterized by several pronounced conduct problems (cluster nos. 6, 7, & 8) showed a lower autonomic activity–reactivity in terms of adrenaline excretion than did those without conduct problems. From the complete main cohort in IDA a representative subsample was drawn for the purpose of complementing the psychological data with physiological information. Measures of adrenaline excretion were obtained in two independent situations at age 13 for this physiological subsample and complete data were obtained for 97 boys (Johansson et al., 1973). It was found that, according to expectations, the adrenaline excretion in these two situations was significantly lower ($p < .001$) for boys in the multi-problem cluster (nos. 6–8) than for boys in the well adjusted cluster (no. 1).

Patterns of adult adjustment problems

In the present study, adult adjustment problems are reflected in three aspects of the data: criminal offenses, alcohol problems, and psychiatric problems (having a DSM III diagnosis other than substance abuse). Data for these aspects of maladjustment were obtained from official records. Records from all parts of Sweden were accessed with permission of the appropriate authorities. Data were obtained for all individuals for whom school data at age 13 were available, except for 2 subjects who had died.

The official records data used here covered the period before age 18 and the period from ages 18 through 23. During the later age period, 148 subjects of the total sample were found in criminal records, 92 subjects were found in alcohol records, and 60 subjects had been under psychiatric care. Of particular interest, and supporting the idea of a person approach to the study of maladjustment, was the observation that many individuals were found in more than one of the records (Table 2).

Of those who had criminal records 52% were also in at least one of the two other types of records; of those who were found in alochol records, 76.1% also appeared in at least one of the two other types of records; and of those who had been under psychiatric care, 58.3% were also in at least one of the other types of records. The problem overlap was significantly larger ($p<.01$) than expected by chance for all three problems (according to χ^2 tests in which the presence/absence of a problem was cross-tabulated against the presence/absence of any of the other two problems). The statistical analysis also showed that being in only one record actually appeared significantly less often ($p<.01$) than could be expected from a random model (Magnusson, 1988).

Longitudinal relations between patterns of overt adjustment problems in childhood and adult maladjustment

In many studies within the variable-oriented tradition, strong relationships have been found between, on the one hand, indicators of early antisocial behaviors, like the ones studied here, and, on the other hand, later antisocial behavior problems like criminality and alcohol abuse. An overview of this research is given by Robins (1984). She also pointed out the difficulties in unconfounding different relationships, since problems tend to be correlated. Applying a person perspective, the obvious approach is to study the relationships between childhood and adulthood configurations or patterns of problems. In this way, a problem in isolation is not considered as psychologically significant per se; it achieves its significance when seen in combination with other problems.

The next step in the present study was to connect the individual patterns of adjustment problems found at age 13 with the problem combinations found at adult age. Although this connection can be made in different ways, our results are based on an analysis of the correspondence and noncorrespondence between the different adjustment patterns in childhood and the

Table 2. *Frequency of recorded criminal offences, alcohol abuse, and psychiatric care for males ages 18 through 23*

Official record	No. of individuals
Criminality record only	71
Alcohol record only	22
Psychiatric care only	25
Criminal and alcohol records	48
Criminal record and psychiatric care	13
Alcohol record and psychiatric care	6
Criminal record, alcohol record, and psychiatric care	16
Total	201

different combinations of adjustment problems in adulthood. The basic results for this kind of analysis can be shown as a cross-tabulation of cluster membership at age 13 against the number of adjustment problem combinations at ages 18 through 23, (i.e., an 8×8 contingency table). An exploratory testing of types (i.e., cells being more frequented than expected by chance) and of antitypes (i.e., cells being less frequented than expected by chance) was performed with an exact, single-cell test (using the computer program EXACON, Bergman & El-Khouri, 1987). To reduce the risk of chance significant results when evaluating many tests on the same data set, the 1% significance level was chosen. In Table 3 the significant types and antitypes are given.

As seen in Table 3, as expected, having no overt adjustment problems at age 13 is significantly related to an absence of registered problems at adult age. Only for the two most severe multi-problem clusters at age 13 does the relationship to the adult combinations of adjustment problems reach a significant level. Having severe conduct problems at age 13 (cluster no. 7) is related to having registration for both "criminality" and "alcohol abuse" at adult age, and having a broad and severe spectrum of overt adjustment problems (cluster no. 8) is significantly related to appearing in all three kinds of records. As compared to the boys in the well adjusted cluster, the risk for a boy in cluster 7 of having official records for both "criminality" and alcohol abuse is 5.5 times higher, and the risk for a boy in cluster 8 of having all three kinds of records is 20.1 times higher. It is also of interest to note which pattern combinations tend not to concur. In this case, the significant antitypes are consistent with and confirm the interpretation of these results.

The results in Table 3 indicate that no studied overt problem patterns in childhood other than those reflected in clusters 7 and 8 had a strong and

Table 3. *Significant longitudinal streams from cluster membership at age 13 to adult patterns of adjustment problems: Ratios of observed to expected frequency*

Cluster at age 13	Adult pattern of adjustment problems			% of sample	Ratio of observed/ expected frequency
	Criminality	Psych. care	Alcohol abuse		
Significant types					
Cluster 1 (well adjusted)	no	no	no	44.9	1.10
Cluster 7 (severe aggression, hyperacitivity)	yes	no	yes	1.7	3.40
Cluster 8 (multiple problems)	yes	yes	yes	0.6	7.32
Significant antitypes					
Cluster 1 (well adjusted)	yes	no	yes	2.5	0.61
Cluster 1 (well adjusted)	no	no	yes	0.9	0.50
Cluster 7 (severe aggression, hyperactivity)	no	no	no	2.8	0.55
Cluster 8 (multiple problems)	no	no	no	1.9	0.62

Note: Only streams significant at the 1% level are included in the table (using a one-tailed hypergeometric test of the appropriate collapsed table).

significant relation to any adult combination of adjustment problems. That is, children characterized by only a single adjustment problem, or by a combination of less pronounced problems, were not significantly overrepresented in any combination of adult adjustment problems. This is important information underscoring the fruitfulness of considering patterns of problems, rather than single-problem indicators, in research on the developmental process underlying adult maladjustment.

One must also be aware that chance fluctuations may influence the results and that, presumably, the power of detecting less strong relationships may not be high. Only one nonsignificant tendency will be discussed here. For cluster 6, which is characterized by hyperactive behaviors combined with school problems, the only tendency found was official records for criminality. One might wonder why this cluster is not related to adult adjustment problems as cluster 7 is, since the two clusters are fairly similar except that cluster 6 is characterized by "underachievement" in addition to the other problems. One explanation may be the lower power when testing the longitudinal streams for cluster 6, since it consists of only 12 subjects. Another explanation may be the presence of "underachievement," which can be viewed as a marker of not-below-average intelligence (since there is a positive correlation between the degree of underachievement and intelligence). A not-below-average intelligence may operate as a protective factor.

Early behavior problems and registered adjustment problems as precursors of adult registered adjustment problems

Of course, the above perspective, although incorporating the study of patterns, is rather restricted in that only overt behavior problems are included as antecedent information for explaining individual differences in the adult patterning of adjustment problems. For instance, many studies have pointed to the significance to later antisocial problems of early contacts with the authorities with regard to criminality or alcohol abuse (Torstensson, 1987). To illustrate one possible extension of the pattern analysis, an analysis was performed in order to shed light on the following questions:

1. Are severe patterns of behavior problems in school only important for adult antisocial behavior to the extent that they are involved in the process leading to early difficulties with the authorities which, in turn, influence the process leading to adult antisocial behavior (Model 1 in Figure 1)?
2. Or should such severe childhood patterns also be seen as indicators of personality types that increase the likelihood of adult antisocial behavior, even if there are no early problems with the authorities (Model 2 in Figure 1)?
3. Or should early behavior problems and early problems with the authorities be seen as mainly independent factors influencing adult adjustment problems (Model 3 in Figure 1)?
4. Or do early behavior problem pattern indicate basic personality types that are at risk for developing both adolescent and adult antisocial behavior, and the strong relation between them is mainly a reflection of this fact (Model 4 in Figure 1)?

One way of illuminating these questions is to study the simultaneous relation between, on the one hand, early patterns of behavior problems and early registration (before age 18) with regard to criminality and or alcohol abuse and, on the other hand, adult registration for both criminality and alcohol abuse (the most conspicuous problem pattern found in Table 2). The relevant information is given in Table 4.

Being registered before the age of 18 apparently increases the risk of adult registration from 3.5% to 27%, and belonging to one of the two most severe multi-problem clusters at age 13 increases the risk of adult registration to 30.5% (as compared to 5.1% for the well adjusted cluster). However, early registration, even when belonging to the well adjusted cluster, leads to a substantially increased risk of adult registration (18.6% as compared to the group with no early problems at 2.8%). Belonging to one of the two

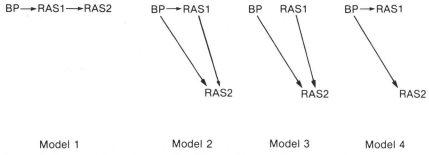

Figure 1. Four models for the role of behavior problems at school (BP) and registered antisocial behavior in adolescence (RAS1) in the development of adult-registered antisocial behavior (RAS2).

Table 4. *Adults (%) characterized by both criminality and alcohol abuse according to cluster membership at age 13 and early registration for criminality and/or alcohol abuse*

Cluster at age 13	Early registration for criminality and/or alcohol abuse		
	Yes	No	All
1 (well adjusted)	18.6	2.8	5.1
2–5 (some problems)	20.0	4.0	8.5
7, 8 (severe problems)	48.5	7.7	30.5
All	27.0	3.5	9.1

multi-problem clusters, but not being registered early, only leads to a moderately increased risk of adult registration (7.7% as compared to 2.8%). It appears that the main factor is the presence of early registration, but that belonging to one of the two multi-problem clusters increases the risk of adult registration further (from 18.6% to 48.5%). A logit model was fitted to Table 4 and it was found that the log–odds ratios were described as satisfactory by an additive model including early registration ($p < .001$) and cluster membership ($p < .05$).

In conclusion, it appears that the results support Model 2 or Model 3 in Figure 1. If Model 1 were true there would be no relationship between early behavior problems and adult problems controlling on early registration; but there is such a relationship, and therefore this model can be rejected. If Model 4 were true there would be no relationship between early and late registered adjustment problems for a given category of early behavior problems; but there is such a relationship and also this model is rejected. It would appear that Model 2 rather than Model 3 is preferable, since there is a strong connection between early behavior problems and early registration ($\chi^2 = 49.53$, df $= 2$, $p < .001$). However, it is possible that these factors influence adult adjustment independently of each other though they are statistically correlated (e.g., both factors are influenced by the same basic home-background factors). A more decisive choice between Models 2 and 3 presupposes analyses which are out of the scope of this chapter.

Discussion

In our view, the person-oriented approach takes account of interactions among operating factors in a direct way. Moreover, it deals with and presents data in terms that are directly applicable to individuals, in contrast to the traditional regression models, which yield results referring to what Lewin called "the average person" (Lewin, 1931), who simply does not exist.

As was emphasized in the introduction to the chapter, variable-oriented research is of course important and necessary, and a person-oriented approach should be seen as complementary not competing. However, let us briefly mention some limitations of a variable-oriented approach within a developmental context. In a variable-oriented approach, data treatment is dominated by the use of linear regression models. This can be exemplified by the frequent use of correlation coefficients as expressions of pairwise relationships between variables, for instance between a predictor and an outcome measure, and as a basis for factor analysis, for path analyses, for LISREL, and so on. Two factors potentially limit the use of linear regression models for the study of developmental issues. The first one is the existence of strong interactions among single aspects of individual functioning and among environmental factors as they influence individual functioning. This issue has been dealt with and eloquently demonstrated by Hinde and Dennis (1986). Of course, to a certain extent interactions can be handled within, for instance, structural equation modeling, but these possibilities are limited (Bergman, 1988b). Secondly, the existence of strong inter-individual differences in growth rate actually invalidates many of the results that have been presented both from cross-sectional and longitudinal studies using linear regression models (Magnusson, 1985).

Another limitation of variable-oriented research, as it is often reflected in the traditional regression analytic approach, is connected with the psychological interpretation of the role of a certain aspect in the total dynamic functioning of an individual. Take, for example, one central aspect of a person's social network, namely poor peer relations. Our analyses showed that poor peer relations may have different implications depending upon whether they occur alone or in the context of a syndrome including conduct problems. Only in the latter case was there a strong relation to later adjustment problems. Presumably, there are also fundamental differences in the etiology of the problem for these two groups. The same kind of reasoning can be made for other aspects of individual functioning, such as aggression.

With regard to aggression, for example, Magnusson and Bergman (1988) have demonstrated that aggression in its extreme form usually occurs together with other conduct problems, and that the longitudinal relationship between aggression and later criminality or alcohol abuse disappeared when the group of children characterized by a syndrome of several adjustment problems, including aggression, were excluded from the analysis. This result implies that the often-found relationship between aggression in childhood and later adjustment problems cannot be interpreted uncritically in terms of the role aggression plays in the development of these adjustment problems. It is possible that the other factors that also characterize the highly aggressive child are the crucial ones. The implications of correlated problems have also been discussed by Robins (1984).

The results from a variable-oriented approach and those from a person-oriented one provide basically different perspectives, and one cannot automatically translate results obtained with one of these approaches into meaningful statements in the language of the other approach. Nevertheless, we would like to emphasize the following point: The issue of aggression discussed above is a particular instance of the more general question regarding the extent to which pairwise correlations between overt adjustment problems can be explained by the existence of a limited number of boys and girls who are characterized by all or several of these problems, that is, by syndromes rather than by single problems. Of course, this question is complicated to illuminate. For instance, what do we mean by the phrase "explained by"? To what extent would the results reported above for aggression be "explained by" the removal of children high in hyperactivity, thereby indicating the possibility that this factor can also be viewed as basic in the same way as the syndrome pattern? There are other questions as well, concerning the translation of results obtained with a person approach into a variable-oriented language and vice versa, which we cannot address here.

The analysis of factors antecedent to adult adjustment problems was here restricted to the inclusion of patterns of overt behavior problems. Further analyses will involve studying the role of environmental factors in terms of patterns and of examining the role of protective factors, both in the environment and in the individual, by including them among the variables on which the patterning is based. Of course, this will not be problem free. Two immediate problems are the increased loss of cases as information about more variables per individual is demanded and the methodological difficulties of analyzing the increasing number of patterns that can result from adding more variables. For instance, in Table 4 limiting the number of persons characterized by certain pattern combinations, after including environmental patterns would result in further subdivisions seriously limiting the statistical power of the analysis.

The analyses presented here, and the studies which are being planned, emphasize one important need in longitudinal studies of individual development. Besides needing to be conducted over a long period of time from childhood to adulthood, longitudinal studies should include a broad set of factors, including psychological and biological factors in the individual and a comprehensive set of factors in the environment, if we truly want to understand how these factors in continuous interaction with each other contribute to the developmental process of individuals.

References

Bergman, L. R. (1988a). You can't classify all of the people all of the time. *Multivariate Behavioral Research, 23*, 425–441.

Bergman, L. R. (1988b). Modelling reality: Some comments. In M. Rutter (Ed.), *Studies of psychosocial risk: The power of longitudinal data.* Cambridge: Cambridge University Press.

Bergman, L. R., & El-Khouri, B. (1987). Exacon: A Fortran 77 program for the exact analysis of single cells in a contingency table. *Educational and Psychological Measurement, 47*, 155–161.

Bergman, L. R., & Magnusson, D. (1983). *The development of patterns of maladjustment* (No. 50). University of Stockholm, Department of Psychology, Reports from the project Individual Development and Adjustment.

Bergman, L. R., & Magnusson, D. (1984a). *Patterns of adjustment problems at age 10: An empirical and methodological study* (No. 615). University of Stockholm, Reports from the Department of Psychology.

Bergman, L. R., & Magnusson, D. (1984b). *Patterns of adjustment problems at age 13: An empirical and methodological study* (No. 620). University of Stockholm, Reports from the Department of Psychology.

Bergman, L. R., & Magnusson, D. (1987). A person approach to the study of the development of adjustment problems: An empirical example and some research strategy considerations. In D. Magnusson & A. Öhman (Eds.), *Psychopathology: An interactional perspective.* New York: Academic Press.

Block, J. (1971). *Lives through time.* Berkeley, CA: Bancroft Books.

Cairns, R. B. (1986). Phenomena lost: Issues in the study of development. In J. Valsiner (Ed.), *The individual subject and scientific psychology.* New York: Plenum.

Hinde, R. A., & Dennis, H. (1986). Categorizing individuals: An alternative to linear analysis. *International Journal of Behavioral Development, 9*, 105–119.

Johansson, G., Frankenhaeuser, M., & Magnusson, D. (1973). Catecholamine output in school children as related to performance and adjustment. *Scandinavian Journal of Psychology, 14*, 20–28.

Kirkegaard-Sörensen, L., & Mednick, S. A. (1977). A prospective study of predictors of criminality. In S. A. Mednick & K. O. Christiansen (Eds.), *Biosocial bases of criminal behavior.* New York: Gardner Press.

Lewin, K. (1931). Environmental forces. In C. Murchison (Ed.), *A handbook of child psychology*, (2nd ed., pp. 590–625). Worcester, MA: Clark University Press.

Loeber, R., & Dishion, T. (1983). Early prediction of male delinquency: A review. *Psychological Bulletin, 94*, 68–99.

Magnusson, D. (1985). Implications of an interactional paradigm for research on human development. *International Journal of Behavioral Development, 8*, 115–137.

Magnusson, D. (1988). Individual development from an interactional perspective, Vol. 1. In D. Magnusson (Ed.), *Paths through life: A longitudinal research program.* Hillsdale, NJ: Erlbaum.

Magnusson, D., & Bergman, L. R. (1984). On the study of the development of adjustment problems. In L. Pulkkinen & P. Lyytinen (Eds.), *Human action and personality essays in honour of Martti Takala, Jyväskylä studies in education, psychology and social research.* Jyväskylä, Finland: University of Jyväskylä.

Magnusson, D., & Bergman, L. R. (1988). Individual and variable-based approaches to longitudinal research on early risk factors. In M. Rutter (Ed.), *Studies of psychosocial risk: The power of longitudinal data.* Cambridge: Cambridge University Press.

Magnusson, D., & Duner, A. (1981). Individual development and environment: A longitudinal study in Sweden. In S. A. Mednick and A. E. Baert (Eds.), *Prospective longitudinal research.* Oxford: Oxford University Press.

Magnusson, D., Duner, A., & Zetterblom, G. (1975). *Adjustment: a longitudinal study.* Stockholm: Almqvist & Wiksell.

McCord, J. A. (1983). A longitudinal study of aggression and antisocial behavior. In K. T. van Dusen & S. A. Mednick (Eds.), *Prospective studies of crime and delinquency* (pp. 269–275). Boston: Kluwer-Nijhoff.

Milligan, G. W. (1981). A review of Monte Carlo tests of cluster analysis. *Multivariate Behavioral Research, 16*, 379–407.

Olweus, D. (1985). Aggression and hormones. Behavioral relationship with testosterone and adrenaline. In D. Olweus, J. Block, & M. Radke-Yarrow (Eds.), *The development of antisocial and prosocial behavior: Research, theories, and issues.* New York: Academic Press.

Robins, L. N. (1966). *Deviant children grow up.* Baltimore: Williams and Wilkins.

Robins, L. N. (1984). Longitudinal methods in the study of development. In S. A. Mednick, M. Harway, & K. M. Finello (Eds.), *Handbook of longitudinal research, Vol. 1: Birth and childhood cohorts* (pp. 31–54). New York: Praeger.

Roff, J. D., & Wirt, R. D. (1984). Childhood aggression and social adjustment as antecedants of delinquency. *Journal of Abnormal Child Psychology, 12*, 111–126.

Rutter, M. & Giller, H. (1983). *Juvenile delinquency: Trends and perspectives.* Harmondsworth, Middlesex: Penguin.

Torstensson, (1987). Drug abusers in a Metropolitan cohort (No. 25). University of Stockholm. Report from Project Metropolitan.

Ward, J. H. (1963). Hierarchical grouping to optimize an objective function. *Journal of the American Statistical Association, 58*, 236–244.

West, D. J., & Farrington, D. P. (1973). *Who becomes delinquent? Second report of the Cambridge study in delinquent development.* London: Heinemann.

Wishart, D. (1982). *Clustan: User manual.* Edinburgh: Program Library Unit, Edinburgh University.

7   Long-term perspectives on parental absence

JOAN McCORD

For more than half a century, juvenile delinquency has been attributed to the deleterious influence of parental absence. During the early 1920s, for example, Slawson (1923) compared boys in New York State reformatories with boys in New York City public schools; the delinquents were twice as likely to be from families with a parent absent. In London (Burt, 1925) and Chicago (Shaw & McKay, 1932), in rural California (Merrill, 1947) and urban Massachusetts (Glueck & Glueck, 1950), studies produced similar results. Single-parent families were more common among incarcerated delinquents than among unselected populations. So convincing were the data by midcentury that Daniel Moynihan in 1965 issued a call to encourage two-parent families among American blacks in order to reduce crime.

The call for action marshaled interest in rethinking the issue, and several of the resultant studies failed to show that parental absence contributed to crime. Among blacks (Austin, 1978; Chilton & Markle, 1972; Robins & Hill, 1966) as well as whites (Grinnell & Chambers, 1979; Hennessy et al., 1978), boys from single-parent families were not more likely to become delinquent than those from two-parent homes.

Yet over the last several years, a spate of articles linking single-parent families to antisocial behavior and varieties of conduct disorders has justified renewed interest in considering parental absence as a potential marker along a devious pathway from childhood to adulthood. This recent literature has shown, for example, that in a national cohort of Great Britain a higher proportion of 5-year-olds living with one parent than of those living either with a parent and step-parent or with two biological parents appeared to be "antisocial" (Wadsworth et al., 1985). Studies in the United States have detected unusually high levels of "acting out" among boys whose parents had been divorced 6 years before (Hetherington et al., 1985), as well as delinquency 10 years after parental divorce (Wallerstein, 1985). Truancy was more frequent among youths reared in homes without fathers than among those reared in homes with two natural parents (Dornbusch et al., 1985;

116

Rickel & Langner, 1985). Higher stages of drug use (Kandel et al., 1978), too, have been reported by students who also reported that their fathers were absent (Brook et al., 1985). And in the sample of noninstitutionalized teenagers included in Cycle III of the Health Examination Survey, youths reared only by their mothers reported more contact with police, running away from home, and smoking than did youths reared by two biological parents (Goldstein, 1984; Dornbusch et al., 1985).

Some of the recent investigators of parental absence have attributed negative effects to personality differences between parents who stay together and those who do not (e.g., Brook et al., 1985). Alcoholism and criminality appear relatively frequently among parents in unstable marriages (McCord, 1982), and lack of education as well as poverty tend to characterize single parents (Wadsworth et al., 1985).

Differences have also been attributed to mediating conditions presumably brought about by break-up of the family. Single parents tend to have little help in rearing their children (Ensminger et al., 1983). They also seem to be less active participants in their children's lives (Dornbusch et al., 1985; McCord, 1982; Steinberg, 1987). And, as compared with expectations based on their parents' achievements, the children of single parents are less likely to work at attaining high educational or occupational status (Wallerstein, 1985).

Convincing as the relationships between being reared by single parents and problem behaviors may appear, a reasonable argument can be made that this is a case of mistaken identity. Crimes associated with poverty, disorganization, and urban clutter will be associated with single-parent families coincidental to the fact that single-parent families tend to be associated with poverty, disorganization, and urban clutter.

Studies that depend on measures of reaction to criminal behavior risk creating evidence for a self-fulfilling prophecy. If policemen, teachers, principals, psychologists, or parents believe that problems will occur among children reared in single-parent families, they are more likely to look for and therefore detect problems among children reared in single-parent families.

Homes that are broken would not necessarily be tranquil if both parents were present; so a contrast between ideal intact homes and broken homes is probably misleading. Several studies have indicated that living in discordant homes with two parents could be more damaging than living in homes with solo mothers (Nye, 1957; Rutter, 1971; West & Farrington, 1973; Power et al., 1974; McCord, 1982).

Attempting to discover more about how differences in family structures affect development, the present research examines the effects of child rearing patterns together with effects of family structure.

A study of child rearing and family structure

The sample

Subjects for this study were drawn from cases in a project designed to prevent delinquency. The project included boys born between 1926 and 1933 who lived in congested, urban areas near Boston, Massachusetts. Counselors visited their homes about twice a month over a period of more than 5 years. Typically the boys were between their 10th and 16th birthdays at the time of these visits. Their counselors recorded what they saw and heard (Powers & Witmer, 1951). These records provided data upon which to classify the families along many dimensions.

Scoring family variables

In 1957, we coded records describing the 232 families of the 253 boys who had remained in the program after an initial cut in 1941 (McCord & McCord, 1960). Codes included ratings of family structure and conflict, esteem of each parent for the other, parental supervision and disciplinary characteristics, parental warmth and aggressiveness, and parental alcoholism.

Family structure was defined in terms of whether or not the child was living with his natural (biological) parents. A parent was coded as absent if for at least 6 months prior to the boy's 17th birthday, the boy's domicile was not the same as that of the parent. Families were placed into one of three groups. If a boy was reared by his two natural parents, with neither absent for as long as 6 months, his family was classified as "intact." If a boy's father was absent a minimum of 6 months prior to the boy's 17th birthday and his mother did not remarry, the family was classified as "mother-alone." If the mother was absent at least 6 months or the boy had a stepfather, the family was placed into the heterogeneous classification of "broken." Among the 232 families, 130 were intact, 60 were mother-alone, and 42 were broken.

Boys from mother-alone families ranged in age from birth to 16 at the time of their loss. Their median age was 7. Boys from broken homes ranged in age from birth to 15 at the time of their loss. Their median age at the break was 3. Intact families had a median of 5 children, with a range of 1 to 16. Mother-alone families ranged in size from 1 to 12, and also had a median of 5 children. Families in broken homes ranged from 1 child to 12, but tended to be smaller than the other two types, with a median of 4 children.

A majority of the mothers had been married only once, but 4 mothers in the mother-alone families, 13 in the broken homes, and 9 in the intact families had been married at least twice. In the mother-alone families, 23 fathers had died and 37 were living. In the broken homes, 29 lacked a father and 30 lacked a mother, including 17 for whom both parents were absent. Deaths accounted for 9 of the absent fathers and 19 of the absent mothers.

In rating families on the quality of interactions, coders evaluated data from reports the counselors made almost immediately after each visit with a boy or his parents. Information about absent parents in mother-alone homes or broken homes came from their concurrent interactions with the boys or their mothers. Substitute parents in broken homes were also rated. Thirteen fathers and 13 mothers were substitute parents.

Parental conflict was a rating based on counselors' reports of disagreements about the child, values, money, alcohol, or religion. Ratings could be "no indication," "apparently none," "some," or "considerable." Parents were classified as evidencing or not evidencing considerable conflict.

A rating of each parent's esteem for the other was based on evidence indicating whether or not a parent showed respect for the judgment of the other. Ratings could be "no indication," "moderate or high," or "low." In the present research, each parent was classified as showing or not showing moderate or high esteem for the other.

Ratings for the mother's self-confidence were based on how she reacted when faced with problems. If she showed signs of believing in her ability to handle the problems, she was rated as self-confident. Alternative ratings were "no indication," "victim or pawn," and "neutral."

Maternal restrictiveness was rated as "subnormal" if a mother permitted her son to make virtually all his choices without her guidance. Alternative ratings were "no indication," "normal," and "overly restrictive."

Supervision described the degree to which the boy's activities after school were governed by an adult. Supervision could be rated "present," or alternatively, "sporadic," "absent," or "no information."

The level of expectations placed upon a child were considered "high" if they involved doing well at school and performing tasks at home or included unusually high standards for school or home. Alternative ratings were "moderate," "low," and "no information."

Discipline by each parent was classified into one of six categories: "consistently punitive, including very harsh verbal abuse," identified a parent who used physical force to control the boy. "Consistent, nonpunitive," identified a parent who used praise, rewards, or reasoning to control the boy. Alternative categories were "erratically punitive," "inconsistent, nonpunitive," "extremely lax, with almost no use of discipline," and "no information." Fathers were difficult to classify for consistency if their discipline was nonpunitive; so in the present research their discipline was coded as "consistently punitive" or "other." Mother's discipline was coded as "consistent," "nonpunitive" or "other."

A mother's role in the family was classified as "leader," "dictator," "martyr," "passive," "neglecting," or "no indication." The leadership role involved participating in family decisions. Mothers in the present study were classified either as being or not being leaders.

The attitude of a parent toward the boy was classified as "affectionate" if that parent interacted frequently with the child, without being generally critical. Alternative classifications were "passively affectionate" (if the parent was concerned for the boy's welfare, but there was little interaction), "passively rejecting" (if the parent was unconcerned for the boy's welfare and interacted little), "actively rejecting" (if the parent was almost constantly critical of the boy), "ambivalent" (if the parent showed marked alternation between affection and rejection of the child), and "no indication."

The aggressiveness of each parent was rated as "unrestrained" if that parent regularly expressed anger by such activities as shouting abuse, yelling, throwing or breaking things, or hitting people. Alternative classifications were "no indication," "moderately aggressive," or "greatly inhibited."

To estimate reliability of the coding, two raters independently read a 10% random sample of the cases. Agreement on these ratings ranged from 76% to 96%. Since chance agreement between raters varies in relation to distribution, the Scott (1955) Interrater Reliability Coefficient, π, was computed to indicate improvement over chance (Table 1).

The 14 variables describing family interactions were dichotomized and introduced into a clustering procedure, Varclus, which searches for combinations of variables to identify unidimensional factors in such a way as to maximize variance among cluster centroids (SAS, 1985). The first cluster included (in order of contribution) mother's discipline, self-confidence, affection for her son, and role. The factor appeared to represent mother's competence. A second dimension included (in order of contribution) mother's esteem for the father, father's esteem for the mother, parental conflict, father's affection for his son, and father's aggressiveness. The factor appeared to represent father's interaction with the family. A third dimension included (in order of contribution) maternal restrictiveness, supervision, and expectations. The factor represented family control. A fourth dimension included father's punitiveness and mother's aggressiveness, weighted in opposite directions. The factor appeared to measure something like disciplinarian. This factor was dropped, however, because 75% of the families scored at the midpoint. Table 2 shows descriptive characteristics of the clusters representing mother's competence, father's interaction, and family control.

To stabilize and simplify the scales, items in each factor were given equal weights and scored so that the scales would yield higher scores for more socially desirable behaviors: greater mother's competence; more approving, less aggressive father's interaction; and greater family control. Scores on

Table 1. *Interrater reliability (2 raters on 10% random sample)*

Characteristic	Percent agreement	Scott π^a
Family structure	96	.92
Family conflict	80	.55
Father's esteem for mother	84	.68
Mother's esteem for father	88	.76
Mother's self-confidence	84	.60
Mother's restrictiveness	84	.65
Boy's supervision	88	.76
Expectations for boy	76	.35
Father's discipline	88	.52
Mother's discipline	84	.62
Mother's leadership	96	.91
Mother's attitude to son	84	.68
Father's attitude to son	84	.57
Mother's aggressiveness	92	.56
Father's aggressiveness	84	.41
Father's alcoholism	96	.91

$^a\pi = (P_o - P_e)/(1 - P_e)$　P_o = percent agreement observed and $P_e = (p)^2 + (q)^2$, where p = proportion having the characteristic and $q = 1 - p$.

"mother's competence" ranged from 0 to $+4$; on "father's interaction," from -2 to $+3$; and on "family control," from -1 to $+2$. Each factor was dichotomized as close to the median as possible in order to describe a family as above or below the median.

Information from childhood included criminal records for the families of the boys. These had been gathered in the late 1930s and again a decade later. These records were used to identify which fathers were criminals. A father was considered a criminal if he had been convicted for a *Federal Bureau of Investigation Type-1 Index* crime (theft, breaking and entering, assault, murder, rape, attempted murder, or attempted rape). The designation of alcoholic was given to a father if he had lost jobs because of drinking or had marital problems attributed primarily to excessive drinking, if welfare agencies repeatedly noted that heavy drinking was the source of his problems, if he had received treatment for alcoholism, or if he had been convicted at least three times for public drunkenness.

Measurement of outcomes

Between 1975 and 1980, when they ranged from age 45 to age 53, the former youth study participants were retraced. Twenty-four were found through

Table 2. *Cluster analysis*

Group variable	R-square		Scoring coefficient
	Highest	Second	
Mother's competence			
Mother's consistency	.553	.104	.386
Mother's self-confidence	.479	.087	.359
Mother's affection	.472	.084	.357
Mother's role	.422	.054	.337
Father's interaction			
Father's esteem for mother	.669	.053	.320
Mother's esteem for father	.720	.058	.332
Parental conflict	.532	.049	− .286
Father's affection for son	.323	.045	.222
Father's aggressiveness	.312	.050	− .219
Family control			
Mother's restrictiveness	.710	.096	− .478
Supervision	.692	.154	.472
Demands	.360	.054	.341

Correlations	A	B	C
A. Mother's competence	1.00		
B. Father's interaction	0.29	1.00	
C. Family control	0.41	0.31	1.00

their death records. Of the remaining 208 men in the present study, 202 (97%) were located; 169 (81%) responded to a questionnaire or to an interview, or both.

Police and court records had been collected in 1948. These records of juvenile delinquency were combined with records gathered in 1979 from probation departments in Massachusetts and in other states to which the men had migrated. Information from departments of mental health, clinics for treatment of alcoholism, voter registrations, death records, and street directories also provided data used in the present study. None of the workers gathering information from the records had access to information about childhood. The interviewer had no access either to childhood records or to official records.

Two measures assessed juvenile behavior. For the narrower one, juvenile delinquency, conviction for any crime prior to reaching age 18 was used as the criterion. Fifty boys had been convicted for such serious crimes as auto theft, breaking and entering, and assault; 19 had been convicted only for such relatively minor crimes as truancy, trespassing, or destruction of property. The second, juvenile deviance, picked up what West and

Farrington (1977) referred to as a delinquent life-style. Nineteen boys who had not been convicted for crimes but had been heavy smokers or had a delinquent reference group were included in the juvenile deviance category. Both smoking and reference groups had been coded in 1957.

In the 10% random sample of cases coded independently to assess reliability, there was no disagreement for coding whether or not a boy smoked "more than occasionally." Coders agreed whether or not a youth had a delinquent reference group in 84% of the cases which were read to assess reliability, $\pi = .54$. Among those convicted for serious crimes, 31 (62%) had also been heavy smokers or had delinquent reference groups. Among those convicted only for minor crimes as juveniles, 6 (32%) had delinquent reference groups and none had been heavy smokers.

The third measure of outcome identified men convicted for the more serious street crimes that appear on the FBI *Type-1 Index*. By this standard 77 men were criminals. Of the 50 juveniles convicted for serious crimes, 21 also were convicted as adults; additionally, 27 men not convicted as juveniles were convicted as adults.

A fourth measure of outcome was alcoholism. Both the questionnaire and the interview included the CAGE test for alcoholism (Ewing & Rouse, 1970). In this test, respondents are asked if they ever have felt the need to cut down on drinking, felt annoyed by criticism of their drinking, felt guilty about drinking, or had taken a morning eye-opener. A man was considered an alcoholic if he responded affirmatively, as do alcoholics (Mayfield et al., 1974), to at least three of these questions. A man was also considered an alcoholic if he had received treatment for alcoholism or if he had been arrested at least three times for public drunkenness or driving while intoxicated. Too, he was considered an alcoholic if he described himself as an alcoholic or if he was arrested twice for alcoholism and answered affirmatively to two of the CAGE questions. By these criteria, 71 men were identified as alcoholics.

The fifth measure of outcome was occupational achievement. Information on occupational status was coded according to the Hollingshead Occupational Scale (Hollingshead & Redlich, 1958). Seventy-five men were working in white collar occupations. Since all the men had lived in deprived areas during childhood, white collar work could serve as a measure of occupational achievement.

Data analysis

The strength of relationships between variables describing family background and outcome was tested using χ^2. In addition, a measure of Proportional Improvement over Chance (PIC) was developed to assess the degree to which information about family factors improved ability to predict whether an individual would have a particular outcome. Use of a proportional chance criterion (Huberty, 1984) assumes that only the distribution of outcomes is known. PIC is defined as

$$PIC = (o-e)/(1-e),$$

where

o = proportion correctly identified, $e = p^2 + q^2$,
p = proportion of the population in which a specified outcome has occurred, the base rate, and $q = 1-p$.

The PIC formula compares observed and expected proportions, where expected values are based on the base rate of the dependent variable and observed values are based on the selection ratio for the predictor variable. Comparison between observed and expected proportions that are correctly identified shows the difference that can be attributed to knowledge of the predictor variable. PIC expresses improvement as the actual improvement divided by possible improvement, possible improvement being the difference between what would be predicted correctly by chance and perfect prediction. PIC therefore gives a picture of the degree to which knowledge of the independent variable would improve the accuracy of predicting the dependent variable.[1]

To avoid confounding the impact of family structure with that of covarying child-rearing effects, the intact, broken, and mother-alone families were compared with family interaction variables controlled. Both because of the heterogeneous nature of the broken home group and because it included parent substitutes, only intact and mother-alone families were used in developing models for the outcome variables.

Boys reared in intact or mother-alone families were reared by their natural mothers. The fathers described were the biological parents, whether present or absent from the home. Among these two groups, stepwise logistic regressions (Dixon, 1985) were used to identify direct and indirect contributions of paternal absence in the development of criminality, alcoholism, and deviance. Using as criteria .15 to remove and .10 to enter, the procedure tested effects of family structure, mother's competence, father's interaction with the family, family control, their two-way, three-way, and four-way interactions, plus father's alcoholism, father's criminality, their interaction, and their two-way and three-way interactions with family structure.

Results and discussion

Comparisons for the impact of child rearing—ignoring differences in family structure—showed that mother's competence, father's interaction with the family, and family control were related to delinquency, juvenile deviance, crime, and achievement. Poor child rearing of each of these types reliably increased risk of juvenile deviance (Table 3). Low mother's competence also reliably increased risk for serious criminal behavior, whereas weak family control also reliably increased risk of juvenile delinquency.

A father's alcoholism increased the probability of delinquency, juvenile deviance, and crime as well as alcoholism. A father's criminality increased the probability of delinquency and crime (Table 4).

Perhaps unexpectedly, neither a father's alcoholism nor a father's criminality provided better than chance predictions of occupational achievement.

Differences among parents in relation to family structure might account

Table 3. *Child-rearing variables and outcome (Percentage in family category for whom outcome was true)*

A. Mother's competence:	Low ($N=109$)	High ($N=123$)	χ^2	PIC
Juvenile delinquent	44	17	20.11****	.15
Juvenile deviant	53	24	20.39****	.26**
Criminal	46	22	14.91****	.16*
Alcoholic	34	28	1.08	−.08
Occupational achievement	25	41	6.99***	.04

B. Father's interaction:	Bad ($N=109$)	Good ($N=123$)	χ^2	PIC
Juvenile delinquent	41	20	13.11***	.09
Juvenile deviant	54	24	22.91****	.28****
Criminal	44	24	10.91***	.13
Alcoholic	32	29	0.22	−.12
Occupational achievement	26	39	4.32*	.00

C. Family control:	Weak ($N=107$)	Strong ($N=125$)	χ^2	PIC
Juvenile delinquent	45	17	21.72****	.17*
Juvenile deviant	56	22	27.77****	.31****
Criminal	44	24	10.32**	.13
Alcoholic	36	26	2.26	−.04
Occupational achievement	26	39	4.32*	.00

*$p < .05$
**$p < .01$
***$p < .001$
****$p < .0001$

Table 4. *Father's deviance and outcome (Percentage in father's category for whom outcome was true)*

A. Father an alcoholic:	No (N = 159)	Yes (N = 73)	χ^2	PIC
Juvenile delinquent	24	42	8.25**	.17*
Juvenile deviant	31	52	9.03**	.22**
Criminal	28	45	6.94**	.18*
Alcoholic	25	44	8.78**	.19*
Occupational achievement	36	27	1.71	−.17*

B. Father a criminal:	No (N = 179)	Yes (N = 53)	χ^2	PIC
Juvenile delinquent	26	42	4.55*	.20*
Juvenile deviant	35	47	2.49	.17*
Criminal	30	45	4.53*	.20*
Alcoholic	29	36	0.89	.13
Occupational achievement	36	25	2.11	.24**

*$p < .05$
**$p < .01$

for these differences in outcome. To check this possibility, broken, intact, and mother-alone families were compared for the variables used to describe child rearing and paternal deviance (Table 5).

Maternal competence was found not to be related to family structure. Father's interaction was most likely to be good and fathers were least likely to be alcoholic or criminal in intact homes. Although boys were most likely to be supervised in intact homes, overall family control did not differ significantly in relation to family structure.

To disentangle the impact of family structure from that of covarying differences in family interactions, families below the median and above the median were separately compared for each of the outcomes. The results are presented in Table 6.

Within each type of family structure, sons of the less competent mothers were more likely to be juvenile delinquents ($p < .05$). Among less competent mothers, a trend ($.10 > p > .05$) suggested that intact families may be protective against juvenile delinquency.

Boys from intact homes were more likely to be juvenile delinquents, deviants, or criminals if their father's interactions were bad than if those interactions were good ($p < .001$). With father's interaction controlled,

Table 5. *Family structure, child rearing, and paternal deviance* (*Percentage of each family type for which description was true*)

	Broken (N = 42)	Intact (N = 130)	Mother-alone (N = 60)
Mother competence: High	52	55	50
Mother consistently nonpunitive	33	32	23
Mother self-confident	31	28	28
Mother affectionate to son	50	45	52
Mother a leader	60	65	58
Father's interaction: Good****	38	69	28
Father, high esteem for Mother****	36	62	18
Mother, high esteem for Father****	29	62	28
Much family conflict****	33	21	57
Father aggressive	14	14	22
Father affectionate to son**	12	35	15
Family control: Strong	45	60	47
Mother little control over boy	36	31	47
Boy was supervised**	40	67	47
High demands placed on boy	26	26	22
Father was an alcoholic***	31	23	50
Father had criminal record*	21	17	37

*$p < .05$
**$p < .01$
***$p < .001$
****$p < .0001$

differences among intact, broken, and mother-alone families were not statistically reliable.

Strong family control appeared to reduce the likelihood of juvenile deviance ($p < .01$) and delinquency ($p < .05$) in both intact and mother-alone families. Intact homes gave no protection against delinquency, crime, or alcoholism for those whose families provided weak control. On the other hand, among the families with strong control, boys reared in intact families were least likely and boys from broken homes were most likely to become juvenile delinquents ($p < .05$).

Only among intact families was paternal alcoholism or criminality related to the sons' juvenile delinquency, deviance, criminality, or alcoholism ($p < .05$). Among families with alcoholic or criminal fathers, slight trends suggested that being present in intact homes might increase the probability of transmitting alcoholism and criminality, respectively. These trends were

Table 6. *Child rearing, family structure, and outcome (Percentage in family category for whom outcome was true)*

Outcome	Juvenile deliquent	Juvenile deviant	Criminal	Alcoholic	Occupational achievement
Mother's competence: Low					
Broken (N: 20)	60**	70**	50*	40	26
Intact (N: 59)	34*	44**	39*	31	26
Mother-alone (N: 30)	53**	60*	57**	37	21
Mother's competence: High					
Broken (N: 22)	18	27	18	23	43
Intact (N: 71)	15	21	23	25	41
Mother-alone (N: 30)	20	30	23	37	40
Father's interaction: Bad					
Broken (N: 26)	42	58	38	35	36
Intact (N: 40)	43***	58***	50¹	25	15**
Mother-alone (N: 43)	40	49	42	37	31
Father's interaction: Good					
Broken (N: 16)	31	31	25	25	33
Intact (N: 90)	16	20	21	29	43
Mother-alone (N: 17)	29	35	35	35	29
Family control: Weak					
Broken (N: 23)	39	52	39	35	30
Intact (N: 52)	44****	54****	44**	37	25
Mother-alone (N: 32)	50*	63**	47	34	25
Family control: Strong					
Broken (N: 19)	37[a]	42	26	26	41
Intact (N: 78)	10[a]	17	21	22	40
Mother-alone (N: 28)	21[a]	25	32	39	37

[a] Significant differences related to family structure, controlling on type of child rearing, χ^2, df = 2, $p < .05$.

* Significant differences related to child rearing, controlling on type of family structure, χ^2, df = 1, $p < .05$.

** χ^2, df = 1, $p < .01$.

*** χ^2, df = 1, $p < .001$

**** χ^2, df = 1, $p < .0001$

not statistically reliable. Among families without alcoholic or criminal fathers, a trend ($.10 > p > .05$) suggested that intact families might be protective against juvenile delinquency and deviance (Table 7).

The importance of having an intact home might depend upon the possibility this gives for having at least one good parent. To check this explanation, the families were divided into four groups, depending on

Table 7. *Risk, family structure, and outcome (Percentage in family category for whom outcome was true)*

Outcome	Juvenile delinquent	Juvenile deviant	Criminal	Alcoholic	Occupational achievement
Father an alcoholic[a]					
Broken (*N*: 13)	46	69	38	38	31
Intact (*N*: 30)	30	40	43	50	27
Mother-alone (*N*: 30)	53	57	50	40	27
Father a criminal[a]					
Broken (*N*: 9)	22	33	11	22	22
Intact (*N*: 22)	45	55	55	27	27
Mother-alone (*N*: 22)	45	45	50	50	24
Father an alcoholic or a criminal[a]					
Broken (*N*: 17)	35	53	29	29	29
Intact (*N*: 44)	36*	45*	45**	41*	32
Mother-alone (*N*: 35)	46	49	49	43	24
Father neither an alcoholic nor a criminal					
Broken (*N*: 25)	40	44	36	32	39
Intact (*N*: 86)	17	24	22	21	35
Mother-alone (*N*: 25)	24	40	28	28	40

[a] Five fathers among broken, 8 among intact, and 17 among mother-alone families were both alcoholic and criminal.

* Proportion is significantly greater than that among families having the same type of family structure but in which the father is neither alcoholic nor criminal, χ^2, df = 1, $p < .05$.

** χ^2, df = 1, $p < .01$.

mother's competence and father's interaction (Table 8). Consonant with this explanation, the father's good interactions reduced the risk of juvenile deviance among families in which the mother showed low competence ($p < .05$).

Juvenile deviance reflected parental competence. Risks were highest when a boy lacked even a single competent parent. They were lowest when the mother was competent and the father's interactions were good. Effects of having only a competent mother or only a "good" father were approximately the same. Being reared by a competent mother and a father whose interactions were good seemed to reduce risks of delinquency, deviance, and crime, while increasing the probability for occupational achievement.

Stepwise logistic regression was used to identify the contribution of family structure to models that predicted each of the outcomes. In each model, family stucture was considered as possibly having a main effect and

Table 8. *Mother's competence, father's interaction, and outcome (Percentage in family category for whom outcome was true)*

Mother's competence:	Low		High	
Father's interaction:	Bad	Good	Bad	Good
Juvenile delinquent	51[b]	35	28	10[a]
Juvenile deviant	63[a]	39	41	14[a]
Criminal	52[b]	37	33	16[a]
Alcoholic	33	35	30	26
Occupational achievement	25	24	29	49[a]

[a] Proportion significantly different from all other values in the same row, $p < .05$.
[b] Proportion significantly greater than for high–bad and high–good, but not for low–good.

as interacting either with the family variables (mother's competence, father's interaction, family control) or with descriptions of paternal deviance (father's alcoholism, father's criminality). Additionally, main and interaction effects of the three family variables were considered, as were main and interaction effects of father's alcoholism and father's criminality.[2]

Table 9 indicates the variables that contributed to the models predictive of each of the outcomes.[3]

Independent of interaction with mother's competence, father's interaction, family control, father's alcoholism, or father's criminality, family structure appeared to influence only juvenile delinquency. Independent of interaction with other terms, mother's competence appeared to influence juvenile delinquency, juvenile deviance, and criminality; father's interaction appeared to influence juvenile delinquency and occupational achievement; family control appeared to influence juvenile deviance; father's alcoholism appeared to influence juvenile delinquency and juvenile deviance; and father's criminality appeared to influence criminality.

These models suggest that child-rearing differences related to the parents' behavior have greater effects than do differences in family structure. Independent of context, parental absence contributed only to juvenile delinquency. The models also show that the impact of parental absence depends upon maternal competence, paternal interaction and behavior, and family control.

The present study reexamined family structure as a potential influence on the development of deviance and of occupational achievement. By considering families whose socioeconomic backgrounds were similar, it was possible to eliminate poverty, disorganization, and blighted urban conditions as

Table 9. *Stepwise logistic regression (coefficients)*

Terms[a]	Juvenile delinquent	Juvenile deviant	Criminal	Alcoholic	Occupational achievement
Structure	−1.05***	—	—	—	—
MC	−1.24****	−0.75**	−0.80***	—	—
FI	0.73*	—	—	—	0.51**
Cntl	—	−0.92****	—	—	—
FAlc	0.57*	0.67**	—	—	—
FCrim	—	—	0.57**	0.31	—
Struc*MC	1.07***	0.47	0.74**	—	—
Struc*FI	1.34****	−0.78**	−0.54**	—	—
Struc*Cntl	−0.95***	—	−0.55*	—	—
Struc*MC*FI	1.08**	0.92**	0.46	—	0.50**
Struc*MC*Cntl	1.12***	0.36	—	—	—
Struc*FI*Cntl	−0.82**	—	−0.40	−0.32	—
Struc*MC*FI*Cntl	0.63	−0.38	—	—	0.29
Struc*FAlc	−0.82**	−0.71*	—	0.47*	—
Struc*FCrim	—	0.59*	—	−0.34	—
Struc*FAlc*FCrim	−0.38	−0.50*	—	—	−0.45*
MC*FI	−0.97**	−0.51	−0.62*	—	—
MC*Cntl	−1.18***	—	—	—	—
FI*Cntl	0.91**	—	0.55*	—	—
MC*FI*Cntl	−0.59*	—	—	—	—
FAlc*FCrim	—	0.37	—	—	—
Constant	—	—	—	−0.65**	−0.91****

[a] Struc = family structure; MC = mother's competence; FI = father's interaction; Cntl = family control; FAlc = father's alcoholism; FCrim = father's criminality.

$*p < .05$
$**p < .01$
$***p < .001$
$****p < .0001$

alternative explanations for outcomes that differentiated the behavior of boys from broken and intact homes.

Case records based on repeated visits to the homes of 232 boys allowed analyses that included the dynamics of family interactions. These indicated that children reared in broken and mother-alone families also frequently had alcoholic or criminal fathers and had been exposed to parental conflict. These conditions could explain why single-parent families seem to produce children with problem behaviors.

Parental absence is one of several conditions that seem to increase juvenile delinquency. However, these increases might represent differential reactions to similar behavior, depending upon whether the child was from an intact family. Giving credence to this possibility is the fact that neither juvenile deviance nor serious criminal behavior was related to parental absence unless other conditions also contributed to risk.

The analyses clearly suggest that parental behavior has a stronger impact than family structure. With the exception of juvenile delinquency, the impact of family structure depended on interaction with variables describing maternal competence, paternal behavior, and family control.

The importance of these interactions can be illustrated by dividing the 48 co-variate patterns into three groups in relation to juvenile deviance: those in which none of the boys appeared to be juvenile deviants, those in which all appeared to be juvenile deviants, and those in-between. Twenty-nine boys fell into the first category and 16 fell into the second. Of the 29 who were not juvenile deviants, 18 (62%) were from mother-alone families with competent mothers; only 2 (12.5%) of 16 juvenile deviants were from such homes. Effects of parental absence largely depended on the competence of the remaining parent. Separation seemed to have little or no adverse effect when the alternative was an intact family with conflict, low parental esteem, paternal alcoholism, or criminality.

Intact families appear to offer some protection against the impact of maternal incompetence on juvenile deviance. Yet, the greatest benefits from intact families seem to come from the presence of two competent, congenial parents.

Acknowledgments

The author would like to express appreciation to Lee Robins for careful and astute criticism of this manuscript. The author thanks Richard Parente, Robert Staib, Ellen Myers, and Ann Cronin for their work in tracing the men and their records, and Joan Immel, Tom Smedile, Harriet Sayre, Mary Duell, Elise Goldman, Abby Brodkin, and Laura Otten for their careful coding of the follow-up. She also wishes to express appreciation to the Department of Probation of the Commonwealth of Massachusetts, the Division of Criminal Justice Services of the State of New York, to the Maine State Bureau of Identification, and to the states of California, Florida, Michigan, New Jersey, Pennsylvania, Virginia, and Washington for supplemental data about the men. This study was partly supported by U. S. Public Health Service research grant MH 26779, National Institute of Mental Health (Center for Studies of Crime and Delinquency). Of course, only the author is responsible for the statistical analyses and for the conclusions drawn from this research.

Notes

1 A significance test for PIC uses χ^2 with one degree of freedom.
2 The focus of the analyses was on detecting the contribution of family structure to the outcomes. Therefore, possible interaction between paternal deviance and the other descriptions of family (mother's competence, father's interaction, and family control) were not considered for the models.

3 χ^2 goodness of fit (df $= 8$), for juvenile delinquency was 7.10 ($p = .526$); for juvenile deviance, 6.05 ($p = .642$); for criminality, 6.89 ($p = .549$); for alcoholism, 7.394 ($p = .495$); and for occupational achievement, 3.838 ($p = .87$).

References

Austin, R. L. (1978). Race, father-absence, and female delinquency. *Criminology, 15*, 487–504.

Brook, J. S., Whiteman, M., & Gordon, A. S. (1985). Father absence, perceived family characteristics and stage of drug use in adolescence. *British Journal of Developmental Psychology, 2*, 87–94.

Burt, C. (1925). *The young delinquent.* New York: Appleton.

Chilton, R. J. & Markle, G. E. (1972). Family disruption, delinquent conduct and the effect of subclassification. *American Sociological Review, 37*, 93–99.

Dixon, W. J., (1985). *BMDP statistical software 1985.* Berkeley: University of California Press.

Dornbusch, S. M., Carlsmith, J. M., Bushwall, S. J., Ritter, P. L., Leiderman, H., Hastorf, A. H., & Gross, R. T. (1985). Single parents, extended households, and the control of adolescents. *Child Development, 56*, 326–341.

Ensminger, M. E., Kellam, S. G., & Rubin, B. R. (1983). School and family origins of delinquency: Comparisons by sex. In K. T. Van Dusen & S. A. Mednick (Eds.), *Prospective Studies of Crime and Delinquency* (pp. 73–97). Boston: Kluwer-Nijhoff.

Ewing, J., & Rouse, B. A. (1970). *Identifying the hidden alcoholic.* Paper presented at the 29th International Congress on Alcohol and Drug Dependence, Sydney, NSW Australia.

Glueck, S., & Glueck, E. T. (1950). *Unraveling juvenile delinquency.* New York: Commonwealth Fund.

Goldstein, H. S. (1984). Parental composition, supervision, and conduct problems in youths 12 to 17 years old. *Journal of the American Academy of Child Psychiatry, 23*(6), 679–684.

Grinnell, R. M., Jr., & Chambers, C. A. (1979). Broken homes and middle-class delinquency: A comparison. *Criminology, 17*, 395–400.

Hennessy, M., Richards, P. J., & Berk, R. A. (1978). Broken homes and middle-class delinquency: A reassessment. *Criminology, 15*, 505–528.

Hetherington, E. M., Cox, M., & Cox, R. (1985). Longterm effects of divorce and remarriage on the adjustment of children. *Journal of the American Academy of Child Psychiatry, 24*(5), 518–530.

Hollingshead, A. B., & Redlich, F. C. (1958). *Social class and mental illness.* New York: John Wiley & Sons.

Huberty, C. J. (1984). Issues in the use and interpretation of discriminant analysis. *Psychological Bulletin, 95*(1), 156–171.

Kandel, D. B., Kessler, R. C., & Margulies, R. Z. (1978). Antecedents of adolescent initiation into stages of drug use: A developmental analysis. In D. B. Kandel (Ed.), *Longitudinal research on drug use,* (pp. 73–99). New York: John Wiley & Sons.

Mayfield, D., McLeod, G., & Hall, P. (1974). The CAGE questionnaire: Validation of a new alcoholism screening instrument. *American Journal of Psychiatry, 131*, 1121–1123.

McCord, J. (1982). A longitudinal view of the relationship between paternal absence and crime. In J. Gunn & D. P. Farrington (Eds.), *Abnormal offenders, delinquency, and the criminal justice system* (pp. 113–128). Chichester: John Wiley & Sons.

McCord, W., & McCord, J. (1960). *Origins of alcoholism.* Stanford, CA: Stanford University Press.

Merrill, M. A. (1947). *Problems of child delinquency.* New York: Houghton Mifflin.

Nye, F. I. (1957). Child adjustment in broken and in unhappy unbroken homes. *Marriage and Family Living, 19,* 356–361.

Power, M. J., Ash, P. M., Shoenberg, E., & Sirey, E. C. (1974). Delinquency and the family. *British Journal of Social Work, 4,* 13–38.

Powers, E., Witmer, H. (1951). *An experiment in the prevention of delinquency: The Cambridge-Somerville youth study.* New York: Columbia University Press.

Rickel, A. U., & Langner, T. S. (1985). Short- and longterm effects of marital disruption on children. *American Journal of Community Psychology, 13*(5), 599–611.

Robins, L. N., & Hill, S. Y. (1966). Assessing the contribution of family structure, class and peer groups to juvenile delinquency. *Journal of Criminal Law, Criminology and Police Science, 57,* 325–333.

Rutter, M. (1971). Parent-child separation: Psychological effects on the children. *Journal of Child Psychology and Psychiatry, 12,* 233–260.

SAS Institute. (1985). *SAS user's guide: Statistics.* Cary, NC: SAS Institute.

Scott, W. A. (1955). Reliability of content analysis: The case of nominal scale coding. *Public Opinion Quarterly, 19*(3), 321–325.

Shaw, C., & McKay, H. D. (1932). Are broken homes a causative factor in juvenile delinquency? *Social Forces, 10,* 514–524.

Slawson, J. (1923). Marital relations of parents and juvenile delinquency. *Journal of Delinquency, 8,* 280–283.

Steinberg, L. (1987). Single parents, stepparents, and the susceptibility of adolescents to antisocial peer pressure. *Child Development, 58,* 269–275.

Wadsworth, J., Burnell, I., Taylor, B., & Butler, N. (1985). The influence of family type on children's behavior and development at five years. *Journal of Child Psychology and Psychiatry, 26*(2), 254

Wallerstein, J. S. (1985). Children of divorce: Preliminary report of a ten-year follow-up of older children and adolescents. *Journal of the American Academy of Child Psychiatry, 24,* 545–553.

West, D. J., & Farrington, D. P. (1973). *Who becomes delinquent?* London: Heinemann.

West, D. J., & Farrington, D. P. (1977). *The delinquent way of life.* London: Heinemann.

8 Adult outcome of institution-reared children: Males and females compared

MICHAEL RUTTER, DAVID QUINTON, AND JONATHAN HILL

The study of the long-term effects of adverse experiences in early life has involved a variety of controversies and has raised a number of crucial research issues (Rutter, 1981, 1987a). Initially, there were rather strong claims that maternal deprivation in infancy led to permanent, irreversible damage (Bowlby, 1951). This proposition was subjected to severe academic criticism (O'Connor, 1956; Orlansky, 1949; Yarrow, 1961), and it became clear that a life of early adversities can have a number of diverse outcomes, with long-term effects heavily dependent on the nature of subsequent life experiences (Clarke & Clarke, 1976). The pendulum swung and critics argued that there was very little continuity in psychological development; such continuity as there was being dependent on individuals' interpretation of their experiences (Kagan, 1984).

In recent years there has been a limited swinging back of the pendulum, as investigators have been faced with evidence demonstrating a rather complex mix of both continuities and discontinuities (Rutter, 1987a). Some of that evidence stemmed from our follow-up into adult life of girls reared in institutions or Group Homes, to which they had been admitted when young because of some form of family breakdown (Quinton et al., 1984; Quinton & Rutter, 1988; Rutter & Quinton, 1984). Our study produced some striking findings both in terms of the major impact of experiences in early adult life and in terms of the various mediating variables that might constitute links in the chain extending over two decades from adversities in infancy to functioning in the mid-20s. The data led to a set of conclusions about some of the factors that might underlie both continuities and discontinuities. Nevertheless, with any complex set of findings, there is always a concern that the fascinating patterns found might be specific to the particular sample studied and therefore of limited generalizability. In particular, our findings on protective mechanisms that produced resilience in the face of adversity (Rutter, 1979, 1985a, 1987b, in press a), an issue little investigated until very recently, needed to be confirmed by another study. Accordingly, we report here a parallel study of males reared in the same institutions as were the female sample. The methods and measures both initially and at follow-up were exactly the same for the two sexes. Only the interviewers were partially different, although there was substantial overlap (J. H. interviewed nearly half of the men but none of the women).

Replications are rarely exact and, of course, this partial replication (partial in the sense that the institutions were the same, but the sample was different) involves a sex difference. That constitutes a potentially important feature in view of the obvious sex differences in patterns of both child (Earls, 1987; Eme, 1979) and adult psychopathology (Weissman & Klerman, 1977). Also, however, it seems that boys are more likely than girls to show disturbance following at least some types of psychosocial adversity (Rutter, 1970, 1982, in press a; Zaslow & Hayes, 1986), perhaps due in part to boys' greater exposure to stress experiences (Gove & Herb, 1974). If that is so, it may be particularly useful to compare the adult outcome of men and women when they have experienced the same set of adverse experiences, namely, an institutional upbringing and all that that implies.

It is important to note that, even here, the comparability may be more apparent than real. The adult staff in group children's homes are almost entirely female (Quinton & Rutter, 1988), a feature that may differ in its impact on girls and boys. Also, boys' tendency to respond to stress or adversity with oppositional behavior rather than distress may cause them to receive less sympathetic reactions from staff (Rutter, in press b). There is growing evidence that parental responses to the behavior of boys differ from that to similar behavior in girls (Hinde & Stevenson-Hinde, 1987); the responses of other care-givers are also likely to differ. Finally, findings are beginning to accumulate to suggest that emotional/behavioral disturbance in childhood may lead to rather different forms of adult psychopathology in males and females (Kandel & Davies, 1986; Quinton et al., this volume; Robins, 1986). In particular, it appears that conduct disturbance in childhood predisposes to both antisocial and non-antisocial varieties of personality disorder in adult life, the former being more characteristic in males and the latter in females (Rutter, 1987c; Zeitlin, 1986). For all these reasons it is necessary to view the comparison of institution-reared men and women as an opportunity to look for possible differences by sex as well as for replication.

The follow-up of institution-reared females

Research goals

The initial planning of the investigation derived from a concern to determine the extent to which parenting breakdown in one generation was followed by similar breakdown in the next. The findings from the female follow-up showed that there were across-generation continuities: women who had experienced a breakdown in their own upbringing were much more likely than other women to experience serious difficulties in rearing their own children. An appreciable minority could not cope for one reason or another and had to give up the care of their children to other people. At the same time, the outcome proved to be quite heterogeneous, with some women functioning very well (Quinton & Rutter, 1988).

The investigation was also begun to explore the factors involved in individual differences in responses to stress, adversity, and disadvantage. The answers we obtained proved illuminating in their demonstration that risk and protective factors continued to be operative right into adult life (Rutter, 1985*a*, 1987*b*). In fact the most powerful protective mechanism to counter the ill effects stemming from adversities in childhood proved to be the emotional support of a nondeviant spouse with whom the women had a close, confiding, harmonious relationship.

The third reason for the follow-up study was an interest in tracing the developmental processes by which some deprived children went on to have beneficial experiences in adult life whereas others continued to suffer stress and disadvantage. The data pointed to a diverse range of mechanisms which combined to produce a chain of indirect linkages. Because the chain extended from infancy to adulthood, quite strong continuities over long periods of time were evident in certain circumstances. However, because the chain relied on multiple links, each one dependent on the presence of some particular set of features, there were many opportunities for the chain of adversity to be broken. Consequently, discontinuities were also prominent. There were many striking findings on the ways in which both continuities and discontinuities operated. For example, we found that positive experiences at school could do much to counter the ill effects of adverse experiences within the home. Also, we found that a crucial mediating variable was the woman's concept of being able to take action to control what happened to her, of acting positively rather than just reacting passively. We sought to measure this characteristic through an assessment of the extent to which each woman used "planning" in her choice of marriage partner and in her choice of work or career.

A fourth reason for embarking on the study was a wish to investigate the operation of protective mechanisms (Rutter, 1987*b*). By this term we meant not just positive influences, but rather processes that countered risk effects. The notion requires the demonstration of some form of interaction by which the beneficial effects either are evident only in the presence of risk or are potentiated in risk circumstances (Rutter, in press *a*). The findings provided several examples of such interaction effects. For example, both positive school experiences and the exercise of planning had little effect in the control group, but a marked effect in the institution-reared group.

Finally, the follow-up study was motivated by a concern to delineate those early features that put children at risk for poor social functioning and psychiatric problems in adult life. Two rather separate issues required attention. First, there was the question of the extent to which the risk derived from genetic or experimental variables. The research design was not one that allowed a rigorous comparison of genetic and environmental effects, but some test was possible by using a measure of parental deviance (a variable that covered criminality as well as psychiatric disorder) as a proxy for genetic risk. The findings suggested that, with females, most of the risk stemmed from adverse experiences rather than from parental deviance. The one exception to that pattern was provided by the emergence of personality disorder, in which both genetic and environmental features seemed influential. The second issue was, which aspect of the various environmental adversities constituted the greatest risk. Two findings from the follow-up of females are relevant in that connection. First, marked disruptions in parenting during the first 2 years of life were associated with a worse outcome in adulthood. Second, the outcome was particularly bad for girls who spent almost all of their childhood years in an institution. They were thereby protected from the ill effects of family discord, neglect, and abuse, but the lack of continuity in parenting (they had upwards of 50 different care-givers) was damaging.

The follow-up of males provided both the opportunity for partial replication (or nonreplication) of those findings and also the chance to determine whether the processes involved for males differed from those operative in females.

Methods

The overall design closely parallels that used in the follow-up study of females. The subjects were boys Children's Homes run on group cottage lines; they were admitted because their parents could not cope, rather than because of any type of disturbed behavior shown by the boys themselves. The original sample size was 123, of whom 91 (74%) were interviewed. Information on a further 4% was obtained from informants. A fifth could not be traced and one had died.

The comparison group of 58 boys (42 of whom were interviewed) comprised a quasi-random general population sample of individuals of the same age, never admitted into care, living with their families in the same general area of inner London.

Both groups were assessed in childhood by means of the same standardized behavioral questionnaire completed by teachers (Rutter, 1967; Rutter et al., 1975).

The data at follow-up derived from standardized investigator-based interviews with subjects and their spouses lasting some 2 to 4 hours, plus official crime records (Quinton & Rutter, 1988). Such interviews differ from the more usual structured respondent-based interviews in that the ratings are made by the investigator on the basis of detailed descriptions of behavior, rather than using the respondent's yes or no to specific closed questions. Necessarily, investigator-based interviews are heavily reliant on skilled interviewing and on explicit specification of rating criteria but, because investigators can be trained on these criteria, it allows both greater comparability in ratings and more subtle differentiations than are possible with respondent-based interviews (see Brown & Rutter, 1966; Graham & Rutter, 1968; Rutter & Brown, 1966; Le Couteur et al., submitted, for more detailed accounts of the approach).

Results

Outcome in adult life

We start with case-control comparisons on overall outcome. Figure 1 gives the data on personality disorder and official criminality among ex-care (i.e., institution-reared) men and women. As used here, *personality disorder* means persistently abnormal interpersonal relationships associated with definitely impaired social functioning, and *official criminality* refers only to a criminal record at or after age 18. Both men and women showed large,

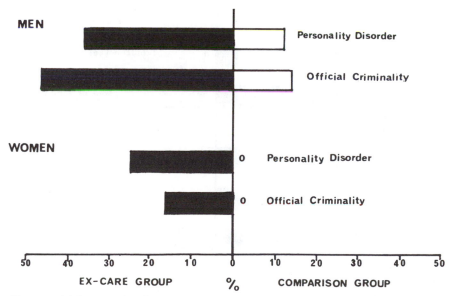

Figure 1. Adult personality disorder and criminality among institution-reared and comparison groups.

statistically significant, case-control differences. However, it was apparent that the rate of psychopathology in the male control group was substantially greater than that in the female controls. It is likely that this finding largely reflects a general sex difference, with criminality and personality disorder more common in men. However, in addition, it seemed that by chance the male control group tended to come from somewhat more deviant families. Thus, the control men were three times as likely as the control women to have alcoholic or criminal fathers (18% vs. 5%). Overall, 38% of the men compared with 24% of the women had one or more parents with a history of definite psychiatric disorder, alcoholism, or criminality, a difference that fell short of statistical significance.

For both sexes there were case-control differences in family functioning, but once more the male control group appeared more deviant than the female control group (Figure 2). However, it is also evident that, for men, the case-control differences are less striking than they were for personality disorder and criminality, and none reached statistical significance.

It is especially interesting that scarcely any of the men had had children taken into care because of a breakdown in parenting. It seems that the maintenance of parenting, and perhaps also of the marriage, may depend more on the wife/mother than the husband/father. For that to be the explanation, however, it would be necessary that most of the institution-

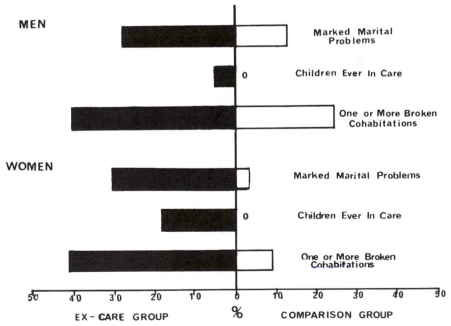

Figure 2. Marital and parenting problems.

reared men should have married nondeviant women. In fact, that proved to be so. Whereas the ex-care women were much more likely than controls to marry deviant men (52% vs. 19% comparing first spouses for those ever married/cohabited; $p < .02$), the ex-care men showed only a minimal, nonsignificant tendency to be more likely than controls to marry deviant women (27% vs. 17%; N.S.).

It appears that men from deprived backgrounds (with a high rate of psychopathology themselves) are less likely than women from a similar background to be disadvantaged in their choice of spouse. This seems to be because men are less likely than women to seek escape from unhappy family circumstances through pregnancy or marriage. This suggestion is supported by the marked sex difference in teenage parenthood, in age at first cohabitation, and in marriage for negative reasons. The institution-reared women were many times more likely than controls (41% vs. 5%; $p < .0001$) to be a teenage parent, whereas the difference in men was much smaller (8.9% vs. 2.4%) and statistically nonsignificant. The comparable figures for cohabitation at age 18 or younger were 40% versus 5% in women ($p < .0002$) and 18% versus 12% in men (not significant); and for marriage for negative reasons they were 36% versus 0% in women ($p < .0001$) and 12.4% versus 2.4% in men (not significant).

These differences apart, the general pattern of case-control differences in overall social outcome was fairly similar and statistically highly significant for the two sexes (Figure 3). This summary measure takes into account love

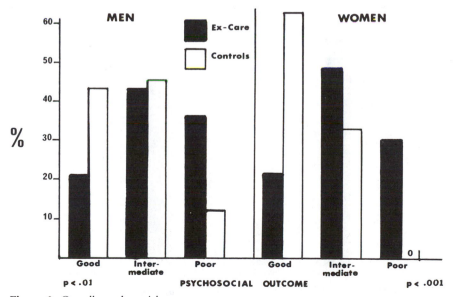

Figure 3. Overall psychosocial outcome.

relationships, marriage, friendships, criminality, psychiatric disorder, work, and autonomy of living conditions. A good outcome required no problems in any of these areas; poor outcome required definite problems in at least three. In both sexes, the institution-reared group had a markedly worse outcome than that of the control group. It is evident, however, that for both men and women, just over one fifth of the ex-care group showed good functioning and only about a third showed poor functioning. Hence, there was considerable heterogeneity to account for.

Childhood predictors of adult outcome

Figure 4 summarizes the findings on the early childhood predictors of poor social functioning in adult life. For both sexes, there was a major, statistically significant, effect of an early disrupted upbringing—meaning that during the first two years of life there had been one or more short-term admissions into foster care, multiple separations through parental discord or disorder, persistent family discord, or admission into long-term institutional care. For women there was no effect of parental deviance that was independent of early disruption. The rating of parental deviance meant that one or both parents had a criminal record or had been treated for psychiatric disorder, alcoholism, or dependency on hard drugs (using information from the Social Security records for these assessments). For men, in contrast, parental deviance did relate statistically to outcome after an early disrupted upbringing had been taken into account. It should be noted that of course,

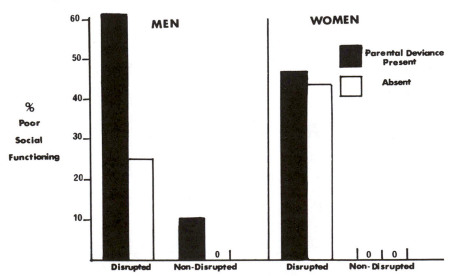

Figure 4. Effects of parental deviance and early disrupted upbringing on social functioning in adulthood in ex-care group.

the subjects in the "non-disrupted" group had had rearing that was markedly atypical in many respects, both in terms of suboptimal early upbringing and later disruption. Further analyses showed that this apparent difference between males and females was not primarily a function of a sex difference in the effects of parental deviance. Rather it reflected the fact that in males all instances of poor social functioning were associated with personality disorder whereas in females, although this was usually the case, it was not always so. In both sexes parental deviance was significantly associated with an outcome diagnosis of personality disorder (these findings are not included here).

The children in the institution-reared sample had been admitted to the Group Foster Homes because of a concern that they were at risk from being reared in severely disrupted families or from a breakdown in parenting. It is chastening, therefore, to note that of those admitted before age 2 who remained in the institution until age 16 or older, 44% of males and 45% of females showed poor social functioning at follow-up, giving little indication that institutional admission had proved protective. Of course, it is possible that their outcomes might have been even worse had the children remained with their biological parents.

The next issue to consider is the role of deviant behavior in childhood as a mediating variable leading to a poor social outcome in adult life. To examine this question we used both an abnormal score on the teacher's behavior questionnaire and juvenile delinquency, as reported in the official crime records. Childhood deviance was defined as the presence of either feature. Figure 5 shows the findings for females. (The data for controls on the right side of the figure do not include the findings for deviant girls because the numbers were so small.) The outcome in adult life was somewhat worse for those who showed behavioral deviance in childhood, but the differences were modest in size and the overall effect of childhood deviance after controlling for case-control differences fell short of significance. Moreover, it is obvious that the adult outcome for nondeviant females in the ex-care group was much worse than that in the controls. We may conclude that childhood deviance plays some role as a mediator, but in females its role was only moderate in strength.

Figure 6 shows the same comparison for males. The pattern was generally similar, although the mediating role of childhood deviance was stronger (and statistically significant) within the ex-care group. What is more striking, however, is that in men, as distinct from women, the case-control difference, although still statistically significant, was greatly reduced once childhood deviance had been taken into account. The nondeviant boys in the ex-care group did have a significantly worse outcome than their controls, but the difference was much less marked than in girls. A linear logistic analysis on the total data set, pooling the groups and the sexes, confirmed

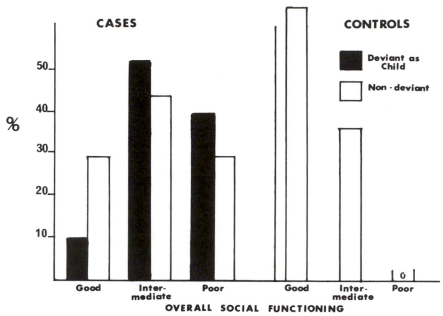

Figure 5. Effect of childhood deviance on social functioning as adults (females).

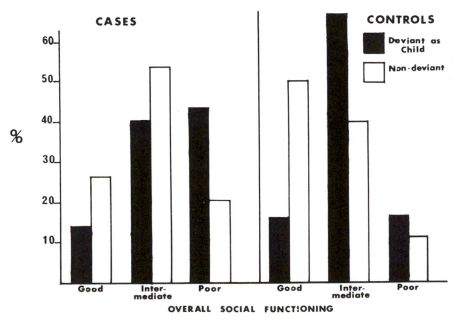

Figure 6. Effect of childhood deviance on social functioning as adults (males).

these conclusions. There was a strong and highly significant group by sex interaction and a less strong but statistically significant main effect of childhood deviance, after taking into account the interaction term; no other effects reached significance. However, the coefficient for the three-way group by sex by childhood deviance interaction was quite high (a huge standard error meant that the effect was insignificant), suggesting that probably there were far too few subjects in the key cells for an adequate test of the interaction.

Factors in adolescence and adult life associated with outcome

We turn now to factors operating later in life, focusing on those that proved important in women. As already mentioned, the most powerful protective factor in women was marital support, a rating based on a harmonious marriage to a nondeviant spouse with demonstrated warmth and definite confiding. Those who were unmarried and non-cohabiting were rated as lacking marital support. The data in Figure 7 refer only to the ex-care group. It is obvious that the findings for men were almost identical to those for women. In both sexes, there was a powerful, and statistically highly significant ($p = .001$), protective effect from the presence of a supportive spouse.

It is important to note that this finding could reflect either the effect of the

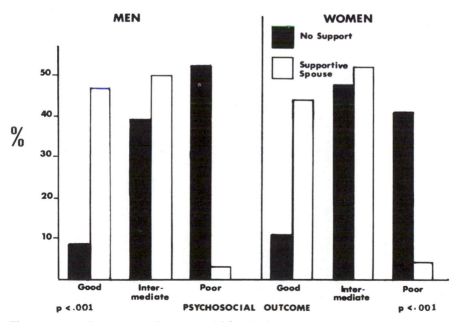

Figure 7. Marital support as a factor in social functioning (ex-care groups).

spouse on the subject or of the subject on the spouse. That is, the behavior of the subject could have resulted in a loss of marital support. Doubtless, there were two-way interactions but attention to historical data showed that there was indeed a support effect (Quinton et al., 1984; Quinton & Rutter, 1988).

In our study of institution-reared females "planning" constituted an important mediating variable through its effect on choice of marital partner and on actions to shape the adult environment in a favorable direction. "Planning" is a composite variable combining planning for work (meaning some definite choice of job or career other than the clearly ludicrous or improbable) and planning for marriage (meaning marriage after an acquaint-anceship of 6 months or more, plus a positive choice of partner and not just because of external pressure or as a means of escape from an intolerable situation). Planning was considered present if criteria were met for both work and marriage, or if met for work and the subject had never cohabited (on the grounds that, in these circumstances, remaining single was likely to reflect positive planning). Figure 8 compares the findings for men and women. It is apparent, once more, that the figures for the two sexes were broadly similar, although the relationship between planning and overall psychosocial outcome was somewhat stronger in women. The young people who planned had a markedly better outcome, with the effects of planning statistically significant in both sexes. We need to ask now, as we did for the women, how that effect came about.

In that connection, it is necessary first to examine the findings in the

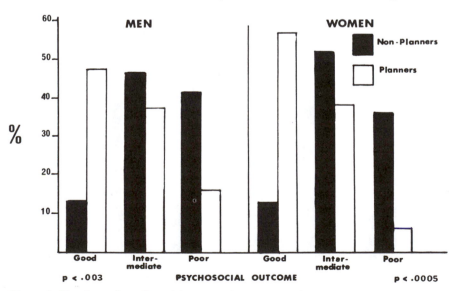

Figure 8. Planning and psychosocial outcome (ex-care groups).

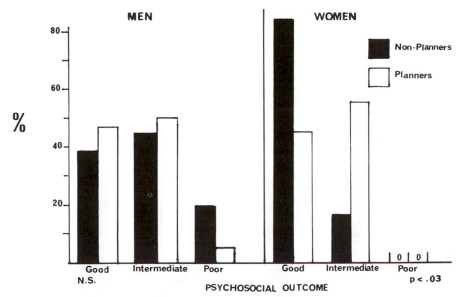

Figure 9. Planning and psychosocial outcome (control groups).

control groups (Figure 9). The pattern is strikingly different from that in the ex-care group. For men there was no significant association between planning for work and psychosocial outcome. For women there was a just-significant association, but it went in the opposite direction, with non-planners having a better outcome. In short, planning provides a true protective mechanism, that is, one that is operative in the face of serious adversity but which has no effect in ordinary circumstances (Rutter, 1987*b*). The finding immediately suggests that the effects of planning are likely to be indirect and that planning is not simply a proxy for better overall behavioral functioning. How then did planning exert its effect?

Figure 10 points to the probable answer for females, namely, that planning made it much more likely that the institution-reared women would land up with marital support. The planning measure was again the composite of work and marriage. This effect was not seen, however, for either male or female controls and was not significant for institution-reared men. The probable explanation for control subjects is that before marriage, they mixed with a much more normal peer group than did the institution-reared and, hence, that even random allocation would make it quite likely that they would marry a well functioning mate. Also, most came from supportive families who were likely to help guide them, whereas this was manifestly not the case in the ex-care group. Further examination of the data indicated that there were two probable reasons that planners among institution-reared men did not receive significantly more marital support than non-planners. First,

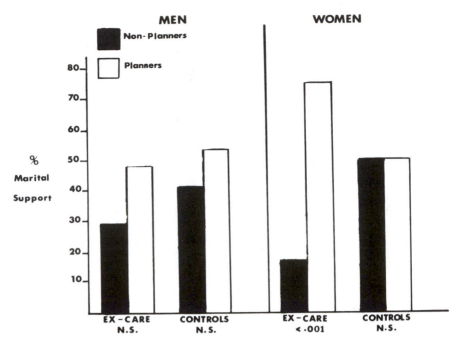

Figure 10. Planning and marital support (all groups).

among ex-care men, a third (6 of 17) of those who planned for marriage were not work planners. This pattern did not occur in the male controls (1 of 17) or in either the ex-care or control group women (1 of 13 and 1 of 15, respectively). There was a significant association for ex-care men between planning for marriage and marital support, but this was not paralleled in work planning as it was for women. Secondly, as already noted, ex-care men were less likely than their female counterparts to land up with deviant spouses and, hence, less likely to lack marital support, as defined here.

These findings raised the question of what led to marital support for the ex-care men. It was not that well functioning women were more likely to pick nondeviant men as spouses. Deviant behavior in childhood and adolescence was unrelated to marital support in either the male or female ex-care or control groups. The lesser difference in men between the ex-care and control group in marital problems (see Figure 2) and in the proportion with a deviant spouse, together with the findings on planning suggest that, at least in the ex-care group, marital choice may have been more strongly determined by the women than the men. Perusal of the interview protocols suggested that, in at least some cases, the apparent planning for marriage by ex-care men may have been a consequence of planning by their wives-to-be rather than by the men themselves.

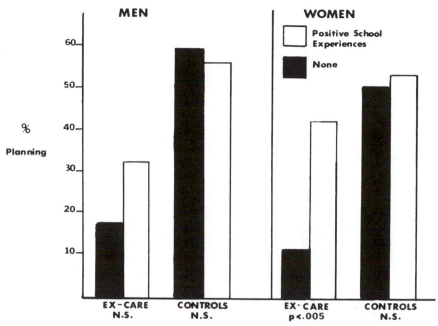

Figure 11. The effect of positive school experiences on planning.

The next question is why some young people in the ex-care groups exerted planning whereas others did not. The data in Figure 11 point to a possible explanation. The women who had had positive school experiences were more likely to exhibit planning for work and for marriage. The effect was greater for women than men, the latter showing an effect in the same direction but statistically nonsignificant. This finding for men is in keeping with the suggestion that planning for marriage may sometimes stem from the female spouse (since the association in ex-care men was somewhat stronger between positive school experiences and planning for work). Yet again, this protective effect of positive school experiences was seen only for the ex-care group and not for the controls. Why? We suggest that the benefits of good school experiences were much greater for the institution-reared sample just because they have so few other sources of self-esteem, satisfaction, and accomplishment. Most of the controls, in contrast, had rewarding experiences at home and, therefore, the additional good experiences at school made less difference; they already had ample sources of self-esteem.

Figure 12 puts both planning and marital support into the analysis together in order to determine the extent to which they had independent effects. Marital support had the stronger effect; moreover, the effect applied in both planners and non-planners. A linear logistic analysis showed a significant main effect for marital support and a lesser effect for planning

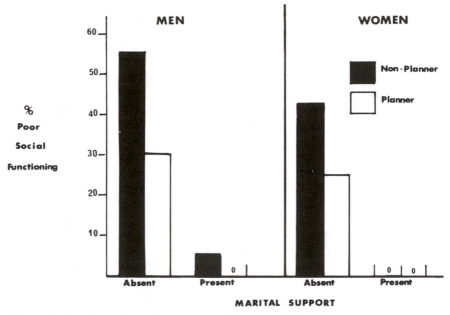

Figure 12. Planning and marital support in relation to social functioning (ex-care groups).

that fell short of statistical significance and no significant interaction effect overall. If by good fortune, non-planners landed up with marital support, the protective effect applied just as strongly. However, especially in males, it seemed that there might be some independent effect of planning that was separate from the presence of marital support. It may be inferred that the planning characteristic probably had an impact on other aspects of people's lives apart from marriage, although the marriage effect was particularly strong.

Conclusions

We may conclude that the data on the adult outcome of institution-reared males have provided a powerful confirmation of many of the key findings from the earlier comparable follow-up in females. In both cases there was a strong effect on adult outcome stemming from seriously adverse experiences in childhood; but in both there was a marked heterogeneity in outcome. This heterogeneity was associated in a meaningful fashion with later experiences. In particular, marital support in early adult life (meaning a harmonious marriage to a nondeviant spouse) provided a powerful protective effect. Most strikingly, this protective mechanism showed the operation of an interactive process, with the effects evident in the *presence* of adversity but not in its absence.

In these respects, the pathways from infancy to adult life seemed similar in men and women. The risk for maladaptive social functioning in adult life started at the beginning with birth to parents, of whom one or both showed chronic deviance in the form of psychiatric disorder, criminality, or drug dependence. The findings suggested that there was a significant direct effect on a personality disorder in adult life that was not mediated by environmental conditions, at least as measured in the study. The research design was not one that allowed any test for genetic influences, but the finding of a small direct effect is compatible with other evidence suggesting that personality disorder is partially influenced by genetic variables (Crowe, 1983).

There was also a strong effect of a disrupted early upbringing, an effect that held after controlling for parental deviance. In those individuals without personality disorder there was no direct effect of parental deviance on adult social functioning. The implication is that the parental abnormalities put the children at risk primarily because they led to a series of adverse experiences, rather than because there was a genetic risk that was independent of later environmental circumstances. This inference is consistent with the evidence from studies of children born to mentally ill parents (Rutter 1987; *a* in press *b*).

It should not be assumed, however, that the environmental risk was necessarily independent of the genetic background. Our data did not allow any examination of gene-environment interactions (Kendler & Eaves, 1986), but the findings from other investigations have suggested that genetic factors may sometimes serve to increase susceptibility to adverse environmental circumstances (Cadoret, 1985; Cadoret et al., this volume).

This environmental risk factor that stood out in our findings was disrupted early parenting, as shown by multiple parent–child separations, repeated short-term admissions into foster care, persistent family discord, or early admission into long-term institutional care. This composite variable brought together several different types of adverse experience including a changing pattern of personal care-giving that is likely to jeopardize the formation of secure parent–child attachment (Rutter, 1981); family discord that is associated with severe quarreling, hostility, and sometimes scapegoating of individual children (Rutter, 1985*b*); and a harmonious, but loveless, upbringing in an institutional setting that lacked continuity in personal care-giving (Quinton & Rutter, 1988). Evidence from other research suggests that each of these three types of experience is associated with a substantial psychiatric risk. Indeed, the longitudinal study by Hodges and Tizard (1989, *a* & *b*) suggested that the ill effects of an early institutional upbringing to some extent persist, even when the later years of childhood as spent in a stable, harmonious family environment.

Nevertheless, our own findings, as well as those of others, indicate that in ordinary circumstances early family adversities all too often lead to later family adversities (Quinton & Rutter, 1988). Thus, children who are admitted to institutions in infancy because of a breakdown in parenting usually experience further hazards in the late teens, either because they return to the same severely discordant families from which they were "rescued" a dozen years previously, or because they lack any home to which they can go on leaving the Group Homes. In other words, in many cases the continuing psychiatric risk derives not from any irreversible effect in infancy, but rather from a continuity in disadvantageous environmental circumstances that continue to impinge in ways that prolong and intensify the risks. Yet, the data showed substantial heterogeneity in outcomes, indicating the need to account for major discontinuities, as well as continuities, in development. In that connection, marital support from a nondeviant spouse stood out as a factor associated with a powerful protective effect. It seemed that, to some degree, adult experiences could modify the effect of adversities experienced in childhood. What exactly were the pathways leading from childhood to adult life? The findings on this issue showed an interesting mixture of similarities and differences between men and women.

In women, it was possible to trace out several key linkages that served to create a chain of indirect connections leading to both continuities and discontinuities. Positive school experiences were associated with an in-creased likelihood that the girls would exert planning in choosing marital partners and in selecting work careers; such planning was associated with a greater probability of marrying a nondeviant spouse with whom there would be a harmonious marital relationship; and, in turn, the marital support was associated with better social functioning in adult life. Of course, there should be great caution in moving from these statistical associations to causal inferences. It is possible that all of these variables (i.e., school experiences, planning, and marital support) represented some enduring quality of the individual rather than any environmental effect. We undertook a range of statistical analyses (Quinton & Rutter, 1988) to test for that possibility and it appeared that that was not likely to be the explanation. Thus, our contemporaneous independent measures of childhood deviance (i.e., teachers' questionnaire ratings and official crime records) did not account for the pattern of findings. It is possible that unmeasured qualities of the subjects played a role that we could not assess, but that did not seem to be the main story. It is not that individual characteristics were unimportant, to the contrary. Planning played a major role in choice of marital partner, but there was a substantial effect of marital support that held even after taking planning into account. In other words, to an important extent, individual qualities influenced environmental circumstances. There is growing evidence that to some extent people select and shape their own environments (Caspi et al., 1987 & this volume; Scarr & McCartney, 1983). In so doing, individual characteristics are themselves modified.

The findings for men were consistent with chain effects of this kind, but the effects were less marked than for females and often fell short of statistical significance. Two main sex differences were apparent. First, in men there was a strong effect of childhood deviance on adult functioning; a similar, but weaker effect was evident in females. In both sexes, planning exerted a direct statistical effect on adult social functioning but, again, this was somewhat greater in males than females. We may infer that the young people's behavior in childhood and adolescence was associated with social functioning in adult life for reasons that were independent of marital support. That inference is in keeping with both the evidence that conduct disorder in childhood predisposes to personality disorder in adult life (Robins, 1978; Rutter & Giller, 1983) and also the evidence that temperamental qualities in childhood are associated with later social functioning (Sigvardsson et al., 1987). However, the mechanisms underlying this apparently direct pathway from childhood to adult life are not clearly understood. Is it that once maladaptive social functioning becomes well established in childhood it tends to become self-perpetuating through a deviant personality organization, or is it that such social dysfunction has consequent or "knock-on" effects on personal interactions, which then create psychosocial risks? There is both experimental and naturalistic evidence that aggression and conduct disturbance in boys leads people to treat them differently from other children (Brunk & Henggeler, 1984; Dodge, 1983; Maccoby & Jacklin, 1983); such differential treatment in some cases is associated with an increased tendency for the behavior to be perpetuated.

The second sex difference concerned the choice of marriage partner. The ex-care men were less likely than the ex-care women to marry a deviant spouse, and their own planning style seemed to play a lesser role in marital choice. The implication is that, at least for this group of institution-reared individuals, the characteristics of the women may have been more important in the processes leading to selection of marital partner. The suggestion must remain tentative in the absence of direct evidence on marital choice mechanisms, but the possibility warrants further study. Of course, another possibility is that it is the effect of pregnancy that creates the difference. Among the women it was common for pregnancy to play an important part in the processes associated with marriage to an unsupportive deviant man. In part this may reflect a tendency for the girls to seek escape from an unhappy family background by starting their own family. However, probably more often the pregnancy arose as a consequence of a pervasive lack of planning. Similarly, the fact that they did not seek an abortion or adoption in infancy may have involved a lack of decision rather than any considered choice. Brown and his colleagues (1986) showed that the style of girls' responses to an illegitimate pregnancy is associated with their subsequent social outcome. In our society, an unwanted pregnancy has less effect on the men concerned than on the mothers. For obvious reasons, we have less valid data on the illegitimate children fathered by the ex-care men than on the pregnancies of the women. In any event, pregnancies played a less central role in adult transitions for men than for women.

Finally, there was a sex difference in the pathways to the next generation. An institutional upbringing showed a stronger association with marked marital problems and broken cohabitations in women than in men and a much stronger association with a breakdown in parenting, which led to offspring being taken into foster care. It seems that, in our society, the success or failure of parenting may depend more on the mother than on the father.

In conclusion, the findings of this follow-up into adult life of institution-reared men and women showed a complex mixture of both straight and devious pathways from childhood to adult life, the patterns being to some extent similar in the two sexes and to some extent different.

Acknowledgments

The study reported in this chapter was undertaken under a contract from the DHSS/SSRC Joint Working Party on Transmitted Deprivation and with the support of a grant from the Joseph Rowntree Memorial Trust. Jonathan Hill was supported by a Medical Research Council Training Fellowship; thanks are also expressed to the John D. and Catherine T. MacArthur Foundation. We are grateful to Christine Liddle who participated in the planning and interviewing and to Andrew Pickles for statistical advice. Thanks are due to Joy Maxwell for preparation of the figures and to Helen Journeaux for careful preparation of the manuscript and for checking of the references.

References

Bowlby, J. (1951). *Maternal care and mental health*. Geneva: World Health Organization.

Brown, G. W., Harris, T. O., & Bifulco, A. (1986). Long-term effects of early loss of parent. In M. Rutter, C. Izard, & P. Read (Eds.), *Depression in young people: Developmental and clinical perspectives* (pp. 251–296). New York: Guilford Press.

Brown, G. W. & Rutter, M. L. (1966). The measurement of family activities and relationships: A methodological study. *Human Relations, 19,* 241–263.

Brunk, M. A., & Henggeler, S. W. (1984). Child influences on adult controls: An experimental investigation. *Developmental Psychology, 20,* 1074–1081.

Cadoret, R. J. (1985). Genes, environment and their interaction in the development of psychopathology. In T. Sakai & T. Tsuboi (Eds.), *Genetic aspects of human behavior* (pp. 165–175). Tokyo: Igaku-Shoin.

Caspi, A., Elder, G. H., & Bem, D. J. (1987). Moving against the world: Life-course patterns and explosive children. *Developmental Psychology, 23,* 308–313.

Clarke, A. M., & Clarke, A. D. B. (1976). *Early experience: Myth and evidence.* London: Open Books.

Crowe, R. R. (1983). Antisocial personality disorders. In R. E. Tarter (Ed.), *The child at psychiatric risk* (pp. 214–227). Oxford: Oxford University Press.

Dodge, K. A. (1983). Behavioral antecedents of peer social status. *Child Development, 54,* 1386–1499.

Earls, F. (1987). Sex differences in psychiatric disorders: Origins and developmental influences. *Psychiatric Developments, 1,* 1–23.

Eme, R. F. (1979). Sex differences in childhood psychopathology: A review. *Psychological Bulletin, 86,* 574–595.

Gove, W. R., & Herb, T. R. (1974). Stress and mental illness among the young: A comparison of the sexes. *Social Forces, 53,* 256–265.

Graham, P. & Rutter, M. (1968). The reliability and validity of the psychiatric assessment of the child. II. Interview with the parent. *British Journal of Psychiatry, 114,* 581–592.

Hinde, R. A. & Stevenson-Hinde, J. (1987). Implications of a relationship approach for the study of gender differences. *Infant Mental Health Journal, 8,* 221–235.

Hodges, J., & Tizard, B. (1989 *a*). IQ and behavioural adjustments of ex-institutional adolescents. *Journal of Child Psychology and Psychiatry, 30,* 53–75.

Hodges, J., & Tizard, B. (1989 *b*). Social and family relationships of ex-institutional adolescents. *Journal of Child Psychology and Psychiatry, 30,* 77–97.

Kagan, J. (1984). *The nature of the child.* New York: Basic Books.

Kandel, D. B., & Davies, M. (1986). Adult sequelae of adolescent depressive symptoms. *Archives of General Psychiatry, 43,* 255–262.

Kendler, K. S., & Eaves, L. J. (1986). Models for the joint effect of genotype and environment on liability to psychiatric illness. *American Journal of Psychiatry, 143,* 279–289.

Le Couteur, A., Rutter, M., Lord, C., Rios, P. Robertson, S., Holdgrafter, M., & McLennan, J. (in press). Autism diagnostic interview: A standardized investigator based instrument. *Journal of Autism & Developmental Disorders.*

Maccoby, E. E., & Jacklin, C. N. (1983). The "person" characteristics of children and the family as environment. In D. Magnusson, & C. Allen (Eds.), *Human development: An interactonal perspective,* (pp. 75–91). New York: Academic Press.

O'Connor, N. (1956). The evidence for the permanently disturbing effects of mother-child separation. *Acta Psychologica, 12,* 174–191.

Orlansky, H. (1949). Infant care and personality. *Psychological Bulletin, 46,* 1–48.

Quinton, D., & Rutter, M. (1988). *Parenting breakdown: The making and breaking of intergenerational links.* Aldershot, England: Avebury.

Quinton, D., Rutter, M., & Liddle, C. (1984). Institutional rearing, parenting difficulties and marital support. *Psychological Medicine, 14,* 107–124.

Robins, L. (1978). Sturdy childhood predictors of adult antisocial behaviour: Replications from longitudinal studies. *Psychological Medicine, 8,* 611–622.

Robins, L. N. (1986). The consequences of conduct disorder in girls. In D. Olweus, J. Block, & M. Radke-Yarrow (Eds.), *Development of antisocial and prosocial behavior: Research, theories and Issues* (pp. 385–414). New York: Academic Press.

Rutter, M. (1967). A children's behaviour questionnaire for completion by teachers: Preliminary findings. *Journal of Child Psychology and Psychiatry, 8,* 1–11.

Rutter, M. (1970). Sex differences in children's responses to family stress. In E. J. Anthony & C. Koupernik (Eds.), *The child in his family* (Vol. 1, pp. 165–196). New York: John Wiley & Sons.

Rutter, M. (1979). Protective factors in children's responses to stress and disadvantage. In M. W. Kent & J. E. Rolf (Eds.), *Primary prevention of psychopathology: Vol. 3: Social competence in children* (pp. 49–74). Hanover, NH: University Press of New England.

Rutter, M. (1981). *Maternal Deprivation Reassessed (2nd ed.).* Harmondsworth, England: Penguin.

Rutter, M. (1982). Epidemiological-longitudinal approaches to the study of development. In W. A. Collins (Ed.), *The concept of development: Minnesota symposium on child psychology, Vol. 15.* Hillsdale, NJ: Lawrence Erlbaum.

Rutter, M. (1985a). Resilience in the face of adversity: Protective factors and resistance to psychiatric disorder. *British Journal of Psychiatry, 147,* 598–611.

Rutter, M. (1985b). Family and social influences on behavioural development. *Journal of Child Psychology and Psychiatry, 26,* 349–368.

Rutter, M. (1987a). Continuities and discontinuities from infancy. In J. Osofsky (Ed.), *Handbook of Infant Development* (2nd ed., pp. 1256–1296). New York: John Wiley & Sons.

Rutter, M. (1987b). Psychosocial resilience and protective mechanisms. *American Journal of Orthopsychiatry, 57,* 316–331.

Rutter, M. (1987c). Temperament, personality and personality disorder. *British Journal of Psychiatry, 150,* 443–458.

Rutter, M. (1987d). Parental mental disorder as a psychiatric risk factor. In R. E. Hales & A.J. Frances (Eds.) *American Psychiatric Association's Annual Review* (Vol. 6, pp. 647–663). Washington, DC: American Psychiatric Association.

Rutter, M. (in press a). Psychosocial resilience and protective mechanisms. In J. Rolf, A. Masten, D. Cicchetti, K. Nuechterlein, & S. Weintraub (Eds.), *Risk and protective factors in the development of psychopathology.* New York: Cambridge University Press.

Rutter, M. (in press b). Psychiatric disorder in parents as a risk factor for children. In D. Shaffer, I. Philips, N. Enver, N. Silverman, V. Q. Anthony, (Eds.), *Prevention of psychiatric disorders in child and adolescent: The project of the American Academy of Child and Adolescent Psychiatry.* OSAP Prevention Monograph No. 2, Office of Substance Abuse Prevention. Washington, DC: Government Printing Office.

Rutter, M.L., & Brown, G. W. (1966). The reliability and validity of measures of family life and relationships in families containing a psychiatric patient. *Social Psychiatry, 1,* 38–53.

Rutter, M., Cox, A., Tupling, C., Berger, M., & Yule, W. (1975). Attainment and adjustment in two geographical areas. I. The prevalence of psychiatric disorder. *British Journal of Psychiatry, 126,* 493–509

Rutter, M., & Giller, H. (1983). *Juvenile delinquency: Trends and perspectives.* Harmondsworth, England: Penguin.

Rutter, M., & Quinton, D. (1984). Long-term follow-up of women institutionalized in childhood: Factors promoting good functioning in adult life. *British Journal of Developmental Psychology, 2,* 191–204.

Scarr, S., & McCartney, K. (1983). How people make their own environments: A theory of genotype environmental effects. *Child Development, 54,* 424–435.

Sigvardsson, S., Bohman, M. & Cloninger, C. R. (1987). Structure and stability of childhood personality: Prediction of later social adjustment. *Journal of Child Psychology and Psychiatry, 28,* 929–946.

Weissman, M. M., & Klerman, G. L. (1977). Sex differences and the epidemiology of depression. *Archives of General Psychiatry, 34,* 98–111.

Yarrow, L. J. (1961). Maternal deprivation: toward an empirical and conceptual re-evaluation. *Psychological Bulletin, 58,* 459–490.

Zaslow, M. J., & Hayes, C. D. (1986). Sex differences in children's response to psychosocial stress: toward a cross-context analysis. In M. E. Lamb, A. L. Bron, & B. Rogoff (Eds.), *Advances in developmental psychology, Vol. 4.* Hillsdale, NJ: Lawrence Erlbaum.

Zeitlin, H. (1986). *The natural history of disorder in childhood.* Institute of Psychiatry Maudsley Monograph, No. 29. Oxford: Oxford University Press.

9 Antecedents and consequences of cocaine use: An eight-year study from early adolescence to young adulthood

MICHAEL D. NEWCOMB AND PETER M. BENTLER

The use of cocaine has spread to many segments of society and has shown relatively rapid increases in prevalence among adolescents and young adults (Abelson & Miller, 1985; Adams et al., 1986; Clayton, 1985; Gottheil, 1986; O'Malley et al., 1985; Washton & Gold, 1987). Although national epidemiological samples indicate that about one quarter of all young adults have tried cocaine at least once, some more limited geographical samples have revealed prevalence rates over 40% (Newcomb & Bentler, 1988a). It is apparent, then, that cocaine use may have a significant impact on the health and psychological functioning of the nation. Thus, it is imperative to determine in a rigorous manner the unique predictors and consequences of cocaine use in order to appraise more accurately the effects of the current cocaine epidemic (Gold et al., 1986). Such data would provide valuable information for both prevention and treatment of cocaine involvement, as well as characterize natural patterns of use.

Some investigators have suggested that cocaine involvement can arise as the result of a psychological predisposition for use, specifically characterized by some type of affective or mood disorder (Khantzian & Khantzian, 1984). From this perspective, cocaine is chosen because of its stimulant and euphoric effects that help medicate, at least temporarily, a dysphoric emotional state. Some limited empirical support has been found for this hypothesis. Newcomb and Bentler (1986a) found that only depression, out of several other measures of psychopathology, increased cocaine use over a one-year period during adolescence. Mixed support has been found for this effect over a longer period of time from adolescence into young adulthood (Kandel et al., 1985; Newcomb & Bentler, 1986b). Also in support of the predisposition notion is the research demonstrating that certain cocaine abusers have been treated successfully with antidepressant medication (Gawin & Kleber, 1984). Similarly, Gawin and Kleber (1985) found that about one half of a treatment sample of cocaine abusers had a secondary diagnosis of an affective disorder. Despite these few intriguing empirical findings in support of the psychological predisposition theory (Khantzian, 1987), very few of these hypotheses have been supported empirically in

158

general population surveys (Newcomb et al., 1987). In other words, while a great deal of psychopathology appears to co-exist with cocaine abuse in clinic and treatment samples (Gold et al., 1985), such associations appear far less frequently in general population samples (Clayton, 1985).

Other predictors of cocaine use have included parental attitudes toward drug use, parents' actual drug use, intention to use cocaine, cannabis use, peer and adult models of cocaine use, deviance or lack of social conformity, higher income, lack of headache proneness, and disinterest in academic pursuits (Kandel et al., 1985; Mills & Noyes, 1984; Newcomb & Bentler, 1986*a* & *b*). However, since these studies specifically examined cocaine as the only dependent or outcome variable, it is not possible to determine whether these are, in fact, unique predictors of cocaine use, or whether, more likely, they represent predictors of drug use in general with cocaine use as only one component.

On the other hand, some researchers have suggested that there are unique consequences to cocaine use. Although many of these outcomes are short-term effects attributable to the pharmacological effects of the drug (Gold et al., 1985) and can be as severe as toxic psychosis and death (Estroff, 1987; Wetli, 1987), the longer-term nonfatal consequences are not as well established. For instance, we found that cocaine use over a one-year period during adolescence was not associated with an increase in various types of psychopathology, including depression, insomnia, thought disorganization, and headache proneness (Newcomb & Bentler, 1986*a*). In this same sample at an older age, heavy use of cocaine was associated with some slight impairment in cognitive functioning, increased depression, and some health problems (Castro et al., 1988), although these effects were quite small. In further studies of this same sample, we found that cocaine use during early and late adolescence increased the number of sexual relationships, increased the number of aggressive or confrontational acts, reduced the number of theft episodes, reduced the degree of happiness with being close to someone, and increased the chances of divorce in young adulthood (Newcomb & Bentler, 1988*a*).

In general, most studies of cocaine antecedents and consequences have not attempted or been able to separate the relationships of these processes to cocaine use from their relationship to other drugs (Kandel et al., 1986). It is well known and has been frequently demonstrated that cocaine is rarely used in isolation, but is one aspect of a lifestyle involving polydrug use (Castro et al., 1987; Kandel et al., 1985; Mills & Noyes, 1984; Newcomb & Bentler, 1986*a* & *b*). In fact, one of the most consistent predictors of cocaine use has been prior use of marijuana (Kandel et al., 1985; Newcomb & Bentler, 1986*a*. In one sample, cocaine use was so highly related to marijuana use that Kandel et al. (1985) could not create a "cocaine use only" category.

These findings lead naturally to an obvious question. Are there unique predictors and consequences of cocaine use that are distinct from use of other drugs, and in particular, use of other illicit drugs? Kandel and co-workers (Kandel et al., 1985; Kandel & Logan, 1984) have observed that the lifetime patterns of use for cocaine are unique compared to other drugs. For instance, the hazard rates for use of all drugs except cocaine reach a peak during late adolescence and decline thereafter. For cocaine, however, the hazard rate continues to rise well into young adulthood. Thus, it is certainly possible that there may be some unique predictors or consequences of cocaine involvement, since it seems to begin later and continue into a different stage of life than other drugs do.

The study

The analyses presented in this study attempt to answer this question by using a latent-variable structural modeling method that can capture a general tendency to use drugs while retaining the unique aspects of cocaine, alcohol, and other illicit drug use. Latent constructs of general drug use are used to represent the overlap between using several drugs, which has generally been called polydrug use. This represents a continuous measure, ranging from no drug involvement at the low end to high involvement with many drugs at the upper end. The portion of unique variance not captured by this general drug use construct represents use of a particular drug that is not part of a polydrug-use lifestyle; in particular, the unique contribution of cocaine use is tested for having specific antecedents or consequences. In this way we are able to determine and separate (if they occur) unique predictors and outcomes of cocaine use from the general tendency toward polydrug use (the drug use latent construct).

The data are from three equally spaced collection points spanning 8 years from early adolescence to young adulthood. An attempt is made to separate a latent factor of cocaine involvement from a general drug use factor in late adolescence and young adulthood. Three additional constructs were assessed with multiple indicators at all three time points and represent possible antecedents and consequences of cocaine and drug use, based on the literature discussed above (see recent reviews by Newcomb, 1987, and Sadava, 1987). These include academic orientation, social conformity, and emotional distress. The degree of successful social integration was measured in both late adolescence and young adulthood and is reflected in a construct of social support. Social support has proven to be an excellent predictor of positive psychosocial functioning and successful attainment of normative roles in life (Newcomb & Bentler, 1988b; Sarason & Sarason, 1985). Finally, three indicators of subjectively perceived trouble with drugs were measured during young adulthood and are used to represent a consequences factor of drug problems.

Subjects

Data were obtained from participants in an 8-year longitudinal study of adolescent development and drug use (Newcomb & Bentler, 1986c, 1988a). Data for this study were taken from 654 subjects who participated at three equally spaced assessment points: year 1 (early adolescence), year 5 (late adolescence), and year 9 (young adulthood).

This study began in 1976 with a group of 1,634 students in the 7th, 8th, and 9th grades. An excessively large student pool was chosen to yield about 1,000 complete triads of a student, his or her close friend, and his or her parent. Informed consent was obtained from both teenagers and their parents, and each participant was informed that his or her responses were protected legally by a grant of confidentiality from the U.S. Department of Justice. Unfortunately, we do not have detailed information regarding the total sampling frame (or universe of subjects) from which our initial sample was drawn. All students were located at 11 Los Angeles County schools which were roughly representative of schools in the county in terms of socioeconomic status and ethnicity. We selected 5 lower socioeconomic status schools, 3 of high status, and 3 of medium status. The larger number of lower status schools was intended to offset an expected lower level of participation among students and parents from the lower socioeconomic status schools. The schools were located in 5 school districts. Data were again collected 4 years later (in 1980) when the subjects were late adolescents, and 4 years after that when the participants were young adults (1984). At the young adult follow-up, data were collected from 739 subjects of our original sample (654 provided data at all three assessments). This represents a 45% retention rate over the entire 8-year period of the study.

Table 1 presents a description of the sample as young adults. To determine the representativeness of the subjects followed into adulthood, we compared our sample with other national samples and individuals in studies similar to ours. When characteristics (e.g., income and living arrangements) of our participants were compared with national surveys of young adults (Glick & Lin, 1986; Johnston et al., 1987; Miller et al., 1983) and other samples of young adults (Donovan, Jessor, & Jessor, 1983; Kandel, 1984), very similar patterns were noted. For instance, the U.S. Bureau of the Census reported that in 1984, 45% of 20-to-24-year-olds lived with their parents (Glick & Lin, 1986). This prevalence rate is quite similar to the 48% we found in our sample of the same age.

One would expect heavier drug users to drop out of a long-term study, leaving the resulting sample unrepresentative of the population. To evaluate such an effect, we compared reported drug use from our sample and a national representative sample of young adults (Miller et al., 1983). Lifetime prevalence levels were equal for hallucinogens, heroin, sedatives, analgesics,

Table 1. *Description of sample*

Variable	Number of subjects	Percent of sample
Total	654	100
Sex		
Male	192	29
Female	462	71
Age		
21	253	39
22	214	33
23	170	26
24	17	2
Ethnicity		
Black	97	15
Hispanic	64	10
White	432	66
Asian	61	9
Current life activity		
Military	17	3
Junior college	79	12
University	139	21
Part-time job	89	14
Full-time job	305	47
None	25	4
Income last year		
None	62	9
Less than $5,000	215	33
Between $5,000 and $15,000	300	46
Over $15,000	76	12
Current living arrangements		
Alone	27	4
With parent(s)	311	48
Spouse	68	10
Spouse and child(ren)	43	7
Cohabitation	58	9
Dormitory	37	6
With roommates	81	12
Other	29	4

and cigarettes, whereas our sample reported significantly higher prevalence of use of cannabis, cocaine, stimulants, tranquilizers, and alcohol. Prevalence rates of our sample were also compared with those provided for the Western U.S. region in the national survey and were found not to differ significantly. Clearly, we did not lose a higher proportion of drug users as a result of attrition than cross-sectional surveys lose by non-response (see Newcomb & Bentler, 1988a, for further details).

A series of analyses were run to determine whether the attrition in sample size from 1976 to 1984 (junior high school to young adulthood) was the result of any systematic influence. Data obtained in 1976 were compared for those who did and did not provide completed questionnaires in 1984. These group were contrasted in terms of use of 13 different drug substances and 25 personality traits in 1976. Using the Bonferroni procedure to adjust for multiple simultaneous comparisons, not one of these 38 variables was significantly different in the remaining sample from those lost. The average (absolute) point biserial correlation for these 38 tests was .04, whereas the average squared correlation was .002. The largest difference accounted for less than 1% of the variance between groups and was not significant when using the Bonferroni method to correct for chance. These analyses indicate that very little of the attrition rate between 1976 and 1984 was due to self-selection based on drug use or personality traits.

To tease out any remaining differences, a stepwise multiple regression analysis was run using the 38 1976 drug use and personality variables as the predictor pool, and retention in 1984 as the criterion variable. Using this procedure, 9 variables were chosen to differentiate the groups. Although significant, this equation, created by selecting all of the best predictors, accounted for less than 5% of the variance between groups. Those who continued in the study reported more beer use, less cigarette use, less attractiveness, more generosity, more intelligence, more vulnerability, less liberalism, less orderliness, and more trustful qualities in 1976 than those who did not continue in this study.

In a hierarchical fashion, we then added sex and ethnicity (as dummy variables) to the attrition prediction equations. Sex accounted for 1% of the unique variance in attrition (equivalent to its zero-order association with attrition), and ethnicity accounted for less than 3% of the unique attrition variance. Although quite small, these additional effects indicate that those who were most likely to continue in the study were female, white, Asian, and not black. There were no differential effects for Hispanics. These attrition effects, however, were surprisingly small, considering the lengthy period of the study and the large loss of subjects.

Measures used

The description of the variables is organized according to the latent factors they are hypothesized to reflect. Variables reflecting latent factors of drug use, academic orientation, social conformity, and emotional distress were assessed at each time point (years 1, 5, and 9). Variables for social support latent factors were assessed in late adolescence and young adulthood, and variables for a latent construct of drug problems were gathered only in young adulthood. Finally, in years 5 and 9, more detailed measures of cocaine use were collected and used to reflect constructs of cocaine involvement (one in each year).

Drug use factors. Multiple indicators for latent variables of drug use were measured at all three time points through assessment of the subjects' frequency of use of alcohol (sum of beer, wine, and liquor), illicit drugs (including marijuana, hashish, stimulants, sedatives, inhalants, psychedelics, narcotics, and PCP), and cocaine. Responses in year 1 were given for lifetime frequency of use, whereas responses in years 5 and 9 were for the past 6 months. In years 5 and 9 we attempted to identify a separate latent factor of cocaine involvement. In year 5, the indicators for this factor were cocaine frequency (which also loaded on drug use) and the number of times of being "super-high" on cocaine (during the past 6 months). In year 9, the indicators for cocaine involvement were cocaine frequency (also loading on drug use), frequency of using cocaine at work or school during the past 6 months (Newcomb, 1988), and dealing cocaine (amount of cocaine sold during the past 6 months).

Academic orientation. Indicators for a construct of academic orientation were assessed at all three time points. In years 1 and 5, two single items were used as indicators of this latent construct: grade-point average (coded in the standard way) and educational aspirations (ranging from only partial high school to a doctoral degree). In year 9, two single items were used to represent a latent construct of academic orientation: educational plans (ranging from no more formal education to a doctoral degree) and educational aspirations (ranging from partial high school to a doctoral degree).

Social conformity. Three personality traits from the Bentler Psychological Inventory (BIP) (Bentler & Newcomb, 1978; Newcomb & Bentler, 1988a) were used as indicators of a social conformity latent construct at all three time points. These three measures were law abidance, (lack of) liberalism, and religious commitment (Stein et al., 1986).

Emotional distress. Indicators for an emotional distress construct were assessed at all three time points. Year 1 indicators were (lack of) self-acceptance and (lack of) cheerfulness (both from the BPI). In years 5 and 9, the indicators were (lack of) self-acceptance, depression (Newcomb et al., 1981, 1986), and self-derogation (Kaplan, 1975).

Social support. In years 5 and 9, a latent construct of social support was reflected in four multi-item scales: good relationship with parents, good relationship with family, good relationship with adults, and good relationship with peers. The scales assess the amount of respect, support, and inclusion experienced with the four categories of relationships (Newcomb & Bentler, 1986*d*).

Problems with drugs. A problems-with-drugs latent construct was reflected in three scales in the young adult assessment. Trouble with alcohol and trouble with drugs were assessed as present or absent during each of the previous 4 years. Problems with alcohol or drugs within the last 3 months (Stein et al., 1987) was measured on a scale of no difficulty to great difficulty.

Analysis strategy

First, the prevalence of alcohol, illicit drugs, and cocaine was examined over the 8 years, separately for men and women. Three-wave longitudinal latent-variable models (Bentler, 1980, 1986*a*; Bentler & Newcomb, 1986) were used to analyze the data using the EQS structural equations program (Bentler, 1986*b*). A latent-variable confirmatory factor analysis was performed to ascertain that the measured variables reflect the hypothesized latent constructs in a reliable manner. Then, a structural or path model was developed to identify the across-time influences, based on the measurement model previously established. Cross-time influences are not limited to the restricted forms imposed by Jöreskog's 1977 model (Bentler, 1987; Newcomb & Bentler, 1988*a*). The standard LISREL model as developed by Jöreskog (1977) tests only for relationships (paths, correlations) between latent factors. This method does not easily allow detection of paths or effects from the nonfactor or unique portions of variance (i.e., cocaine use not captured by general drug use). The more general model, available in the EQS program (Bentler, 1986*b*), permits direct tests of the common or latent factor (general drug use) and the unique or nonfractor variance of the specific drug use variables (i.e., cocaine frequency) as predictors and consequences over time.

Although several of the manifest variables were not normally distributed, maximum likelihood estimates were used owing to the large size of the model. Current distribution-free methods cannot accommodate the number of variables contained in the present study. Elliptical methods were not appropriate since the kurtoses were not homogeneous (Bentler, 1983). Recent research and theory development indicate that maximum likelihood estimators are quite robust over normality violations (Harlow, 1985; Mooijaart & Bentler, 1986) and the results should not be biased by the necessary use of this method.

Results

Drug use prevalence trends

To analyze prevalence of drug use, all three measures of drug use were dichotomized into use or non-use of the particular category of drugs. In year 1, these measures reflect the lifetime prevalence of alcohol, illicit drugs, and cocaine use, while in years 5 and 9, these measures reflect prevalence during the past 6 months.

The prevalence rates are plotted in Figure 1 separately by sex. As is evident, alcohol remained consistently high, illicit drug use increased during adolescence and then decreased into young adulthood, and cocaine rose steadily from early to late adolescence and then into young adulthood.

Differences in prevalence were calculated between males and females for each drug category at each time point. None of these tests was significant. Next, point-biserial correlation tests were used to compare the sexes on the frequency of use for each category of drugs at each time point (reflecting the intensity rather than prevalence of use). In this case, men reported significantly more frequent alcohol use during late adolescence ($r = -.07$) and young adulthood ($r = -.12$) than women did. No other significant differences in drug use frequency were found. (For more detailed breakdowns of changes in drug use over time, see Newcomb & Bentler, 1987.)

Confirmatory factor analysis (CFA) model

The first step in our multivariate analyses was to assess the adequacy of our hypothesized measurement model. In other words, we needed to demonstrate that the variables we had chosen to reflect the latent factors in fact reflected these constructs in a statistically reliable manner. This was accomplished with a confirmatory factor analysis or CFA model. The hypothesized measurement model was summarized in this chapter in the section regarding measures. For example, a latent construct of social conformity was hypothesized to account for the variation in three measured scales: law abidance, liberalism, and religious commitment.

An initial CFA model was run which (1) fixed all factor variances at unity (in order to identify the model); (2) allowed all constructs (latent factors) to correlate freely; and (3) included across-time correlations between residual variables on repeated measures (e.g., between the residuals of law abidance at the three time points). This initial model did not adequately reflect the data ($\chi^2 = 1724.86$, df $= 821$, $p<.001$), although the Normed Fit Index (NFI, per Bentler & Bonett, 1980) was sufficiently large (.86) to suggest that modifications should yield an acceptable fit. Factor intercorrelations for this initial model are presented in the upper triangle of Table 2.

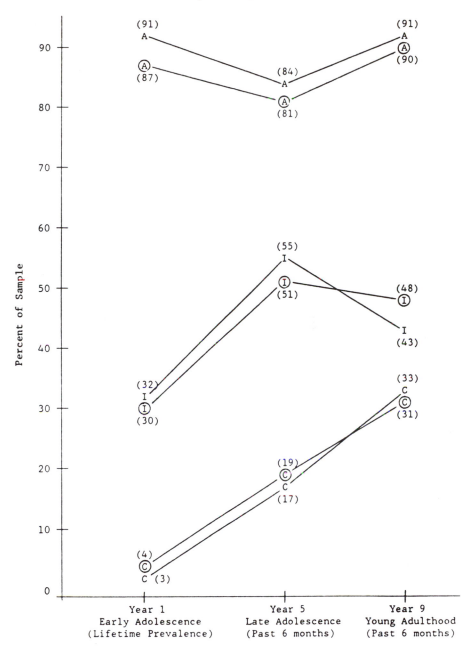

Figure 1. Prevalence of alcohol, cocaine, and other illicit drug use across 8 years from early adolescence to young adulthood. Results are plotted separately by sex. A = alcohol; I = illicit drugs; C = cocaine; circled letters represent females.

Table 2. *Latent-factor intercorrelations for the initial (upper triangle) and final (lower triangle) confirmatory factor analysis*

Factors	1	2	3	4	5	6	7
Early adolescence							
1. Drug use	1.00	−.26***	−.77***	.16**	.44***	.43***	−.15**
2. Academic orientation	−.26***	1.00	.33***	−.39***	−.22**	−.18**	.86***
3. Social conformity	−.63***	−.35***	1.00	−.33***	−.49***	−.36***	.29***
4. Emotional distress	.16**	−.41***	−.32***	1.00	.02	.04	−.20**
Late adolescence							
5. Drug use	.47***	−.21**	−.48***	.02	1.00	.82***	−.32***
6. Cocaine involvement[a]						1.00	−.26***
7. Academic orientation	−.14**	.78***	.30***	−.24***	−.31***		1.00
8. Social conformity	−.55***	.18*	.63***	−.06	−.75***		.36***
9. Emotional distress	−.04	−.24***	−.15**	.31***	.19***		−.34***
10. Social support	−.13*	.30***	.33***	−.31***	−.32***		.48***
Young adulthood							
11. Drug use	.37***	−.16**	−.36***	.02	.67***		−.26***
12. Cocaine involvement	.26***	−.17**	−.26***	−.05	.44***		−.12*
13. Academic orientation	−.14**	.69***	.17**	−.16**	−.27***		.77***
14. Social conformity	−.36***	.02	.53***	−.01	−.55***		.07
15. Emotional distress	−.01	−.25***	−.07	.34***	.13**		−.26***
16. Social support	.02	.35***	.21**	−.36***	−.19**		.40***
17. Drug problems	.21***	−.06	−.21***	.10*	.33***		−.17**

[a] In the final CFA model factors 5 and 6 were perfectly correlated ($r = 1.00$) and were combined into one factor (5).

*$p < .05$
**$p < .01$
***$p < .001$

The Lagrange Multiplier modification indices (Bentler, 1986c; Bentler & Chou, 1986) were used to determine where the model could be modified in order to improve the fit. Based on an examination of these indices, correlations between several dozen pairs of residuals were added to the model. These modifications resulted in a model that adequately reflected the data ($\chi^2 = 784.42$, df = 750, $p = .17$, NFI = .94). In fitting this final CFA model, the correlation between year 5 drug use and year 5 cocaine involvement reached unity, indicating that these two latent factors could not be kept separate. As a result, in the final CFA model, all year 5 cocaine variables were allowed to load on year 5 drug use, and the year 5 cocaine involvement factor was eliminated. Factor intercorrelations for this final confirmatory factor analysis model are presented in the lower triangle of Table 2. All hypothesized factor loadings were significant, and the standardized factor loadings from this final CFA model are given in Table 3. To test whether adding the correlated residuals disturbed the fundamental associations among the latent constructs, the factor intercorrelations

8	9	10	11	12	13	14	15	16	17
−.42***	−.01	−.10*	.41***	.30***	−.12*	−.29***	−.02	.01	.20***
.14*	−24***	.27***	−.17**	−.15*	.68***	.00	−.25**	.12*	−.04
.62***	−.10*	.25***	−.38***	−.25***	.18	.53***	−.05	.09*	−.24***
−.04	−.30***	−.23**	.00	−.06	−.15**	.02	.31***	−.22***	.09
−.79***	.23***	−.28***	.75**	.45***	−.29***	−.55***	.15**	−.13**	.46***
−.52***	.11**	−.15***	.59***	.45***	−.22***	−.34***	.08**	−.07*	.27***
.30***	−.31***	.32***	−.26***	−.11*	.75***	.05	−.26***	.16**	−.19**
1.00	−.32***	.49***	−.65***	−.40***	.23***	.80***	−.20***	.29***	−.35***
−.33***	1.00	−.64***	.13***	.04	−.24***	−.10*	.48***	−.38***	.19**
.65***	−.81***	1.00	−.23***	−.15**	.20***	.27***	−.40***	.61***	−.26***
−.62***	.13**	−.28***	1.00	.79***	−.26***	−.75***	.12**	−.13**	.52***
−.45***	.07	−.14**	.56***	1.00	−.17**	−.42***	.05	−.07	.40***
.24***	−.25***	.30***	−.21***	−.18***	1.00	.05	−.19***	.12**	−.11*
.79***	−.17**	.36***	−.74***	−.52***	.01	1.00	−.22***	.23***	−.28***
−.25***	.51***	−.53***	.11**	.06	−.20***	−.29***	1.00	−.53***	.28***
.49***	−.57***	.81***	−.14**	−.08	.29***	.40***	−.86***	1.00	−.22***
−.35***	.17**	−.26***	.41***	.35***	−.12*	−.26***	−.26***	−.22***	1.00

between the initial and final CFA models (Table 2) were correlated. This correlation was higher than .95, indicating that the model modifications did not alter the basic pattern of factor intercorrelations.

Structural model analyses

The final stage in data analyses was the creation of a structural or path model, which included regression effects representing unidirectional influences of one variable upon another. As a rule we do not include regression paths within time, since their causal interpretation is ambiguous. Within-time associations were captured as correlations between constructs, factor loadings, or correlated residuals. The regression effects in which we were most interested were those across time that could have a plausible "causal" basis.

Since many of the correlated residuals added in the CFA model modifications may simply be another way to capture regression effects across time, the empirically determined correlated residuals across time were deleted in the initial structural model. This was done in hopes of capturing these associations as true, across-time causal paths (partial regression effects). All constructs in early adolescence were allowed to correlate freely,

Table 3. *Standardized factor loadings for the final confirmatory factor analysis*

Factor/variable	Factor loadings[a]		
	Early adolescence	Late adolescence	Young adulthood
Drug use			
Alcohol frequency	.68	.69	.54
Illicit drug use frequency	.60	.90	.89
Cocaine frequency	.15	.75	.45[b]
Times super-high on cocaine		.56	
Cocaine involvement			
Cocaine use at work			.65
Dealing cocaine			.59
Academic orientation			
Grade-point average	.51	.47	.75
Educational aspirations	.45	.71	.75
Educational plans			.85
Social conformity			
Law abidance	.64	.59	.57
Liberalism	−.57	−.48	−.45
Religious commitment	.38	.38	.44
Emotional distress			
Self-acceptance	−.74	−.83	−.91
Cheerfulness	−.48		
Depression		.87	.86
Self-derogation		.56	.74
Social support			
Good relationship with adults		.62	.46
Good relationship with parents		.65	.53
Good relationship with family		.58	.45
Good relationship with peers		.42	.57
Drug problems			
Trouble with alcohol			.49
Trouble with drugs			.61
Tabule with drugs or alcohol			.64

[a] All factor loadings are significant ($p < .001$).
[b] Also loads cocaine involvement in young adulthood (.50).

as were all factor residuals within late adolescence and within young adulthood. All late adolescent constructs were initially predicted from all early and late constructs, whereas all young adult constructs were initially predicted from all early and late adolescent constructs.

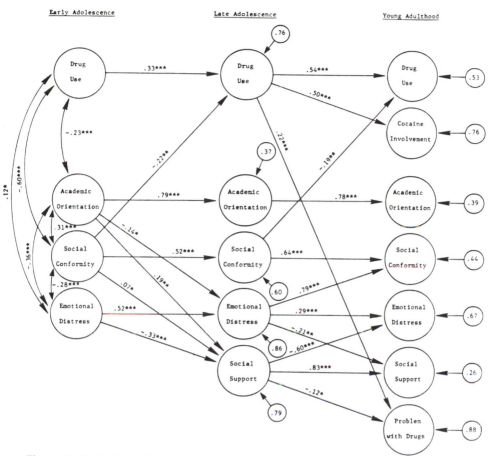

Figure 2. Final path model depicting significant effects between latent constructs. Covariance are correlations; regression path estimates are standardized (*p<.05; **p<.01; ***p<.001); and residual variables are variances. Nonstandard regression effects that include at least one measured variable are listed in Table 4. The information given in Table 4 and that given in Figure 2 are based on the same final structural model and are presented separately for clarity.

This beginning model was overfit by adding across-time regression paths (based on the Lagrange Multiplier modification indices) and then by deleting nonsignificant parameters (as suggested by MacCallum, 1986). The final model included only significant paths, since nonsignificant correlations and paths were removed systematically. The removal of these nonsignificant parameters was guided by the multivariate Wald test (Bentler & Chou, 1986), which ensures that deleting multiple effects can be done without losing significant parameters. This results in a more parsimonious model that is not cluttered by unnecessary (nonsignificant) parameters, and the remaining effects are thus more readily interpretable.

Table 4. *Direct across-time causal paths from the final structural model that are not depicted in figure 1*

Early adolescence	Late adolescence	Young adulthood	Standardized parameter estimate[a]
DRUG USE	Grade-point average		−.08*
DRUG USE	Self-derogation		−.16***
Alcohol frequency	SOCIAL CONFORMITY		−.19***
Illicit drug use frequency (R)	Grade-point average		−.07*
Illicit drug use frequency (R)		Cocaine frequency	.09**
ACADEMIC ORIENTATION	Liberalism		.08*
Grade-point average (R)	Good relationship with parents		.07*
Grade-point average (R)	Good relationship with peers		.10**
Grade-point average (R)		Self-derogation	−.08**
Educational aspirations (R)	Educational aspirations		.09**
SOCIAL CONFORMITY	Alcohol frequency		−.13**
SOCIAL CONFORMITY	Self-acceptance		−.08*
Law abidance (R)	Self-derogation		.10**
Cheerfulness (R)	Times super-high on cocaine		−.06*
	Alcohol frequency (R)	Cocaine frequency	.06*
	Alcohol frequency (R)	Law abidance	−.10**
	Alcohol frequency	Good relationship with peers	−.06*
	Alcohol frequency	SOCIAL CONFORMITY	−.15***
	Illicit drug use frequency (R)	Self-derogation	.06*
	Illicit drug use frequency (R)	Trouble with drugs	.19***
	Cocaine frequency (R)	Dealing cocaine	.12***

ACADEMIC ORIENTATION	Good relationship with family	.08**
Educational aspirations (R)	Liberalism	.09*
Educational aspirations (R)	Depression	−.06*
SOCIAL CONFORMITY	Law abidance	.22***
SOCIAL CONFORMITY	Trouble with alcohol	−.09*
Law abidance (R)	Alcohol frequency	−.13***
Law abidance (R)	COCAINE INVOLVEMENT	−.17***
Law abidance	DRUG PROBLEMS	−.07**
Liberalism (R)	Self-acceptance	.05*
Liberalism	Trouble with drugs or alcohol	.16***
Religious commitment (R)	Educational expectations	.06*
Self-acceptance (R)	Trouble with alcohol	−.12***
Self-acceptance	EMOTIONAL DISTRESS	−.28***
Self-acceptance	SOCIAL SUPPORT	.11**
Depression	SOCIAL CONFORMITY	−.43***
Self-derogation (R)	Law abidance	−.09**
Self-derogation (R)	Self-acceptance	−.07*
Self-derogation	Trouble with drugs or alcohol	.09**
Good relationship with parents (R)	Alcohol frequency	.07*
Good relationship with parents	Dealing cocaine	−.09**
Good relationship with adults (R)	Depression	−.07**
Good relationship with peers (R)	Law abidance	−.08*

Note: Latent variables are indicated with capital letters and manifest variables are in lowercase letters.

[a] Significance level determined by a critical ratio of the unstandardized parameter estimate divided by its standard error.

[b] (R) denotes variable residual.

*$p < .05$
**$p < .01$
***$p < .001$

173

The final structural model fits the data quite well ($\chi^2 = 840.80$, df $= 813$, $p = .24$, NFI $= .93$). Associations among the latent factors are graphically displayed in Figure 2, whereas the across-time paths that include at least one observed variable are listed in Table 4 with their standardized regression weight. The relationships presented in Figure 2 and those listed in Table 4 are based on the same final structural model and are presented separately only for reasons of clarity. Two-headed arrows represent correlations, and single-headed arrows reflect causal paths. All effects listed in Table 4 are directional, across-time effects reflecting causal paths. Correlations among residual variables, including between residual pairs of identical measured variables across time, are not presented, since these are not particularly interesting and will not be interpreted. They represent small associations in the model that are necessary to achieve an acceptable fit, but that are not germane to the larger theoretical issues in the model.

Figure 2 represents a rather standard latent variable path model. The measurement error portion is not included, since this remained virtually identical to that presented in Table 2. The effects described in Table 4, on the other hand, represent types of influence that have not been typically reported in the literature. The resulting model is not a standard LISREL model, since LISREL was not designed to permit such effects as those shown in Table 4 (Bentler, 1987; Newcomb & Bentler, 1988a). It is these nonstandard effects, however, that permit us to separate antecedents and consequences of cocaine use from those of polydrug use. This is particularly important since the year 5 cocaine involvement latent factor collapsed with the year 5 general drug use factor, leaving only the measured variables to reflect unique effects for cocaine.

Correlations among factor residuals at years 5 and 9 were in the same direction as the analogous CFA factor correlations but slightly smaller. (These are not presented here.)

Discussion

Summary of empirical findings

The findings captured in our CFA and structural models address several substantive issues in addition to drug use. However, we have focused on the antecedents and consequences of drug and cocaine use.

Results from the CFA models provide correlations among the 17 latent constructs, which are disattenuated for measurement error. As such, these correlations represent the true, or error-free, associations among the constructs. These correlations form the basis upon which the structural model linking latent factors in a causal sequence is built.

In the final CFA model one of the most noteworthy findings was that cocaine involvement and drug use during late adolescence could not be separated empirically; these constructs were perfectly correlated and needed to be combined into one factor. However, it was possible to maintain these separate factors in young adulthood, even though they were moderately to highly correlated. In the final CFA model (Table 2), early adolescent drug use was significantly correlated with less academic orientation and less social conformity at all three time points, more emotional distress (at early adolescence only), more drug use, more cocaine involvement, and more drug problems at the other two time points, and less social support during late adolescence (but not young adulthood). Late adolescent drug use was significantly correlated with less social conformity, more emotional distress, and less social support at years 5 and 9, and with more drug problems during young adulthood.

In the final structural model (Table 4 and Figure 2), the following antecedents or predictors of drug use were found. Drug use in both late adolescence and young adulthood was predicted from earlier drug use and a lack of social conformity. Late adolescent alcohol use was predicted from a lack of earlier social conformity, whereas the number of times super-high on cocaine was predicted from less cheerfulness in year 1. Young adult cocaine involvement was predicted from low law abidance and drug use in late adolescence. Young adult alcohol use was predicted from earlier low law abidance and good relationship with parents. Young adult cocaine frequency was predicted from early adolescent illicit drug use and late adolescent alcohol use. Dealing cocaine in young adulthood was predicted from using cocaine and having poor relationship with parents during late adolescence. Finally, the precursors of drug problems in young adulthood were earlier drug use, lack of social support, and lack of law abidance. Late adolescent low social conformity, low self-acceptance, high frequency of illicit drug use, high liberalism, and high self-derogation generated various types of trouble with drugs and alcohol in young adulthood.

Turning to the consequences of drug use, we found that early adolescent drug use increased later drug use, decreased grade-point average, and decreased self-derogation, all in late adolescence. In regard to specific substances, early adolescent alcohol use reduced social conformity in late adolescence, early adolescent illicit drug use reduced grade-point average in late adolescence, and increased cocaine frequency in young adulthood, whereas early adolescent cocaine use had no direct effects on later variables. Late adolescent drug use increased later drug use, cocaine involvement, and drug problems as young adults. Late adolescent alcohol use decreased social conformity, increased cocaine use, reduced law abidance, and reduced good relationships with parents during young adulthood. Illicit drug use during late adolescence increased self-derogation and increased trouble with drugs in year 9. Finally, the only direct consequence of either of the two late adolescent cocaine variables was an effect of cocaine frequency to increase dealing cocaine as a young adult.

Interpretation of findings

The prevalence rates across the 8-year span of the study revealed that alcohol remained constantly high, illicit drug use increased during adolescence and decreased into young adulthood, and cocaine use increased steadily through adolescence into young adulthood. Some of the changes may reflect historical period effects rather than maturational changes (Bachman et al., 1988), although the present study design did not allow us to choose between these two interpretations. No sex differences in prevalence were noted. These prevalence trends indicate that something different is occurring with cocaine as compared to other illicit drug use. These findings corroborate Kandel's patterns of hazard rates for drug use initiation (Kandel et al., 1985; Kandel & Logan, 1984) and indicate that cocaine is not simply an experimental drug among teenagers, but is increasingly initiated as youngsters advance into young adulthood and perhaps beyond. Thus, the possible limiting effect of experimental drug use for teenagers may not characterize cocaine involvement, which apparently attracts older individuals.

These patterns are in accord with our findings regarding the separability of general drug use from cocaine involvement. In general, cocaine involvement during adolescence could not be separated from polydrug involvement, and there were few distinct antecedents or consequences of cocaine involvement, as distinct from general drug use. However, factors of drug use and cocaine involvement could be kept separate in young adulthood, reflecting the possibility that a cocaine lifestyle may evolve at an older age and does not emerge among teenagers, supporting results from other studies. Nevertheless, these two factors of drug use in young adulthood were not differentially predicted from prior influences.

Despite this general conclusion that cocaine involvement and general drug use are not highly distinguishable, at least during adolescence, several small but intriguing differential effects were found. Only the number of times super-high on cocaine was directly predicted from any of the emotional distress variables; times super-high on cocaine at year 5 was directly predicted from low cheerfulness in year 1. If a lack of cheerfulness can be construed as at least a mild dysphoric mood, this provides some evidence for an effectiveness antecedent of cocaine *abuse*, as reflected in the times super-high on cocaine, and distinct from cocaine *use*, as reflected in the frequency measure. This corroborates and substantially extends other research (Kandel et al., 1985; Newcomb & Bentler, 1986*a*), which did not separate unique aspects of cocaine use from general drug involvement, nor use from abuse. Frequency of cocaine use in young adulthood was uniquely predicted by an 8-year earlier antecedent of illicit drug use, as well as by late adolescent alcohol use. Thus, involvement with illicit drugs (primarily marijuana) at a very early age was a precursor for much later cocaine involvement, as suggested by previous research that examined much shorter time periods (Kandel et al., 1985; Newcomb & Bentler, 1986a). Getting more heavily involved with cocaine as a young adult by selling the drug was uniquely predicted by earlier use of cocaine and by feeling alienated from parents and their socializing influence.

The associations with self-derogation varied with period of time. Year 1 drug use reduced self-derogation during late adolescence, in support of Kaplan's (1986) general theory of deviant adaptations and self-feelings. In contrast, late adolescent illicit drug use increased self-derogation as a young adult. It appears that drug use may enhance self-feelings during the teenage years, perhaps due to involvement in peer cultures favorable to drug use (Kaplan, 1986) or to precocious development characteristic of teenage drug users (Newcomb, 1987; Newcomb & Bentler, 1988a). On the other hand, illicit drug use appears to damage self-feelings as the teenager matures into young adulthood and confronts the expanded role responsibilities of adulthood.

Although the effects for self-derogation differed by age period, such effects were not found for other consequences of drug use; these remained fairly consistent for adolescence and young adulthood. General consequences of drug use included reducing grade-point averages, decreasing social conformity, generating later drug use, and contributing to drug problems.

Finally, there were some similar and different predictors of general drug use versus experiencing problems with drugs. Predictors of general drug use included a lack of social conformity (including its specific indicators) and prior drug use. Although these were also predictors of drug problems (including its various indicators), additional predictors of trouble with drugs or alcohol included negative self-feelings, such as low self-acceptance and high self-derogation, and low social support. Thus, it appears that at least two predictive distinctions between drug use and problematic use of drugs are negative self-feelings and poor social integration. In other words, the distinction between use and abuse of drugs is partially determined by the psychological status of the individual and his or her success at social connectedness, and not entirely by the drug use per se. This conclusion is consistent with other research (Carman, 1979).

In conclusion, we found that cocaine involvement was not distinct from general drug use for teenagers and only modestly separable for young adults, in whom a cocaine lifestyle may be emerging. The only unique outcome from early cocaine use was dealing cocaine later in life. Early psychological distress uniquely increased intense use of cocaine, as well as contributed to having problems with drugs. Thus, overall the theories suggesting specific antecedents and consequences of cocaine use were not generally supported in this community sample. It remains possible that these theories are appropriate in drug treatment patients, who have abused cocaine more seriously.

Acknowledgments

This research was supported by grant DA01070 from the National Institute on Drug Abuse. The assistance of Julie Speckart and Julie Verette is gratefully acknowledged.

References

Abelson, H. I., & Miller, J. D. (1985). A decade of trends in cocaine use in the household population. In N. J. Kozel & E. H. Adams (Eds.), *Cocaine use in America: Epidemiologic and clinical perspectives*. Rockville, MD: National Institute on Drug Abuse.

Adams, E. H., Gfroerer, J. C., Rouse, B. A., & Kozel, N. J. (1986). Trends in prevalence and consequences of cocaine use. *Advances in Alcohol and Substance Abuse, 6*, 49–72.

Bachman, J. G., Johnston, L. D., O'Malley, P. M., & Humphrey, R. H. (1988). Explaining the recent decline in marijuana use: Differentiating the effects of perceived risks, disapproval, and general lifestyle factors. *Journal of Health and Social Behavior, 29*, 92–112.

Bentler, P. M. (1980). Multivariate analysis with latent variables: Causal modeling. *Annual Review of Psychology, 31*, 419–456.

Bentler, P. M. (1983). Some contributions to efficient statistics in structural models: Specification and estimation of moment structures. *Psychometrika, 48*, 493–517.

Bentler, P. M. (1986a). Structural modeling and *Psychometrika*: An historical perspective on growth and achievements. *Psychometrika, 51*, 35–51.

Bentler, P. M. (1986b). *Theory and implementation of EQS: A structural equations program*. Los Angeles: BMDP Statistical Software.

Bentler, P. M. (1986c). *Lagrange multiplier and Wald tests for EQS and EQS/PC*. Los Angeles: BMDP Statistical Software.

Bentler, P. M. (1987). Latent variable structural models for separating specific from general effects. Prepared for Health Services Research Conference: Strengthening Causal Interpretations of Non-experimental Data, Tucson.

Bentler, P. M., & Bonett, D. G. (1980). Significance tests and goodness of fit in the analysis of covariance structures. *Psychological Bulletin, 88*, 588–606.

Bentler, P. M., & Chou, C. P. (1986). *Statistics for parameter expansion and construction in structural models*. Paper presented at the American Educational Research Association meeting, San Francisco.

Bentler, P. M., & Newcomb, M. D. (1978). Longitudinal study of marital success and failure. *Journal of Consulting and Clinical Psychology, 46*, 1053–1070.

Bentler, P. M., & Newcomb, M. D. (1986). Personality, sexual behavior, and drug use revealed through latent variable methods. *Clinical Psychology Review, 6*, 363–385.

Carman, R. S. (1979). Motivations for drug use and problematic outcomes among rural junior high school students. *Addictive Behaviors, 4*, 91–93.

Castro, F. G., Newcomb, M. D., & Bentler, P. M. (1988). Depression and poor health as antecedents and consequences of cocaine use. *Psychology and Health*, 2, 157–186.

Castro, F. G., Newcomb, M. D., & Cadish, K. (1987). Lifestyle differences between young adult cocaine users and their nonuser peers. *Journal of Drug Education, 17*, 89–111.

Clayton, R. R. (1985). Cocaine use in the United States: In a blizzard or just being snowed. In N. J. Kozel & E. H. Adams (Eds.), *Cocaine use in America: Epidemiological and clinical perspectives*. Rockville, MD: National Institute on Drug Abuse.

Donovan, J. E., Jessor, R. & Jessor, L. (1983). Problem drinking in adolescence and young adulthood: A follow-up study. *Journal of Studies on Alcohol, 44*, 109–137.

Estroff, T. W. (1987). Medical and biological consequences of cocaine abuse. In A. M. Washton & M. S. Gold (Eds.), *Cocaine: A clinician's handbook* (pp. 23–32). New York: Guilford.

Gawin, F. H., & Kleber, H. D. (1984). Cocaine abuse treatment: Open pilot trial with desipramine and lithium carbonate. *Archives of General Psychiatry, 41*, 903–909.

Gawin, F. H., & Kleber, H. D. (1985). Cocaine use in a treatment population: Patterns and diagnostic distinctions. In N. J. Kozel & E. H. Adams (Eds.), *Cocaine use in America: Epidemiologic and clinical perspectives*. Rockville, MD: National Institute on Drug Abuse.

Glick, P. L., & Lin, S. (1986) More young adults are living with their parents: Who are they? *Journal of Marriage and the Family, 48*, 107–112.

Gold, M. S., Galanter, M., & Stimmel, B. (1986). Cocaine: A new epidemic. *Advances in Alcohol and Substance Abuse, 6*, 1–6.

Gold, M. S., Washton, A. M., & Dakis, C. A. (1985). Cocaine abuse: Neurochemistry, phenomenology, and treatment. In N. J. Kozel & E. H. Adams (Eds.), *Cocaine use in America: Epidemiologic and clinical perspectives*. Rockville, MD: National Institute on Drug Abuse.

Gottheil, E. (1986). Cocaine abuse and dependence: The scope of the problem. *Advances in Alcohol and Substance Abuse, 6*, 23–30.

Harlow, L. L. (1985). *Behavior of some elliptical theory estimators with nonnormal data in a covariance structures framework: A Monte Carlo study*. Doctoral dissertation, UCLA.

Johnston, L. D., O'Melley, P. M., & Bachman J. G. (1987). *National trends in drug use and related factors among American high school students and young adults, 1975–1986.* Rockville, MD: National Institute on Drug Abuse.

Jöreskog, K. G. (1977). Structural equation models in the social sciences: Specification, estimation, and testing. In P. R. Krishnaiah (Ed.), *Application of statistics* (pp. 265–287). Amsterdam: North-Holland.

Kandel, D. B. (1984). Marijuana users in young adulthood. *Archives of General Psychiatry, 41*, 200–209.

Kandel, D. B., Davies, M., Karus, D., & Yamaguchi, K. (1986). The consequences in young adulthood of adolescent drug involvement: An overview. *Archives of General Psychiatry, 43*, 746–754.

Kandel, D. B., & Logan, J. A. (1984). Periods of risk for initiation, stabilization, and decline in drug use from adolescence to early adulthood. *American Journal of Public Health, 74*, 660–666.

Kandel, D. B., Murphy, D., & Karus, D. (1985). Cocaine use in young adulthood:

Patterns of use and psychosocial correlates. In N. J. Kozel & E. H. Adams (Eds.), *Cocaine use in America: Epidemiologic and clinical perspectives.* Rockville, MD: National Institute on Drug Abuse.

Kaplan, H. B. (1975). Increase in self-rejection as an antecedent of deviant responses. *Journal of Youth and Adolescence, 4,* 438–458.

Kaplan, H. B. (1986). *Social psychology and self-referent behavior.* New York: Plenum.

Khantzian, E. J. (1987). Psychiatric and psychodynamic factors in cocaine dependence. In A. M. Washton & M. S. Gold (Eds.), *Cocaine: A clinician's handbook* (pp. 229–240). New York: Guilford.

Khantzian, E. J., & Khantzian, N. J. (1984). Cocaine addiction: Is there a psychological predisposition? *Psychiatric Annals, 14,* 753–759.

MacCallum, R. (1986). Specification searches in covariance structure analyses. *Psychological Bulletin, 100,* 107–120.

Miller, J. D., Cisin, I. H., Gardener-Keaton, H., Harrell, A. V., Wirtz, P. W., Abelson, H. I., & Fishburne, P. M. (1983). *National survey on drug abuse: main findings 1982.* Rockville, MD: National Institute on Drug Abuse.

Mills, C. J., & Noyes, H. L. (1984). Patterns and correlates of initial and subsequent drug use among adolescents. *Journal of Consulting and Clinical Psychology, 52,* 231–243.

Mooijaart, A., & Bentler, P. M. (1986). Robustness of normal theory statistics in Structural equation models. (MS.)

Newcomb, M. D. (1986). Nuclear attitudes and reactions: Associations with depression, drug use, and quality of life. *Journal of Personality and Social Psychology, 50,* 906–920.

Newcomb, M. D. (1987). Consequences of teenage drug use: The transition from adolescence to young adulthood. *Drugs and Society, 4(1),* 25–60.

Newcomb, M. D. (1988). *Drug use in the workplace: Risk factors for disruptive substance use among young adults.* Dover, MA: Auburn House.

Newcomb, M. D., & Bentler, P. M. (1986a). Cocaine use among young adults. *Advances in Alcohol and Substance Abuse, 6,* 73–96.

Newcomb, M. D., & Bentler, P. M. (1986b). Cocaine use among adolescents: Longitudinal associations with social context, psychopathology, and use of other substances. *Addictive Behaviors, 11,* 263–273.

Newcomb, M. D., & Bentler, P. M. (1986c). Drug use, educational aspirations, and work force involvement: The transition from adolescence to young adulthood. *American Journal of Community Psychology, 14,* 303–321.

Newcomb, M. D., & Bentler, P. M. (1986d). Loneliness and social support: A confirmatory hierarchical analysis. *Personality and Social Psychology Bulletin, 12,* 520–535.

Newcomb, M. D., & Bentler, P. M. (1987). Changes in drug use from high school to young adulthood: Effects of living arrangement and current life pursuit. *Journal of Applied Developmental Psychology, 8,* 221–246.

Newcomb, M. D., & Bentler, P. M. (1988a). *Consequences of adolescent drug use: Impact on the lives of young adults.* Beverly Hills, CA: Sage.

Newcomb, M. D., & Bentler, P. M. (1988b). Impact of adolescent drug use and social support on problems of young adults: A longitudinal study. *Journal of Abnormal Psychology, 97,* 64–75.

Newcomb, M. D., Bentler, P. M., & Fahy, B. (1987). Cocaine use and psychopathology: Associations among young adults. *International Journal of the Addictions, 22,* 1167–1188.

Newcomb, M. D., Fahy, B., & Skager, R. (1988). Correlates of cocaine use among adolescents. *Journal of Drug Issues, 18*, 327–354.

Newcomb, M. D., Huba, G. J., & Bentler, P. M. (1981). A multidimensional assessment of stressful life events among adolescents: Derivation and correlates. *Journal of Health and Social Behavior, 22*, 400–415.

Newcomb, M. D., Huba, G. J., & Bentler, P. M. (1986). Life change events among adolescents: An empirical consideration of some methodological issues. *Journal of Nervous and Mental Disease, 174*, 280–289.

O'Malley, P. M., Johnston, L. D., & Bachman, J. G. (1985). Cocaine use among American adolescents and young adults. In N. J. Kozel & E. H. Adams (Eds.), *Cocaine use in America: Epidemiologic and clinical perspectives*. Rockville, MD: National Institute on Drug Abuse.

Sadava, S. W. (1987). Interactional theories. In H. T. Blane & K. E. Leonard (Eds.), *Psychological theories of drinking and alcoholism*. New York: Guilford Publications.

Sarason, I. G., & Sarason, B. R. (1985). *Social support: Theory, research, and applications*. The Hague, The Netherlands: Martinus Nijhoff.

Stein, J. A., Newcomb, M. D., & Bentler, P. M. (1986). Stability and change in personality: A longitudinal study from early adolescence to young adulthood. *Journal of Research in Personality, 20*, 276–291.

Stein J. A., Newcomb, M. D., & Bentler, P. M. (1987). An eight-year study of multiple influences on drug use and drug use consequences. *Journal of Personality and Social Psychology, 53*, 1094–1105.

Washton, A. M., & Gold, M. S. (1987). Recent trends in cocaine abuse as seen from the "800 COCAINE" hotline. In A. M. Washton & M. S. Gold (Eds.), *Cocaine: A clinician's handbook* (pp. 10–22). New York: Guilford.

Wetli, C. V. (1987). Fatal reactions to cocaine. In A. M. Washton & M. S. Gold (Eds.), *Cocaine: A clinician's handbook* (pp. 33–54). New York: Guilford.

10 Conduct problems as predictors of substance abuse

LEE N. ROBINS AND LAWRENCE McEVOY

The association between behavior problems of childhood and substance use is well established. Studies of adolescent drug users (Johnston et al., 1978; Jessor & Jessor, 1977; Kandel et al., 1978; Robins et al., 1978) have found that they have an excess of early sexual behavior, poor school performance, low aspirations for academic achievement, nonconformity with parents' rules, and often associations with other youngsters who are similarly deviant. While use of psychoactive substances in childhood is not listed among the symptoms of conduct disorder in the official diagnostic nomenclature of the American Psychiatric Association, DSM-IIIR (1987), it is recognized as an "associated feature," so that its presence should serve to raise the clinician's level of suspicion that the diagnosis is present, without directly contributing to the diagnosis. According to DSM-IIIR, among children with conduct disorder, "regular use of tobacco, liquor, or nonprescribed drugs and sexual behavior that [begin] unusually early for the child's peer group in his or her milieu are common."

To be "unusually early for his or her milieu," substance use would clearly have to occur by early adolescence in the United States because almost all young people have had some exposure to psychoactive substances by age 18. Over 90% have had an alcoholic drink, two thirds have smoked tobacco, and more than half have tried marijuana (Johnston et al., 1987). Smoking typically begins around age 13 or 14 (7th or 8th grade), and use of alcohol and drugs at about age 15 or 16 (9th or 10th grade).

While substance *use* appears in the Associated Features for Conduct Disorder, substance *abuse*, defined as social, psychological, or physiological symptoms resulting from the use of psychoactive substances, does not. This would seem a reasonable omission, because the development of substance abuse problems usually requires a number of years of use, by which time the youngster is past the age at which he is likely to be given a conduct disorder diagnosis (although DSM-IIIR allows the diagnosis in adults so long as it had its onset in childhood). However, occasionally problems with substances do begin in childhood or adolescence, and this fact is noted and related to conduct problems in the "Age of Onset" section of the text on Psychoactive Substance Use disorders, as follows:

182

Alcohol Abuse and Dependence usually appear in the 20s, 30s, and 40s. Dependence on amphetamine or similarly acting sympathomimetics, cannabis, cocaine, hallucinogens, nicotine, opioids, and phenylcyclidine (PCP) or similarly acting arylcyclohexylamines more commonly begin[s] in the late teens or twenties. When a psychoactive substance abuse disorder begins in early adolescence, it is often associated with conduct disorder and failure to complete school.

Although neither statement specifically claims that conduct disorder determines more than the timing of drug use or drug abuse, there are 3 hypotheses about a possible causal role for conduct disorder, all of which are consistent with these two observations from DSM-IIIR.

1. Conduct disorder could lead to more substance users and thereby increase the proportion of the population at risk of developing substance abuse.
2. Conduct disorder could lead to earlier use than would otherwise occur, and early use itself might increase the risk of developing substance abuse.
3. Conduct disorder might increase the risk that use will progress into abuse, whether onset begins early or late.

Exploring these three hypotheses, which are not mutually exclusive, is the goal of this chapter. Additional goals, assuming that conduct disorder is found to be a plausible contributor to the rate of substance abuse, will be to ask whether the proper definition of the causal variable is conduct disorder, considered as a diagnostic syndrome, or whether only certain of the symptoms used to make the diagnosis account for its relationship with substance use. If the syndrome as a whole is predictive, we will ask whether the standard categorical definition of conduct disorder best explains its predictive power or whether a dimensional definition would be more useful. Finally, we will ask what conduct disorder can tell us about the repeated finding that women have less substance abuse than men. Do women have a special immunity to substance abuse beyond that provided by a lower frequency and severity of conduct disorder?

The ECA Project

The Epidemiological Catchment Area (ECA) study, conducted in five U.S. sites in 1979–1985 provided data for our study. It sampled 20,000 members of the adult population age 18 or older residing both in households and in institutions. Respondents were interviewed three times over a 1-year period, with the middle interview consisting of a very limited number of questions.

Method

Because the purpose of the study was to ascertain the prevalence of major *adult* mental disorders over the lifetime, conduct disorder was not a target diagnosis. However, antisocial personality was one of the target diagnoses, and to make that diagnosis, it was necessary to learn whether at least three childhood conduct problems had occurred before age 15. Respondents were therefore asked about each of 10 childhood behaviors, and if a behavior had occurred, they were asked the age at which it first occurred. The behaviors asked about do not cover all of the items listed as symptoms of conduct disorder in DSM-IIIR. Omitted is information about forced entry into buildings, weapon use, cruelty to animals and people, and forcing sex on others. Three items are covered that are not mentioned as symptoms of conduct disorder in DSM-IIIR: school discipline problems, school expulsion, and arrests. DSM-IIIR items covered by our interview include lying, stealing, running away from home, fighting, truancy, and vandalism, although with respect to vandalism we do not make the distinction between firesetting and other destructive acts as DSM-IIIR does. Thus, although there is considerable overlap between conduct problems covered and the symptoms in the official nomenclature for conduct disorder, there is not a perfect correspondence.

Among the childhood behaviors contributing to the diagnosis of antisocial personality is psychoactive substance use (alcohol or drugs) before age 15. Early substance use, as noted above, is not a symptom of conduct disorder in DSM-IIIR but only an "Associated Feature." In this chapter we will not count it as a conduct problem, but instead explore age of first use of substances as a possible consequence of conduct problems and as an independent predictor of substance abuse. We will date first substance use as the earlier of two ages, the age at first using an illicit drug and age first drunk. We asked for age first drunk rather than age at first drink, because it is difficult to distinguish first self-initiated drink from sips of wine at family dinners or tastes of parents' drinks. We felt safe in assuming that getting drunk was usually self-initiated. In any case, the decision probably made little difference in the results, since Johnston et al. (1987) found that both first drink and first time drunk typically occurred in 9th or 10th grade.

Information about conduct problems and initiation of substance use before age 15 was taken only from the first interview, since the subjects were all past the age of risk for these events. Problems as a result of substance use (i.e., substance abuse) reported in either the first or third interview were counted. The problems include psychological and physical dependence, social problems, withdrawal symptoms, medical problems, and emotional or mental health problems. Problems resulting from the use of each of seven categories of substances were ascertained: alcohol; cannabis; cocaine;

amphetamines; barbiturates, other sedatives, and minor tranquilizers; hallucinogens; and heroin or other opiates.

Information about childhood problems, substance use, and substance-related problems were all ascertained retrospectively. Despite our concern about the ability to recall whether these events had occurred, and particularly the ages at which they occurred, we were pleased to note that the order in which substances were first used in adolescence and the relative frequency of specific conduct problems were highly consonant with results from previous surveys in which adolescents were recalling much more recent events. We believe, therefore, that adults are able and willing to report reasonably accurately on behaviors in childhood and adolescence.

Results were reported for the sample weighted to compensate for design effects (e.g., interviewing only one person per household regardless of number in the household, and oversampling institutional residents in all five sites, the elderly in three sites, and blacks in one site), nonresponse, and differences between the demographic characteristics of the sampled areas and the United States as a whole. As a result, our report is our best estimate of the relationships between conduct problems and substance abuse in the United States.

Rather than report statistical significance of differences, which is of trivial interest in a sample so large that a difference of even 1% or 2% can be statistically significant, we report relative risks and population-attributable risks as estimates of more interest for predicting the future of patients or for planning preventive programs.

The sample

In previous analyses of these data, we found that the number of persons who had never used alcohol was small in all age and sex groups, but that there was a more sizeable minority of teetotalers in North Carolina than in the other ECA samples (Helzer & Burnham, in press). Illicit drug use was generally limited to those born after 1945; that would be those under age 25 in 1969, when illicit drug use moved from special inner city populations of the United States into the general population (Robins et al., 1986). We also found, as have many others, that males have more use of illicit drugs than females and that males exceed females in both alcohol and drug dependence. We compared the sample members who reported ever having used an illicit drug to the total sample, weighted to the national population's demographic characteristics with respect to age, sex, and location (Table 1).

Drug users were overrepresented in the Los Angeles sample and underrepresented in the Durham, North Carolina, sample. Durham's lower rate is probably explained by its high rate of abstainers from alcohol, a substance that has been called the "gateway" to illicit drugs.

Table 1. *The sample*

	Base sample (%)	Drug-using sample (%)
Number	19,873	5,611
Weighted to the nation		
Conduct problems before 15		
0–1	68	41
2–3	21	33
4–6	9	21
7–9	2	5
Age		
Under 30	31	61
Over 35	58	22
Males	48	56
Weighted to local populations		
Residence		
New Haven	24	23
Baltimore	22	21
St. Louis	14	14
Durham	19	16
Los Angeles	21	26
	100	100

Drug users were young (61% were under age 30 when interviewed and only 22% were over 35) and predominantly male (56%). In contrast, the total sample had an average age of 40 and contained slightly more women than men, reflecting their longer life expectancy.

Drug users more often had a history of conduct disorder than did the sample as a whole. If we define conduct disorder as having had 4 or more conduct problems before age 15, only 11% of the total population had conduct disorder, as compared with 26% of the drug users. As Figure 1 shows, the higher rate of conduct problems among males than females explains the predominance of males among drug users; when number of conduct problems is held constant, as many women as men have used drugs. Figure 1 also clearly shows the association between youth and drug experience.

The high rate of conduct problems in those who had ever used illicit drugs supports our first hypothesis. One way in which conduct problems increase the risk of substance abuse is by increasing the number exposed to illicit drugs over their lifetimes. It is not just that those with conduct problems use drugs earlier than they otherwise would.

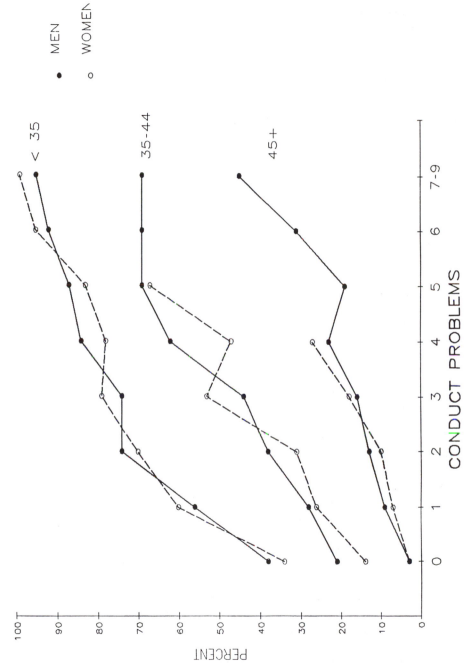

Figure 1. Drug use by age and conduct problems (for categories containing at least 20 respondents).

187

Conduct disorder as a predictor of drug abuse by users

We now investigate the hypotheses that conduct disorder increases the risk of substance abuse among users either by reducing the age of first exposure or by other mechanisms. To investigate these issues, we will restrict the sample to users of illicit drugs. By doing so, we ensure that our sample has been exposed to both alcohol and illicit drugs, because all illicit drug users have drunk alcohol. Limiting the sample to drug users leaves us with a sample of 5,611 persons, who constitute a weighted 33% of the total sample. As already noted, this is a young, predominantly male sample.

Measurement of substance abuse

To decide how best to reduce the description of problems with various substances to a single measure of substance abuse, we categorized responses to questions about problems with each substance two ways: as positive diagnoses according to DSM-III criteria and as the presence of any symptom. We then did factor analyses and Guttman scale analyses, comparing results for these two definitions of abuse with substances in seven versus four categories (alcohol, cannabinoids, "pills" [sedatives, amphetamines, and hallucinogens], and "hard drugs" [cocaine and opiates]). The progression from alcohol to cannabinoids to other drugs has been reported in many other studies (Kandel et al., 1978; Brunswick, 1979; O'Donnell et al., 1976). The progression from pills to hard drugs is less well established, but worked well in the current study.

Analyses were done for each of the five sample sites independently, with weighted and unweighted data. The option of using four drug categories rather than seven and of counting a category as positive when a problem occurred attributable to any drug in that category (rather than requiring that full diagnostic criteria be met) gave a single-factor solution in every site, with high factor loadings that were almost identical whether we used weighted or unweighted data. This option also produced a Guttman scale in each site, with the categories ranked from low to high as expected from previous studies: alcohol, cannabinoids, pills, and hard drugs, with coefficients of reproducibility all above .92 and coefficients of scalability all above .62.

In order to choose whether to use this four-category, any-problem option as a Guttman scale (a score of 0 to 4 is based on the highest level of substance with which a problem occurred) or as a simple count of the number of categories out of four in which a problem had been experienced, we correlated these two options with a number of outcomes we expected to find associated with substance abuse (e.g., job problems, arrest, illegal occupations, marital problems). Both were highly correlated with each of these outcomes, but the count of categories with at least one problem had slightly stronger correlations with these outcomes than did the Guttman scale.

Table 2. *Substance abuse problems among users of illicit substances*

No. of categories with problems	All drug users		Substances that caused problems	
	%	No. of users with this no. of problems	Substance	%
None	36	1744	None	100[a]
One	35	1761	Alcohol	69[a]
			Marijuana	27
			Pills	4
				100
Two	18	972	Alcohol & marijuana	70[a]
			Alcohol & pills	15
			Marijuana & pills	13
			Marijuana & hard drugs	1
			Alcohol & hard drugs	1
				100
Three	8	451	Alcohol, marijuana, pills	90[a]
			Marijuana, pills, hard drugs	4
			Alcohol, marijuana, hard drugs	3
			Alcohol, pills, hard drugs	3
				100
Four	3	260	All four	100[a]
	100	5188		

[a] These categories fit the Guttman scale. They sum up to 83% of all users: $(100\% \times 36\%) + (69\% \times 35\%) + (70\% \times 18\%) + (90\% \times 8\%) + (100\% \times 3\%) = 83\%$.

Therefore, in the current report, we measured substance abuse by the number of substance categories (out of four) in which at least one problem occurred.

The similarity of our count of categories with problems to a Guttman scale is shown in Table 2. When problems were caused by only one substance, that substance was alcohol (as predicted by the Guttman scale) in 69% of cases. When there were problems with two substances, they were the predicted alcohol and cannabinoid in 70% of cases. When there were problems with three substances, they were the predicted alcohol, cannabinoid, and pills in 90% of cases. The five "ideal types" that correspond to the Guttman scale accounted for 83% of all users of illicit drugs.

Table 3. *Demographics of substance abuse problems among drugs users (Rows add to 100%)*

	Number of drug categories with problems		
	None (%)	One or Two (%)	Three or Four (%)
Total	36	35	11
Sex			
Men	24	61	14
Women	52	41	7
Age			
18–29	36	52	12
30–34	38	51	11
35 +	35	57	8
Ethnic group			
Black	39	55	6
Hispanic	35	56	9
White	36	53	11

Among illicit drug users, 64% developed at least one drug problem. Most of those with a problem (55%) had only one, and this was usually with alcohol. Only 11% had problems in three or four drug categories, logically implying that they have a problem with some drug other than marijuana. Since it is drugs other than marijuana that appear to have the most serious long-term effects, we were particularly interested in predictors of problems with three or four categories of substances.

Demographic predictors of abuse

Male drug users were twice as likely as female users to develop a problem, and twice as likely to have problems in three or four substance categories (Table 3). There was little difference by ethnic group among those with some substance abuse problem, but white drug users were more likely than other users to have problems with three or four substances (11% vs. 6% for blacks). Age groups differed little in the proportions of those who had experienced *any* problem with substances, but the oldest group of drug users had the fewest members with problems in three or four substances.

When we look at age and sex effects simultaneously (Table 4), we find sex differences much more striking than age differences. The oldest male group (i.e., males with the lowest rate) exceeds the youngest female group (i.e., females with the highest rate) both in number who ever had a substance abuse problem and the number who had problems with three or four categories of drugs.

Table 4. *Sex and age as predictors of substance abuse problems among users*

Categories of substance abuse	Men			Women		
	18–29 (%)	30–34 (%)	35+ (%)	18–29 (%)	30–34 (%)	35+ (%)
Number of users	1,733	613	608	1,395	480	342
None	23	27	26	51	53	55
One or two	61	57	65	42	41	40
Three or four	16	16	9	7	6	5
	100	100	100	100	100	100

Table 5. *Individual conduct problems before age 15 as predictors of problems with three or four substances*

Conduct problem	Users with this problem (%)	Relative risk if problem present	Population attributable risk (%)
Stealing	37	3.6	49
Truancy	59	2.3	44
Expulsion, suspension	29	3.6	43
Fighting	31	3.0	39
School discipline problem	21	3.3	32
Lying	22	2.5	25
Arrest	14	3.1	23
Vandalism	14	3.0	22
Running away	15	2.7	21

Conduct problems: Syndrome or individual predictors?

Of the 9 conduct problems before age 15 about which we had information, the most common was truancy, occurring in three fifths of these drug users (Table 5). Next most common was stealing, reported by more than one third (37%). Only one in seven had been arrested, run away from home, or committed acts of vandalism before age 15.

To learn whether specific behaviors could predict which users would develop substance abuse, we compared their relative risks for predicting problems in three or four categories. (The *relative risk* is calculated by dividing the proportion with problems in three or four categories when the conduct problem was present by the proportion with problems in three or four categories when the conduct problem was absent.) Stealing and expulsion from school tied for first place, with a relative risk of 3.6. But every one of the conduct problems had a relative risk above 2, a common cut-off point for labeling a factor as important. This narrow range means that no particular behavior among drug users can be identified as much more predictive of substance abuse than any other.

Relative risks associated with particular behaviors could be used by a clinician as a basis for predicting whether a youngster who has used drugs is at high risk of becoming a substance abuser. But relative risks are not very useful as a basis for selecting drug users from the general population for enrollment in treatment or prevention programs. The success of such programs depends not only on whether the future course of substance abuse can be altered for the individuals selected, but also on whether the individuals who have been selected account for a high enough proportion of all probable future users so that changing their risk profile would make a major contribution to reducing the substance-abusing population. To select the proper set of individuals, it is necessary to know not only which predictors have the highest relative risks, but also how common each of these risk factors is. Changing the prospects of substance abuse only for youngsters with very rare risk factors, even if they would otherwise surely become abusers, would have little impact on the number of substance abusers in the population. A measure of risk popular with epidemiologists because it combines information about strength of the risk factor with information about its frequency is "population attributable risk" ot PAR (Last, 1983):

$$\frac{p(RR-1)}{1+p(RR-1)}$$

The numerator is prevalence of the risk factor in the population times the relative risk minus one. The denominator is 1 plus the numerator.

We find that our nine conduct problems vary more in their PARs than in their relative risks, although even for the PAR, the ratio of the largest to the smallest is only slightly greater than 2 (49%:21%). Stealing has the highest PAR because it both has a high relative risk and is a common behavior problem. By identifying those who have stolen among our drug-experienced youngsters, we identified half of all who would develop serious substance abuse (according to our definition of problems in at least three categories of substances). Assuming we knew how to modify their risks, we would have to work with one third of all drug-using children to achieve this result.

Truancy has the next highest PAR because, although it has the lowest

Table 6. *Individual conduct problems and substance abuse problems before age 15*

| No. of conduct problems | N | Substance categories with problems | | | |
		None (%)	1–2 (%)	3–4 (%)	Total (%)
None	891	62	35	2	100
One	1015	48	49	3	100
Two	932	34	58	8	100
Three	707	27	60	13	100
Four	519	20	65	15	100
Five	426	18	61	21	100
Six	311	12	59	29	100
Seven	191	3	53	44	100
Eight	134	3	41	56	100
Nine	49	0	46	54	100

Table 7. *Conduct problem cut-points to predict substance abuse*

Conduct problem cut-points	Proportion of drug users who would qualify (%)	Relative risk of abuse of three or four substances	Population attributable risk (%)
1+	81	5.9	80
2+	59	7.5	80
3+	40	5.2	63
4+	26	4.4	47
5+	17	4.6	38
6+	10	4.9	28
7+	5	5.5	18
8+	2	5.6	10
9	1	5.0	3

relative risk among our conduct problems, it is by far the most common of them. But if we were to use truancy as the indicator of risk, we would have to work with almost three fifths of all drug-using children to prevent less than half of the future substance abuse. The rare behaviors, arrest, vandalism, and running away, would each require working with only one seventh of all children, but at best would prevent less than one fourth of all substance abuse.

If instead of looking at individual conduct problems, we count the number present, we get a very different result (Table 6). Now we get a 27-fold difference between those who have eight or nine types of conduct problems and those who have none (55%:2%). And the risk of substance abuse rises regularly with each increase in conduct problems up to eight, indicating that for predicting substance abuse, conduct problems function well as a dimensional predictor.

When we calculate relative risks and PARs for number of conduct problems, we compare substance abuse rates in those with at least a given number of conduct problems with rates in those with fewer conduct problems (Table 7). Every possible cut-point has a higher relative risk than any individual behavior problem in Table 5, and cut-points of 1, 2, or 3 have higher population attributable risks than any of the individual problems.

Choosing a cut-point requires making a compromise between the PAR, which measures the maximum possible social benefits of the intervention (assuming it was completely successful), and the cost of the intervention, as measured by the proportion of the population that would have to receive the intervention. Clearly we would not use a cut-point of one, because the PAR (benefit) is just as high with a cut-point of two, while the proportion of the population receiving the intervention drops from 81% to 59%. Nor would we be likely to choose a cut-point of 9, because the cut-point of 8 provides more than three times the benefit at only twice the cost. Between cut-points 2 and 8, the choice would be made depending on available resources and on how expensive the available interventions were believed to be.

Using a count of conduct problems is much preferable to using individual behavioral items. A cut-point of 4, for example, would identify about as many future substance abusers as would stealing (47% vs. 49%), but would require intervening with considerably fewer drug-using youngsters (26% vs. 37%). A cut-point of 5 would identify as many prospective substance abusers as would fighting, but would require intervening with only 17% of all drug-using youngsters instead of 31%. Clearly the number of behaviors is a more efficient predictor than type of conduct problems, and our future analyses will use only number.

It is of practical utility to treat the count as a dimension rather than as a categorical value, because that allows varying the cut-point with the costs and benefits of intervention. A categorical definition of conduct disorder (e.g., three or more of the listed behaviors) does not encourage this flexibility. But this advantage inheres in dimensionality only if there is no clear diagnostic threshold. If there were such a threshold, the relative risk would decline as the cut-point moved above it, making the PAR drop more precipitously with increasingly restrictive cut-points than it does in Table 7. The steadiness of the relative risk above a cut-point of 2 or more shows that there is no other diagnostic threshold for conduct problems. Thus, we conclude that for predicting substance abuse, conduct disorder can be treated as a dimensional variable within the range of 2 or more to 8 or more conduct problems, allowing cut-points to be selected for intervention on the

Table 8. *Conduct problems and age of first substance use*

No. of conduct problems	Mean ages		
	First drunk	First drug use	First of either
None	17.6	21.3	17.5
One	16.3	19.8	16.1
Two	15.8	18.9	15.7
Three	15.6	18.5	15.4
Four	14.7	17.8	14.4
Five	14.3	17.6	14.1
Six	14.1	16.3	13.8
Seven	12.8	16.5	12.6
Eight	12.9	16.1	12.6
Nine	12.0	14.5	12.1

basis of resources and the expected cost-benefit ratio of the selected intervention.

Age of first substance use

Having found that conduct disorder does predict substance abuse among drug users, and therefore its impact is not limited to increasing the number of users, we next want to test the hypothesis that its effect can be explained by its causing precocious use of psychoactive substances. For precocious use to be such a mechanism, conduct problems would have to predict age of first substance use, age of first substance use would have to predict substance abuse, and the effect of age of first use would have to persist when the number of conduct problems was held constant.

We found a striking relationship between number of conduct problems and early use of both drugs and alcohol (Table 8). There is more than a 5-year difference in average age at first substance use between those with no conduct problems (a mean age of 17.5 years) and those with nine or more conduct problems (a mean age of 12.1 years). The predictions of age at first drunkenness and age at first use of an illicit drug are equally strong. (It is noteworthy that at every level of conduct problems, first drunkenness precedes first use of illicit drugs by more than 2 years, showing the sturdiness of the alcohol-use-prior-to-drug-use sequence.)

Both early drunkenness and early use of illicit drug predict that drug users will progress to substance abuse (Table 9). No respondent who delayed getting drunk until age 25 (or never did) had problems in three or four categories, and two thirds had no substance abuse problems at all; only 3% of those who delayed illicit drug use beyond age 25 had problems with three

Table 9. *Ages of onset and number of categories of substance abuse problems (percentage)*

| | Age at first: | | | | | | | |
| | Drug use | | | | Drunkenness | | | |
	<15	15–19	20–24	25+	<15	15–19	20–24	25+
No problem	13	35	45	46	16	40	55	66
One or two categories	60	53	50	51	64	51	42	34
Three or four categories	27	12	5	3	20	9	3	0
	100	100	100	100	100	100	100	100

or four categories of substances, and half had no substance abuse problems at all. In contrast, one out of five of those who were first drunk before age 15 and one out of four of those who first used a drug this young ended up with problems in three or four categories, and less than one out of six escaped problems altogether.

It seems plausible, then, that conduct problems might influence later substance abuse by influencing the age at which substance use begins. The final step is to see whether age of first use continues to have a strong effect when the number of conduct problems is held constant. We find that age of onset has little or no effect if there are no conduct problems (Figure 2). Abuse is extremely rare for those free of conduct problems, no matter how early substance use began. At every other level of conduct problems, however, the earlier that use begins, the greater is the likelihood of substance abuse. Thus, it is plausible that one way in which conduct problems influences substance abuse is by lowering the age of introduction to psychoactive substances.

If this were the only mechanism through which conduct problems affected the substance abuse of users, then the relationship between conduct disorder and substance abuse would disappear when age of first use is controlled. This occurred only when substances were first used at age 20 or later. For those first using substances before age 20, the number of conduct problems was an even better predictor of substance abuse than was age of onset (before or after age 15). Among those beginning substance use before age 15 with seven or more conduct problems, more than half developed serious substance abuse; with only one conduct problem, only 5% did so, despite the early exposure. When first use occurred between ages 15 and 19, there is still a large effect from number of conduct problems, but the control for age of first use somewhat reduced their impact.

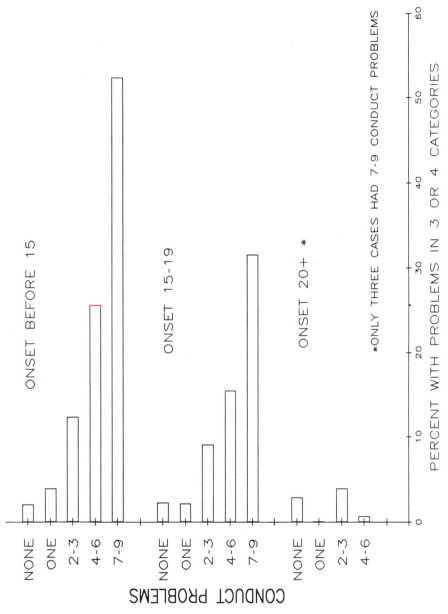

Figure 2. Conduct disorder and substance abuse in relation to age at first substance use.

The results show an interaction between conduct disorder and age of first use. Clearly in this general population of drug users, substance abuse virtually required both having at least some early behavior problems and beginning use of substances before age 20. For those first using substances earlier than that and having at least some conduct problems, the number of conduct problems did affect chances of developing substance abuse by being negatively correlated with the age of beginning use. Children with multiple conduct problems became substance abusers in part because they first used psychoactive substances before the age at which it is common "for the child's peer group in his or her milieu," but that is not the only way in which multiple conduct problems predicted substance abuse. They also predicted which earlier users would develop serious substance abuse.

These results convey an important message: Any delay in the introduction to alcohol or drugs appears to reduce the risk of severe substance abuse problems, even among youngsters whose high level of conduct problems makes them especially susceptible to developing substance abuse. But a second message is that, unless delay is past adolescence, youngsters with conduct disorder who use drugs will still have an elevated level of risk. We do not know what the mechanism is that links their level of conduct problems to susceptibility to substance abuse. In the absence of such understanding, preventive efforts will have to be limited to reducing use of substances, or at least attempting to postpone their use, and trying to reduce levels of conduct disorder by interventions early in childhood.

Sex differences

Our final concern has to do with the sex of the user. As noted earlier (Table 4), drug using women were much less likely than men to develop substance-related problems. Do women have some special immunity to substance-related problems, or do they have fewer of the predictors we have already identified? In an early study (Robins et al., 1962) we found that women's apparent immunity to alcoholism was explained only by the fact that few women drink heavily; among heavy drinkers, women's rate of alcoholism was equal to men's. This finding has been confirmed by others (Reich et al., 1975; Cloninger et al., 1978). We might expect then, that women drug users have fewer conduct problems than men and begin substance use later, and that if we were to control on these two predictors, their advantage would disappear.

When we look at users of drugs (Table 10), we find that women do, in fact, have fewer conduct problems than men (an average of 1.8 out of 9 before age 15 vs. 2.9 for men), and they do begin substance use later, first getting drunk about a year and a half later than males (at an average age of 16.6) and beginning their illicit drug use about a quarter of a year later than males (at age 19.2).

Table 10. *Sex differences in conduct problems and age at first substance use among users of illicit drugs*

	Men	Women
Mean number of conduct problems before 15 (of 9)	2.9	1.8
Mean age first drunk	15.1	16.6
Mean age first illicit drug use	18.9	19.2

When we look at sex differences, controlling both on age of first substance use and number of conduct problems (Figure 3), we find that women, like men, require both conduct problems and first use of substances before age 20 in order to develop later substance abuse, and that delaying first use past age 15 does reduce risk, but that conduct problems are powerful predictors within age of first use groups. Among those who began substance use at the "normal" time—between ages 15 and 18—males continue to have a somewhat higher risk of substance abuse than females, even when controlling on conduct problems, although differences are much less than in the total sample of users. However, among those who begin substance use before age 15, females develop substance abuse as frequently or more frequently than males with the same level of conduct problems. These results might be explained by the fact that early use of substances is even more deviant for girls than for boys, since the normal age of beginning is a bit later for girls.

We found little difference between the nature of predictors of substance abuse for male and female drug users, and that the striking difference in their rates of substance abuse seems to depend on the fact that males have much more conduct disorder than females and tend to begin substance use younger. To compare the two sexes with respect to these two predictors of substance abuse more systematically, we can use receiver operating characteristic (ROC) curves (Erdreich & Lee, 1981; Hanley & McNeil, 1982). These curves use all possible cut-off points for number of conduct problems and age of first drug use for males and females. If conduct problems or age of first drug use was not at all predictive of substance abuse, its curve would lie on the diagonal of the square. The variable's power of prediction is measured by the difference between the one half of the square that lies to the right of the diagonal and the area of the square lying to the right of the ROC curves.

For both men and women who have used drugs, conduct problems are a better predictor of later substance abuse than is age at which substance use began. (Compare areas below the curve in the top and bottom charts in Figure 4.) And conduct problems are equally predictive for men and women, although the best cut-off point is lower for women than men (3 conduct problems vs. 4 for men; the cut-off point nearest the upper left corner is the best one). Age of first substance use is a better predictor for women than for

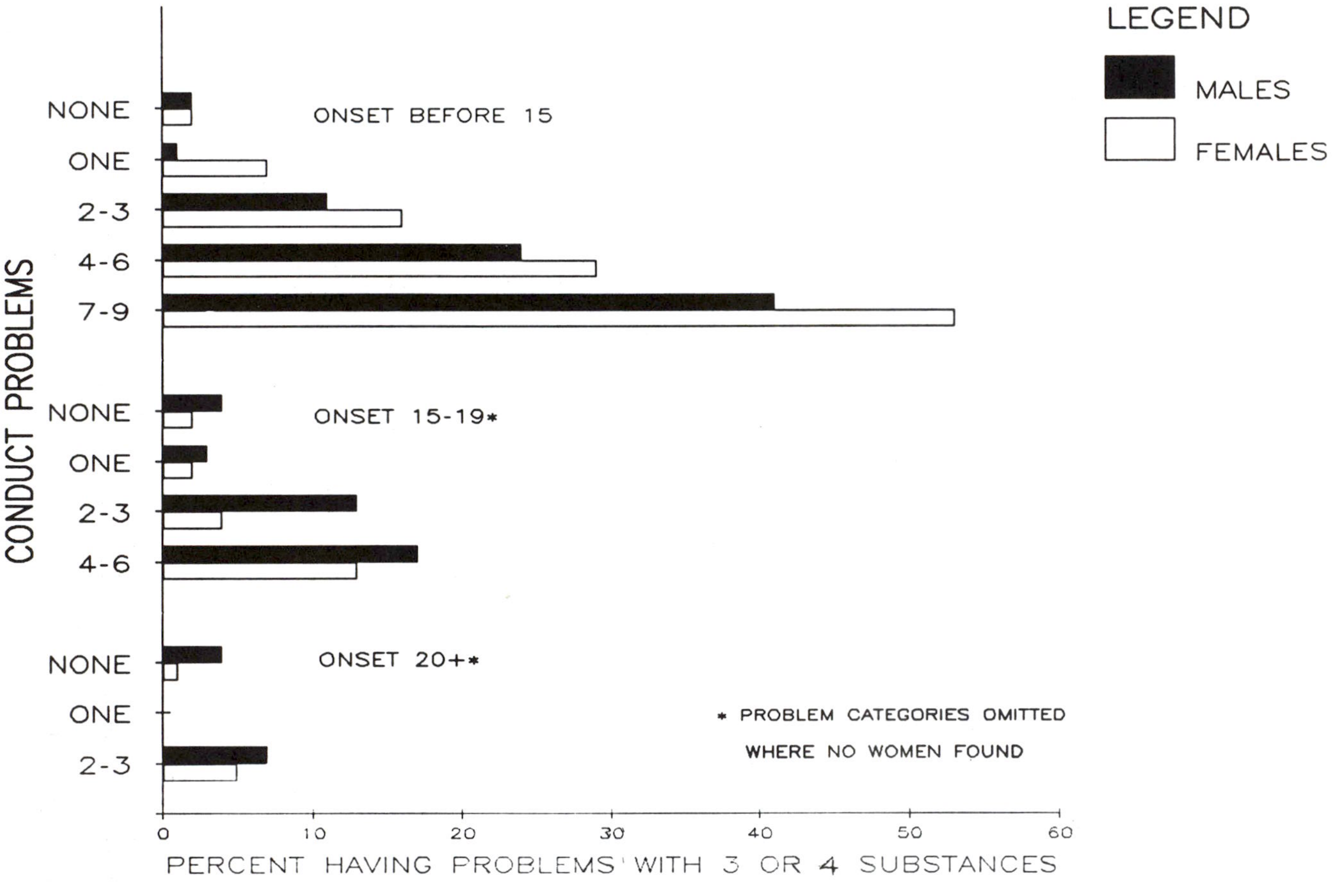

Figure 3. Sex differences among drug users in number of conduct problems and age at first substance use.

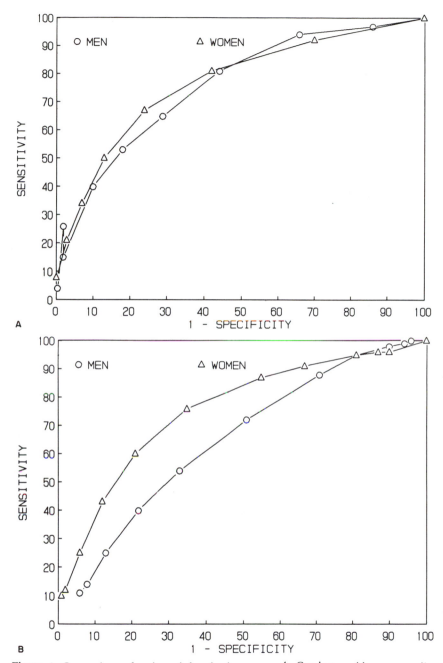

Figure 4. Comparison of male and female drug users. *A.* Conduct problems as predictor of later abuse. *B.* Age at first substance use as predictor of later abuse.

men, as shown in the lower chart in Figure 4 (and the best cut-off point is later for woman than men, below age 16 vs. below age 15 for men).

Conclusions

To answer the questions we posed initially: All three of our hypotheses were supported. The connection between conduct disorder and substance abuse is partly explained by the fact that youngsters who have conduct problems are more likely than others to be exposed to illicit drugs. Among those who use illicit drugs, the more conduct problems, the earlier use begins, and early use is itself an independent predictor of abuse. But unless initial use is delayed into adulthood, the more conduct problems the more likely is there to be substance abuse, regardless of when use starts. Thus conduct problems are a remarkably powerful predictor, affecting substance abuse through two identified mechanisms and independently as well.

Gender, unlike conduct problems, appears to have little direct predictive value with respect to susceptibility either to substance use or substance abuse. Although it has an indirect effect through influencing the number of conduct problems and the date at which substance use begins, girls with a history of conduct problems who start substance use early have as great a risk of later substance abuse as do boys with a similar history.

Because conduct problems continue to predict substance abuse even when we control for exposure and timing of exposure, we know those two mechanisms do not fully explain the effect of conduct problems on substance abuse. We have found that it is not the presence or absence of *particular* conduct problems that makes the difference. Further understanding of how conduct problems contribute to substance abuse will probably require information about how they influence adolescent social relationships and environments, and how they contribute to adult statuses that facilitate or inhibit heavy use of psychoactive substances. Likely adult candidates are unemployment, marital disruption, and incarceration, all known correlates of conduct disorder. Because we cannot accurately determine the temporal order of these correlates of conduct disorder relative to substance abuse in our retrospective study, we cannot test these adult outcomes as critical intervening variables between conduct disorder and substance abuse. A longitudinal research design would be particularly valuable in further explaining how conduct disorder contributes to substance abuse, because it would allow distinguishing these probable pathways of influence from the consequences of substance abuse.

We also cannot be content with our finding that one of the important mechanisms by which conduct disorder affects the risk of substance abuse is by lowering the age of first exposure to psychoactive substances. We do not yet understand why early use should be so much more dangerous than later use. It is not simply that it is an indicator of a personality profile consistent with dependence, since it is potent even for youngsters with very mild conduct problems. One wonders whether there might be a biologically critical period of high susceptibility to drug effects that ends in middle adolescence when pubertal changes are complete.

Until we have a better understanding of these age effects, and what the other intervening mechanisms are between conduct disorder and substance abuse, efforts at prevention would seem to call for reducing the number of conduct problems, avoiding the use of psychoactive substances altogether, or at least postponing their use past age 15, or better yet, 19. While it is true that substance users with no history of conduct problems seem to have little risk for substance abuse even when they begin use very young, beginning use before age 15 appears to increase the risk for substance abuse among youngsters with minimal, moderate, and severe conduct problems. Even juvenile delinquents probably have a better future if they avoid early substance use and so minimize their risk of becoming abusers. Mrs. Ronald Reagan has instigated a "Just say no" campaign against drugs. With conduct disordered youngsters, if that fails, a campaign to "Just say later" could also be useful.

Acknowledgments

This research was supported by the Epidemiological Catchment Area Program (ECA). The ECA is a series of five epidemiological research studies performed by independent research teams in collaboration with staff of the Division of Biometry and Epidemiology (DBE) of the National Institute of Mental Health (NIMH). The NIMH principal collaborators are Darrel A. Regier, Ben Z. Locke, and Jack D. Burke, Jr.; the NIMH project officer is Carl A. Taube. The principal investigators and co-investigators from the five sites are; from Yale University, U01 MH 34224, Jerome K. Myers, Myrna M. Weissman, and Gary L. Tischler; from the Johns Hopkins University, U01 MH 33870, Morton Kramer and Sam Shapiro; from Washington University, St. Louis, U01 MH 33883, Lee N. Robins and John E. Helzer; from Duke University U01 MH 35386, Dan Blazer and Linda George; and from University of California, Los Angeles, U01 MH 35865, Marvin Karno, Richard L. Hough, Javier I. Escobar, and M. Audrey Burnham. This work was also supported by Research Scientist Award MH 00334, USPHS Grants MH 17104, MH 31302, and DA-04001, and the MacArthur Foundation Risk Factor Network.

References

American Psychiatric Association (1980). *Diagnostic and statistical manual of mental disorders* (3rd ed.). Washington, DC: Author.
American Psychiatric Association (1987). Diagnostic and statistical manual of mental disorder (3rd ed. rev.). Washington, DC: Author.
Brunswick, A. F. (1979). Black youth and drug use behavior. In G. Beschner, A.

Friedman (Eds.) *Youth drug abuse; Problems, issues, and treatment.* Lexington, MA: Lexington Books.

Cloninger, C. R., Christiansen, K.O., Reich, T., & Gottesman, I. I. (1978). Implications of sex differences in the prevalences of antisocial personality, alcoholism, and criminality for familial transmission. *Archives of General Psychiatry, 35,* 941–951.

Erdreich, L. S., & Lee, E. T. (1981). Use of relative operating characteristic analysis in epidemiology. *American Journal of Epidemiology, 114,* 649–662.

Hanley, J. A., & McNeil, B. J. (1982). The meaning and use of the area under a receiver operating characteristic (ROC) curve. *Radiology, 143,* 29–36.

Helzer, J. E., Burnham, A. (in press). Alcohol abuse and dependency. In L. N. Robins & D. A. Regier (Eds.), *Psychiatric disorders in America.* New York: The Free Press.

Jessor, R., & Jessor S. L. (1977). *Problem behavior and psychosocial development— A longitudinal study of youth.* New York: Academic Press.

Johnston, L. D., O'Malley, P. M., & Bachman, J. G. (1987). *National trends in drug use and related factors among American high school students and young adults.* (DHHS Publication No. ADM 87–1535). Washington, DC: U.S. Public Health Service.

Johnston, L., O'Malley, P., & Eveland, L. (1978). Drugs and delinquency. In D. Kandel (Ed.), *Longitudinal research on drug use: Empirical findings and methodological issues.* Washington, DC: Hemisphere–John Wiley & Sons.

Kandel, D., Kessler, R., & Margulies, R. (1978). Adolescent initiation into stages of drug use: A developmental analysis. In D. Kandel (Ed.), *Longitudinal research on drug use: Empirical findings and methodological issues.* Washington, DC: Hemisphere–John Wiley & Sons.

Last, J. M. (1983). *A dictionary of epidemiology.* New York, Oxford, Toronto: Oxford University Press.

O'Donnell, J., Voss, H. L., Clayton, R. R., Slatin, G. T., & Room, R. G. (1976). *Young men and drugs—A nationwide survey.* (Research Monograph No. 5). Rockville, MD: National Institute on Drug Abuse.

Reich, T., Winokur G., & Mullaney J. (1975). The transmission of alcoholism. In R. R. Fieve, D. Rosenthal, & H. Brill (Eds.), *Genetic research in psychiatry.* Baltimore: Johns Hopkins University Press.

Robins, L., Bates W. M., & O'Neal P. (1962). Adult drinking patterns of former problem children. In D. J. Pittman & C. R. Snyder (Eds.), *Society, culture, and drinking patterns,* New York: John Wiley & Sons.

Robins, L. N., Helzer, J. E., Przybeck, T. (1986). Substance abuse in the general population. In J. Barret & R. M. Rose (Eds.), *Mental disorders in the community.* New York: Guilford.

Robins, L. N., Hesselbrock, W. E., & Helzer J. E. (1978). Polydrug and alochol use by veterans and non-veterans. In D. E. Smith, S. M. Anderson, M. Buxton, N. Gottlieb, W. Harvey, & T. Chung (Eds.), *A multicultural view of drug abuse,* Cambridge, England: Schenckman.

Yamaguchi, K., & Kandel, D. B. (1984). Patterns of drug use from adolescence to young adulthood: II. Sequences of progression. *American Journal of Public Health, 74,* 668–672.

11 Continuities and discontinuities in temperament

STELLA CHESS AND ALEXANDER THOMAS

Considerable attention has been paid to the issue of continuity over time in the research studies of temperament. If such continuity exists it would provide a basis for predictability of behavior from infancy to later life. Also, it would provide evidence that temperament is a stable constituent of the individual's psychological structure.

Statistical analyses of continuity

We calculated the inter-year product–moment correlations for the first 5 years of life in 133 middle-class subjects of our New York Longitudinal Study (NYLS) for nine categories of temperament, which we categorize and rate. These categories are activity level, regularity of biological functions, approach or withdrawal tendencies to new situations, adaptability to change, sensory threshold, quality of mood (whether predominantly positive or negative), intensity of mood expression (whether positive or negative), distractibility, and a combined category of persistence and attention span.

We have also identified three temperamental constellations of functional significance. *Difficult temperament* comprises the combination of irregularity, withdrawal, slow adaptability, high intensity, and relatively negative mood. *Easy temperament* is the opposite: regularity, approach, quick adaptability, low or moderate intensity, and predominantly positive mood. *Slow-to-warm-up temperament* comprises the combination of withdrawal, slow adaptability, and mild intensity. This last constellation can be equated with the shy, but not anxious individual. (The details of our interview methods, definitions of categories, and scoring methods can be found in Thomas & Chess, 1977.)

We use these nine categories and three constellations because we have found them useful and sometimes crucial in advising parents and teachers in the management of problems arising with individual children in child care and school settings. For adolescents and adults, insight into their own temperamental characteristics is often helpful in understanding their own behavior and in developing strategies to minimize undesirable expressions of one or another temperamental trait or pattern.

In our quantitative analysis of correlations for each of the nine categories through the first 5 years of life, we found statistically significant correlations from one year to the next for all categories except approach/withdrawal, distractibility, and persistence. As the time between the years being compared was increased from 1 year to 2, 3, or 4 years, the number of significant correlations decreased. The number of significant correlations was greatest for the categories of activity level and adaptability. Approach/ withdrawal, distractibility, and persistence, the three categories with the lowest inter-year correlations, are also the three categories with skewed distribution curves for each of the first 5 years. The other six categories, with higher inter-year correlations, all approximate normal distribution curves. This suggests that a lack of sufficient differentiation of the subjects for approach/withdrawal, distractibility, and persistence may be at least partially responsible for the low level of inter-year correlations.

Correlations from childhood to early adult life

We also calculated correlations between temperament in years 1 through 5 and early adult temperament (Chess & Thomas, 1984). The adult temperament scores were obtained by pooling the scores of three raters: a naive interviewer, one of us (A.T.) who sat in on the interviews, and a naive scorer, who made her ratings from audio tapes. A test of reliability among those raters showed correlations averaging .44. An adult temperament questionnaire was also administered to approximately half the sample. The retrieval rate for early adult life follow-up was 100%. There was only one significant correlation between each of the first 2 years of life and the young adult: intensity in year 1 and persistence in year 2. For year 3, the significant correlations increased to 2 (adaptability and approach/withdrawal), with a third (quality of mood) almost reaching the $p < .05$ level. For year 4 the correlations increased sharply, to include the three identified in year 3 plus intensity. For year 5 the significant correlations disappeared entirely.

The significant correlations in years 3 and 4 comprise elements of the easy versus difficult temperament constellation. In view of this finding, the issue of continuity in this temperamental pattern was explored further. We were especially interested in this analysis, inasmuch as children with difficult temperament are especially vulnerable to the development of behavior disorders, as found in the NYLS and in studies in a number of research centers in the United States and abroad (Thomas et al., 1968; Graham et al., 1973; Maziade et al., 1985; Turecki & Tonner, 1985). The demands for socialization in the early years (uninterrupted night sleeping, acceptance of strange places and people, learning the rules of discipline and peer relationship, expression of frustration without prolonged temper tantrums, etc.) are especially stressful for these children. In addition, many of the parents react negatively to such a child's difficulty, with either self-blame and guilt, anger at the child, inconsistent or rigid demands, attempts at appeasement, or some combination of these reactions, which serve to increase the child's stress and difficulties in mastering social expectations.

For purposes of this analysis, an overall easy-difficult temperament score was constructed by taking the means of the scores of the five categories making up the easy-difficult constellation. The inter-year correlation for adjacent first years was significant for each successive pair of years, with values ranging from .29 to .44. Years 1 to 3 and 2 to 4 were significant, but at a lower level, but not 3 to 5; years 1 to 4 were not significant, but years 2 to 5 and 1 to 5 were significant. Correlations between each of the first 5 years and early adult life were significant for year 3 (.31) and year 4 (.37), but not for year 5 (.15). These findings were confirmed when using the early adult temperament questionnaire. The increase in correlations for the first 4 years can be understood as the result of the continuing nature of the child–parent interaction over those years. Many of the parents responded to the child's difficult behavior by such methods of handling as rigid demands for compliance, and unsympathetic and even angry reactions which were intensified by the child's difficult behavior. It was not that the parents were basically hostile or rejecting of their child. Rather they were unprepared for the child's expression of difficult temperament, as compared to the behavior of other children, found their child-care activities burdensome and even frustrating, and hence reacted in ways that were inimical to the child's best interests and to their relationship with him or her. We have no explanation for the lack of correlation for year 5.

Difficult temperament in year 3 was also found to be negatively correlated with overall early adult adjustment. No significant correlation between any single temperamental trait and early adult adjustment was identified.

We found no significant differences in these analyses between males and females.

Other studies of consistency of temperament

McDevitt (1986) has recently reviewed a number of other studies of consistency of temperament in the infancy and childhood years, as well as the NYLS findings into early adult life. Unfortunately, with the current lack of consensus among researchers as to the definition, categorization, and rating of temperament, the literature reveals a plethora of studies using different concepts, variables, methods, and time intervals, though the majority of studies have used our model. Definitive conclusions from this review are therefore not possible. McDevitt concludes, however, that several issues and trends are apparent. First, "there is fairly good evidence that temperamental characteristics show some significant (non zero) stability from birth to adulthood." Second, "in the first 3 months of life there is insufficient reliable variance in temperament measures to detect many of the possible links." Third, "more global concepts and measures of temperament appear more stable than more narrowly defined ones. . . . What seems to emerge. . . is the general notion that continuities in temperament are more enduring and more easily detected as the level of analysis becomes less specific, situational or contextual and more global and general. On the other hand, as the generality of a concept or measure increases, its sensitivity and ability to provide useful information clinically or theoretically decreases" (pp. 35, 36).

Theoretical concerns

Disparities of method

A number of the difficulties in attempting to predict later psychological development from infancy data have been detailed by Rutter (1970). These include the amount of development still to occur; modifiability of psychological development by the child's subsequent experiences; the effect of intrauterine environment on the characteristics of the young infant, and the disappearance of these effects over time; the effects of differing rates of maturation; and differences in the function being tested in infancy and maturity, so that a test in infancy may not measure the same attribute as a test in later childhood or adult life.

With regard to temperament scores, Rutter points up several additional methodological problems, such as the reliance on adjectives parents use to describe their children's behavior, the possibility of selective bias in determining which episodes of behavior the parent or other observer reports, and the problem of separating the content from the style of behavior. Most important, he feels, is the effect the changing context of the child's behavior might have on the temperament ratings.

The last problem raised by Rutter bears on a knotty issue in all developmental research. A specific characteristic may have significant continuity in an individual or a group from one age period to another. Yet the changing context of the child's behavior and the emergence of new forms at later age–stage levels of development may give the same characteristic very different forms of expression. The problem, therefore, is one of determining when dissimilar behavior over time reflects the same characteristic—whether it be temperament, motivation, cognition, values and standards, or psychopathology—and when the same behavior reflects different characteristics at different age periods. In regard to temperament specifically, the behavioral criteria for any temperamental trait must necessarily change over time as the child's psychological functioning develops and evolves. Thus, for example, a 2-year-old may have loud temper tantrums, and at 18 years be described as hot-tempered. Both behaviors, though phenomonologically different, will fit the definition of intense negative mood expression. Or a 2-month-old may show withdrawal responses by the first reactions to the bath or a new food, and a 10-year-old by the first reactions to a new peer group or academic subject.

The temperamental identity or dissimilarity of different behaviors over time is, of course, not self-evident. It involves theoretical concepts of the developmental process, and investigators with different theoretical frameworks will disagree as to whether specific behaviors at different age periods reflect the same psychological characteristic or not. At issue is the determination of the validity and heuristic value of any theoretical concept, as well as the internal consistency of its application to specific behavioral phenomena.

In addition to the issues raised by Ruter, several other methodological problems regarding the determination of consistency over time have been apparent in the NYLS. A child's characteristic expression of temperament may be blurred at any specific age period by routinization of functioning. Thus, an infant who shows marked withdrawal reactions to the bath, new foods, and new people may, a year or two later, show positive responses to these same stimuli because of repeated exposure and final adaptation. If, at the same time, few new situations and stimuli are experienced, the withdrawal reaction may not be evident. Adaptation and routinization of activities, may, in the same way, blur the expression of other temperamental traits, such as irregularity, slow adaptability, and negative mood expression. Limitation of opportunity for physical activity may lead to frequent restless movements, which may be interpreted as high activity or even hyperactivity. Specific single items of behavior may sometimes be significant in temperamental consistency from one age period to another, but quantitative scoring methods can hardly give proper weight to the importance of such functionally significant items.

Another rather subtle issue in the rating of temperament sometimes arises. A child may have withdrawal reactions to the new and be slow to adapt, and these characteristics may be clearly evident in the child's behavior and easily rated. However, as the child grows older, if allowed to adapt at a comfortable pace and with a wide variety of life experiences, by adolescence and early adult life the youngster will develop a solid sense of self-confidence in the ability to master and enjoy new situations after an initial brief period of discomfort. Such an adolescent or young adult may then respond to a question about new situations by stating unequivocally that he or she likes them, looks forward to them, and even seeks them out. Closer inquiry may be necessary to elicit the fact that he or she still suffers from initial discomfort in a new situation, but has developed behavioral techniques to adapt at his or her own pace and to mask initial distress from others. However, if faced with a radically new set of expectations and demands, which cannot be linked with earlier successful experiences, such a person may show an active recurrence of childhood difficulties with the new. Another issue is that idiosyncratic maturational changes, which can affect behavioral development and temperament significantly, can arise in later childhood and adult life. We have seen several striking examples in our NYLS subjects.

Finally, the question of consistency of temperament over time cannot be studied globally. One or several temperamental traits may show striking continuity in some individuals from one specific age period to another, and the other attributes may not. At other age periods the reverse may be true. The originally consistent traits may not show the correlations, whereas other patterns may now do so.

Let us presume, and hope, that substantial, perhaps even dramatic progress will be made in resolving these various methodological problems. What then? It is a reasonable prediction that we will find the short- and long-term correlations of continuity in temperament may reach the 50% level. This is an optimistic estimate, but conceivable. But this will still leave us with certain fundamental issues unresolved.

1. Our findings pertain to group trends and not to those of individual children. Group trends can provide us with much useful information, such as cross-cultural studies, but they cannot necessarily give us an accurate assessment or prediction for any individual child. Even a correlation coefficient of 50%, if this is ever attained, still leaves 75% of the variance unaccounted for.

2. The concern with the issue of consistency in temperament has tended to put into the background the study of discontinuity or change, an equally important aspect of psychological development. McCall has even emphasized that "some of us have argued that change is the essence of developmental disciplines... and that we should be just as vigorous in describing change, whether in individual differences or developmental functions and whether in mental development or temperament, as we are in the search for stability and continuity" (1986, p. 16). Actually, continuity and change are not mutually exclusive. A temperamental characteristic or pattern may be continuous throughout one time period and then change, and the opposite may also occur. Also, one temperamental attribute may be consistent over time in an individual and another attribute may change.

3. As a number of writers have emphasized (Rutter, 1982; McCall, 1986; Schaffer, 1986), the study of continuity and discontinuity in itself is of secondary importance to the larger issue of the processes and mechanisms that result in either similarity or change in a temperamental trait over time. This issue is fundamental to developmental studies in general.

The goodness-of-fit model

In our search for a heuristically useful theoretical model, we rejected the influential psychoanalytical and behaviorist concepts, if only because they both assumed a single dynamic process which shaped the developmental sequences in all children. What was necessary, we felt, was a theoretical framework which could answer the questions: Why does one child show a smooth consistent course in his temperament? Why does another show great variability over time? Why does one interaction between temperament and environment produce an uninterrupted healthy developmental course, another show variability in the level of functioning at different age periods, and still another show progressively severe behavioral disorder over time? Our solution was the formulation of the "goodness-of-fit" model.

As we have used this concept, goodness of fit results when the environmental expectations, demands, and opportunities are consonant with the individual's temperament and other characteristics so that he can master them effectively. There is poorness of fit, on the other hand, when the environmental demands are excessive for the individual's capacities, so that excessive stress and an unhealthy developmental course may be the result (Thomas et al., 1968).

Goodness of fit does not imply an absence of stress or conflict; quite the contrary. Stress and conflict are inevitable concomitants of the developmental process, in which new expectations and demands for change and progressively higher levels of functioning occur continuously as the child grows older. Demands, stresses, and conflicts, when consonant with the child's developmental potentials and capacities for mastery, will be constructive in their consequences. The issue involved in disturbed behavioral functioning is rather one of *excessive* stress resulting from poorness of fit and dissonance between environmental expectation and demands and the capacities of the child at a particular level of development.

The goodness-of-fit model cannot be reduced to any simple formula to be applied like a blueprint to all children or adults. There are innumerable child–environment combinations that can promote either a goodness or poorness of fit, depending on the individual characteristics of the child, the parent, the teacher, or the peer group. In one child, goodness of fit may promote consistency in temperament over time, while in another child it will promote a change in one temperamental attribute or another. The same variability of influence is true for a poorness of fit. The issue is to individualize the analysis of child–environment interaction in each case, if the dynamic mechanisms are to be identified. This principle can be illustrated by several subject histories from the NYLS, which also illustrate the complexity of rating consistency and change in temperament.

Case illustrations and their implications

Specific NYLS case histories

Carl requested an interview with one of us (S. C.) after his first term in college because of feelings of depression and inability to cope with the academic and social situation at college. He had made no new real friendships and found studying difficult, an experience he could not recall ever having had before. He had done well academically in high school, had many friends in the community, found school enjoyable, and had a wide range of interests. In the interview he was alert, energetic, articulate, and in very good contact. He did not appear depressed, but rather bewildered at what was happening, exclaiming, "This just isn't me!" It was clear that he had a strongly positive self-image and could not reconcile this with his current difficulties.

Our anterospective longitudinal data showed that in infancy and the toddler-age period Carl had had one of our most difficult temperament patterns, with intense, negative reactions to new situations and slow adaptability only after many exposures.

Fortunately, the father, himself a mild-mannered and patient individual, recognized on his own that his youngster's behavior, while stressful to the family, was not abnormal. He commented spontaneously to our interviewer that once Carl adjusted to anything new, he then showed a zestful enthusiastic involvement (the positive side of his intensity of reactions), which was a pleasure to watch. He even called the boy's loud shrieking a sign of "lustiness," which he clearly considered preferable to his own mild even temper. The mother, on the other hand, kept feeling that there must be something wrong with her as a mother; otherwise why would the child behave so differently from most of the other young children she knew, but the father reassured her.

As a result of the parents' understanding and their patient, consistent, and low-keyed handling of his violent outbursts, Carl did not become a behavior problem. In his middle childhood and high school years he met very few radically new situations. He lived in the same community and went through the neighborhood schools with the same schoolmates and friends. Academic progression was gradual and new subjects were not introduced abruptly. He had sufficient time to adapt to new demands and became enthusiastically involved with a number of activities. As a result, he developed an appropriate positive and self-confident self-image.

When Carl went off to college away from home, however, he was suddenly confronted with a whole series of new situations simultaneously: strange surroundings, an entirely new peer group, new types of faculty approaches, school schedules, and curriculum. He also became involved in a complex emotional relationship with a girl who had a number of psychological problems; it was the first time he had to cope with such a difficult personal experience. Again, as with the many new adaptive demands of early childhood, his temperamental patterns of withdrawal from the new and intense negative reactions were expressed. Other possible reasons for his difficulties were explored—dependency needs for his parents, sexual conflict, anxiety over academic demands, peer competition—but no evidence of any these was elicited.

Only one discussion was necessary with Carl, and consisted primarily in clarifying for him his temperamental pattern and the behavioral techniques he could use for adaptation. Actually, Carl had begun to take these steps on his own: reducing the number of new academic subjects covered, disciplining himself to study each subject daily for a specific time, attenuating his involvement with the girl, and making a point of attending peer social activities, no matter how uncomfortable he felt. When seen again at the end of the academic year his difficulties had disappeared and his functioning was now on his previous positive level. He was told that similar negative reactions to new experiences might occur in the future. His response was "That's all right. I know how to handle them now."

Carl sought consultation again about 7 years later when he was 26. This was 4 years after his 22-year follow-up interview, when he had been found to be doing well socially and academically. At this later consultation he was cheerful and exuberant, but had a number of body tics. Carl launched into an enthusiastic description of his many activities and plans. He had gone into the computer field, was pursuing an innovative idea of his own, and was planning to start his own firm. At the same time he was absorbed in his harpsichord, and wanted to take a year off for serious musical work. Carl was also deeply involved with a young woman and both were seriously considering marriage. In addition, he was dabbling in photography and trying to maintain his athletic activities. When asked, "When do you sleep?" he replied promptly, "That's one of my problems. I don't get enough sleep, and I'm always tired. But I really came to ask you why I have all these tics." His physician (S.C.) laughed to herself because the answer was so obvious. She told him that with all his activities, plans, and dilemmas as to which decisions to make that he must be under great tension. This was excessive stress, but not anxiety, and combined with his physical fatigue was clearly the cause of his tics. He had to face the realities of life, set priorities, make decisions, cut down on his activities, even eliminate some, and get enough sleep.

When seen in the most recent follow-up at age 29, 3 years later, he was as zestful as ever, but relaxed. His tics had entirely disappeared. He had given up the idea of taking a musical year off, was doing well in his work, and had started his own company. He was engaged to be married and made sure he spent enough time with his fiancée. He wished he could still pursue his other interests energetically but recognized the need to put them in the background. The only residue of his temperamental withdrawal tendencies was his description of himself as "generally reserved," with a few good friends, a few casual ones, "but I keep most people at a distance."

Now that he is a mature young adult, we can say that Carl's temperament has changed. The change from negative to positive mood and from withdrawing to approaching situations appears permanent. This is no doubt shaped by his high self-esteem and many interests and abilities, which enable him to embark on new projects and tasks in graduated steps and thus explore new situations with enthusiasm. His intensity remains, but is now an asset rather than a liability, except that he has to be careful not to let this positive intensity lead him to accrue commitments of time and energy that he cannot fulfill. His relative reserve in making new friendships may be evidence of persistent mild discomfort with the new, but it appears at most to be of minor significance and has not interfered with his making good relationships with people in his work.

An important issue is the degree to which an individual progressively achieves insight into his own temperament through later childhood and adolescence and into adult life. With this insight can come an appreciation of the kinds of situations in which the expression of one or another temperamental attribute would be undesirable and require conscious control if optimal functioning is to be developed and maintained.

The effect of such insight can be either positive or negative. If the person has a strongly positive self-image and confidence in his capacities and abilities, as in Carl's case, then this insight can be used productively.

Another example from the NYLS is a young woman, Ellen, who had a difficult temperament as a child. Her parents were intelligent and well-meaning, but they did not understand Ellen's behavior and responded to her inconsistently and with frequent scolding. As a result of this poorness of fit, the child developed a mild behavior disorder with excessive resistance and crying to any criticism, even if given gently, overreaction to her younger sister's teasing, with loud screams and shouts of "leave me alone," similar intense negative responses to any change in family plans, and a strong tendency to be a worrier and apprehensive. The parents came for advice, and were quickly responsive to an explanation of Ellen's temperament and the need for firm but quiet, patient, and consistent management. The girl's symptoms disappeared within a year, and her social and academic development progressed smoothly thereafter. When interviewed recently in our current follow-up, she was launched successfully on a professional career, was happily married, and functioning well socially. She continued to be intensely expressive, but it was now predominantly positive instead of negative. Ellen explained that she is afraid of expressing anger. "I'm afraid it will come out violently. I put the cork on and it simmers." She tries to avoid confrontations, which may lead to an explosion of anger. However, she does not avoid such issues if they are important, but finds another way to face them without a direct confrontation. In summary, Ellen, as a young adult, retains some features of difficult temperament, including intensity of expression. She also still has discomfort with new situations ("I was always that way") but does not let this interfere with her involvement and mastery of any important new situation or demand. It is her negative mood expression which has changed dramatically, due to her self-insight. She now rates near the high level of positive mood, instead of the rating of high level of negative mood she had as a child.

However, if insight into one's temperament occurs in a person with a self-derogatory self-image, the result may be counterproductive. An example of Norman, one of our NYLS subjects, with the temperamental traits of high distractibility and low persistence. He is of superior intelligence and did well in elementary school. However, his father, a hard-driving worker with the opposite traits of low distractibility and high persistence, could not accept his son's need for breaks in any prolonged task and his apparent "forgetfulness" when distracted. The father refused to accept our explanations of Norman's behavior and the boy's need for acceptance and encouragement. Instead, he equated his son's behavior with irresponsibility and lack of character and will power, criticisms which he made openly and frequently to the boy. Norman grew to appreciate that he lacked his father's stick-to-it-iveness and that he was easily distracted, but he also accepted his father's derogatory judgments on these characteristics. By adolescence he was highly self-critical and said, "My father doesn't respect me, and let's face it, why should he?" A true poorness of fit, if there ever was one. Norman's insight only discouraged him and increased his lack of persistence. He dropped out of several colleges for lack of effort and went from one job to another, without persisting long enough at any to stimulate any motivation to continue. Several courses of psychotherapy were ineffective, inasmuch as Norman, with his negative self-image, could not grasp the fact that he could modify his distractibility and low persistence when it was important for his own functioning.

The life histories of Carl and Norman indicate that in some families the father may play a highly important and even dominant role in a child's development, as compared to the mother's influence. This has indeed been evident in a number of NYLS families. In some instances the father's influence has been a healthy one, as in Carl's development; in other cases the father has been an unhealthy influence, as in Norman's case. But these evidences of the significance of the father's role in the young child's development sharply contradict the professional ideology prevalent in recent decades, which gave primary and even unique importance to the mother's attitudes and child-care functioning. The past decade has seen increasing attention to the place of the father in the child-rearing process (White & Newberger, 1983), but a one-sided emphasis on the mother's influence still crops up all too frequently in the developmental literature (Chess & Thomas, 1982).

Implications of the goodness-of-fit model

Our qualitative analysis of individual life histories, using the goodness-of-fit model, has been based on the need to deal with the multivariate nature of temperament itself and the many ways in which the interaction between the child's temperament and other characteristics and between temperament and environment over time can reinforce, modify, or change temperamental attributes, as well as other behavioral traits of the individual. Other developmental psychiatrists and psychologists have also advocated indi- vidualized approaches to the study of behavioral development, such as an "idiographic approach" (Rutter, 1980, p. 5), a biopsychosocial model (Engel 1977), a systems theory model (Marmor 1983), and a life-span developmen- tal perspective (Baltes et al., 1980). Other workers have used concepts very similar to our goodness-of-fit formulation, though they may use other terms, such as "match and mismatch" (Greenspan, 1981; Murphy, 1981; Stern, 1977).

Whether we use the goodness-of-fit model or any other theoretical approach, the analysis of the mechanisms of temperamental continuity and change, as well as the analysis of other behavioral characteristics, cannot rely on any fixed blueprint formula which can be applied to all families in all cultures. Individual families in the same culture can vary tremendously, as our experience with the NYLS has demonstrated. Even more so, different cultures, with varying value systems and expectations, can have a decisive influence. A goodness of fit in one culture may be a poorness of fit in another, and vice versa. The social psychologists Super and Harkness have given special attention to this issue of cross-cultural differences and emphasized the value it may have for expanding our knowledge of temperament and its functional significance. "The study of temperament and development in a variety of cultural contexts promises more than the isolation of pathways to group differences. It leads us instead to fundamental questions about the organization, function, and development of behavior that are difficult to answer—even to ask—in a single environment. Exploration of the issues raised by comparative research will contribute much to our understanding of human temperament" (1986, pp. 145–146).

Our goodness-of-fit model and its theoretical and practical implications will undoubtedly be refined and modified as experience accumulates with the utilization by researchers and clinicians of this concept and related formulations. One intriguing possibility is related to the issue of parental perception and bias in reporting their children's behavior. It is generally agreed that the parent is the most valuable source of information on the child's behavior in the wide range of situations and experiences that the youngster encounters in daily life and in kind of adaptations he or she makes over time. At the same time, there is evidence, not surprisingly, that the reports of some parents may show a subjective bias when compared to objective reports of an outside observer (Bates & Boyles, 1984). Carey (1970) also used his infant temperament questionnaire to obtain from mothers both ratings of specific behaviors as well as their global general impressions of their children's temperament. In about 25% of the cases he found that the mothers markedly minimized the child's more difficult temperamental characteristics in their general statements as compared to their questionnaire responses.

The findings on parental perceptions have been considered a methodological problem in obtaining an accurate assessment of a child's temperament from the parents' descriptions. On one level this is true and highlights the need to minimize this difficulty by emphasizing objective descriptive reports from a wide variety of life situations which minimize value judgments as much as possible. On another level, however, differences between a parent's global, subjective judgment of the child, and the objective descriptions of specific behaviors may open up one method of assessing goodness of fit. For example, the objective scoring of a parent questionnaire or interview may rate the child as having a difficult temperament, but the parent will give a strong positive statement of the child's character. Rather than viewing this discrepancy as a methodological problem, it might also signify that, for that parent, the child's difficult temperament is not creating a negative response, so that a goodness of fit is likely to exist. We ourselves have not had the opportunity to explore this hypothesis, but it appears worth considering for future research.

Other approaches to the study of continuity and discontinuity

We have emphasized the individualized qualitative approach to the study of continuity and change in temperament, because of its emphasis on the analysis of the richness of data on the behavior of real children and adults in real-life situations. Qualitative analysis can be a most powerful instrument in studies of normal and deviant psychological development. Piaget, Vygotsky, and Freud, as well as a host of other investigators who have made significant contributions to developmental psychology and psychiatry, have relied primarily on this qualitative approach. However, the qualitative approach does have its limitations. It may be inadequate for deciding the relative validity of competing conclusions from the same data set, and it lacks the precision provided by mathematics and the computer for methods of quantitative analysis. In turning to quantitative methods, McCall has pointed out that temperament researchers may need complicated models because of temperament's multivariate and conceptual nature. He suggests that "temperament research will be an ideal context for the use of path analysis, structural equations, and a variety of techniques based on similar statistical principles," at the same time that he warns that "structural equations have become a fad, and it is being used in contexts that exceed its purpose and limitations" (1986, p. 22).

We are just now starting our analyses of our recently completed follow-up of our NYLS subjects and are planning to explore the usefulness of structural equations for these analyses, especially for the issue of continuity and discontinuity.

Another promising direction of study of continuity and change involves the analysis of similarity and differences in the ratings of temperament in different life contexts, both contemporaneously and over time. Such an analysis is bound to be complex, but our impression from some of our individual case studies is that it could be highly productive.

The study of temperament promises to continue the expansion in scope and diversity it has witnessed in recent years. Within this framework, the issue of continuity and discontinuity will undoubtedly remain one of major interest, both for its relevance to our understanding of temperament and its pertinence for a number of basic questions in developmental psychology and psychiatry. Dunn has recently summarized the issues for future research in the stability of temperament:

We need to identify which factors affect which children and which dimensions of temperament, at which developmental stages, and to distinguish endogenous from exogenous sources of variation. The causes of stability may well be different for different dimensions of temperament and for different children. Do some children remain "stable" in particular temperamental dimensions because they actively "niche-pick" and seek particular kinds of social environment? Do others remain stable because their parents consistently respond to and encourage certain styles of behavior? How can we best address the question of what processes are involved in the patterns of stability and change that we find? (1986, p. 166)

These are challenging questions. Their answers will not be simple and will undoubtedly reveal the processes of continuity and change in temperament to be complex, interrelated, and to constitute an integral part of the overall interactional process between the individual and the environment at sequential age-stage developmental periods.

References

Baltes, P. B., Reese, H. W., & Lipsitt, L. P. (1980). Life-span developmental psychology. *Annual Review of Psychology, 31*, 65–110.

Bates, J. E., & Boyles, K. (1984). Objective and subjective components in mothers' perceptions of their children from age 6 months to 3 years. *Merrill-Palmer Quarterly, 30*, 111–130.

Carey, W. B. (1970). A simplified method of measuring infant temperament. *Journal of Pediatrics, 77*, 188–194.

Chess, S., & Thomas, A. (1982). Infant bonding: Mystique and reality. *American Journal of Orthopsychiatry, 52*, 213–222.

Chess, S., & Thomas, A. (1984). *Origins and evolution of behavior disorders.* New York: Brunner/Mazel.

Dunn, J. (1986). Commentary: Issues for future research. In R. Plomin & J. Dunn (Eds.), *The study of temperament: Changes, continuities and challenges* (pp. 163–171). Hillsdale, NJ: Lawrence Erlbaum Associates.

Engel, G. L. (1977). The need for a new medical model: A challenge for biomedicine. *Science, 196*, 129–135.

Graham, P., Rutter, M., & & George S. (1973). Temperamental characteristics as predictors of behavior disorders in children. *American Journal of Ortho-psychiatry, 43*, 328–339.

Greenspan, S. I. (1981). *Psychopathology and adaptation in infancy and early childhood.* New York: International Universities Press.

Marmor, J. (1983). Systems thinking in psychiatry: Some theoretical and clinical implications. *American Journal of Psychiatry, 140*, 833–838.

Maziade, M., Capéraà, P., Laplante, B., Boudreault, M., Thivierge, J., Cote, Rs., & Boutin, P. (1985). Value of difficult temperament among 7-year-olds in the general population for predicting psychiatric diagnosis at age 12. *American Journal of Psychiatry, 142*, 943–946.

McCall, R. B. (1986). Issues of stability and continuity in temperament research. In R. Plomin & J. Dunn (Eds.), *The study of temperament: Changes, continuities and challenges.* (pp. 13–25). Hillsdale, NJ: Lawrence Erlbaum Associates.

McDevitt, S. (1986). Continuity and discontinuity of temperament in infancy and early childhood: A psychometric perspective. In R. Plomin & J. Dunn, (Eds.), *The study of temperament: Changes, continuities and challenges* (pp. 27–38). Hillsdale, NJ: Lawrence Erlbaum Associates.

Murphy, L. B. (1981). Explorations in child personality. In A. I. Rabin, J. Aronoff, A. M. Barclay, & R. A. Zucker (Eds.), *Further explorations in personality* (pp. 161–195). New York: John Wiley & Sons.

Rutter, M. (1970). Psychological development: Predictions from infancy. *Journal of Child Psychology and Psychiatry, 11*, 49–62.

Rutter, M. (1980). Introduction. In M. Rutter (Ed.), *Scientific foundations of developmental psychiatry* (pp. 1–7). London: Heinemann.

Rutter, M. (1982). Chairman's closing remarks. *Temperamental differences in infants and young children.* Ciba Foundation Symposium 89, pp. 294–298.

Schaffer, H. R. (1986). Child psychology: The future. *Journal of Child Psychology and Psychiatry, 27*, 761–779.

Stern, D. (1977). *The first relationship.* Cambridge: Harvard University Press.

Super, C. M., & Harkness, S. (1986). Temperament, development and culture. In R.

Plomin & J. Dunn (Eds.), *The study of temperament: Changes, continuities and Challenges* (pp. 131–150). Hillsdale: NJ: Lawrence Erlbaum Associated.

Thomas, A., & Chess, S. (1977). *Temperament and development.* New York: Brunner/Mazel.

Thomas, A., Chess, S., & Birch, H. G. (1968). *Temperament and behavior disorders in children.* New York: Brunner/Mazel.

Turecki, S., & Tonner, L. (1985). *The difficult child.* New York: Bantam.

White, K. M. & Newberger, E. H. (1983). Parenting and its problems. In M. D. Levine, W. B. Carey, A. C. Croker, & R. T. Gross (Eds.), *Developmental–behavioral pediatrics* (pp. 209–223). Philadelphia: W. B. Saunders.

12 The creation of interpersonal contexts: Homophily in dyadic relationships in adolescence and young adulthood

DENISE KANDEL, MARK DAVIES, AND
NAZLI BAYDAR

Interpersonal influences are crucial to the psychosocial development of the individual. It is in the context of family and peer groups that individuals become socialized and acquire the values, attitudes, and skills necessary to their functioning as members of society. Social interactions not only contribute to the development of the individual, but social ties also provide one with sources of support in times of stress. Paradoxically, rather than diminishing the role of environmental factors, recent advances in the understanding of genetic factors in the etiology of behavior and the emphasis on multifactorial genetic models have given environmental factors increased importance. Behavior is clearly the result of both biological and environmental influences.

However, the dichotomy between biological and environmental factors is not as clearly demarcated as it would appear; under certain circumstances, individuals create their own environment (Scarr & McCartney, 1983). An important feature of individuals' developments is that contexts vary in the extent to which affiliation is voluntary. The child is born into a family, a predetermined context. As individuals mature, they become engaged in the selection and formation of their own contexts. Such opportunities generally increase with age up to a certain point, after which they constrict rather than expand. Thus, the opportunities for shaping one's context vary with age, also probably with social status, and involve different target individuals or groups at different stages of the life cycle. In childhood, and especially in adolescence, individuals join peer groups and form friendships. In adulthood, most individuals enter into relatively permanent intimate relationships with another adult. While friends still remain a potential important social force, in adulthood the most important interpersonal relationship is that with partner or spouse. In our society, parents are predetermined but friends and spouses are selected.

Such choices are important for an individual's further development. For although choices are made, in part, as a function of the individual's prior attributes, values, and personality characteristics, involvement in the new relationship has further effects and influences on that individual. The bases

221

on which social ties are created and the extent to which there is or is not continuity in the underlying processes over time remain unexplored areas of research.

In this chapter, we consider the bases on which others are selected for intimate relationships at two different stages of the life cycle. The investigation takes a life-course perspective and assesses the similarities and differences between pairs of friends in adolescence and married pairs in adulthood.

The fundamental assumption of the analysis is that the bases underlying affiliation will be reflected in *homophily*, that is, the degree of similarity between the two members of the pair on a particular attribute. There are role changes associated with progression through the life course and associated changes in types of interpersonal interactions. The extent to which there may be developmental continuity in the bases of interpersonal affiliations has yet to be determined, as has the extent to which the bases of affiliation at a later stage in the life cycle are influenced by earlier experiences.

Although we have panel data over a 13-year period, we do not have the repeated measures that would be required to study dynamically at each time period the process underlying the formation of intimate relationships and to differentiate selection from socialization. Instead, we examine the similarity between members of dyads at two points in time.

It is important to keep in mind that observations of similarity among individuals at one point in time could result from two processes: selection and socialization. Indeed, theories of interpersonal behavior (Homans, 1961; Thibaut & Kelly, 1959; Heider, 1958; Newcomb, 1961) assume that similarity between individuals induces liking (interaction, attraction) and correlatively that liking engenders similarity. There is much empirical evidence to support the proposition that interpersonal attraction and strength of liking are related to degree of similarity on various attributes, such as attitudes, values, behaviors, and personality traits (see Berscheid, 1985; Blankenship et al., 1984; Byrne, 1971; Duck & Gilmour, 1981; Lazarsfeld & Merton, 1954; Lott & Lott, 1965; Neimeyer & Mitchell, 1988; Newcomb, 1961). Homophily among friends could result from a selection process leading to assortative pairing, and homophily among spouses could result from assortative mating, such that individuals with prior similarity on some attributes of mutual importance purposefully select each other as friends or mates. Alternatively, homophily could result from a socialization process in which individuals who associate with each other, irrespective of their prior similarity, influence one another over time. The two processes are not mutually exclusive and both probably take place, as we documented in an earlier phase of this research (Kandel, 1978a). In following a cohort of adolescents over a six-month interval, we found that both processes play a role in the formation, maintenance, and dissolution of friendships. Prior homophily on behaviors and attitudes, such as marijuana use or delin-quency, was a determinant of interpersonal attraction (Kandel, 1978*a*). Homophily increased further as the result of sustained association. Thus, homophily between friends at one point in time resulted from two complementary processes: adolescents who shared certain prior attributes tended to choose each other as friends and tended to influence each other as the result of continued association. Selection and socialization were approximately equal in importance (Kandel, 1978*a*). Although homophily is a result of both interpersonal attraction and interpersonal influence, in this study we interpret it mainly as an index of attraction.

In this chapter we deal with the following issues: (1) What are the levels of homophily in intimate relationships at different phases of the life cycle, in friendship dyads in adolescence and in marital dyads in adulthood? (2) How does homophily vary across domains for variables that are relevant at both periods and for variables that are relevant only at one phase of the life cycle, or for which information is only available at one time period, either in adolescence or in adulthood? (3) What is the extent of continuity or discontinuity in homophily in intimate relationships over time? In order to answer this question, we need first to characterize individuals according to the homophily of the dyads to which they belong and then we must see whether those who belong to highly homophilous pairs at one point in their lives also tend to do so at another point.

Study of dyads in adolescence and adulthood

Subjects

Three different subsamples have been used in the analyses: adolescent-best-school-friends dyads, young adult-spouse/partner dyads, and triads of young adults matched to a best friend in adolescence and a spouse/partner in adulthood. Each relational sample represents a different subset of cross-sectional and longitudinal data sets from an ongoing follow-up study.

In the first phase of the study, in 1971, a statewide survey was carried out on a random sample of adolescents representative of the public high school population in grades 9 through 12 in New York State and drawn from 18 schools throughout the state. Selected homerooms were sampled in 13 schools, and in 5 schools the total student body was surveyed. The data were obtained from structured, self-administered questionnaires given in class-rooms.

In 1980 and 1984, follow-up personal interviews in young adulthood were conducted on a subsample of adolescents formerly enrolled in the 10th and 11th grades in the initial sample schools. The target population for the follow-up was drawn from the enrollment lists of half the homerooms from grades 10 and 11 in the 18 schools and included students who were absent from school at the time of the initial study. The 1,222 young adults (566 men and 656 women) reinterviewed in 1984 represent 75% of the original target adolescent sample. In 1984, a mailed survey was carried out with the participants' spouses and partners. Seventy-three percent ($N = 561$) returned the questionnaire.

Adolescents. In order to investigate homophily in adolescent friendships, we used a sample of 1,132 adolescent-best-school-friend dyads. In 1971, all students in the five high schools sampled in their entirety were asked to nominate their best friend in school. A friend could be nominated from any grade in the school. Students generated an identification number according to fixed rules for themselves and their friend, identical to the number the friend constructed for himself/herself (Kandel, 1978*b*).

Matches on the basis of these numbers produced 1,132 dyads, in which the chooser was attending the 10th and 11th grades. These matches represented 38% of the students in these grades. The low proportion is explained by the facts that a certain number of students failed to produce numbers either for themselves or their friends; some of the numbers produced were incomplete or incorrect; and some best friends were absent on the days of data collection. The choice did not have to be reciprocated for a dyad to be included. Among the dyads, 633 were same sex–female dyads, 403 were same sex–male dyads, and 96 were cross–sex dyads (56 from male choosers and 40 from females). It should be noted that the best school friend is the best friend overall, in and out of school, for 79% of adolescents. The subsample of 10th and 11th graders was selected for the present analyses, because the adult follow-up was restricted to students from these two grades, and we wanted to match these former adolescents to their spouse as well as to their best school friend.

Adults. In order to investigate homophily in marital dyads, we used the total sample of 561 adult-spouse/partner dyads (abbreviated as marital dyads) obtained in 1984. Of the 561 dyads, 62 were partnerships of 6 months or longer in duration and the remainder were spouses; in 48%, focal respondents were males.

In order to examine homophily over time, we used a sample of 100 triads composed of young adults matched to a best school friend in adolescence in 1971 and a spouse/partner in adulthood in 1984; in 41 of these triads, the focal respondent was a male. In 3 cases the friend became a spouse. In 1971, the target in-school sample of 10th and 11th graders included 536 adolescents matched to a best friend; 185 such dyads were included in the 1984 follow-up cohort. The 100 cases included in the triads were a subset of the

536. The 100 friendship pair members who were also in marital dyads included 55 females from female–female friendships and 4 females from cross-sex friendships; 35 males from male–male friendships and 6 males from cross-sex friendships.

Thus, whether in adolescence or in adulthood, most intimate friendships are formed with a person of the same sex. More friendship dyads in our sample were female than male.

When we examined similarities between friends and between married pairs, we used all identified dyads; when studying stability of homophily over time, we were limited to the 100 cases who were members of both friendship and marital pairs.

Analytical strategy

The statistic used to measure homophily at one point in time is *weighted kappa*, unless the variable is nominal, in which case *unweighted kappa* is used (Cohen, 1960; Fleiss, 1973; Strauss, 1973). Traditional correlation measures are not adequate to measure concordance or homophily, since they do not control for possible marginal differences between types of dyad. The kappa statistics, in contrast, measure the amount of concordance observed in a symmetric table over what would be expected by chance. The formula for kappa is

$$\kappa = \frac{p_o - p_c}{1 - p_c}$$

p_o = proportion of sample observed in concordance
p_c = proportion of sample that would have been concordant if the variables of interest were independent.

For ordinal variables, weighted kappa takes deviations from the diagonal into account in computing concordance. Discordant observations from the main diagonal are weighted inversely to their distance from the diagonal. For nominal variables, unweighted kappa scores all deviations from the diagonal as discordant. A value of one reflects perfect concordance; a value of zero reflects concordance merely at chance level. Unequal marginal distributions reflect discordance in a number of dyads and set an upper limit below one on the value of kappa.

The analysis of homophily over time required a more complex methodology.

The analysis proceeded in two stages. In the first stage, we examined the degree of homophily in different domains in adolescence and in adulthood. I the second stage, we examined dyadic homophily over time on selected items from adolescence to adulthood. The results are presented for males and females together, since few differences appeared between the sexes.

Results of the study

The variables on which homophily was examined represent important domains of a person's life in adolescence and in adulthood. Some of these domains are relevant at both periods, others are not. They include sociodemographic attributes, drug use, attitudes, interpersonal quality of interactions with parents in adolescence and with spouse in adulthood, school-related activities and leisure-time activities in adolescence, and health, fertility and parenting in adulthood. Selected measures are described in the Appendix.

From the available data, two kinds of comparisons can be made: comparisons of the relative importance of factors identical in adolescence and in adulthood, factors specific to adolescence or to adulthood.

Homophily in adolescence and adulthood: Comparison on three domains

Comparison of characteristics that were available both in adolescence and in adulthood reveals similarities and divergences on homophily in the two life phases. The discussion focuses on results for the largest number of friendship and marital dyads available. Data for the 100 longitudinal cases, which are part of the focal respondent-best-friend-spouse triads, are also presented in the tables. They show that patterns of homophily in this selected sample are very similar to those observed in the larger group. However, because of the smaller size of the longitudinal sample, the levels of statistical significance are often lower.

The bases of homophily on sociodemographic background are almost identical at both time periods: the most important variable is ethnicity (Table 1).[1] Religion is next in importance in adulthood, but less important than age in adolescence. (Although the follow-up sample came from only 10th or 11th grade, all grades in each high school in the original survey were sampled, so that matched cases could come from all grades. However, the age range is limited to a maximum of 4 years.) The relatively low value on homophily for age in the marital dyads reflects the fact that spouse pairs in our sample are rarely of the exact same age. For all other demographic attributes, which involve class of origin, the values are low and remarkably similar in adolescence and in adulthood.

Homophily on drug use (Table 2) is relatively high and generally higher for illicit than licit drugs at both life phases. Both lifetime and current measures were used for married persons, because drug use may have been discontinued before they met or early in the marriage, whereas for the

Table 1. *Homophily in adolescent friendship and adult marital dyads: Sociodemographic characteristics (weighted kappas)*

	All cross-sectional		Longitudinal	
	Friendship dyads	Marital dyads	Friendship dyads	Marital dyads
Ethnicity[a]	.606***	.639***	.338[§]	.265**
Age	.443***	.032**	.280***	.086**
Religion[a]	.234***	.479***	.161*	.482***
Father's place of birth[a]	.202***	.213***	.167*	.011
Mother's place of birth[a]	.176***	.241***	.019	−.098
Father's education	.083***	.071**	.111[§]	.008
Mother's education	.072***	.116***	.041	.011
Total N	(1,132)	(561)	(100)	(100)

[a] Unweighted kappas
[§] $p < .10$
* $p < .05$
** $p < .01$
*** $p < .001$

Table 2. *Homophily in adolescent friendship and adult marital dyads: Frequency of drug use (weighted kappas)*

	All cross-sectional			Longitudinal		
	Friendship dyads (lifetime)	Marital dyads (lifetime)	Marital dyads (last yr)	Friendship dyads (lifetime)	Marital dyads (lifetime)	Marital dyads (last yr)
Cigarettes	.336[a]***	.222***	.320***	.303***	.134*	.203*
Hard liquor/alcohol	.246***	.132***	.248***	.280***	.323***	.372***
Beer/wine	.208***	—	—	.298***	—	—
Marijuana	.445***	.371***	.461***	.436***	.379***	.283***
Psychedelics	.353***	.298***	.175***	.132*	.202**	.000
Cocaine	.176***	.453***	.388***	.000	.559***	.514***
Sedatives	.291***	.323***	.226***	−.033	.490***	.000
Stimulants	.236***	.230***	.091***	.205**	.413***	.181***
Minor tranquilizers	.191***	.303***	.113***	−.042	.266***	.000
Total N	(1132)	(561)	(561)	(100)	(100)	(100)

[a] Combines lifetime and current use (see Appendix).
* $p < .05$
** $p < .01$
*** $p < .001$

Table 3. *Homophily in adolescent friendship and adult marital dyads: Attitudes and depression (weighted kappas)*

	All cross-sectional		Longitudinal	
	Friendship dyads	Marital dyads	Friendship dyads	Marital dyads
Educational expectations/ attainment[a]	.295***	.426***	.328***	.431***
Religiosity	.205***	.539***	.169*	.647***
Political orientation	.139***	.180***	.082$	.127*
Depressive symptoms	.116***	.009	.142**	−.008
Total N	(1132)	(561)	(100)	

[a] Expectations for adolescent friendship dyads; attainment for adult marital dyads.
$ $p<.10$
*$p<.05$
**$p<.01$
***$p<.001$

Table 4. *Homophily in adolescent friendship dyads: Relationships with parents and school and leisure activities (weighted kappas)*

	All	Longitudinal
Relationship with parents		
Closeness to father	.065***	.161**
Closeness to mother	.078***	.094*
Parent-peer orientation	.166***	.138*
School activities		
Overall self-reported grade average	.306***	.221**
Classes cut per week	.276***	.286***
Time spent on homework	.229***	.255***
Days absent from school	.142***	.091$
Leisure activities		
Index of peer activity	.254***	.291***
Participating in political activities	.219***	−.031
Time spent listening to records	.159***	.190**
Index of minor delinquency	.187***	.177**
Index of major delinquency	.185***	.089
Time spent reading for pleasure	.164***	.174**
Time spent watching TV	.124***	.251**
Total N	(1,132)	(100)

$ $p<.10$
*$p<.05$
**$p<.01$
***$p<.001$

adolescents, most drug use had been recent. In adolescence, homophily is highest on marijuana, followed closely by psychedelics. In adulthood, homophily is high on marijuana, but even slightly higher on cocaine. Although we might expect socialization effects to be more evident for recent use than for lifetime use, the lower values on current use for three drugs—psychedelics, sedatives, and stimulants—reflect a maturational effect. The use of illicit drugs declines with age, especially for drugs that are less commonly used.

Table 3, dealing with various attitudes, displays what is perhaps the most striking difference between the two life periods, namely the increase in homophily with respect to religiosity as individuals moved from adolescence to adulthood. In adulthood, concordance on religiosity, as indexed by participation in religious services, is very high. Concordance on educational attainment among marital partners, although lower than on religiosity, is also relatively high and represents a slight increase over the degree of homophily on educational aspirations observed in adolescent friendship pairs. There is a lack of concordance on depression for marital pairs.

Thus, ethnicity, education, and drug use are areas of concordance that are common both in adolescence and adulthood. Religiosity is much more important in adulthood than in adolescence, probably because most religious activities are family oriented.

Homophily in adolescence

Certain domains could only be examined in adolescence: relationships with parents, school-related activities, and leisure-time activities, including delinquency.

Relationships with parents (Table 4) show relatively low levels of similarity between friends. Homophily on school-related activities and performance show higher levels, as does homophily on leisure-time activities.

Homophily in adulthood

Among the domains that could be investigated only in adulthood, those pertaining to spouses' evaluation of the quality of the marital relationship show a fair degree of agreement (Table 5). Spouses (and partners) agreed on the degree of closeness that characterized their relationship and on the satisfaction they derived from it.

There is also a fair degree of agreement on child-rearing practices (Table 6), especially those having to do with limit-setting, in which the referrent behavior is relatively specific, such as whether "the child is allowed to stay up as late as he/she wants" or "how often the parents take away privileges."

Table 5. *Homophily in adult marital dyads: Quality of the relationship (weighted kappas)*

	All	Longitudinal
Closeness of relationship	.341***	.307***
Satisfaction	.315***	.277***
Depends on spouse for advice	.117***	.189**
He/she is affectionate	.198***	.290***
Total N	(561)	(100)

**p<.01
***p<.001

Table 6. *Homophily in adult marital dyads: Parenting (weighted kappas)*

	All	Longitudinal
All parents		
Difficulty in being parent	.142***	.127$
How often parents kiss and hug children	.122**	.032
Total N	(331)	(56)
Parents of children age 2 and over		
How often child is allowed to watch as much TV as he or she wants	.240***	.334***
How often child is allowed to stay up as late as he or she wants	.402***	.545***
How often parents agree on bringing up the child	.234***	−.041
How close parents feel to the child	.124**	.042
How often parents talk about what they did wrong	−.022	−.014
How often parents spank or slap the child	.284***	.205*
How often parents yell at the child	.111**	.023
How often parents act cold or unfriendly	.022	−.079
How often parents take away privileges	.314***	.378***
Total N	(250)	(44)

$p<.10
*p<.05
**p<.01
***p<.001

Homophily observed with respect to fertility expectations is very high (Table 7). Homophily on this characteristic is the second highest observed in the marital dyads (ethnicity is the highest). The lack of homophily on obesity is surprising, since one would expect both selection and lifestyle after marriage to lead to similarity on that dimension.

Table 7. *Homophily in adult marital dyads: Health and fertility (weighted kappas)*

	All	Longitudinal
Ratio of health	.163***	.101
Obesity ratio	.083***	.096*
Ever seen mental health professional	.267***	.439***
Feelings about life as a whole	.238***	.207**
Number of children expected	.582***	.625***
Total *N*	(561)	(100)

*p<.05
**p<.01
***p<.001

Homophily over time

Although individuals involved in intimate relationships, whether in adolescence or in adulthood, tend to share certain characteristics, there are variations in the degree of homophily across dyads and across dimensions. We can assume that some individuals are involved in dyads that are homophilic on a particular dimension of interest and across dimensions, while other individuals are part of non-homophilic, discordant dyads.

Theories of interpersonal attraction lead us to assume further that homophilic dyads are more intimate, provide greater satisfaction to their members, and have greater influence over them than non-homophilic ones (Berscheid, 1985; Byrne, 1971). From a developmental perspective, one important question is, to what extent are individuals consistent over time in the degree to which they tend to affiliate with similar others? That is, to what extent do individuals remain consistent in the degree to which they create congruent environments for themselves? Is congruence in adolescent friendships related to congruence in adulthood marital dyads?

Some information about the consistency of homophily at different stages of life can be provided if we quantify the degree of homophily experienced in adolescent and marital dyads for persons for whom we have information at both ages and see whether these quantities are correlated.

There is little guidance in the literature on how to describe an individual in terms of the degree of homophily experienced in dyadic relationships. There have been discussions on how to define dyads based on the behaviors of dyad members, especially for marital dyads (Thompson & Williams, 1982; Thompson, 1986; Mirowsky & Ross, 1987; Glass & Polisar, 1987; Cook & Dryer, 1984; Schumm et al., 1984; Klein, n.d.). The reverse, defining an individual according to dyadic characteristics, is rarely discussed (for an exception, see Kenny, 1988). This methodological problem, however, is another perspective on the issue raised by David Magnusson in this volume (see Chapter 6) on how to move from single variable analysis to more complex conceptualizations of individual attributes. While Magnusson focuses on the aggregation or patterning of single individual attributes, we focus on how to define emergent group characteristics and the characterization of the individual according to these interpersonal contextual attributes.

Our solution was to define latent variables for dyadic homophily in a factor-analytic, LISREL–based measurement model (Jöreskog & Sorbom, 1984). For each domain of interest, two such latent variables were defined, one for homophily in adolescence and the other for homophily in adulthood. Each latent variable was assumed to cause variation in two indicators, the responses of the two dyad members. We focused on three domains: education, attendance at religious services, and marijuana use. In adolescence, the indicators were the respondent's and best friend's responses to questions on each of the three domains; in adulthood, the indicators were the responses of the focal respondent and his or her spouse (or partner). In order to estimate the continuity of an individual's tendency to form homophilic dyads over time from adolescence to adulthood, we estimated a LISREL model in which we examined the correlation over time of the two latent constructs, as presented in Figure 1. A key feature is that the regression parameters in the measurement model are all fixed to equal 1.0, so that the observed covariance in the dyad reflects itself in the variance of the latent variable. Stated differently, this implies that each member of the dyad shares a common constant and that the variance of the latent variable reflects population variability of these common constants. Thus, the latent variable can be interpreted as an index of homophily in the dyad.

Several other parameters are included in the model to control for other processes that might influence homophily. First, we allowed correlated error between the respondent's adolescent and adult reports to account for correlation due to other factors unrelated to homophily but which cause correlation over time for a particular indicator. A similar parameter allowed for correlated error between the best friend's and spouse's reports to account for correlation due to other factors unrelated to homophily but which cause correlation over time between the respondent's best friend and spouse for a particular indicator. Our a priori assumption was that this correlation would be close to zero, because the similarities between the best friend and the spouse are likely to be due to their affiliation with the focal respondent only. This parameter was included to maintain symmetry in the correlated error structure. The final parameter in the model, and that of greatest interest, is the correlation of the latent variables over time, which we interpret as the correlation between homophily in adolescence and homophily in adulthood.

The model was estimated separately for educational expectations and

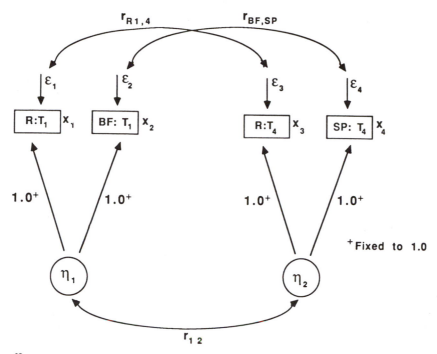

η_1 : Explains covariance between R and BF @ T_1

η_2 : Explains covariance between R and SP @ T_4

r_{12} : Correlation for tendency to be homophilous overtime.

$r_{R1,4}$: Correlation due to idiosyncratic factors unrelated to homophily that cause variation at T_1 and T_4 in the respondent.

$r_{BF,SP}$: Correlation due to idiosyncratic factors unrelated to homophily that cause variation in BF and Spouse.

R : Respondent

BF : Best friend

SP : Spouse

Figure 1. LISREL model for one-variable homophily model from adolescence to adulthood.

attainment, for attending religious services, and for marijuana use. In adolescence, we measured educational aspirations and lifetime frequency of marijuana use; in adulthood, we measured educational attainment and frequency of marijuana use within the last year. Table 8 presents several descriptive results along with the continuity of homophily over time. Part I of the table indicates the fraction of variance in an indicator for each respondent that is due to concurrent homophily. Part II presents the over time correlation of dyadic homophily; part III presents the correlations of

Table 8. *Continuity of dyadic homophily over time from adolescent friendship pairs to adult marital dyads on three variables*[a]

	Educational expectation/ attainment	Attendance at religious services	Marijuana use
I. Fraction of indicator variance due to homophily in:			
Adolescence			
Respondent	.38	.25	.55
Best friend	.46	.27	.69
Adulthood			
Respondent	.52	.72	.36
Spouse	.57	.80	.36
II. Continuity of dyadic homophily over time	.63*	.38*	.46*
III. Idiosyncratic residual correlation over time			
Respondent	.58***	.49**	.31*
Best friend/spouse	−.08	−.02	−.52**
IV. Goodness-of-fit statistics			
χ^2 (df = 1)	.38	.49*	.22
$p<$	ns	ns	ns

[a] Coefficients based on estimation of LISREL model displayed in Figure 1.
  *$p<.05$
 **$p<.01$
***$p<.001$

the residuals over time; and part IV indicates the goodness of fit of the models. The latter statistics indicate that the models adequately explain the observed covariance matrices. In order to measure homophily at a well defined point in time, the one-year rather than lifetime measure of marijuana use was chosen for the marital dyad.

The fraction of variance due to homophily is similar to a proportion of explained variance and reflects the extent to which the behavior of a particular individual reflects similarity in the dyad on that particular dimension. The fraction of variance in the indicators due to homophily sharply increases for attending religious services from approximately 26% in adolescence to approximately 76% in adulthood. It increases slightly for educational expectations and attainment from about 42% in adolescence to approximately 54% in adulthood; and for marijuana use, it decreases from 62% in adolescence to 36% in adulthood. These values reflect the extent to which individual members of dyads are influenced by the overall dyadic homophily, which in the LISREL model is represented by the latent variable. The rankings of the proportions of variance explained by the latent homophily variable among the three variables of interest will parallel ranking of homophily as measured by the kappas.

Table 9. *Overtime correlations and homophily in adolescence and adulthood on three individual behaviors*

	Correlations between		Homophily in		Continuity in
	adolescence and adulthood (focal respondent) Pearson R	Best friend and spouse Pearson R	friendship dyads kappas[a]	marital dyads kappas[a]	dyadic homophily
Educational expectations/ attainment	.64***	.24***	.30***	.43***	.63***
Religiosity	.40***	.15**	.20***	.54***	.38***
Frequency of marijuana use[b]	.33***	.05*	.44***	.46***	.46***

[a] Weighted kappas.
[b] Lifetime in adolescence, last year in adulthood.
*p<.05
**p<.01
***p<.001

The continuity of dyadic homophily from adolescence to adulthood is quite high for educational expectations and attainment ($r = .63$) and lower for marijuana use ($r = .46$) and attending religious services ($r = .38$). Persons who experience high congruency of values and behaviors with friends in adolescence also experience high congruency with their spouse in adulthood.

Residuals measure idiosyncratic components of an individual's behavior. As expected, the correlations of residuals from adolescence to adulthood for the respondent are relatively high, while the correlations of the residuals between the best friend and the spouse show a different pattern.[2]

As a summary, Table 9 displays the continuity in dyadic homophilies over time, the correlations over time in individual behaviors between adolescence and adulthood for focal respondents and for best friends and spouses, as well as the cross-sectional dyadic homophily values at each time period, which we had examined earlier (see Tables 2 and 3). Levels of dyadic homophily over time are related to dyadic homophily at each point in time, but not necessarily to continuity of individual behaviors over time.

Discussion and conclusions

These data contribute to resolving a fundamental issue raised by the lifecourse perspective: the degree to which there is continuity or discontinuity in development. A major conclusion to be drawn from this study is that there is continuity from adolescence to adulthood in the extent to which individuals seek to affiliate with other individuals similar to themselves. The degree of homophily in intimate relationships in adulthood is related to the degree of homophily in intimate relationships in adolescence. Thus, individuals appear to seek and create with their spouses the same degree of consonant social environment they sought and created with their peers in adolescence. The principal finding is that tolerance for a nonconsonant environment or lack of such tolerance is a stable trait. However, it must be kept in mind that homophily as measured in these models contains two components which cannot be estimated separately: dyads form because of similarity, and dyads may grow to be more similar over time. The continuity of homophily from adolescence to adulthood reflects both processes.

There are similarities as well as divergences between adolescence and adulthood in the dimensions around which homophily and consonance characterize intimate relationships. Ethnicity and the use of licit and illicit drugs are important bases of interpersonal association both in adolescence and adulthood. Religiosity, fertility expectations, and perceived qualities of interpersonal relationships among family members are important in adulthood. The important role of ethnicity as a basis for affiliation at both life phases illustrates the importance of similarity as a basis for interpersonal attraction. We also know that, in adolescence, sex is an even more important basis of friendship than race (Kandel, 1978b). We noted that in adolescence as well as in adulthood the best friend is of the same sex in nearly 90% of the cases (Baydar & Kandel, 1988). Both race and sex are the most visible distinguishing attributes of an individual.

We would like to suggest further that next to visible biological attributes, homophily is highest on those domains of life that are most salient to an individual's role at different phases of the life span. A study of perceived similarity and understanding among married couples found that salience on four issues was especially high, namely work, family size, physical discipline of the children, and leisure time (White, 1985). These areas were more salient than economic contribution, chores, who gives more in the relationship, and women's rights issues. While we did not measure work-related values and attitudes in our study, we did find that homophily was most important for factors that pertain to family size, discipline of the children, and leisure time activities, i.e. drug use. In addition, we found religiosity, one dimension that was not highlighted by White (1985), to be very important. Other investigators, however, have found religiosity to be a most important determinant of marital satisfaction (Filsinger & Wilson, 1984; Heaton, 1984; Wilson & Filsinger, 1986), especially for women (Hansen, 1987).

Although there is a tendency to seek individuals similar to oneself, not everyone has this tendency to the same degree. How individuals come to be socialized to seek out similar others on those very dimensions that are important to them is one of many questions that cannot be answered by our inquiry. However, race may have great importance because, together with sex, it is that variable which is a most visible indicator both of biological and cultural similarity. To the extent that individuals seek out and create particular environments, they maximize genetic and cultural homogeneity.

Acknowledgments

Work on this research has been partially supported by research grants DA00064, DA01097, DA03196, and DA02867 and a research scientist award DA00081 from the National Institute on Drug Abuse and an award from the John D. and Catherine T. MacArthur Foundation. Partial support for computer costs was provided by Mental Health Clinical Research Center Grant MH 30906–07 from National Institute of Mental Health to the New York State Psychiatric Institute. The research assistance of Christine Schaffran is gratefully acknowledged. The manuscript benefited greatly from the insightful and detailed editorial suggestions made by Lee Robins and Michael Rutter.

Appendix: Definition of selected variables

Cigarettes:
  For friendship dyads, current use:
    1 = never, 2 = once or twice ever, 3 = former use, 4 = occasionally,
    5 = less than pack per day, 6 = pack per day or more.
  For marital dyads, lifetime:
    0 = never, 1 = less than 10 times, 2 = 10–99 times, 3 = 100 to 999 times,
    4 = 1,000 times or more.
  For marital dyads, last year:
    0 = no use, 1 = once a year, 2 = several times a year, 3 = once a month,
    4 = 2–3 times a month, 5 = once a week, 6 = 2–3 times a week,
    7 = 4–6 times a week, 8 = daily.

Beer/Wine:
  For friendship dyads only, current use:
    1 = never, 2 = less than once a month, 3 = once a month, 4 = 2–3 times a
    month, 5 = once a week, 6 = several times a week, 7 = daily.

Hard liquor/Alcohol, marijuana, and all other drugs:
  For friendship dyads, lifetime:
    1 = never, 2 = 1–2 times, 3 = 3–9 times, 4 = 10–39 times, 5 = 40–59
    times, 6 = 60 or more. (For LISREL, three new categories were created:
    1 = never, 2 = 1–9 times, 3 = 10 +.)
  For marital dyads, lifetime and last year: Same categories as for cigarettes.
  For LISREL, marijuana use last year was coded as: 0 = never, 1 = used but
  not in last year, 2 = less than once a month, 3 = once a month or more.

Educational expectations (friendship dyads):
   1 = won't finish high school, 2 = high school only, 3 = technical or business school, 4 = some college, 5 = college, 6 = graduate or professional school. (For LISREL, 1 and 2, and 3 and 4 were combined.)

Educational attainment (marital dyads):
   9 = 9 years or less, 10 through 16 = years of education, 18 = MA or graduate school, 20 = PhD or professional school. (For LISREL, 4 categories were created: 9 – 12, 13 – 15, 16, 17 and over.)

Religiosity (frequency of attending religious services):
   For friendship dyads:
      1 = rarely or never, 2 = 1–3 times a month, 3 = 1–2 times per week, 4 = every day.
   For marital dyads:
      1 = never, 2 = several times a year, 3 = once a month, 4 = 2 – 3 times a month, 5 = once a week, 6 = several times a week, 7 = every day.
      (For LISREL, at both time periods the coding was: 1 = less than once a month, 2 = less than once a week, 3 = once a week or more.)

Political orientation:
   For friendship dyads:
      1 = very conservative, 2 = conservative, 3 = moderate, 4 = liberal, 5 = very liberal, 6 = radical.
   For marital dyads:
      1 = conservative, 2 = moderate, 3 = liberal, 4 = radical.

Depressive symptoms:
   An average score based on how much subject has been bothered in the past year by feeling unhappy, sad, or depressed; feeling hopeless about the future; feeling too tired to do things; having trouble going to sleep or staying asleep; feeling nervous or tense; worrying too much about things (six items).

Closeness to father and mother:
   Closeness to father:
      An average score index based on four items relating to the adolescent's relationship with father: how often he praises or encourages the adolescent, how much the adolescent wants to be like the father when an adult, how close the adolescent feels to father, and how much the adolescent depends on the father for advice and guidance.
   Closeness to mother:
      Constructed similarly to closeness-to-father index, using parallel items as apply to mother, but with one additional item: frequency of talking about personal problems with mother.

Parent-peer orientation:

Measures whether the respondent feels greater understanding from parents or friends, and relies more on opinions of parents or friends (two items).

Index of peer activity:

Measures the frequency of getting together with friends outside of school, dating, attending parties, hanging around with a group of kids, and driving around with friends (five items).

Index of minor delinquency:

Based on whether respondents had within the past 3 months been sent out of a classroom by a teacher, taken things of little value (worth less than $2) that did not belong to them, taken things of some value ($2 to $50) that did not belong to them, been drunk, cheated on a class test, run away from home or stayed out all night without their parents' permission, and drove too fast (seven items).

Index of serious delinquency:

Based on whether respondents had ever taken a car for a ride without the owner's permission, banged up something that did not belong to them on purpose, taken things of large value (worth over $50) that did not belong to them, and held up or robbed a person (four items).

Notes

1 The sex-specific analyses obscure the fact that in adolescence homophily on sex is higher than on ethnicity. Males tend to select males as friends and females select females (Kandel, 1978*b*).
2 For education and religious services, these correlations are not significantly different from zero. For marijuana use, the correlation is high and negative, because the observed covariance between best friend and spouse is much lower than would be predicted from the homophily model. To compensate for the fact that homophily predicts more covariance than is observed, the correlation of the residuals terms is negative. The negative correlation coefficient should not be interpreted as discontinuity in marijuana use between best friend and spouse, since it represents the correlation of the residual variation after similarities with the focal respondent and the correlation of these similarities over time have been taken into account.

References

Baydar, N., & Kandel, D. (1988). Friendship networks, intimacy and illicit drug use in young adulthood: A comparison of two competing theories. Unpublished manuscript.

Berscheid, E. (1985). Interpersonal attraction. In G. Lindzey & E. Aronson (Eds.), *The handbook of social psychology* (pp. 413–484). New York: Random House.

Blankenship, V., Hnat, S. M., Hess, T. G., & Brown, D. R. (1984). Reciprocal interaction and similarity of personality attributes. *Journal of Social and Personal Relationships, 1,* 415–432.

Byrne, D. (1971). *The attraction paradigm.* New York: Academic Press.

Cohen, J. (1960). A coefficient of agreement for nominal scales. *Educational and Psychological Measurement, 20,* 37–46.

Cook, W., & Dryer, A. (1984). The social relations model: A new approach to the analysis of family-dyadic interaction. *Journal of Marriage and the Family,* August, 679–687.

Duck, S., & Gilmour, R. (Eds.) (1981). *Personal relationships 1: Studying personal relationships.* New York: Academic.

Filsinger, E. E., & Wilson, M. R. (1984). Religiosity, socioeconomic rewards, and family development: Predictors of marital adjustment. *Journal of Marriage and the Family, 46,* 663–670.

Fleiss, J. (1973). *Statistical methods for rates and proportions.* New York: John Wiley & Sons.

Glass, J., & Polisar, D. (1987). A method and metric for assessing similarity among dyads. *Journal of Marriage and the Family, 49,* 663–668.

Hansen, G. L. (1987). The effect of religiosity on factors predicting marital adjustment. *Social Psychology Quarterly, 50,* 264–269.

Heaton, T. B. (1984). Religious homogamy and marital satisfaction reconsidered. *Journal of Marriage and the Family, 46,* 729–733.

Heider, F. (1958). *The psychology of interpersonal relations.* New York: John Wiley & Sons.

Homans, G. C. (1961). *Social Behavior: Its elementary forms.* New York: Harcourt Brace.

Jöreskog, K., & Sorbom, D. (1984). *LISREL VI: Analysis of linear structural relationships by the method of maximum likelihood.* Mooresville, IN: Scientific Software.

Kandel, D. B. (1978a). Homophily, selection and socialization in adolescent friendships. *American Journal of Sociology, 84,* 427–436.

Kandel, D. B. (1978b). Similarity in real life adolescent pairs. *Journal of Personality and Social Psychology, 36,* 306–312.

Kenny, D. A. (1988). Interpersonal perception: A social relations analysis. *Journal of Social and Personal Relationships, 4,* 247–261.

Klein, D. M. (n.d.). The problem of multiple perception in family research. University of Notre Dame.

Lazarsfeld, P. F., & Merton, R. K. (1954). Friendship as a social process. In M. Berger, T. Abel, & C. H. Page (Eds.), *Freedom and control in modern society* (pp. 18–66). Princeton, NJ: Van Nostrand.

Lott, A. J., & Lott, B. E. (1965). Group cohesiveness versus interpersonal attraction: A review of relationships with antecedent and consequent variables. *Psychological Bulletin, 64,* 259–309.

Mirowsky, J., & Ross, C. E. (1987). Belief in innate sex roles: Sex stratification versus interpersonal influence in marriage. *Journal of Marriage and the Family, 49,* 527–540.

Neimeyer, R. A., & Mitchell, K. A. (1988). Similarity and attraction: A longitudinal study. *Journal of Social and Personal Relationships, 4,* 131–148.

Newcomb, T. M. (1961). *The acquaintance process.* New York: Holt, Rinehart & Winston.

Scarr, S., & McCartney, K. (1983). How people make their own environments: A theory of genotype environment effects. *Child Development, 54*, 424–435.

Schumm, W. R., Barnes, H. L., Bollman, S. R., Jurich, A. P., & Milliken, G. A. (1984). Approaches to the statistical analysis of family data. *Home Economics Research Journal.*

Simpson, I. H., & England, P. (1981). Conjugal work roles and marital solidarity. *Journal of Family Issues, 2*, 180–204.

Strauss, D. J. (1973). Measuring endogamy. *Social Science Research, 6*, 225–245.

Thibaut, J., & Kelly, H. (1959). *The social psychology of groups.* New York: John Wiley & Sons.

Thompson, E. (1986). Two into one: Modeling couple behavior. (Working Paper 86–15). Madison: University of Wisconsin, Center for Demography and Ecology.

Thompson, E., & Williams, R. (1982). Beyond wives' family sociology: A method for analysing couple data. *Journal of Marriage and the Family, 44*, 999–1008.

White, J. M. (1985). Perceived similarity and understanding in couples. *Journal of Social and Personal Relationships, 2*, 45–57.

Wilson, M. R., & Filsinger, E. E. (1986). Religiosity and marital adjustment: Multidimensional interrelationships. *Journal of Marriage and the Family, 48*, 147–151.

13 Common and uncommon pathways to adolescent psychopathology and problem behavior

PATRICIA COHEN, JUDITH S. BROOK, JACOB
COHEN, C. NOEMI VELEZ, AND MARC GARCIA

A long-term longitudinal study of the period from early childhood through late adolescence may help to clarify two major issues in developmental research: Do some aspects of early experiences have common, important, and pervasively enduring effects with respect to both later psychological distress and later problem behavior?

To what extent do specific influential early experiences affect specific areas of later functioning?

In particular, it has long been known that there are correlations between substance abuse, delinquency, and emotional problems of adolescents. Jessor and Jessor (1977) have conceptualized both substance abuse and conduct problems as members of the class of "problem behavior," which tends to increase in prevalence over the high school to early post–high school years. Therefore, the question of specificity naturally arises: Do these problems have the same course? Do they have the same risk factors?

In the study to be reported here, an early experience variable that constitutes comparable risk for both psychological distress and problem behavior in adolescence is considered a common pathway. If, on the other hand, it is related differentially to psychological distress as compared to problem behavior, it is then identified as a specific risk or "uncommon pathway." The purpose of the current investigation, then, is to identify early risks exerting influence on later problems broadly or specifically.

At present there is no general consensus among investigators as to the specific or common early determinants of the later development of psychopathology or drug abuse. Indeed, there are few longitudinal data available to examine the early antecedents of both psychological problems and problem behavior in a single methodological and conceptual framework (Baumrind, 1967; Kellam et al., 1982).

In the past decade, a few investigators such as Kohn (1976) and the Jessors (1977) have called attention to the fact that research has tended to focus on the study of very specific occurrences in adolescence. Drug use, delinquency, and emotional disorders have rarely been considered simultaneously, but rather have been treated as distinct outcome variables. One notable exception to this trend is a study of the first-grade antecedents of both teenage substance abuse and psychological well-being. Findings by Kellam and his colleagues (1982) suggest that mothers' educational expectations and mothers' own psychological well-being appear to be common predictors for both psychiatric symptoms and substance abuse among teenagers, although their relative potency for predicting problems of each kind was not assessed.

Although psychological distress and problem behavior share some common elements, our study was undertaken on the conviction that they are not simple functional equivalents, and that their differential antecedents are as important for developing an understanding of their natures as are their common pathways.

The study: Domains of early experience

The three domains of early experience that are believed to be of great importance by developmentalists—context, parent characteristics, and parenting behaviors—were included in the present study, as well as a measure of early biological risk. In making general predictions about the overall importance of these domains for psychological distress or problem behavior, we will be guided by the findings of other investigators of these problems.

The first domain, context, consists of indices reflecting generally supportive or stressful characteristics of the setting, such as crime in the neighborhood, socioeconomic status, and residential instability. Urban or rural location of residence was also considered, since location effects have been reported by several investigators (Costello et al., 1985; Offord et al., 1986; Rutter, Cox et al., 1975). Context attributes may be related to both psychological distress and problem behavior, but on past evidence they are expected to be more related to problem behavior and especially substance abuse, tending to shape the form of expression of problems.

The second domain, family and parent attributes, includes parental sociopathy and parental history of mental illness, divorce, and remarriage. Psychopathology is believed to aggregate in families and thus parental psychopathology is expected to relate to a child's emotional distress. On the other hand, parental sociopathy may be expected to relate more specifically to problem behavior, certainly including acting out or externalizing behavior, and possibly substance abuse as well. Family dissolution and remarriage are stresses that may result in any of these problems (Rutter, Yule, et al., 1975).

The third domain, parent–child interaction and relationship, should also be of importance in predicting both distress and problem behavior in adolescence. The relative impact on these different outcomes is more difficult to predict and probably can be expected to vary as a function of the aspect of parenting considered. Variables related to parental control and supervision, maternal and paternal involvement in the child, and the strictness and consistency of rules may be related particularly to problem behavior. Power-assertive punishment techniques have been shown to relate to aggressive behavior in the child. Parental aspirations for the child may speak to the child's overall confidence and to positive aspects of the parent–child relationship, and therefore may relate more to emotional disorder. Finally, on the basis of prior research, biological risk may be expected to be related to emotional problems, to behavior problems, and possibly to drug abuse as well (Cohen et al., 1989*b*).

The sample and data set

The current study is based on data from a longitudinal study of a random sample of children in families living in two upstate New York counties. Families were originally sampled in 1975 when the children were ages 1 to 10 (see Kogan et al., 1977, for a detailed description of the original sampling plan and study procedures) and were recontacted for interview in 1983 when they were aged 9 to 18. Interviews of mothers in the original survey were completed by trained lay interviewers, and covered a broad range of emotional, behavioral, and temperamental difficulties in children, as well as a number of descriptors of the family and of child-rearing practices.

In the current analyses we examine only those children who were ages 5 to 10 at the time of the original interviews and ages 13 to 18 at the time of the follow-up, a limit of age range designed to allow for development of conduct and drug problems. Eighty-eight percent of the families of this older sample were located at the time of the follow-up, and nearly 80% were interviewed. This sample is representative of families with children of these ages in the northeastern United States, with the exception of a higher rate of Catholic religious background and fewer minority families, both due to the characteristics of the sampled counties (Table 1).

At the time of the follow-up both mothers and youth were interviewed separately but simultaneously in their homes by pairs of trained lay interviewers. Interviews typically took about 2 hours each.

The measures

Dependent variables. Three variables were selected from among those available in this study to represent substance abuse, behavior problems, and emotional problems. The measures of behavior problems and emotional problems were the Child Behavior Checklist (CBCL) Externalizing and Internalizing Symptom Scales (Achenbach & Edelbrock, 1983) as reported by mothers at the time of follow-up. These widely used measures

Table 1. *Demographic characteristics of families of*
13-to-18-year-olds (N = 423)

Mean age = 15.54 years
Median family income = $32,500
Income range: under $4,000 to over $75,000
Intact families: 74%
Race: 94% white
Religion: 57% Catholic, 39% Protestant

discriminate fairly well between clinical and nonclinical samples, and have
been shown to be useful in many studies based on nonclinical samples as
well. Alpha internal consistencies in the current study were .87 for the
externalizing scale and .77 for the internalizing scale. Scaled diagnostic
syndrome scores were also generated by our research group, based on
reports by both mother and youth. Analyses using these scores produced
findings similar to those involving the CBCL scales, but will not be reported
here because the wide use of the CBCL makes its findings more readily
understood. However, the measure of substance abuse used here was
derived from the pooled parent and child diagnostic interview responses. It
includes answers to questions regarding both consumption and related
problems for alcohol, marijuana, and other drugs, and is measured with an
internal consistency of .89.

Although substance abuse as measured here is clearly a "problem
behavior," the status of the CBCL externalizing-symptom scale is more
ambiguous. Certain of its components, such as aggressive behavior and
delinquent acts, clearly fall within the domain of problem behavior,
whereas others, such as hyperactivity or impulsiveness, probably do not.
This measure as a whole is broadly viewed as a reflection of behavioral
symptoms of mental disorder. The CBCL internalizing symptom scale,
which includes items on depression and anxiety among others, is more
unambiguously a measure of emotional distress.

As might be expected, these measures were intercorrelated. Substance
abuse and externalizing symptoms correlated .27, while internalizing and
externalizing symptoms were correlated .58, a magnitude consistent with
that reported in other samples (Achenbach & Edelbrock, 1983). Internalizing symptoms and substance abuse were not significantly related ($r = .09$).

Risk factors. With one exception all risk factors were measured at the time of
the original interview, 8 years prior to the assessment of the problems of the
child.

Biological risk. This was assessed by a single pooled measure of early somatic risk. This measure includes pre- and perinatal problems as well as illnesses, accidents, and hospitalizations in early childhood. It was shown in previous analyses to predict future psychopathology (Cohen, et al., 1989b).

Context. Five indicators of potential differential risk associated with the environmental context of the family were included in the current study:

1. Urban setting
2. Neighborhood crime
3. Residential instability
4. Low socioeconomic status
5. Social isolation

All were measured in the original interview. Differences in rates of problems associated with urban as compared with rural residence have been implicated by Rutter et al. (1975), although other differences in populations they studied may have accounted for differential rates. The second potential risk factor, neighborhood crime, was measured by a two-item index. Family residential instability was measured by the number of moves in the previous 5 years and the length of time at the current address. Low socioeconomic status (SES) is one of the most commonly measured risk factors for problems during childhood and adolescence, as well as adulthood. One of the elements of low SES, median income of the neighborhood, was originally included as a separate risk factor. However, its high correlation with family SES (.70) resulted in a redundancy of measurement that lowered the power of either to be shown to contribute independently to later problems. In additon, the risk of developing externalizing symptoms associated with family socioeconomic status was found to be conditional on neighborhood median income. The negative effects of low SES were much greater when the family also lived in a poor neighborhood.

A final measure of environmental context risk for later problems was a scale of social isolation, reflecting the contacts (or lack of them) with other children in various settings.

Family. Five risk factors associated with parent characteristics and family structure were included:

1. Parental treatment for mental health
2. Parental sociopathy
3. Low maternal availability
4. Mother-only family
5. Mother–step-father family

Parental mental health treatment history is known to be one of the most potent risk factors for childhood psychopathology. Mothers were asked about their own and the fathers' treatment histories, but the nature of the mental illness treated was not determined. An index of parental sociopathy, including problems with alcohol, drugs, or the police on the part of either or both parents, was created from maternal responses to questions on the original maternal interview. Three variables shown in studies by Rutter and Sandberg (1985) to present a cumulative risk for childhood psychopathology were pooled, because we hypothesized that all three would lower maternal availability to the child. These were maternal ill health, maternal employment, and many siblings. Finally, two family structures potentially posing a risk to children were measured at the time of the follow-up. These were living in a mother-only family, and living with a mother and step-father. These were each coded as dummy variables so that simultaneous consideration in a regression equation produced the contrast of each with the children in intact families.

Parent–child interaction. Five risk factors reflecting the quality of parenting were measured in the original interview:

1. Paternal involvement
2. Maternal inattention
3. Power-assertive punishment
4. Absence of rules
5. Low educational aspirations and expectations

A measure of paternal involvement reflected the time the father spent with the child as well as his involvement in decisions related to the child. An index of maternal inattention was created from several measures reflecting the recency and frequency of medical and dental check-ups, maternal awareness of vaccinations and inoculations, use of vitamins, and other aspects of "investment" in the child. Power-assertive punishment techniques, including screaming at the child, threatening, hitting, isolating, and taking away privileges, have been shown to be powerful risk factors for children's problems (Eron et al., 1971; Patterson, 1982). An absence of rules and inconsistency in enforcing rules have been implicated in the development of problems (Baumrind, 1967). Finally, parents' low educational aspirations and expectations for the child have been shown to be a risk factor for subsequent problem behavior (Kellam et al., 1982). Each of these measures of parenting was measured with two or more items from the maternal interview, resulting in roughly normally distributed scales.

The method

Three methodological aspects of the current study should be noted. First, risk factors had been measured prospectively, 8 years prior to the measurement of the emotional and behavioral problems. Prospective assessment minimizes the possible confusion of risk factors for child problems with effects of the child problems on the purported risk factor. The danger of confusion is particularly salient with regard to the parent–child interaction, which is known to be affected by such "reverse" effects (Maccoby & Martin, 1983). On the other hand, we have not covaried problems measured in early childhood for two reasons. First, a number of early risks predate these problems, such as sociopathy in the parents and early somatic problems, and therefore effects on later childhood psychopathology may well be mediated by effects on earlier childhood psychopathology, without negating a causal effect. Second, other early risks may be useful as harbingers of risk in late childhood and adolescence even if their mechanisms are not clear. For example, other analyses (Cohen & Brook, 1987) suggest that power-assertive punishment in early childhood is not a risk factor for development of new or additional problems in late childhood unless its use continues. This finding means that the causal influence of power-assertive punishment on children's problems operates over a shorter span of time than the interval actually measured (in our study, 8 years).

A second methodological strength of the current study is the simultaneous consideration of risk factors from multiple domains. Many studies have examined only one or two domains of these risk factors at a time (e.g., Furstenberg et al., 1987). The difficulty with this approach is that the same youths may be identified by several risk factors, each of which claims to "explain" their behavior problems. But the risk factors studied in these various tests may not be independent. When the predicative power of an established risk factor disappears with the simultaneous consideration of another risk, the causal impact of the first factor should be questioned. Under such circumstances, both theory and policy are likely to require revision.

Finally, the comparison of the partial or direct effects of risk factors on different outcome variables has typically proceeded informally. Investigators are often forced to note that a risk has been significant for one outcome but not for another, or that some estimate of magnitude of effect appears to be larger for one outcome than another without any formal statistical comparison of the differences. Thus, the identification of common and uncommon, or specific, risks has proceeded as once did the interpretation of overall F tests for differences among several groups, or the interpretation of the meaning of complex interactions; that is, informally. Of course, a risk factor may be significant for one outcome but not for another without affecting the two outcomes in a *significantly* different way. Such a finding is consonant with the conclusion that the risk factor has an equivalent effect on the two outcomes. The risk factor may be significantly related to two different outcomes, but have a significantly larger effect on one than the other. In order to provide a simultaneous test of the significance of the differences, between the various effects of risk factors, we devised a procedure that we call *net regression*, because it provides an overall test of the net differences in the partial regression coefficients, as well as a test of each risk factor.

In this procedure, an ordinary least-squares equation is produced for each of two standardized dependent variables, Y and Z, using all risk factors of interest. (In our case, we also included as co-variates age, sex, and the age-by-sex interaction.) The two predicted or estimated dependent variables, $\breve{Y}$ and $\breve{Z}$, are then produced. Their equations are, of course, the sum of the regression-weighted risk factors plus a constant. This sum for $\breve{Y}$ is then subtracted from Z, and this new variable, $Z - \breve{Y}$, is regressed on the original set of predictors (risk factors). The overall R for this equation and its associated F provides a test of the significance of the aggregate differences in risk factors, and each partial regression co-efficient and its t indicates the magnitude and significance of the difference in risk for each variable. (The symmetrical analysis of $Y - \breve{Z}$ is totally redundant with this analysis, but may be done to check on the accuracy of the programming.)

Finally, it is important to note that the tests provided by the net regression procedure are not at all the same as those that determine whether one dependent variable (such as externalizing symptoms) accounts for the association between risk factors and the other dependent variable (such as substance abuse). This different question is answered by partialling one dependent variable from the other, and regressing this partialled variable on the risk factors.

Findings

We found, as other studies have, that internalizing is more prevalent in girls than in boys, whereas externalizing is more prevalent among boys. Substance abuse was approximately equally prevalent in the two sexes.

The following analyses show the relationship of each risk factor to the three measures of problems in adolescence. The first set controls only for the relationships of age and sex with risk and outcome variables. The second set of analyses adds controls for all other risk factors. In the third set of analyses the net regression procedure is used to assess the significance of the differences in partial coefficients produced in the second analyses.

Bivariate analyses

Internalizing symptoms. Internalizing symptoms in adolescence were related bivariately with the index of biological risk, and with risk factors from the context group (low SES and social isolation), from the family environment set (parental mental illness and remarriage), and from the parent-child set (Table 2). Contrary to expectation, maternal inattention was inversely correlated with subsequent internalizing symptoms.

Table 2. *Relationships of problem outcomes with individual risks measured 8 years earlier*

	Substance abuse β^a	Externalizing β	Internalizing β
Biological risk			
Early somatic risk	.08§	.15**	.18**
Context			
Urban (vs. rural)	.05	.03	.02
Neighborhood crime	.16**	.14**	.05
Residential instability	−.07	.15**	.06
Low SES	.04	.16**	.16**
Social isolation	.02	.07	.17**
Family environment			
Parental sociopathy	.03	.22**	.09§
Parental mental illness	−.02	.17**	.17**
Low maternal availability	.07	.12*	.05
Single parent home	.06	.13**	.05
Mother–step-father home	.02	.20**	.17**
Parent–child			
Maternal inattention	.16**	.01	−.21**
Low father involvement	.04	.05	.01
Power-assertive punishment	.04	.30**	.12**
Lax, inconsistent rules	.06	.01	.09§
Low educational aspirations	.02	.14**	.09§

^{a} All coefficients are net of child's age, sex, and age by sex.
* $p < .05$
** $p < .01$
§ $p < .10$

Externalizing symptoms. Externalizing symptoms were related bivariately to biological risk, to three factors from the context group to all five measures of family environment, and to two factors from the parent–child set (power-assertive punishment and low educational aspirations). The relationship with power-assertive punishment was the largest of any assessed.

Substance abuse. Substance abuse in adolescence was significantly related to only two risk factors in the bivariate analysis, one from the context set and one from the parent–child set. Children whose early childhood was spent in high crime neighborhoods were more likely to show later substance abuse. The relationship of maternal inattention with future substance abuse is consistent with previous findings regarding the importance of mother–child

Table 3. *Risk factors related independently to each of the indices of emotional and behavioral problems of adolescence*

	Substance abuse β^a	Externalizing β	Internalizing β
Biological risk			
Early somatic risk	.02	.02	.04**
Context			
Urban (vs. rural)	.10	−.01	.04
Neighborhood crime	.16**	−.10$	.01
Residential instability	−.12*	.05	−.01
Low SES	.04	.03	.09$
Social isolation	−.02	.05	.15**
Family environment			
Parental sociopathy	−.01	.12*	.03
Parental mental illness	−.04	.08*	.09*
Low maternal availability	.02	.07	.02
Single parent home	.26$	.25$	.09
Mother–step-father home	.20	.51**	.45**
Parent–child			
Maternal inattention	.17**	.04	−.19**
Low father involvement	.05	.05	.03
Power-assertive punishment	.03	.21**	.05
Lax, inconsistent rules	.04	.03	.11*
Low educational aspirations	.04	.06	.02

^{a} Coefficients are unstandardized regression coefficients; dependent variables are standardized. Analyses control for age, sex, and age by sex.
* $p < .05$
** $p < .01$
$ $p < .10$

attachment and parental control. Although the absence of a relationship with lax and inconsistent rules is surprising, given the fact that contemporaneous structure has been found to be related to drug use (Brook et al., 1986), we have no evidence that it is a *prospective* risk factor.

Partial relationships of risks with future problems

As anticipated, the risk factors were somewhat redundant in their prediction of future problems (Table 3). The biological risk indicator was significant only for internalizing symptoms. Within the context set, in addition to the previously significant relationship of neighborhood crime with future substance abuse, residential instability was also a significant *protective* factor. This finding is less puzzling when one considers the utility of solid peer connections for obtaining and using drugs. None of the context set showed a significant independent relationship with future externalizing symptoms. The measure of early childhood social isolation was significantly related to subsequent internalizing symptoms.

None of the variables reflecting family environment was independently related to substance abuse, although three of them predicted future externalizing symptoms. Two, parental mental illness and remarriage, also were independent risks for internalizing symptoms. The fact that parental mental illness related to both of these outcomes is consistent with the nonspecificity of the questions regarding parental mental illness; that is, internalizing kinds of mental illness such as depression and externalizing kinds of mental illness would both be reflected by this measure.

The risk associated with step-father families for this adolescent sample is consistent with recent reports by Hetherington (1987).

Finally, the parent–child set included variables having independent relationships with each outcome variable: maternal inattention was a risk for substance abuse, power-assertive punishment was a risk for externalizing, and maternal attention and lax rules were risks for internalizing symptoms.

Although early somatic risk was an independent risk for internalizing symptoms only, its effects were not significantly lower for either substance abuse ($t = 1.63$, df = 403) or externalizing ($t = 1.53$, df = 403). This is consistent with evidence based on analyses of measures combining youths' and mothers' reports of disorder, in which perinatal and early somatic problems were shown to be a risk for all three kinds of problems (Cohen et al., 1989b).

Two other risks predicted both internalizing and externalizing symptoms at the zero-order level: low socioeconomic class and low educational aspirations of mother for the child. However, neither of these was significant net of the other risk factors.

Specific or "uncommon" risks

Internalizing and substance abuse. As shown in Table 4, three contextual risks had significantly different effects on substance abuse and internalizing: neighborhood crime (significantly greater for substance abuse than internalizing), residential instability (significantly protective for substance abuse only), and social isolation (significantly greater for internalizing than substance abuse). Within the family environment set, the risk associated with parental mental illness was significantly greater for future internalizing symptoms than for substance abuse. In addition, a trend was noted for a significantly larger effect of remarriage on internalizing than substance

Table 4. *Net regression analysis: Significant differences in risk factors*

	Substance abuse–internalizing β^a	Substance abuse–externalizing β	Internalizing–externalizing β
Biological risk			
Somatic risk	−.02	.00	.02
Context			
Neighborhood crime	.15**	.06	.08§
Residential instability	−.11**	−.17**	−.06
Social isolation	−.16**	−.07	.10*
Family environment			
Parental sociopathy	−.04	−.13*	−.09§
Parental mental illness	−.13**	−.12**	.01
Single mother	.16	.01	.16
Remarriage	−.25§	−.31§	.06
Parent–child			
Maternal inattention	.35**	.12*	−.23**
Power-assertive punish.	−.02	−.18**	−.16**
Lax, inconsistent rules	−.06	.02	.08§

Note: Overall differences (df = 19/403): $F = 8.27^{**}$, $F = 6.80^{**}$, $F = 4.07^{*}$

[a] Coefficients are raw regression coefficients; dependent variables are Outcome A − Predicted Outcome B. All analyses control for age, sex, and age by sex effects. Variables not significant in any analysis are omitted from the table, although present in the equations.

§ $p < .10$
* $p < .05$
** $p < .01$

abuse. In the parent–child set only one risk was significantly different, namely, maternal inattention, which was a risk factor for future substance abuse but a protective factor for internalizing.

Externalizing and substance abuse. The one context variable that differed significantly between substance abuse and externalizing was residential instability, which was a protective factor for substance abuse but not significant for externalizing (see Cohen et al., 1989*a*, for evidence that one component of residential instability is a risk for one component of externalizing). Within the family environment set, both parental mental illness history and parental sociopathy were significantly greater risks for externalizing than for substance abuse. There was a trend, paralleling that for the substance abuse–internalizing comparison, for remarriage to be a greater risk for externalizing. Within the parent–child set, maternal inattention was a greater risk for substance abuse, while power-assertive punishment was a greater risk for externalizing.

Internalizing and externalizing. There were no significantly different risk factors in the biological risk or family environment sets for subsequent externalizing as compared to internalizing symptoms, although there was a trend for parental sociopathy to be more consequential for externalizing symptoms ($t = 1.81$, $p < .10$). However, one context risk factor, social isolation, was a greater risk for internalizing than for externalizing symptoms. It should be noted that the large correlation between internalizing and externalizing symptoms tends to ensure some similarity among predictors.

Within the parent–child set three significant differences or trends were found: maternal inattention was a protective factor for internalizing but not for externalizing, and power-assertive punishment was a greater risk for subsequent externalizing. The difference in risk for lax rules was not significant at the .05 level ($t = 1.76$, df = 403).

Discussion

We have performed a rather stringent test for the impact of risk factors measured 8 years earlier on adolescent substance abuse and externalizing and internalizing symptoms. Table 5 summarizes the findings.

Although early somatic risk did not differ significantly for the three outcome measures, specific risk factors were found within each of the other sets.

Context. One particularly interesting finding in the context set was a change in the sign of residential stability. Residential stability was a risk for future drug abuse, whereas residential instability constituted a risk for externalizing, albeit not an independent one. This finding is consistent with the critical role that availability of drugs plays in drug abuse (Clayton & Voss, 1981; Elliot et al., 1985). Youth who are repeated newcomers to the neighborhood, are perhaps, therefore, less integrated into the networks through which drugs can be obtained.

The risk associated with the neighborhood crime index also deserves comment. Presumably the risk mechanism common to future substance abuse and externalizing symptoms is the modeling of antisocial and illegal behavior. This mechanism has no function with respect to internalizing symptoms. We are not aware of any other work explicitly comparing modeling effects for conduct problems and drug abuse (Huba & Bentler,

Table 5. *Summary of uncommon (specific) risk factors*

	Childhood problems		
	Greater effect on		Less effect on
Biological risk (none)			
Context			
Neighborhood crime	Substance abuse Externalizing	vs.	Internalizing
Residential instability	Externalizing Internalizing	vs.	Substance abuse (protective)
Social isolation	Internalizing	vs.	Externalizing Substance abuse
Family environment			
Parental sociopathy	Externalizing	vs.	Substance abuse Internalizing
Parental mental illness history	Externalizing Internalizing	vs.	Substance abuse
Remarriage	Externalizing Internalizing	vs.	Substance abuse
Parent–child			
Maternal inattention	Substance abuse	vs.	Externalizing
	Externalizing	vs.	Internalizing (protective)
Power-assertive discipline	Externalizing	vs.	Internalizing Substance abuse
Lax, inconsistent rules	Internalizing	vs.	Externalizing Substance abuse

1980). Social isolation, on the other hand, was a risk factor specific to internalizing symptoms.

Family environment. Family variables as a set tended to discriminate externalizing symptoms from substance abuse, with parental mental illness, sociopathy, and remarriage the most specific risks. The absence of a risk for substance abuse associated with parental sociopathy is puzzling. We need to "unpack" this variable to determine whether specific components (parental problems with drugs, alcohol, or the police) are differentially related to substance abuse.

The only family variable that was a significantly lower risk for internalizing than externalizing symptoms was parental sociopathy. The only one significantly greater for internalizing symptoms than for substance abuse was parental mental illness history.

Parent–child. Parental–child relationships showed a complex pattern of specificity, with power-assertive punishment a specific risk for externalizing behavior; inconsistency of rule enforcement a special risk for internalizing symptoms (contrary to prediction); and maternal inattention a risk factor for substance abuse, but a protective factor against internalizing symptoms. That maternal inattention should be a protective influence against internalizing symptoms is curious. Inattentive mothers are employed, in ill health, or engaged with multiple offspring. Perhaps such mothers are likely to overlook children's subjective symptoms, and so fail to report them. Both our data and other research suggest that emotional problems of adolescents are often hidden from their parents.

In sum, these early risk factors showed substantial specificity in predicting symptom patterns 8 years later. Externalizing symptoms shared some risk factors with internalizing disorder and others with substance abuse. Substance use was the outcome with the greatest number of specific context risk factors, and externalizing symptoms was the outcome with the most specific family risk factors. Parent–child relationship variables were consequential for all syndromes, with some specificity for particular aspects.

Acknowledgments

This research was supported by grants, MH36971 and MH30906 from the National Institute of Mental Health, grant DA03188 from the National Institute of Drug Abuse, and the New York State Office of Mental Health.

References

Achenbach, T. M., & Edelbrock, C. (1983). *Manual for the child behavior checklist.* Burlington, VT: University Associates in Psychiatry.

Baumrind, D. (1967). Child care practices anteceding three patterns of preschool behavior. *Genetic Psychology Monographs, 75,* 43–88.

Brook, J. S., Whiteman, M. Gordon, A. S., & Cohen, P. (1986). Some models and mechanisms for explaining the impact of maternal and adolescent characteristics on adolescent stage of drug use. *Developmental Psychology, 22,* 460–467.

Clayton, R. R., & Voss, H. L. (1981). Young men and drugs in Manhattan: A causal analysis. (*Research monograph 39*). Rockville, MD: National Institute of Drug Abuse.

Cohen, P., & Brook, J. S. (1987). Family factors related to the persistence of psychopathology in childhood and adolescence. *Psychiatry, 50,* 332–345.

Cohen, P., Johnson, J., Struening, E. L., & Brook, J. S. (1989a). Family mobility as a risk for childhood psychopathology. In B. Cooper & T. Helgason (Eds.), *Epidemiology and the prevention of mental illness.* London: Routledge and Kegan Paul. (pp. 145–155).

Cohen, P., Velez, C. N., & Brook, J. S. (1989b). Mechanisms of the relationship between perinatal problems, early childhood illness, and psychopathology in late childhood and adolescene. *Child Development, 60,* 701–709.

Costello, A. J., Edelbrock, C., Kalas, R., Kessler, M. K., & Klaric, S. A. (1984). *National Institute of Mental Health Diagnostic Interview Schedule for Children.* Bethesda, MD: National Institute of Mental Health.

Costello, E. J., Edelbrock, C. S., & Costello, A. (1985). Validity of the NIMH Diagnostic Interview Schedule for Children: A comparison between psychiatric and pediatric referrals. *Journal of Abnormal and Child Psychiatry, 13,* 579–595.

Crowell, D. (1987). Childhood aggression and violence: Contemporary issues. In D. Crowell, I. M. Evans, & C. R. O'Donnell (Eds.), *Childhood aggression and violence.* New York: Plenum.

Elliot, D. S., Huizinger, D., & Acton, S. S. (1985). *Explaining delinquency and drug use.* Hollywood, CA: Sage Publications.

Eron, L. D., Walder, L. O., & Lefkowitz, M. M. (1971). *Learning of aggression in children.* Boston: Little, Brown.

Furstenberg, F. F., Brooks-Gunn, J., & Morgan, S. P. (1987). *Adolescent mothers in later life.* New York: Cambridge University Press.

Hetherington, M. (1987). Presidential address. Biennial meeting of the Society for Research in Child Development. Baltimore, MD.

Hoffman, M. L. (1975). Moral internalization, parental power, and the nature of parent-child interaction. *Developmental Psychology, 11,* 228–239.

Huba, G., & Bentler, P. M. (1980). The role of peer and adult models for drug taking at different stages in adolescence. *Journal of Youth and Adolescence, 9,* 449–465.

Jessor, R., & Jessor, S. L. (1977). *Problem behavior and psychosocial behavior: A longitudinal study of youth.* New York: Academic Press.

Kellam, S. G., Simon, M. A., & Ensminger, M. E. (1982). Antecedents in first grade of teenage drug use and psychological well-being: A ten-year community-wide prospective study. In D. Ricks & B. Dohrenwend (Eds.), *Origins of psychopathology: Research and public policy.* New York: Cambridge University Press.

Kogan, L. S., Smith, J., & Jenkins, S. (1977). Ecological validity of indicator data as predictors of survey findings. *Journal of Social Service Research, 1,* 117–132.

Kohn, M. L. (1976). Looking back: A 25-year review of social problems research. *Social Problems, 24,* 94–112.

Loeber, R. (1985). Patterns and development of antisocial child behavior. *Annals of Child Development, 2,* 77–116.

Maccoby, E. E., & Martin, J. A. (1983). Socialization in the context of the family; parent-child interactions. In P. H. Mussen (Ed.), *Handbook of child psychology* (3rd ed., pp. 1–101). New York: John Wiley & Sons.

Offord, D. R., Boyle, M. H., Szatmari, P., Rae-Grant, N. I., Links, P. S., Cadman, D. T., et al. (1986). *Ontario health study: Prevalence of disorder and rates of service utilization.* Hamilton, Ontario: McMaster University Press.

Patterson, G. R. (1982). *Coercive family processes.* Eugene, OR: Castalia.

Rutter, M., Cox, A., Tupling, G., Berger, M., & Yule, M. (1975). Attainment and adjustment in two geographical areas. I. The prevalence of psychiatric disorder. *British Journal of Psychiatry, 126,* 493–509.

Rutter, M., & Sandberg, S. (1985). Epidemiology of child psychiatric disorder: Methodological issues and some substantive findings. *Child Psychiatry and Human Development, 15,* 209–233.

Rutter, M., Yule, B., Quinton, D., Rowland, O., Yule, W., & Berger, M. (1975). Attainment and adjustment in two geographical areas. III. Some factors accounting for area differences. *British Journal of Psychiatry, 126*, 520–533.

Werner, E. E., Burman, J. M., & French, F. E. (1971). *The children of Kauai.* Honolulu: University of Hawaii Press.

14 Continuities in psychiatric disorders from childhood to adulthood in the children of psychiatric patients

DAVID QUINTON, MICHAEL RUTTER, AND
LESLEY GULLIVER

The childhood antecedents of adult psychiatric disorders have come newly into focus with the development of the burgeoning field of developmental psychopathology (Rutter, 1988; Rutter & Garmezy, 1983; Sroufe & Rutter, 1984). With this perspective has come an appreciation that simple models linking adult disorders to single traumatic early experiences or to the press of current events or to biological dispositions do not provide an adequate explanation for most psychiatric problems (Rutter, 1984). An approach is required that considers interactions between behaviors, dispositions, and environments (Magnusson & Ohman, 1987), and which does so within a life history and developmental framework. Such an approach is necessary both to advance knowledge of causation and to advance nosology. Of course, a search for the developmental or experiential antecedents of adult disorders carries with it no assumption that there will be such antecedents in childhood; rather, that our understanding of proximal causes will not be complete until we understand the processes whereby that confluence of causal factors comes about, as well as why some individuals are resistant to their impact (Rutter, 1985).

The study of continuities between disorders in childhood and in adulthood is central to this enterprise for a number of reasons: first, in order to determine which adult problems genuinely have an onset in adulthood in the absence of behavioral or emotional precursors during the childhood years; second, to investigate whether the form of childhood disorder is related to particular adult illnesses, either homotypically or heterotypically; third, to find out whether the risk factors for childhood disorder predict later problems in the absence of childhood onset; and finally, to consider whether childhood disorders showing continuity into adulthood follow a relatively autonomous course or whether the continuity is promoted by environmental or experiential factors. In this last regard, the processes may be complex, with the behaviors associated with disorder partly responsible for the environments that maintain it (Scarr & McCartney, 1983). Assortative mating, for example, may be a process of this kind.

There are, at present, very large gaps in our basic knowledge of child–adult continuities and of linking processes. These gaps arise not only because there have been few epidemiologically based prospective studies of childhood disorder, but also because some childhood disorders, such as childhood depression, have been recognized too recently to allow long-term follow-up. Neurodevelopmental and behavioral antecedents in childhood have been found for schizophrenia, although this clinical picture appears to apply to only about half of schizophrenics (Rutter, 1984). As yet, there are few data on the adult outcome of childhood disorders analogous to adult depression. What is known suggests that where there are identifiable precursors of adult depression, these are as likely to have involved conduct or emotional problems as depression itself (Zeitlin, 1986). A number of experiential precursors to depression have been discussed, including early loss of parent and consequent lack of parental care (Brown et al., 1986), but as yet the available data are predominantly retrospective with a consequent weakness in their ability to identify mediating links such as childhood disorders or effects on cognitions. Emotional disorders, including both generalized anxiety and specific fears, are generally transient in childhood (Rutter & Garmezy, 1983). Where there is continuity with adult disorder, it is more apparent in the broad pattern of emotional disorder than in the specific symptomatology. As yet remarkably little is known about the links between childhood and adulthood in disorders of this kind, a lack of information paralleled by the failure to find factors consistently associated with the appearance of the disorder in childhood itself.

By far the strongest continuities are seen between conduct disorders in childhood and antisocial personality disorders in adulthood (Loeber & Dishion, 1983; Olweus, 1979; Robins, 1978; Rutter & Giller, 1983). In general the data show that, although the majority of childhood conduct problems remit in late adolescence and early adulthood, antisocial personality disorder in adulthood is virtually always preceded by conduct problems in childhood. To some extent the continuities found may be greater than for other disorders because the diagnosis at both points in time takes in a wider range of behaviors, or behaviors that are easier to identify. Nevertheless, the degree of continuity between serious childhood conduct problems and a wide range of psychosocial difficulties in adulthood is substantial (Zoccolillo et al., in unpublished data).

There is a need to set out more clearly the degree to which common childhood disorders have continuity with disorders of a similar type in adulthood and also with other psychiatric and psychosocial problems. There is also the question of which features of the childhood disorder best predict which adult difficulty, together with the reasons for individual differences in prediction. For example, the continuities from conduct disorder to antisocial personality disorder seem weaker in girls than in boys. Other issues in need of study are the reversal in the overall sex ratio for disorders from childhood (Rutter, 1982), the processes that mediate continuities in disorder, and the question of the etiology of disorders in those individuals with their first onset in adult life.

For the identification of the childhood antecedents of many adult psychiatric problems, follow-back strategies and retrospective accounts have been economical and illuminating, but in the end longitudinal studies are necessary, both to circumvent the problems arising from inadequate recording or reporting of childhood symptomatology and also to assess the specificity of those antecedents identified through retrospective or follow-back methodologies. To date the main emphasis in longitudinal research has been on the outcome from aggressive and antisocial behavior, but data on other childhood disorders are now beginning to appear (Earls, 1987).

In our follow-up study of the children of a representative sample of psychiatric patients, three issues are addressed: the degree of continuity between common childhood disorders and adult problems; the onset of disorders in early adulthood for those not showing problems in childhood; and the prediction of adult disorder and poor social functioning from the family factors most predictive of childhood disorder. The data concern the first 115 (64%) cases in a follow-up study of the children of psychiatric patients first studied between 1965 and 1971.

Initial study of patients' families

Sample

Between 1965 and 1971 a 4-year prospective study of a representative sample of adult psychiatric patients and their children was undertaken in order to investigate the links between mental illness in parents and disorders in children (Rutter & Quinton, 1984). The patient sample was identified through the Camberwell Psychiatric Register (Wing & Hailey, 1972), which provided a comprehensive register of all patients living within a single London borough. The study sample was a 2-in-5 random selection from a consecutive series of patients with children under age 15 who attended over a 10-month period, together with a supplementary series taken over a further sampling period of all patients within less commonly occurring groups, including schizophrenics, as well as all male patients. Because the intention of the study was to investigate the development of disorders in children, the sampling criteria in addition selected only those patients who had not attended a psychiatric clinic in the preceding 12 months, with the hope of tracing forwards the impact and consequences of a newly occurring set of parental symptomatic behaviors. One hundred and thirty-seven families with 292 children under age 15 at the time of first contact were chosen for intensive study. Although the sampling criteria were intended to select parents with illnesses of recent onset or with no recent episode (as indicated by no psychiatric contact for at least one year), the high rate of personality disorder (half the families included a parent so affected) indicated that chronic psychiatric problems were common, as this diagnosis required pervasive malfunction extending back to the teenage years.

Because the main focus of the study was the identification of key features of parental mental illness that put children at psychiatric risk, no parallel study of a comparison sample was undertaken. Rather, the analyses concerned systematic, within-group comparisons of diagnostic, family, or other characteristics. However, two samples were used to "calibrate" the findings with general population data: first, a cross-sectional representative sample of families with 10-year-old children living in the same geographical area, and second, age- and sex-matched classroom controls, children whose behavior had been assessed by teacher questionnaires.

Data collection methods

The Rutter "B" Scale (Rutter, 1967) was obtained for all children at school and for two classroom controls for each of the index children at the time of initial contact with the family and at yearly intervals for the next 4 years. (The same controls were followed regardless of changes of class or school.) Patients and their spouses were interviewed in their homes shortly after their contact with psychiatric services, again one year later and again after an interval of 2 years, using investigator-based techniques of known reliability and validity (Brown & Rutter, 1966; Quinton et al., 1976; Rutter & Brown, 1966). This interview included detailed assessments of the psychiatric state of the parents and of up to two randomly selected children per family. In addition, data were collected on patterns of parent–child interaction and on the parents' marriage, social contacts, and support. In the intervening 2 years, mothers (regardless of whether they were patient or spouse) were interviewed on the family circumstances and psychiatric symptoms of herself, her husband, and the selected children.

The psychiatric assessment of the parents was made on an instrument similar to the first version of the Present State Examination (PSE) (Wing, et al., 1967), and the psychiatric assessment of the children was made from a 33-item, semi-structured interview covering common emotional, behavioral, and developmental problems (Graham & Rutter, 1968). For both assessments overall diagnoses were made by clinical judgment on the presence of relevant symptomatology and impaired function in social roles or relationships. Although these clinical assessments have now been superseded by more comprehensive and diagnostically sophisticated instruments, they provided a systematic coverage of common symptomatology in both parents and children on five assessment occasions over a 4-year period, as well as assessments of deviant classroom behavior by teachers blind to parental disorder. These data are therefore particularly strong as a basis for a prospective examination of continuities in common childhood disorders into the early adult years.

Findings

The spouses of patients had high rates of disorder themselves. One quarter of husbands and two fifths of wives showed a socially handicapping disorder at the first assessment. In male spouses, nearly all those with rated problems were considered to have personality disorders, whereas this was true for only one quarter of the female spouses with psychiatric problems. These rates of disorder were very much higher than in the community comparison group (Rutter & Quinton, 1984). The other distinctive feature of the patients' families was the high rate of marital difficulties; 47% either had current marital discord, as evidenced by frequent open arguing and quarreling, or marital breakdown (compared with 14% in the community group). Most psychiatric disorders in patients showed a fluctuating course over the 4 follow-up years with only 11% being symptom free throughout. Persistence was particularly strong for both patients and spouses with an initial diagnosis of personality disorder.

For the children, case–control differences on the "B" Scale were greater for girls than for boys, but approximately one third of patients' children showed deviant behavior at each assessment, boys and girls alike. Differences from controls were greater when persistent problems over the whole period of the study were considered, with problems occurring twice as often in the children of patients. Similar proportions of patients' children had a disorder at the time of the parental interview, a more valid indication of clinically significant problems (34% of boys and 24% of girls showed difficulties at the first assessment). Persistent disorders were more common in boys than in girls (31% vs. 12%), but persistent disorders in both sexes tended to take the form of conduct or mixed conduct and emotional problems. At each assessment, approximately one third of the children had emotional problems only.

The elevated rate of disorder in patients' sons was restricted to those who experienced open family discord and hostility. Parental diagnosis had little explanatory power once marital discord was accounted for, although personality problems in the parents seemed associated with boys' increased vulnerability to discord and hostility. Girls had higher rates of disorder than controls whether or not there was family discord, although there was evidence that chronic exposure to discord also affected girls in the long run. There was also a link between depression in parents and depressive symptomatology in the children, but effects were not found for other emotional problems.

A number of issues made a follow-up of this sample worthwhile. The present chapter discusses the extent of continuities between disorders in childhood and adulthood and whether parental disorders and family discord had "sleeper effects" for the offspring of patients who did not have disorders as children.

Follow-up study of the offspring of adult patients

Sample selection

The offspring followed were all those age 21 or older whose childhood psychiatric status had been assessed in at least two parental interviews or who had participated in a sub-study of childhood temperament (Graham et al., 1973). In all, 181 of the original 292 children met these criteria.

To date, 115 (64%) of the offspring and spouses (if any) have been interviewed. The mean age for males was 26.43 years (SD 3.55), and for females 25.59 (SD 3.34). The interview covered in detail individual recollections of childhood experiences, school life, and work history, together with recall of parental symptomatology, its impact, and the subject's reactions to it. Social functioning in adulthood was assessed in the areas of sexual/marital relationships, friendships, and work, using measures established in the previous study of the adult functioning of institutionalized children (Quinton & Rutter, 1988); current psychiatric disorder was based on a PSE modified to cover the whole of the past year rather than the past month; and lifetime disorder (since age 16) was based on contacts with professional services for psychiatric reasons, together with a brief characterization of these or other reported episodes to allow PSE categorization. A designation of antisocial, inadequate, or other personality disorder was made on evidence of pervasive malfunction across the areas of social functioning from age 16 onwards. This age was chosen so as to avoid overlap with childhood psychiatric data and thus the creation of artifactual continuities.

Since only 64% of the sample provided the total data, it was necessary to check for possible biases (Table 1). No statistically significant differences on any of the comparisons were found, either between the interviewed, and those who refused or were untraced cases, or between the interviewed subjects and the latter two categories combined. If anything, those who refused seemed to come from families with less persistent parental disorder and less marital discord or disruption, and those who are not yet traced rated even higher on these characteristics. Since these differences balance each other, it appears that the interpretation of the results will be more affected by the small sample size than by biases resulting from refusals or inability to locate subjects.

Comparisons on adult circumstances and social functioning were made with a control sample comprised of 84 men and women taken from the

Table 1. *Comparison of subjects interviewed and not interviewed*

	Interviewed $N = 115^a$ %	Refused $N = 31^a$ %	Not traced $N = 31^a$ %
Persistent disorder in father	41	22	46
Persistent disorder in mother	37	34	50
With same two parents throughout the original study	67	74	62
Persistent parental discord or marital breakdown	36	25	42
Child persistently deviant on the teacher questionnaire	24	13	18
Child with persistent psychiatric disorder on parental interview	25	20	15
No differences statistically significant			

^{a} Three dead children and one waiting to be interviewed were omitted from this table. Numbers for individual comparisons vary with missing or not applicable data. The comparisons on child psychiatric disorder and deviance on the teacher questionnaire were made on those always within the age group for this assessment.

Table 2. *Current family circumstances*

	Men		Women	
	Cases $(N = 51)$ %	Controls $(N = 42)$ %	Cases $(N = 64)$ %	Controls $(N = 42)$ %
Currently cohabiting	61	73	67	76
Any broken cohabitations (of those ever cohabiting)	24	26	44	9**
Current marital discord (of those currently cohabiting)	26	14	21	3
Current discord or broken cohabitation (of those ever cohabiting)	35	16	56	9***
Has children	41	51	55	43
Pregnancy/fatherhood by age 19	6	2	28	5***

** χ^2 significant at .01 level
*** χ^2 significant at .001 level

classroom control subjects in the first study. These subjects were, on average, about a year younger than the offspring of patients at follow-up 25.26 years (SD 2.19) for men and 24.34 (SD 1.60) for women. Assessments of adult social functioning were made on the same instrument at that used for the patients' offspring, but no direct comparison was possible on current psychiatric disorder because PSE data were not collected on the comparison group.

Results

Family circumstances. The social and family characteristics of the offspring at follow-up were compared with controls (Table 2). For men, there was little difference in the proportions at follow-up of those who had children, were currently married or cohabiting, or admitted to being a father by age 19. Male offspring were twice as likely as controls to have current marital discord, but the difference was not statistically significant. The figures for the women were strikingly different from the control sample on the proportions with broken cohabitations, early pregnancy, and current marital discord.

The overall differences in social functioning taking both the range and severity of problems into account (Quinton & Rutter, 1988) are given in Figure 1. The offspring of patients showed poorer overall social functioning for both sexes, although the difference was greater for women. The contrast was greatest for the proportions of men and women who had neither a history of psychosocial difficulties nor current problems in any area, although this difference was statistically significant only for women ($\chi = 19.70$, df $= 1$, $p < .001$). All of the men in both the case and control samples with poor social functioning were considered to have personality disorders, as were 80% of female offspring. This diagnosis was not made for any of the comparison women, none of whom showed poor social functioning.

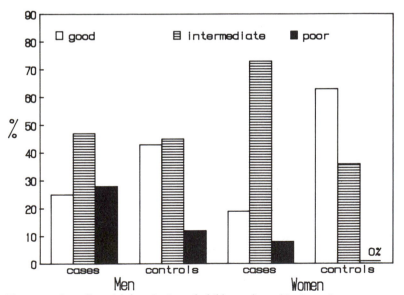

Figure 1. Overall social functioning of children of psychiatric patients.

Continuities in psychiatric disorder. Rutter (1970), using data from the first year of the original study, proposed that different mechanisms might account for the disorders found in the male and female children of psychiatric patients. In boys the effect seemed to be predominantly environmental, whereas genetic influences might be stronger in girls. This argument was based on the following observations: case – control differences for girls were greater than for boys; and for boys, case-control differences were accounted for by an excess of family discord and disruption. No environmental factors were identified that explained the excess of disorder in the daughters of psychiatric patients.

The speculation yielded two predictions: first, that childhood disorders in daughters of parents with affective disorders should show substantial continuity with disorders in adulthood and that these disorders would be affective in nature, whereas this would not be so for boys. Secondly that, since the case – control difference for girls applied predominantly to conduct problems, these should be manifest in adulthood as affective disorders, since the parental disorders were predominantly of this type. This diagnostic switch for girls would partly explain the change in the sex ratio for disorders between childhood and adulthood.

Robins has suggested that data showing a lower level of persistence for conduct disorders in girls may simply imply that the range of outcomes examined was too narrow. The evidence for this view came from the early clinic follow-up study (Robins, 1966) in which antisocial girls as adults showed increased rates of disorder involving anxiety and depression. More recent data from the Epidemiological Catchment Area (ECA) study (Robins, 1986) supported this view, in that women who reported childhood conduct problems showed increased rates of a wide range of adult problems. If "internalizing" disorders in adulthood (affective and anxiety disorders, psychosexual problems, somatization, and the like) were considered along with "externalizing" disorders (drug and alcohol abuse, antisocial personality, etc.), girls showed as much continuity of conduct disorder in adulthood as boys, for whom virtually all outcomes were in the externalizing category. These issues can be examined prospectively in the data from our studies.

Childhood–adulthood continuities in psychiatric disorder. The first requirement for examining child–adult continuities in psychiatric disorders was to assign a childhood diagnosis. Three clearly defined groups were required: a well group, a group with emotional disorders, and a group with conduct problems. The first known parental assessment and the first two known teacher questionnaires (TQ) were used to define these childhood groups. These data were chosen on the principle that the detailed parental account was a satisfactory assessment of the children's functioning over a prolonged period of time and therefore that a single measurement point was adequate, whereas a single TQ was known to have a weak discriminating power (Rutter & Quinton, 1984). The data were restricted to these assessments because they were available for all children. If all available data were considered, children receiving more assessments would have a greater chance of being detected as having problems.

A coding of the presence of disorder was made if either the parental interview or both TQs showed disorder to be present. On this rating, 64 offspring were found to be without childhood psychiatric disorder. Of those with a rating of psychiatric disorder, 21 were rated on the parental interview only, 7 on the TQ only, and 10 on both assessments. Of the 31 subjects with disorder rated as present based on the parental interview, 28 showed disorder also on subsequent parental interview assessments. Seven further offspring were rated on the parental interview as having disorder when teacher information was not available on the first two occasions (5 of these showed disorder also on subsequent parental interview assessments). Six offspring were excluded because they were well on one assessment (TQs or parental interview) and had missing data on the other. A rating of emotional disorder was given if such symptoms were present without any admixture of conduct problems. The conduct disorder diagnosis was made on those with a mixed conduct/emotional picture as well as those with conduct problems only. The remainder constituted the well group.

On this categorization 54% of boys and 27% of girls were considered as having disorder (which, as indicated above, was persistent over several years in almost all cases). Rates were similar (14% vs. 13%) for emotional problems but, as expected, boys much more often showed conduct or mixed problems (40% vs. 15%). The great majority of these disorders were in a moderate range of handicap. The most common conduct problems were fighting, disobedience, lying, and temper tantrums. Delinquency and promiscuity were relatively rare. A rating of "well" here does not rule out the possibility of disorder earlier or later in childhood, nor does a rating of emotional disorder rule out the possibility of the later emergence of conduct problems, a change which would alter the childhood diagnosis.

In all the analyses to be presented, the very small numbers in some cells need to be borne in mind. Statistical significances are given as a guide to interpreting the findings, but larger studies are necessary before the results can be accepted with confidence.

Level of continuity from childhood illness. The relationship between childhood diagnosis and a rating of adult psychiatric problems at or above ID (index of definition) level 5 and/or personality disorder is given in Figure 2. ID level 5 in the PSE threshold level for reliably identifying "cases" in epidemiological studies, using the CATEGO computer scoring system (Wing et al., 1978). The continuities are striking for both childhood emotional and conduct disorders. The differences from the well-in-

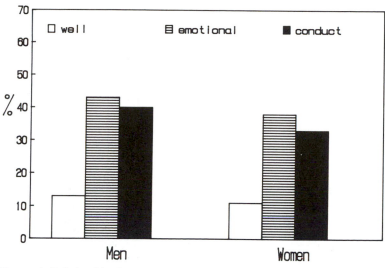

Figure 2. Relationship between childhood diagnosis and adult psychiatric problems (ID level 5).

childhood group fell short of statistical significance when the emotional and conduct diagnoses were considered separately, but were significant at the 1% level when the sexes and diagnoses were combined. There appeared to be no differences in the level of continuity in males or females according to the type of childhood illness. Similarly, the overall level of continuity from any childhood disorder was similar for males and females, with two fifths of boys and one third of girls with childhood illness showing disorder over the year prior to the follow-up interview compared with only one tenth of those showing no disorder over the time of the first study.

Childhood disorder and adult diagnosis. Rutter's predictions and Robins's data involve a switch in diagnosis for conduct-disordered girls who go on to show problems in adulthood. Figures 3 and 4 repeat the above analysis but take adult diagnosis into account. These predictions are clearly confirmed in our data. In neither males nor females did emotional problems in childhood lead to anything but affective problems in adulthood. However, three fourths of males with conduct disorders in childhood who also showed disorder in adulthood had antisocial personality disorders, but this was not so for any of the women. Women with conduct problems in childhood and disorders in adult life showed a persistence of disorder into depressive/anxious symptomatology.

In these analyses the conduct disorder group included those with mixed symptomatology. Unfortunately the low numbers did not allow us to examine statistically whether the switch in girls from conduct disorder to

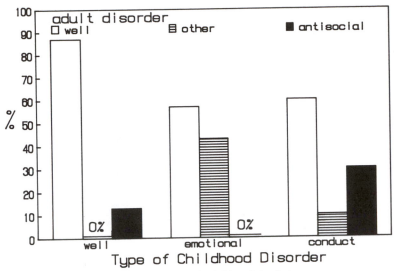

Figure 3. Disorders in childhood and adulthood (males).

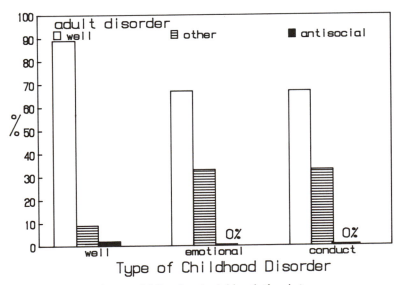

Figure 4. Disorders in childhood and adulthood (females).

internalizing disorders required also the presence of emotional problems in childhood. However, of the 4 boys with pure conduct disorder, 2 showed continuity into adult antisocial behavior, and 2 appeared well. Two of the 3 girls with pure conduct problems had psychiatric disorder in adult life, but in neither case was the problem of an antisocial type. Four of the 12 boys with mixed disorders showed psychiatric disorders in the year prior to the interview, 2 of these being antisocial personality problems. Only one of the 6 girls with mixed disorders showed psychiatric problems at follow-up, and her disorder was depressive in nature. Therefore, it seems unlikely that the differential diagnostic outcome is to be explained primarily by the greater overlap between conduct and emotional problems in the female offspring during the childhood years.

The findings presented here are striking. They show a substantial level of continuity in measures of disorder taken 10 to 15 years earlier with those taken in a one-year psychiatric assessment of subjects in the mid-20s. Moreover, these continuities applied equally to emotional and conduct problems. Indeed, if disorders at ID level 4 are included, over half the adults who had had emotional problems in childhood were rated as showing some psychiatric disorder in early adult life during the year before the interview. (The figures did not change for those with conduct problems in childhood.) Eighty-five percent of those reporting problems at ID level 5 at the time of follow-up also reported continuing or episodic problems since age 16. The great majority of these were persistent and pervasive enough to receive a diagnosis of personality disorder. Of those with current psychiatric problems but no personality disorder, 57% reported previous episodes.

Obviously, it is important to consider whether these findings could be artifactual as a consequence of diagnostic or sampling considerations, although it does not seem likely. For example, the way in which the childhood ratings were constructed would, if anything, overestimate the level of "pure" emotional difficulties, since any change in symptom patterns over childhood would be missed. But the continuity of such problems only to problems in adulthood of a similar type suggests that the childhood diagnostic procedure did define distinct groups. If the childhood designation did not make a genuine separation of diagnostic groups, a similar level of continuity for the emotional and conduct groups would be predicted but not the diagnostically differentiated pattern at outcome.

Onset of disorder in adulthood. The next issue concerns the onset of disorder in adulthood for those offspring not showing psychiatric problems in childhood. This is important in order to establish whether parental disorder is a risk factor for disorder in the adult children when they have not shown psychiatric problems in childhood or adolescence. The existence of this kind of risk is known for those illnesses that have a clear genetic component, but it is not established for the majority of parental disorders in this sample, disorders in which the genetic risk is less apparent (Torgersen, 1983).

In order to determine whether offspring designated as "well" from the original data developed problems later in childhood or adolescence it was necessary to use their own retrospective accounts of difficulties. Thirty-one percent of offspring who originally received no childhood diagnosis developed some emotional or behavioral problem by age 16, and nearly three quarters (71%) of these were emotional problems only. These, together with those considered as showing disorder during the first study, comprise the group with childhood/adolescent problems. The continuities between this rating of childhood difficulties and adult illness are given in Figure 5.

It is clear that the occurrence of adult psychiatric problems was relatively rare in those offspring without difficulties in childhood or early adolescence; only 5% received a diagnosis at ID level 5 over the past year as compared with approximately one third of those with emotional or conduct disturbance. All those with early adult onset were female; two of the disorders were depressive and one was a personality disorder. Since this latter designation requires both chronic and pervasive difficulties, it is likely that the problems stretched back into childhood, but the available data did not allow a designation of childhood disorder on the criteria employed here. The implication is that parental psychiatric disorders of the kind encountered in the parents of these children are not a major risk factor for pathology in early adulthood in the absence of psychopathology in

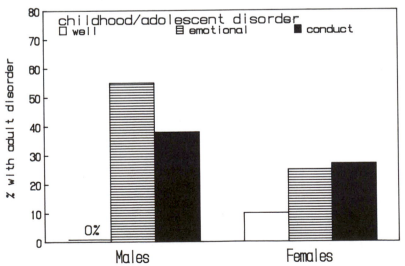

Figure 5. Disorders in childhood/adolescence and disorders in the past year.

childhood and adolescence. These data also suggest that the continuity from childhood/adolescent problems to adult disorder is greater in male offspring for both emotional and conduct problems, but these differences did not reach statistical significance.

Parental pathology, marital problems, and disorders in the adult children. The analysis of the impact of parental disorders in the initial study showed that parental diagnosis carried little risk for children under age 16 in the absence of family discord and disruption (Rutter & Quinton, 1984). This applied to all parental diagnoses, including personality disorder in either parent. Since there is little adult disorder in the offspring in the absence of childhood illness, it would seem that the same conclusion should apply with respect to adult disorder; that is, parental diagnosis would not be a predictor of adult illness in the absence of marital discord or disruption. This prediction is tested in Figure 6 with respect to the diagnosis of parental personality disorder. A subject was rated as having been exposed to marital discord/disruption if the parental marriage showed a discordant pattern for the predominant part of the original study; or if a discordant marriage broke down over this time; or if the parenting figures changed (for example, with the departure of one parent and the arrival of another), regardless of whether parental reports characterized their relationships as predominantly discordant. Offspring in stable single-parent or foster-parent situations were not counted as experiencing discord/disruption over the study period, nor were

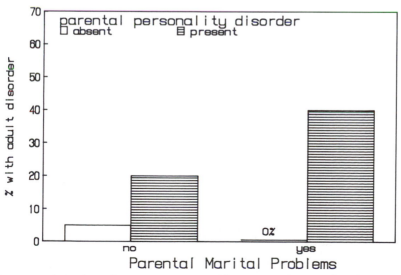

Figure 6. Relationship of parental marital problems, parental personality disorders, and disorders in the past year.

offspring who lost one parent by death, unless the parental marriage was previously discordant. The occurrence of disorders in the past year was strongly related to the experience of persistent parental discord or marital disruption in childhood, with 9% of offspring from nondisrupted or discordant backgrounds showing disorder in comparison with 38% of those with such adverse experiences ($\chi = 9.66$, df $= 1$, $p < .01$). Parental personality disorder in the absence of marital disruption appeared to carry some increased risk for the offspring, increasing twofold when parental personality problems were associated with discordant or disrupted marital relationships. Only 4 subjects experienced persistent discord in the absence of parental personality disorder. None of these was rated as showing disorder currently.

These data may seem to imply that parental personality disorder carries increased psychiatric risk for the offspring in adult life, and that marital discord only does so in association with vulnerabilities stemming from parental personality disorder. However, two caveats are in order. First, there is a modest but nonsignificant increase in adult disorder with parental discord alone if ID level 4 is taken as the criterion level for disorders. Further, personality disorder, by definition, implies chronic environmental stress, whereas discord on its own may be associated with more fluctuating marital and family problems. Therefore the findings may arise through the chronicity of exposure to family discord rather than through an interactive process. Further study of a group with chronic parental marital problems in

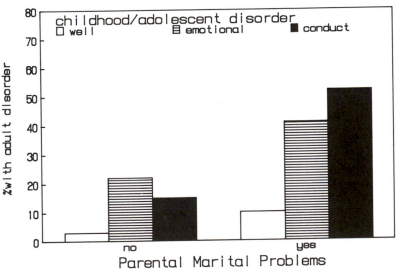

Figure 7. Relationship of parental marital problems, disorders, in childhood/adolescence, and disorders in the past year.

the absence of parental personality disorder would be needed to resolve this issue.

Role of marital discord. Finally, we can consider the role of marital discord as a factor mediating continuities between disorders in childhood and disorders in adulthood (Figure 7).

It is clear that the experience of persistent discord or marital disruption during childhood plays an important role in mediating such continuities. In the absence of persistent discord, disorders in childhood, whether of an emotional or a conduct type, show only modest continuity with adult disorder. In contrast, when childhood disorder was associated with marital difficulties, approximately half of those with emotional or conduct problems by age 16 had psychiatric problems at ID level 5 during the year prior to the interview, or were rated as having personality disorders. Further analyses are necessary to determine whether this finding implies that marital discord acts as an environmental factor maintaining childhood disorder as well as producing it, or whether childhood disorders associated with discord are more severe than those arising outside it. If this were the case, the continuity might be independent of environment once the childhood disorder has become established.

Conclusions

If these findings are confirmed when a larger proportion of the sample has been interviewed, they would point towards a number of important conclusions. But before reviewing these it is necessary to emphasize that the continuities and links uncovered apply to offspring who all had one or both parents with psychiatric disorders. Whether the findings would be the same in a sample without parental illness awaits the results from follow-up studies of nonpatient samples.

Within the sample discussed in this paper several findings stand out. These include the similar level of continuity for emotional and conduct disorders; the confirmation of Robins's finding of a switch in type of disorder for conduct-disordered girls; the low level of adult disorder in the absence of disorder in childhood and adolescence; and the central role of chronic parental marital discord disruption in mediating continuities. Since chronic marital problems were associated in this sample with chronic problems in personality functioning, it is possible that the apparent role of discord is explained by the severity of the parental disorder or by the genetic factors underlying it. However, the much lower risk from personality disorders in the absence of discord points to the direct role of discord in producing and perpetuating child disorder. On the other hand, the strong prediction from its presence is likely to be partly determined by its association with chronic parental illness and chronic family problems. That is, the offspring showing strong continuities in disorder are likely to have been exposed to adverse family environments throughout their childhoods and not just to temporary disturbances associated with episodic illness. This conclusion is probable because the continuity seems little affected by the age of the child at the time the original measures were taken (in our study, ages 6 to 15).

These conclusions are presented with a strength that the sample size does not strictly justify, in order to set out some questions concerning continuities between disorders in childhood and adulthood and the processes mediating them. However, there are strengths in these data that encourage us to attend to them despite the small numbers. These include the systematic coverage of both child and parent disorders and of family relationships over a period of 4 years. As a consequence, we were able to assess the power of enduring family circumstances in early life for predicting continuities in psychiatric disorder from childhood to early adult life. The existence of data on child psychiatric disorders over a 4-year period also meant that we were able to focus on persistent child disorders. The relatively strong continuities into adult life that we found were probably a consequence of that fact.

One of the most interesting findings concerned the differential patterns of continuity according to the type of psychiatric disorder in childhood. Clearly this needs to be tested further through larger prospective investigations. Only then will it be clear whether or under what circumstances the two types of childhood disorder are of equal import in predicting adult difficulties. Nevertheless, our data suggest that the level of continuity from childhood emotional problems may have been underestimated in the past. Of course, it may be that the continuity that was evident in our data stemmed from special features of our sample. In particular, it should be noted that, by definition, all of the children with emotional disorders had mentally ill parents. Also, the emotional disorders that we studied had already shown persistence in childhood. These considerations focus attention on the need to determine the reasons why some emotional disorders in childhood are transient whereas others constitute precursors of adult psychopathology.

The mediating role of seriously disturbed parental relationships in continuities from childhood to adult life also needs further investigation. Our data suggest that they have considerable importance, but again the query is whether this would be equally so if the parents did not have some form of psychiatric disorder. In addition, it is unclear whether the predictive power applies in the absence of emotional or conduct problems in childhood. It is evident that a variety of potential interactions must be examined if we are to elucidate the processes that underlie continuities and discontinuities across the life span.

References

Brown, G. W., Harris, T. O., & Bifulco, A. (1986). Long term effects of early loss of parent. In M. Rutter, C. Izard & P. Read (Eds.), *Depression in young people: Developmental and clinical perspectives* (pp. 251–296). New York: Guilford Press.

Brown, G. W., & Rutter, M. (1966). The measurement of family activities and relationships: A methodological study. *Human Relations, 19,* 241–263.

Earls, F. (1987). On the familial transmission of child psychiatric disorder. *Journal of Child Psychology and Psychiatry, 28,* 791–801.

Graham, P., & Rutter, M. (1968). The reliability and validity of the psychiatric assessment of the child. II: Interview with the parent. *British Journal of Psychiatry, 114,* 581–592.

Graham, P., Rutter, M., & George, S. (1973). Temperamental characteristics as predictors of behavior disorders in children. *American Journal of Orthopsychiatry, 43,* 328–399.

Loeber, R., & Dishion, T. (1983). Early predictors of male delinquency: A review. *Psychological Bulletin 94,* 68–99.

Magnusson, D., & Ohman, A. (Eds.). (1987). *Psychopathology: An interactional perspective.* Orlando, FL: Academic Press.

Olweus, D. (1979). The stability of aggressive reaction patterns in human males: A review. *Psychological Bulletin, 85,* 852–875.

Quinton, D. & Rutter, M. (1988). *Parenting breakdown: The making and breaking of intergenerational links.* Aldershot: Gower.

Quinton, D., Rutter, M., & Rowlands, O. (1976). An evaluation of an interview assessment of marriage. *Psychological Medicine, 6,* 577–586.

Robins, L. N. (1966). *Deviant children grown up.* Baltimore: Williams & Wilkins.

Robins, L. N. (1978). Sturdy childhood predictors of adult outcomes: Replications from longitudinal studies. *Psychological Medicine, 8,* 611–622.

Robins, L. N. (1986). The consequence of conduct disorder in girls. In D. Olweus, J. Block, & M. Radke-Yarrow (Eds.), *Development of antisocial and prosocial behavior: Research theories and issues* (pp. 385–414). New York: Academic Press.

Rutter, M. (1967). A children's behavior questionnaire for completion by teachers: Preliminary findings. *Journal of Child Psychology and Psychiatry, 8,* 1–11.

Rutter, M. (1970). Sex differences in children's response to family stress. In E. J. Anthony & C. Koupernik (Eds.), *The child in his family* (pp. 165–196). New York: John Wiley & Sons.

Rutter, M. (1982). Epidemiological-longitudinal approaches to the study of development. In W. A. Collins (Ed.), *The concept of development* Vol. 15, (pp. 104–144). Minnesota Symposia on Child Psychology. Hillsdale, NJ: Lawrence Erlbaum.

Rutter, M. (1984). Psychopathology and development: 1. Childhood antecedents of adult psychiatric disorder. *Australian and New Zealand Journal of Psychiatry, 18,* 225–234.

Rutter, M. (1985). Resilience in the face of adversity: Protective factors and resistance to psychiatric disorder. *British Journal of Psychiatry, 147,* 598–611.

Rutter, M. (1988). Epidemiological approaches to developmental psychopathology. *Archives of General Psychiatry, 45,* 486–495.

Rutter, M., & Brown, G. W. (1966). The reliability of measures of family life and relationships in families containing a psychiatric patient. *Social Psychiatry, 1,* 38–53.

Rutter, M., & Garmezy, N. (1983). Developmental psychopathology. In E. M. Hetherington (Ed.), *Socialization personality and social development. Vol. 4, Handbook of child psychology* (pp. 775–991). New York: John Wiley & Sons.

Rutter, M., & Giller, H. (1983). *Juvenile delinquency: Trends and perspectives.* Harmondsworth, England: Penguin.

Rutter, M., & Quinton, D. (1984). Parental psychiatric disorder: Effects on children. *Psychological Medicine, 14*, 853–880.

Scarr, S., & McCartney, K. (1983). How people make their own environments: A theory of genotype→environment effects. *Child Development, 54*, 425–435.

Sroufe, L. A., & Rutter, M. (1984). The domain of developmental psychopathology. *Child Development, 55*, 17–29.

Torgersen, S. (1983). Genetics of neurosis: The effects of sampling variation upon the twin concordance ratio. *British Journal of Psychiatry, 142*, 126–132.

Wing, J. K., Birley, J. L. T., Cooper, J. E., Graham, P., & Isaacs, A. D. (1967). Reliability of a procedure for measuring and classifying "present psychiatric state." *British Journal of Psychiatry, 113*, 499–515.

Wing, J. K., & Hailey, A. M. (1972). *Evaluating a community psychiatric service: The Camberwell Register 1964–1971.* London: Oxford University Press.

Wing, J. K., Mann, S. A., Left, J. P., & Nixon, J. M. (1978). The concept of a "Case" in psychiatric population surveys. *Psychological Medicine, 8*, 203–218.

Zeitlin, H. (1986). *The natural history of psychiatric disorders in children.* Oxford: Oxford University Press.

Zoccolillo, M., Rutter, M., Pickles, A., & Quinton, D. The outcome of conduct disorder: Implications for defining adult personaility disorder. Unpublished data.

15   Childhood predictors of psychiatric status in the young adulthood of hyperactive boys: A study controlling for chance associations

SALVATORE MANNUZZA, RACHEL GITTELMAN
KLEIN, PAULA HOROWITZ KONIG, AND
TINA LOUISE GIAMPINO

Despite differing and sometimes problematic methodology, several investigators have noted an excess of antisocial behavior in the eventual adjustment of hyperactive children[1] (Klein & Mannuzza, in press; Weiss & Hechtman, 1986). This association between early hyperactivity and later conduct problems appears to be a reliable, sturdy finding.

In a previous report (Gittelman et al., 1985) we noted that the attention deficit disorder with hyperactivity (ADDH) syndrome offered excellent opportunities for the identification of predictors of outcome because the nature of later dysfunction was relatively uniform (i.e., antisocial disorders), and the prevalence of the latter was relatively high (about 30% in late adolescence/early adulthood). Therefore, in the longitudinal assessment of ADDH, problems associated with identifying risk factors for rare and heterogeneous outcomes were avoided.

Existing research

Two previous studies have reported on predictors of outcome in hyperactive children as young adults. In their 10-year prospective follow-up study, Hechtman et al. (1984) reported on childhood predictors (ages 6–12) of young adult outcome (ages 17–24) in 76 formerly hyperactive children. Childhood predictors included children's cognitive and behavioral characteristics (e.g., IQ, hyperactivity, aggressivity, school performance, peer relations), and family parameters (e.g., socioeconomic status [SES], familial mental health, rearing practices). Outcome variables included measures of emotional adjustment, school performance, work history, police involvement, car accidents, and drug and alcohol use.

Univariate analyses showed numerous significant associations between predictor and outcome variables. Of about 300 correlations, 29 were significant at $p < .05$. Multivariate analyses also provided predictive associations. Among the more salient childhood predictors were IQ, SES, emotional instability, aggressiveness, and parental mental health. However, since no category of outcome was highly associated with a specific predictor

279

variable, the investigators concluded that the interaction of child, social, and family factors better explained their data.

A major strength of the Hechtman study is that formerly hyperactive subjects were followed into adulthood (mean age of 19 years) in a prospective design. However, only 73% of the original cohort were evaluated at 10-year follow-up. Also, due to missing data on certain measures, some analyses were based on less than 50% of the initial sample. Finally, the magnitude of relationships is not presented; it may be that many of the associations, though statistically significant, have little practical or theoretical significance.

Loney et al. (1983) reported on the childhood predictors of outcome in 65 formerly hyperactive subjects who were aged 21 to 23 at follow-up. Predictors included children's characteristics (e.g., IQ, hyperactivity, aggressiveness), demographic variables (e.g., SES, urban/rural residence), and familial factors (e.g., parental strictness and psychopathology). Outcome measures consisted of items from the antisocial personality and alcoholism sections of the *Schedule for Affective Disorders and Schizophrenia—Lifetime Version* (SADS-L; Spitzer & Endicott, 1978), items from the Iowa Crime and Punishment Survey (CAPS: Kramer et al., 1978), and items from the National Survey on Drug Abuse (NSDA: Abelson & Fishburne, 1977).

Multiple regression analyses indicated that early status from all three categories (child characteristics, demographic characteristics, and familial factors) were associated with various outcome measures. The strongest predictors of outcome included IQ, which was negatively correlated with SADS-L diagnoses of antisocial personality and alcoholism, and with some antisocial behaviors from the CAPS; parent psychopathology, which was positively associated with work instability and alcohol-related problems on the SADS-L, and the use of inhalants on the NSDA; childhood aggression, which was significantly associated with objections by others to the subject's drinking (SADS-L), weapon use and police contacts (CAPS), and the use of hallucinogens (NSDA); and urban residence, which correlated with violence when drinking (SADS-L), breaking and entering (CAPS), and the use of opiates, sedatives, and stimulants (NSDA).

However, the diagnoses of antisocial personality and alcoholism at follow-up were very poorly predicted from childhood parameters. Only IQ (negative) and number of siblings (positive) were significantly associated with a diagnosis of antisocial personality; and IQ (negative) was the sole predictor of alcoholism. Therefore, no early clinical, social, or familial characteristic was related to the two most prevalent mental disorders in this group of hyperactive children as young adults. Moreover, the combination of all predictors accounted for less than 10% of the diagnostic variance of these disorders at follow-up.

The clinical relevance of certain outcome measures in the Loney et al. study is difficult to interpret. For example, several predictors (e.g., age at onset, childhood aggression, academic problems, SES, parental strictness) were significantly associated with the use ("Ever tried") of drugs. However, the extent to which ever having used a drug is an important functional aspect of outcome is unclear.

Although both Hechtman et al. (1984) and Loney et al. (1983) report the probability levels of the statistical relationships between childhood and outcome measures, Hechtman et al. do not indicate the frequency or mean severity of the characteristics at either time point, and Loney et al. do so only occasionally. The omission of descriptive information is unfortunate since it restricts the ability to draw general conclusions from the findings and precludes the possibility of determining whether the two studies included similar cases.

Another problematic aspect of the reports is their failure to control for chance associations that are often operative when a large number of variables are entered into multivariate statistical analyses. The degree to which the results may have been affected by chance relationships is unascertainable.

Current study of predictors among hyperactive boys

This report represents an attempt to identify childhood predictors of young adult outcome in a prospective study of hyperactive boys initially evaluated at ages 6 to 12, whose follow-up at ages 16 to 23 (mean age of 18 years) has been reported elsewhere (Gittelman et al., 1985). Predictors found to be associated with outcome by Hechtman et al. (1984) and Loney et al. (1983) were selected for study. These include clinical and cognitive characteristics of the child (parent, teacher, and clinician ratings, IQ, achievement scores), and sociofamilial factors (SES, family stability, parental psychopathology).

Subjects

Subjects were white adolescent males between ages 6 and 12 who had been diagnosed as hyperactive at a no-cost research psychiatric clinic. All had been rated hyperactive by both teachers and parents or clinic staff. Additional childhood criteria included school referral because of behavior problems; Wechsler Intelligence Scale for Children (WISC) IQ of 85 or greater[2]; no psychosis or neurological disorder; and a family that speaks English and has a telephone.

Youngsters who had reached their 16th birthday were included in the follow-up regardless of treatment history. Of the total 103 males who qualified for the study, information was obtained on 101 (98%).

The 101 subjects were between ages 6 and 12 at referral (mean age = 9.3, SD = 1.4), and between 16 and 23 when evaluated at follow-up (mean age = 18.3, SD = 1.5). Follow-up intervals ranged from 5.7 to 11.3 years (mean interval 9.0 years, SD = 1.1).

Childhood predictors

Childhood variables fall into three categories (Table 1).

Clinical characteristics (30 variables). Parent, teacher, and clinical ratings were made. The parent questionnaire (Conners, 1973) was made up of 93 items. The teacher questionnaire (Conners, 1969) consisted of 40 items. All items reflecting ADD symptomatology, conduct problems, and aggressive behavior were identified. The resulting 14 items from each questionnaire are shown in Table 1.

We had no a priori basis for assuming that one convention for scale building would be better than another. Because we wanted to make sure that significant relationships between parent and teacher ratings and outcome were not missed due to injudicious scaling of scores, we included several item combinations with the understanding that the best one would be retained.

In addition to the 14 items from the teacher scale, we used the conduct, inattention, and hyperactivity factors of the Conners scale and the Iowa Aggression factor; the 14 parent and teacher items were also averaged separately, resulting in a mean parent and a mean teacher score. However, the best discrimination between outcome groups was achieved when individual items from each questionnaire were used. For that reason the results for the other score combinations are not presented.

Based on all available information about the child (two teacher ratings, parent and child interviews), the child psychiatrist rated him on two types of aggression: eruptive and unsocialized—scored as absent, maybe present, and present. They were defined as follows:

> *Eruptive aggressive behavior*: Unable to control appropriately his responses towards peers and/or adults. Physically aggressive; impulsive; often reacts to others before understanding the meaning or motives of his words or actions. Gets into numerous fights. Physically disruptive, particularly in classroom where he may hit others with little or no provocation.
>
> *Unsocialized aggressive behavior*: Overtly negative, defiant, hostile, and/or manipulative, evasive, guarded. Attempts to control others. Aggressive, antisocial, overwhelmingly selfish. Denial of anxiety and personal responsibility for feelings and acts. Frequently in hostile conflict with the environment in a variety of social settings (family, school) that do not involve membership in a gang.

Intellectual ability and achievement tests (five variables). Three scores from the

Table 1. *Predictor (childhood) variables*

I. Clinical characteristics
  A. Parent ratings (not at all, just a little, pretty much, very much)
    1. Fights constantly with siblings
    2. Hits or kicks other children
    3. Throws and breaks things
    4. Picks on other children
    5. Wants to run things
    6. Won't obey school rules
    7. Steals from stores
    8. Steals at school
    9. Steals from parents
    10. Denies having done wrong
    11. Feels cheated
    12. Acts as if driven by a motor
    13. Can't keep still
    14. Daydreams
  B. Teacher ratings (not at all, just a little, pretty much, very much)
    1. Quarrelsome
    2. Uncooperative
    3. No sense of fair play
    4. Disturbs other children
    5. Destructive
    6. Steals
    7. Lies
    8. Restless or overactive
    9. Walks around during class
    10. Fiddles with small objects
    11. Excitable
    12. Inattentive
    13. Difficulty in concentrating
    14. Daydreams
  C. Clinical ratings (no, maybe, yes)
    1. Eruptive aggression
    2. Unsocialized aggression
II. Intellectual ability and achievement tests
  A. Wechsler Intelligence Scale for Children (WISC)
    1. Performance IQ
    2. Verbal IQ
    3. Full-scale IQ
  B. Wide Range Achievement Test (WRAT), standard scores
    1. Reading
    2. Mathematics
III. Familial and environmental factors
  A. Socioeconomic status (range: 1–5)
  B. Family stability (range: 1–5)
  C. Parental psychopathology
    1 = No DSM-III mental disorder in either parent
    2 = One or both parents had a DSM-III diagnosis other than antisocial personality and substance use disorder but neither parent had these diagnoses
    3 = One or both parents were diagnosed as having antisocial personality or substance use disorder

Table 2. *Codes for family stability*

Rating Comments

1 Adequate nurturance given child's age. Parents are concerned and involved with the child's welfare. Marital discord is minimal, if any, and does not threaten the integrity of the family. Child lives with both parents.

2 Adequate nurturance given child's age. At least one parent is concerned and involved with child's welfare. Marital discord is somewhat more pronounced than in 1, but does not threaten the integrity of the family. Child lives with one parent who is either single or remarried; has stable relationship with other parent. The home life is similar to 1.

3 Adequate nurturance of child. Marital strife is frequent and threatens the integrity of the family. Stable family life, but there have been at least two moves accompanied by school changes. Child divides week between two homes (i.e., mother and grandparents, or sitter and parents); each setting is stable. Home life is adequate, but parents

separated during period rated. Child lives with one parent who is either single or remarried; has stable relationship with other natural parent. The home life is similar to 2.

4 Neglect of child. Inadequate physical care, inadequate nurturance. However, parent expresses some interest in the child's welfare. Family interaction is marked by frequent arguing, which may be accompanied by physical outbursts. Home life is poor and parents separated during period rated. Child lives with one parent who is either single or remarried; has unpredictable relationship with other parent. Home life is insecure.

5 Extreme lack of parental care. Acting out among family members characterizes the home atmosphere. Either parent may be absent from the home. Unstable adult figures. Parents show minimal interest in the child's welfare.

Note: Ratings reflect current family situation as it has been existing for the past 6 months. Use these ratings as continuous with regard to quality of the home, and use the number judged appropriate if the situation does not conform to statements.

WISC, verbal, performance, and full-scale IQs, were used as measures of intellectual ability.

Two measures of academic achievement were included: standard scores on the reading and arithmetic tests of the Wide Range Achievement Test (WRAT).

Familial and environmental factors (three variables). Socioeconomic status at referral (range: 1–5) was included in accordance with Hollingshead and Redlich (1958) scale.

Family stability was rated on a 1 to 5 scale by a social worker, based on interviews with the mother or both parents (Table 2).

Lifetime psychiatric history of each parent was assessed with the Diagnostic Interview Schedule (DIS: Robins et al., 1981; Robins et al., 1982) at the time of the follow-up. For cases who refused to participate, or could not be located, the Spouse Informant Schedule (SIS) was administered to the husband or wife. The SIS is made up of a subset of DIS items, including sections on psychiatric treatment, alcoholism, drug abuse, antisocial personality, and pathological gambling.

As was the case for the childhood characteristics, there was no a priori knowledge of the best strategy for classifying parental psychopathology. As in the previous instance, we wished to avoid the failure to detect the predictive value of parental mental disorders, should it exist, because of inappropriate coding. Therefore, several means of categorizing the information were used in our preliminary analyses. For example, mental disorders in fathers and mothers were coded separately and together; number of diagnoses was coded; and various combinations of specific diagnoses were analyzed.

The method of coding selected was that which provided the best discrimination between outcome groups.

1 = No DSM-III diagnosis in either parent

2 = DSM-III diagnosis other than antisocial personality disorder (APD) or substance use disorder (SUD) in one or both parents; neither parent has APD or SUD

3 = Either or both parents have APD or SUD

Outcome variables

Subjects were interviewed with the Teenager or Young Adult Schedule (TOYS), a 470-item semistructured interview which was derived from the DIS. Parents of subjects (usually mothers) were interviewed with the Parent Interview (PARI), a 181-item informant interview in which parents were questioned about the subjects. All assessments were made without knowledge of childhood history. (Although not pertinent to this report, the follow-up study included two control groups; for details see Gittelman et al., 1985.) Interviews were conducted by doctoral-level psychologists who inquired only about the individual's adjustment since age 13, in order to keep interviewers blind to childhood status. At the completion of each assessment, DSM-III diagnoses were formulated and justified in a narrative summary.

Two follow-up mental disorders, conduct disorder and ADDH, were selected for study. This decision was prompted by our findings that, compared to normal controls, the formerly hyperactive boys were at a significantly increased risk for ADDH (31% vs. 3%) and for antisocial conduct disorder (27% vs. 8%) in young adulthood (Gittelman et al., 1985). Furthermore, most other diagnoses were rare at follow-up, so that by restricting the outcome to these two disorders, very few subjects would be lost in prediction of later adjustment. Moreover, we found that cases who did not qualify for a mental disorder at follow-up were practically indistinguishable from controls on a host of follow-up measures (Mannuzza et al., 1988). Therefore, defining poor outcome as the presence of a mental disorder encompasses the nature and extent of dysfunction in the sample. This criterion considers ongoing status but not interval diagnoses.

A diagnosis was considered present at follow-up if it was made on the basis of information given by the youngster or the parent.

The three diagnostic (outcome) groups were:

1. Conduct disorder with or without any other diagnosis ($N = 27$).[3]
2. Pure attention deficit disorder ($N = 19$). This group includes subjects with a full ADDH syndrome [Attentional difficulties (A) + Impulsivity (I) + Hyperactivity (H), as well as subjects with any two of the three symptoms *in the absence of* conduct disorder and SUD.
3. No DSM-III diagnosis at follow-up ($N = 50$).[4]

The rationale for including subjects with the syndromes A + H and I + H in the ADDH group warrants discussion. In order to be counted, these symptoms had to be present to a clinically significant degree. That is, they had resulted in either marked subjective discomfort or in functional impairment (e.g., concentration difficulties causing poor school grades, impulsivity leading to numerous regrettable actions). The DSM-III recognizes only A + I as a residual syndrome of ADDH. However, as noted elsewhere (Gittelman & Mannuzza, 1985), this decision may have been unjustified, since hyperactivity does not appear to remit more often than inattention and impulsivity; therefore, it seems reasonable to include any two symptom combinations as reflecting continued ADDH symptomatology.

Data analysis

A multiple discriminant analysis was conducted to assess the relative contribution of the childhood variables in predicting membership in the diagnostic groups at follow-up. In a discriminant analysis, two different sets of equations, canonical and classification, are of interest.

Canonical equations. Predictor variables are statistically reduced to one or more weighted linear combinations (canonical variates) that maximize the average separation between outcome groups, relative to the variance within groups. The maximum number of potential canonical variates (equations) is equal to the number of predictors, or to one less than the number of outcome groups, whichever is smaller. Thus, in the current analyses, two equations are generated.

The second canonical variate represents that linear composite of weights which maximally discriminates outcome groups *after* scores from the first canonical variate have been partialed out. The rationale for generating two equations (when three outcome groups are being studied) is that one canonical variate might distinguish well between outcome groups 1 and 3, but not 2 and 3, and so on. Thus, in certain instances, the second canonical variate may be needed to provide maximum discrimination among all groups. Each canonical variate can be tested for significance.

Classification equations. A separate classification equation (derived from the pooled within-groups covariance matrix and the centroids of the predictor variables) is generated for each outcome group. Each subject's raw scores on predictor measures are entered into the equations, resulting in three values (one for each equation). The subject is then classified into the outcome group corresponding to the equation with the highest score. (This is equivalent to assigning each subject to the outcome group for which he has the greatest probability of membership.)

When all subjects have been classified in this manner, the results are summarized in a percent correctly classified table. This table shows the proportion of subjects in each outcome group who were correctly classified when their data were entered into the classification equations.

The canonical equations address statistical significance; the classification equations concern clinical relevance. For example, canonical variates may be statistically significant, yet the percent correctly classified may be too small for practical utility. Conversely, canonical variates may not be significant, yet a high percentage of subjects in each group could be correctly classified.

The standard discriminant analysis uses all data, including the data from a given subject, in the process of classifying that subject, and is therefore able to capitalize on chance associations between a subject's predictor scores and his outcome. In order to control for chance findings, a jackknife procedure was employed to provide an unbiased estimate of the percent correctly classified. This procedure omits a subject, builds the classification equations on the basis of the remaining sample, and then uses these equations to classify the excluded subject; the process is repeated for every subject in the sample. In this manner, the jackknife procedure ensures that the classifications are based on patterns of associations rather than chance fluctuations.

In the current analysis, all predictor variables were entered concurrently. No adjustments were made for the a priori probabilities of each outcome group; that is, each group was assigned a .33 probability.

Results

The parent ratings noted in Table 3 of aggressive and antisocial behaviors are not especially elevated, suggesting that, on the average, aggressive behavior was not salient. However, the considerable score variance indicates that

Table 3. *Childhood characteristics of conduct disorder, pure ADD, and no-ongoing-disorder groups (N = 96)*

	Outcome group			
Predictor variable	Conduct disorder (N = 27) N (%)	Pure ADD (N = 19) N (%)	No ongoing disorder (N = 50) N (%)	Univariate F
Parent ratings				
fights	1.93 (0.7)	1.53 (0.7)	1.62 (1.0)	1.49
hits/kicks	1.00 (0.8)	0.68 (0.7)	0.88 (0.9)	0.77
throws/breaks	1.00 (1.0)	0.89 (1.1)	0.76 (0.9)	0.54
picks on others	0.96 (0.9)	0.79 (0.8)	1.02 (0.9)	0.48
runs things	1.96 (0.9)	1.42 (0.8)	1.68 (1.0)	1.89
disobeys	1.74 (0.9)	1.42 (1.0)	1.76 (1.0)	0.86
steals/stores	0.33 (0.5)	0.26 (0.6)	0.16 (0.4)	1.26
steals/school	0.22 (0.4)	0.32 (0.6)	0.22 (0.5)	0.27
steals/parents	0.52 (0.7)	0.26 (0.5)	0.24 (0.6)	2.13
denies wrong	2.19 (1.0)	1.74 (0.9)	1.96 (1.0)	1.24
feels cheated	1.48 (0.9)	0.95 (0.9)	1.08 (1.0)	2.21
driven	2.04 (0.9)	1.58 (1.1)	1.98 (0.9)	1.52
restless	2.52 (0.8)	2.58 (0.6)	2.52 (0.8)	0.05
daydreams	1.81 (1.0)	1.37 (1.2)	1.60 (1.0)	1.08
Teacher ratings				
quarrelsome	1.74 (1.1)	1.68 (1.1)	1.94 (1.0)	0.54
uncooperative	1.85 (1.0)	1.58 (0.8)	1.80 (0.9)	0.55
no fair play	1.63 (1.1)	1.16 (1.0)	1.28 (0.9)	1.60
disturbing	2.48 (0.8)	2.63 (0.7)	2.56 (0.8)	0.22
destructive	1.41 (1.0)	0.89 (1.0)	1.30 (1.1)	1.36
steals	0.33 (0.8)	0.47 (1.0)	0.36 (0.7)	0.20
lies	1.37 (1.2)	0.79 (1.1)	1.00 (1.0)	1.87
restless	2.85 (0.4)	2.89 (0.3)	2.90 (0.4)	0.17
walks around	2.44 (0.6)	2.32 (0.8)	2.32 (0.7)	0.33
fiddles	2.22 (0.7)	2.42 (0.8)	2.24 (0.9)	0.37
excitable	2.04 (0.9)	2.53 (0.7)	2.30 (0.8)	2.20
inattentive	2.74 (0.5)	2.53 (0.5)	2.56 (0.6)	1.10
difficulty concentrating	2.63 (0.7)	2.74 (0.6)	2.48 (0.6)	1.24
daydreams	1.37 (1.1)	1.47 (1.0)	1.46 (1.0)	0.08
Clinical ratings				
eruptive aggression				
1	6 (33)	10 (63)	16 (47)	
2	1 (6)	2 (13)	3 (8)	
3	11 (61)	4 (25)	15 (44)	2.20
unsocialized aggression				
1	11 (61)	15 (94)	31 (84)	
2	1 (6)	—	—	
3	6 (33)	1 (6)	6 (16)	1.87

Table 3. (*Continued*)

| Predictor variable | Outcome group | | | Univariate |
	Conduct disorder ($N = 27$) N (%)	Pure ADD ($N = 19$) N (%)	No ongoing disorder ($N = 50$) N (%)	F
Ability, achievement				
WISC PIQ	103 (11)	101 (10)	101 (13)	0.33
WISC VIQ	104 (11)	101 (11)	104 (12)	0.72
WISC FSIQ	104 (11)	101 (9)	103 (11)	0.51
WRAT reading	103 (17)	92 (10)	99 (17)	2.65
WRAT math	94 (9)	93 (7)	93 (9)	0.19
Familial, environmental				
SES[a]	3.63 (1.0)	3.37 (0.9)	3.30 (1.1)	0.91
Family stability				
1	11 (52)	12 (67)	30 (70)	
2	7 (33)	4 (22)	10 (23)	
3	3 (14)	2 (11)	2 (5)	
4	—	—	1 (2)	
5	—	—	—	0.40
Parental psychopathology				
1	14 (52)	11 (58)	32 (64)	
2	4 (15)	6 (32)	12 (24)	
3	9 (33)	2 (11)	6 (12)	1.72

Notes: None of the F values are significant at $p < .05$.
Abbreviations: WISC PIQ = Wechsler Intelligence Scale for Children, performance intelligence quotient; VIQ = verbal intelligence quotient; FSIQ = full-scale intelligence quotient; WRAT = Wide Range Achievement Test.
[a] Figures are means (SD).

some children were indeed rated as being severely aggressive, and consequently, relationships between aggression as perceived by parents and outcome should be detectable. As an example, 20% of the children received ratings of "pretty much" and "very much" on the item "hits or kicks other children," and 21% on "picks on other children." However, the mean ratings on clear antisocial behaviors such as stealing are extremely low, and the rate of stealing may be too low to give it any predictive strength in this sample. A similar pattern is found in the teacher ratings.

Table 3 also shows the univariate F tests for each predictor. None of the F values are significant, indicating that no single childhood variable, by itself, is significantly differentiated among the three diagnostic groups.

Similarly, neither canonical variate was significant: for the first equation,

Table 4. *Percent correctly classified with and without the jackknife procedure*

| | Percent correctly classified as | | | |
	Conduct disorder	Pure ADD	No ongoing disorder	Overall
Without the jackknife	82	84	62	72
With the jackknife	33	21	30	29

| | Percent correctly classified as | | | |
	Conduct disorder	Pure ADD	No disorder since 13	Overall
Without the jackknife	85	95	84	87
With the jackknife	41	16	28	30

$\chi^2 = 61.87$, $p = .84$; and for the second equation, $\chi^2 = 23.09$, $p = .95$. These findings indicate that childhood predictor variables did not significantly differentiate the three outcome groups.

However, the percent correctly classified table (Table 4) shows that 82%, 84%, and 62% of the subjects in the conduct disorder, ADD, and no-ongoing-disorder groups were correctly classified (overall correct classification = 72%).

The majority of misclassifications involved the no-ongoing-disorder group (only 62% correct classification). We considered that this failure to discriminate may have been related to the manner in which the outcome groups were formed. Since ongoing diagnoses were considered for group composition, the no-ongoing-disorder group included subjects with disorders that had remitted prior to follow-up.

To address the possibility that interval diagnoses confounded the results, we "purified" the no-ongoing-disorder group by including only cases that had not received any diagnosis since age 13. These were children whose early ADDH symptoms had remitted before age 13, and who had not developed another disorder.

With the "purified" group, the percent correct classified table now shows that 85%, 95%, and 84% of the subjects in the conduct disorder, ADD, and no-disorder-since-13 groups were correctly classified (see Table 4). Also, overall correct classification increased from 72% to 87%.

Table 4 also shows the percent of correctly classified subjects when analyses are subjected to the jackknife procedure. Percentages drop dramatically; decreases as great as 60% and 70% are observed.

Table 5. *Childhood characteristics and conduct disorder, pure ADD, and no-disorder-since-13 groups* $(N = 71)$

	Outcome group			
	Conduct disorder $(N = 27)$	Pure ADD $(N = 19)$	No disorder since 13 $(N = 25)$	
Predictor variable	N (%)	N (%)	N (%)	Univariate F
Parent ratings				
fights	1.93 (0.7)	1.53 (0.7)	1.36 (1.0)	3.08
hits/kicks	1.00 (0.8)	0.68 (0.7)	0.84 (1.0)	0.74
throws/breaks	1.00 (1.0)	0.89 (1.1)	0.72 (0.8)	0.54
picks on others	0.96 (0.9)	0.79 (0.8)	0.88 (0.9)	0.22
runs things	1.96 (0.9)	1.42 (0.8)	1.52 (1.0)	2.30
disobeys	1.74 (0.9)	1.42 (1.0)	1.52 (1.0)	0.65
steals/stores	0.33 (0.5)	0.26 (0.6)	0.04 (0.2)	2.76
steals/school	0.22 (0.4)	0.32 (0.6)	0.16 (0.5)	0.55
steals/parents	0.52 (0.7)	0.26 (0.5)	0.20 (0.6)	2.04
denies wrong	2.19 (1.0)	1.74 (0.9)	1.84 (1.0)	1.43
feels cheated	1.48 (0.9)	0.95 (0.9)	0.76 (0.9)	4.38*
driven	2.04 (0.9)	1.58 (1.1)	1.84 (1.0)	1.23
restless	2.52 (0.8)	2.58 (0.6)	2.44 (0.7)	0.20
daydreams	1.81 (1.0)	1.37 (1.2)	1.44 (1.0)	1.25
Teacher ratings				
quarrelsome	1.74 (1.1)	1.68 (1.1)	1.80 (1.1)	0.06
uncooperative	1.85 (1.1)	1.58 (0.8)	1.68 (0.9)	0.52
no fair play	1.63 (1.1)	1.16 (1.0)	1.48 (0.9)	1.24
disturbing	2.48 (0.8)	2.63 (0.7)	2.36 (0.9)	0.67
destructive	1.41 (1.0)	0.89 (1.0)	1.16 (1.1)	1.29
steals	0.33 (0.8)	0.47 (1.0)	0.20 (0.6)	0.65
lies	1.37 (1.2)	0.79 (1.1)	0.92 (1.1)	1.75
restless	2.85 (0.4)	2.89 (0.3)	2.88 (0.3)	0.10
walks around	2.44 (0.6)	2.32 (0.8)	2.20 (0.7)	0.76
fiddles	2.22 (0.7)	2.42 (0.8)	2.24 (1.0)	0.35
excitable	2.04 (0.9)	2.53 (0.7)	2.32 (0.7)	2.29
inattentive	2.74 (0.5)	2.53 (0.5)	2.52 (0.6)	1.22
difficulty concentrating	2.63 (0.7)	2.74 (0.6)	2.48 (0.6)	0.96
daydreams	1.37 (1.1)	1.47 (1.0)	1.84 (1.0)	1.15
Clinical ratings				
eruptive aggression				
1	6 (33)	10 (63)	9 (56)	
2	1 (6)	2 (13)	2 (13)	
3	11 (61)	4 (25)	5 (31)	2.54
unsocialized aggression				
1	11 (61)	15 (94)	16 (89)	
2	1 (6)	—	—	
3	6 (33)	1 (6)	2 (11)	2.30

Table 5. (*Continued*)

Predictor variable	Outcome group			Univariate F
	Conduct disorder (N = 27) N (%)	Pure ADD (N = 19) N (%)	No disorder since 13 (N = 25) N (%)	
Ability, achievement				
WISC PIQ	103 (11)	101 (10)	102 (15)	0.22
WISC VIQ	104 (11)	101 (11)	104 (13)	0.68
WISC FSIQ	104 (11)	101 (9)	104 (12)	0.49
WRAT reading	103 (17)	92 (10)	96 (14)	3.30*
WRAT math	94 (9)	93 (7)	93 (10)	0.15
Familial environmental				
SES[a]	3.63 (1.0)	3.37 (0.9)	3.24 (1.3)	0.90
Family stability				
1	11 (52)	12 (67)	13 (68)	
2	7 (33)	4 (22)	5 (26)	
3	3 (14)	2 (11)	1 (5)	
4	—	—	—	
5	—	—	—	0.66
Parental psychopathology				
1	14 (52)	11 (58)	15 (60)	
2	4 (15)	6 (32)	7 (28)	
3	9 (33)	2 (11)	3 (12)	1.13

Note: See Table 3 for abbreviations and notes.
* $p < .05$
[a] Figures are means (SD).

Table 5 shows the univariate F tests for each predictor in the conduct disorder, ADD, and no-disorder-since-13 groups. Two childhood variables differed significantly among groups: "feels cheated" (parent rating) and WRAT reading (both at $p < .05$). However, neither canonical variate was significant: for the first equation, $\chi^2 = 77.25$, $p = .38$; and for the second equation, $\chi^2 = 27.27$, $p = .85$.

As a final attempt to uncover significant associations between childhood characteristics and later outcome, we replaced the conduct disorder group with a SUD (with or without any other diagnosis) group.[5] This new group included 19 subjects, 16 of whom had a concurrent conduct disorder.

Neither canonical variate for the SUD, ADD, and no-ongoing-disorder groups discriminant analyses was significant: for the first equation, $\chi^2 = 85.20$, $p = .18$; and for the second equation, $\chi^2 = 24.18$, $p = .93$. However, when the no-ongoing-disorder group was purified, the first

Table 6. *Childhood characteristics of SUD, pure ADD, and no-disorder-since-13 groups (N = 63)*

Predictor variable	Outcome group			Univariate F
	SUD (N = 19) N (%)	Pure ADD (N = 19) N (%)	No disorder since 13 (N = 25) N (%)	
Parent ratings				
fights	2.00 (0.7)	1.53 (0.7)	1.36 (1.0)	3.09*
hits/kicks	1.11 (0.8)	0.68 (0.7)	0.84 (1.0)	1.10
throws/breaks	1.16 (1.0)	0.89 (1.1)	0.72 (0.8)	1.12
picks on others	1.00 (0.9)	0.79 (0.8)	0.88 (0.9)	0.28
runs things	2.11 (0.9)	1.42 (0.8)	1.52 (1.0)	3.04
disobeys	1.79 (0.9)	1.42 (1.0)	1.52 (1.0)	0.72
steals/stores	0.21 (0.4)	0.26 (0.6)	0.04 (0.2)	1.87
steals/school	0.21 (0.4)	0.32 (0.6)	0.16 (0.5)	0.55
steals/parents	0.58 (0.8)	0.26 (0.5)	0.20 (0.6)	2.26
denies wrong	2.32 (0.8)	1.74 (0.9)	1.84 (1.0)	2.18
feels cheated	1.68 (0.9)	0.95 (0.9)	0.76 (0.9)	6.19**
driven	1.95 (1.0)	1.58 (1.1)	1.84 (1.0)	0.66
restless	2.47 (0.7)	2.58 (0.6)	2.44 (0.7)	0.24
daydreams	1.63 (1.0)	1.37 (1.2)	1.44 (1.0)	0.26
Teacher ratings				
quarrelsome	1.68 (1.2)	1.68 (1.1)	1.80 (1.1)	0.74
uncooperative	1.84 (1.1)	1.58 (0.8)	1.68 (0.9)	0.38
no fair play	1.47 (1.0)	1.16 (1.0)	1.48 (0.9)	0.71
disturbing	2.37 (0.8)	2.63 (0.7)	2.36 (0.9)	0.70
destructive	1.53 (1.0)	0.89 (1.0)	1.16 (1.1)	1.69
steals	0.05 (0.2)	0.47 (1.0)	0.20 (0.6)	1.89
lies	1.16 (1.2)	0.79 (1.1)	0.92 (1.1)	0.53
restles	2.89 (0.3)	2.89 (0.3)	2.88 (0.3)	0.16
walks around	2.37 (0.8)	2.32 (0.8)	2.20 (0.7)	0.29
fiddles	2.11 (0.7)	2.42 (0.8)	2.24 (1.0)	0.61
excitable	1.79 (1.1)	2.53 (0.7)	2.32 (0.7)	4.03*
inattentive	2.79 (0.4)	2.53 (0.5)	2.52 (0.6)	1.56
difficulty concentrating	2.74 (0.5)	2.74 (0.6)	2.48 (0.6)	1.70
daydreams	1.37 (1.1)	1.47 (1.0)	1.84 (1.0)	1.32
Clinical ratings				
eruptive aggression				
1	5 (26)	10 (63)	9 (56)	
2	6 (32)	2 (13)	2 (13)	
3	8 (42)	4 (25)	5 (31)	1.76
unsocialized aggression				
1	14 (74)	15 (94)	16 (89)	
2	1 (5)	—	—	
3	4 (21)	1 (6)	2 (11)	1.94

Table 6 (*Continued*)

| Predictor variable | Outcome group | | | Univariate F |
	SUD (N = 19) N(%)	Pure ADD (N = 19) N(%)	No disorder since 13 (N = 25) N(%)	
Ability, achievement				
WISC PIQ	103 (13)	101 (10)	102 (15)	0.75
WISC VIQ	104 (13)	101 (11)	104 (13)	0.54
WISC FSIQ	104 (13)	101 (9)	104 (12)	0.33
WRAT reading	103 (20)	92 (10)	96 (14)	2.61
WRAT math	93 (8)	93 (7)	93 (10)	0.14
Familial, environmental				
SES[a]	3.47 (0.9)	3.37 (0.9)	3.24 (1.3)	0.27
Family stability	N(%)	N(%)	N(%)	
1	14 (74)	12 (67)	13 (68)	
2	4 (21)	4 (22)	5 (26)	
3	1 (5)	2 (11)	1 (5)	
4	—	—	—	
5	—	—	—	0.16
Parental psychopathology				
1	9 (47)	11 (58)	15 (60)	
2	2 (11)	6 (32)	7 (28)	
3	8 (42)	2 (11)	3 (12)	1.89

Note: See Table 3 for abbreviations and notes.
  * $p < .05$
** $p < .01$
[a] Figures are means (SD).

canonical variate significantly discriminated between SUD, ADD, and no-disorder-since-13 groups ($\chi^2 = 97.22$, $p = .04$).

Table 6 shows the univariate F tests for each predictor in the three diagnostic groups. Three childhood variables differed significantly among the groups: "fights constantly with siblings" (parent rating, $p < .05$), "feels cheated" (parent rating, $p < .01$), and "excitable" (teacher rating, $p < .05$).

With the purified group, the percent correctly classified table showed that 95%, 95%, and 96% of the subjects in the SUD, ADD, and no-disorder-since-13 groups were correctly classified (Table 7). Also, overall correct classification increased from 77% (no ongoing disorder) to 95% (no disorder since 13). Consistent with what had occurred when conduct disorder was used to define an outcome group (see Table 4), percentages dropped dramatically when the jackknife procedure was employed.

Table 7. *Percent correctly classified, including those with SUD*

| | Percent correctly classified as | | | |
	SUD	Pure ADD	No ongoing disorder	Overall
Without the jackknife	95	79	70	77
With the jackknife	47	26	44	41
	Percent correctly classified as			
	SUD	Pure ADD	No disorder since 13	Overall
Without the jackknife	95	95	96	95
With the jackknife	42	42	28	36

Summary and conclusions

Our study of childhood predictors in hyperactive children focused exclusively on diagnosed mental disorders as measures of adjustment at follow-up. Two conclusions can be drawn from our findings. First, mental status in early adulthood cannot be predicted from childhood characteristics with any degree of confidence. When outcome groups with conduct disorder, ADD, and no disorder were constrasted, only two significant associations were found (parent rating "feels cheated," and WRAT reading). When SUD, ADD, and no disorder groups were compared, only three significant associations emerged (parent ratings of "feels cheated" and "fights constantly with siblings," teacher rating of "excitable"). In view of the fact that 38 predictor variables were included in four different outcome clusters (conduct disorder, SUD, no ongoing disorder, purified), the number of significant associations barely exceeded what would be expected by chance alone.

These findings do not appear inconsistent with reports of other investigators who followed hyperactive children. As indicated earlier, Loney et al. (1983) found that, of 14 childhood variables, only two (IQ and number of siblings) were significantly associated with the diagnosis of antisocial personality, and only one (IQ) with alcoholism at follow-up. Moreover, less than 10% of the diagnostic variance was accounted for in the multiple regression analyses.

Our failure to replicate the finding regarding the predictive value of IQ scores may be due to several methodological differences. Loney et al. employed SADS-L diagnostic criteria, whereas we used DSM-III criteria, and our subjects were younger. Differences in prevalence rates might have resulted from these two factors. In addition, Loney included subjects with

IQs of 70 and above, whereas our cut-off was 85, so that the range of IQs was greater in Loney's study. Finally, the childhood clinical characteristics of the two cohorts (many of which might co-vary with IQ) could have differed.

There are several possible reasons for our failure to find predictors of follow-up mental status. Perhaps our childhood measures were poor choices. This is unlikely, since we were guided by other investigators (Hechtman et al., 1984; Loney et al., 1983) in selecting childhood variables with potential for discriminating outcome status. Also, as indicated earlier, we analyzed variables in numerous ways (individual items, means of item clusters, factor scores, several different codings of parental psychopathology, etc.) to select variables that would yield maximum group discrimination, with full awareness of the biases we might be introducing. They did not help. More importantly, many of these measures had been shown to be valid assessments of the children's status, since they were sensitive to treatment effects at the time most of the children were treated in controlled trials (Gittelman-Klein et al., 1976).

Alternatively, the outcome groups as defined may not have been sufficiently distinct to warrant differentiation. In forming our diagnostic groups, we recognized the high degree of co-morbidity between ADD and conduct disorder and attempted to control for this overlap by composing a "pure ADD" group. Perhaps further differentiation (e.g., conduct disorder only, conduct disorder plus ADD, ADD only, other disorders, etc.) is needed to tease out childhood characteristics with prognostic utility. However, the sample sizes obtained when these diagnostic distinctions are implemented are too small to allow for meaningful data analyses.

It seems unlikely that our inability to predict psychiatric status at follow-up is due to the inadequacy of the outcome measures. Several observations argue against this point. First, we used a standard diagnostic instrument with trained interviewers with demonstrated reliability. Second, the diagnoses distinguished clearly between the former hyperactive and control cases (Gittelman et al., 1985). Third, the pattern of co-morbidity in the outcome of the former patients, as derived from the interview, revealed a highly consistent pattern of psychopathology. Compared to cases whose ADDH had remitted, those who maintained the ADDH symptoms were at significantly greater risk for antisocial personality disorder, which, in turn, placed them at risk for SUD. Finally, other mental disorders did not distinguish the former hyperactive and control children, thereby arguing for the specific nature of the psychiatric risks inherent in ADDH (Gittelman et al., 1985). Together, these findings indicate that the follow-up diagnoses were likely to have had satisfactory accuracy.

The second conclusion concerns a caution in interpreting results from studies that have relied on discriminant analysis, factor analysis, and other multivariate procedures. In this study, a large percentage of subjects (95%) were correctly classified when all predictors were included and no control for bias was implemented. However, with the jackknife procedure, markedly different results were obtained. This was true even when the discriminant analysis (i.e., canonical variate) showed significant group differentiation.

The likelihood that the discriminant analyses will capitalize on chance increases as the ratio of predictor variables to subjects approaches 1:1. If there is no true relationship between predictor variables and outcome, but we are using 50 variables to classify 50 subjects, each subject's pattern of scores uniquely identifies that subject, and the weights in the discriminant analysis are assigned such that this "signature" will yield a correct classification. However, the accuracy of the classification equations is based on their ability to identify a particular case, rather than their ability to identify patterns of relationships between the predictor variables and outcome. Therefore, when the classification equations are built without knowledge of a particular subject (as is the case with the jackknife procedure), the accuracy of classification drops markedly.

In conclusion, the use of statistical procedures that control for chance in multivariate analyses seems necessary. This decision is not simply one of choosing a more or less conservative test, but of removing critical sources of bias.[6]

Our failure to find childhood predictors of later psychiatric status in hyperactive children is disconcerting. A different picture may emerge when we examine discrete behavioral indicators of outcome rather than diagnosis, as other have done (Hechtman et al., 1984; Loney et al., 1983).

Notes

1 Diagnosed as ADDH in DSM-III (APA, 1980) and ADHD in DSM-III-R (APA, 1987).
2 One subject with a WISC IQ of 75 was inadvertently included in the follow-up sample. He was maintained in the current analyses for comparability with several other published reports on this sample.
3 Of the 27 cases with conduct disorder, 8 had ADD, 5 had substance use disorder, 11 had ADD and substance use disorder, and 3 had none of these disorders.
4 Five subjects could not be classified into one of the three categories. These subjects had the following disorders: 1 borderline personality disorder, 1 intermittent explosive disorder, 1 ADD (A + I + H) and substance use disorder, 1 ADD (A + I) and substance use disorder, 1 pathological gambling, substance use disorder, and adjustment disorder.
5 We thank Dr. Lee Robins, Washington University, St. Louis, for suggesting this analysis.
6 Efron and Gong (1983) review the jackknife, the bootstrap, cross-validation, and variations of these procedures with specific reference to prediction problems.

Acknowledgments

The authors thank Drs. Donald F. Klein, Michael T. Borenstein, and Donald Ross for their comments and their assistance with the data analyses, and Ms. Noreen Bonagura for locating and recruiting subjects.

This paper was supported, in part, by Public Health Service Grant MH 18579 and by Mental Health Clinic Research Center Grant MH 30906.

References

Abelson, H., & Fishburne, P. (1977). *National survey on drug abuse: II. Methodology.* Rockville, MD: National Institute on Drug Abuse.

American Psychiatric Association. (1980). *Diagnostic and statistical manual of mental disorders* (3rd ed.). Washington DC: Author.

American Psychiatric Association. (1987). *Diagnostic and statistical manual of mental disorders* (rev. 3rd ed.). Washington DC: Author.

Conners, C. K. (1969). A teacher rating scale for use in drug studies with children. *American Journal of Psychiatry, 126*, 884–888.

Conners, C. K. (1973). Rating scales for use in drug studies with children. *Psychopharmacology Bulletin* (special issue), 24–29.

Efron, B., & Gong, G. (1983). A leisurely look at the bootstrap, the jackknife, and cross-validation. *American Statistician, 37*, 36–48.

Gittelman-Klein, R., Klein, D. F., Katz, S., Saraf, K., & Pollack, E. (1976). Comparative effects of methylphenidate and thioridazine in hyperkinetic children. *Archives of General Psychiatry, 33*, 1217–1231.

Gittelman, R., & Mannuzza, S. (1985). Diagnosing ADDH in adolescents. *Psychopharmacology Bulletin, 21*, 237–242.

Gittelman, R., Mannuzza, S., Shenker, R., & Bonagura, N. (1985). Hyperactive boys almost grown up: I. Psychiatric status. *Archives of General Psychiatry, 42*, 937–947.

Hechtman, L., Weiss, G., Perlman, T., & Amsel, R. (1984). Hyperactives as young adults: Initial predictors of adult outcome. *Journal of the American Academy of Child Psychiatry, 23*, 250–260.

Hollingshead, A. B., & Redlich, F. C. (1958). *Social class and mental illness: A community study.* New York: John Wiley & Sons.

Klein, R., & Mannuzza, S. (in press). Long-term outcome of the attention deficit disorder/hyperkinetic syndrome. In T. Sagvolden (Ed.), *Attention deficit disorder and hyperkinetic syndrome.* Hillsdale NJ: Lawrence Erlbaum.

Kramer, J., Loney, J., & Whaley-Klahn, M. A. (1978). *The Iowa crime and punishment survey.* Iowa City: University of Iowa.

Loney, J., Whaley-Klahn, M. A., Kosier, T., & Conboy, J. (1983). Hyperactive boys and their brothers at 21: Predictors of aggressive and antisocial outcomes. In K. T. Van Dusen & S. A. Mednick (Eds.), *Prospective studies of crime and delinquency.* Boston: Kluwer-Nijhoff.

Mannuzza, S., Gittelman, R., Bonagura, N., Konig, P.H., & Shenkar, R. (1988). Hyperactive boys almost grown up: II. Outcome of those without a psychiatric diagnosis at follow-up. *Archives of General Psychiatry, 45*, 13–18.

Robins, L. N., Helzer, J. E., Croughan, J., & Ratcliff, K. S. (1981). National Institute of Mental Health Diagnostic Interview Schedule: Its history, characteristics, and validity. *Archives of General Psychiatry, 38*, 381–389.

Robins, L. N., Helzer, J. E., Ratcliff, K. S., & Seyfried, W. (1982). Validity of the Diagnostic Interview Schedule, version II: DSM-III diagnoses. *Psychological Medicine, 12,* 855–870.

Spitzer, R. L., & Endicott, J. (1978). *Schedule for Affective Disorders and Schizophrenia—lifetime version.* New York: Biometrics Research, New York State Psychiatric Institute.

Weiss, G., & Hechtman, L. T. (1986). *Hyperactive children grown up.* New York: Guilford Press.

16 Early life psychosocial events and adult affective symptoms

REMI J. CADORET, EDWARD TROUGHTON,
LINDA MORENO MERCHANT, AND ALLAN
WHITTERS

In recent years one focus of psychiatric epidemiology has been the importance of genetic factors in adult psychopathology. In this endeavor, adoption studies have been extensively used and have proven to be effective in estimating both genetic and environmental effects (Cadoret, 1986). Despite the fact that adoption designs can determine the effect of environmental factors and gene–environment interaction on human behavior, this aspect of research has been neglected by social psychiatry and other disciplines that study the impact of social structure upon mental health. This literature includes much research on social stressors (Langner & Michael, 1969; Rabkin & Struening, 1976; Brown & Harris, 1978), social buffers to stress (Dean et al., 1980; Eaton, 1978; Andrews et al., 1978; Husaini et al., 1982), and personal coping skills and stress (Wheaton, 1983; Kobasa et al., 1981). In most of this literature genetic effects and gene–environment interactions tend to be confounded with socioenvironmental factors. However for purposes of eventual prevention of psychopathology and for greater understanding of the mechanism of impact of social structure on mental health it is essential to separate genetic from environmental effects. In this chapter we discuss how an adoption study can be applied to the investigation of the role of social events on psychopathology and show that environmental factors can lay the groundwork for later-life affective symptoms.

The study of psychosocial factors

In an earlier study of male adoptees (Cadoret et al., 1985a) major depression was positively correlated with the presence in the adoptive family of an individual with an alcohol problem. In this sample of 242 males, 18 (7.5%) had major depression, but almost half of all males reported one or more lifetime depressive symptoms. One reason for using this male sample again in the current study was to investigate psychosocial factors associated with adult depressive symptoms, especially factors that occurred temporally prior to the onset of symptoms, so that a direction of causality could be determined, while at the same time controlling for other relevant factors such as genetic background. Since manic symptoms are often a part of the affective picture of depression (Akiskal, 1983*a*), we investigated these symptoms at the same time.

Method

Adoption data were available from two Iowa agencies: Iowa Children's and Family Services and Lutheran Social Services, both of Des Moines, Iowa. Adoptees had been selected so that half (probands) came from biological relatives with evidence of psychopathology, and the remaining half (controls) were age- and sex-matched to the probands but were without evidence from the adoption records of biological parent psychopathology. Adoptees were selected so as to range in age from 18 to 40. Each adoptee who participated in the study received a structured psychiatric interview: either the SADS-L (Spitzer & Endicott, 1979); the NIMH-DIS (Robins et al., 1981); or an earlier version of the DIS, based mainly on Feighner diagnostic criteria (Feighner et al., 1972). The adoptive parents were also interviewed with a structured instrument that inquired into adoptee childhood health, development, schooling, and social adjustment and other adoptive family members' health and adjustment problems. These interviews were conducted in person by research assistants who were unaware of the adoptee's biological background (whether proband or control). Details about refusals and sample bias are available elsewhere (Cadoret & Cain, 1980; Cadoret et al., 1985*b*). The refusal rate was approximately 35%. Refusees tended to be older adoptive parents, and the commonest reason for refusal was concern about confidentiality. Biological parent psychopathology was not correlated with adoptive parent assent or refusal.

Environmental factors in the adoptive home were determined from adoption records, the adoptive parent interview, and the adoptee interview. These environmental factors in the adoptive family were categorized as follows:

> Alcohol problem;
> Antisocial problem;
> Other behavior problems;
> Death of adoptive parent;
> Divorce of adoptive parent(s);
> Socioeconomic status (SES) of adoptive home;
> Rural or nonrural adoptive home;
> Adoptee placed in adoptive home at 5 months or later (late age of placement);
> Adoptive parent physical health problem.

These environmental factors were used as discrete or categorical variables in the log-linear models. In the logistic regressions, interval data such as age and number of months prior to final placement were entered as "continuous" variables. In these data, approximately one third of adoptive families had one of the first five factors listed. (For an enumeration of number of families with each environmental condition, see Cadoret et al., 1985*b*.)

Diagnosis of psychopathology in biological backgrounds was determined from records available from the adoption agency. (Criteria for these biological parent diagnoses are in Cadoret & Cain, 1980; Cadoret et al., 1985*b*.) Generally there was not enough clinical information in the adoption records to use research diagnostic criteria such as DSM-III. Accordingly we diagnosed "alcohol problem" in biological parent whenever heavy drinking and some social or medical complication of drinking was present (e.g., fired from job, arrested for public intoxication, hospitalized for detoxification). "Antisocial behavior" was diagnosed by presence of one or more behaviors characteristic of antisocial personality such as felony conviction, physical abuse of family, or poor work history. Biological parent diagnoses were discrete variables and were used as such in the log-linear analyses. Of the 241 males interviewed, 22 (9.1%) biological parents were designated as having an alcohol problem and 41 (17.0%) as having an antisocial problem.

Diagnosis of adult adoptee psychiatric conditions was made from the structured interviews using DSM-III criteria and were used in the analysis as categorical data. However, for many of the analyses in this paper, counts of lifetime number of symptoms of the affective conditions of mania and depression were used as variables. Only interviewed adoptees were used in this study, since we were interested in quantitative psychiatric complaints including numbers and types of symptoms and such subjective information was available only from interviews. Of the 329 males in the study, 241 or 73% were interviewed.

Data analysis utilized standard descriptive statistics but relied mainly on multivariate techniques to demonstrate and separate genetic and environmental effects. Log-linear analysis was used for categorical data analysis. We used BMDP 4F statistical software (Dixon, 1981) to fit log-linear models. When genetic and environmental factors appeared in the same model, the genetic–environment relationship was forced into the model to control for selective placement effects. We also used the multiple regression approach suggested by Plomin et al. (1977) to detect gene–environment interaction.

Results

Determination of main effects. The male sample ($N = 241$) had an average age at interview of 24.8 with a standard deviation of 6.2 and a range of 18 to 40 Results of DSM-III classification of adult male psychopathology appears in Table 1. Substance abuse and antisocial personality were common diagnoses. Major depression was less common, and no diagnosis of mania was

Table 1. *Adult psychopathology (lifetime) in interviewed male adoptees (N = 241)*

DSM-III diagnoses	Number	%
Antisocial personality	34	14.1
Alcohol abuse/dependence	62	25.7
Drug abuse/dependence	28	11.6
Any of above disorders	76	31.5
Major depression	18	7.5
Mania	0	0

Table 2. *Lifetime affective symptoms by type and number in male adoptees (N = 241)*

| Male adoptees | Number of symptoms | | | | | | | |
	0	1	2	3	4	5	6+	Total
Number with depressive symptoms	139	36	18	13	6	7	22	241
Number with manic symptoms	185	22	13	7	9	4	1	241

made. However, affective symptoms reported in the DIS occurred in a considerable number of individuals: 42% of males claimed one or more lifetime depressive symptoms, and 23% reported one or more manic symptoms. The distribution of depressive and manic symptoms appears in Table 2 and shows the usual J-shaped distribution.

In order to relate the affective symptoms to genetic and environmental factors, we fitted them into a model which was based upon previous findings with these data. These prior analyses (Cadoret et al., 1985a & b; 1986) found that antisocial problems in biological relatives predicted increased incidence of antisocial personality in adoptees, and that alcohol problems in biological relatives predicted adult adoptee alcohol abuse and drug abuse. Accordingly we constructed a basic model to control for these known genetic effects, to which we planned to add under outcome the presence of affective symptoms, and test individually the environmental factors listed in the method section for their effect upon adoptee affective symptom outcome. In this modeling we used the following outcome variables. The affective symptoms of depression and mania in Table 1 were used to dichotomize subjects into those who claimed symptoms and those who did not. Adoptee diagnosis that had correlated in other studies with

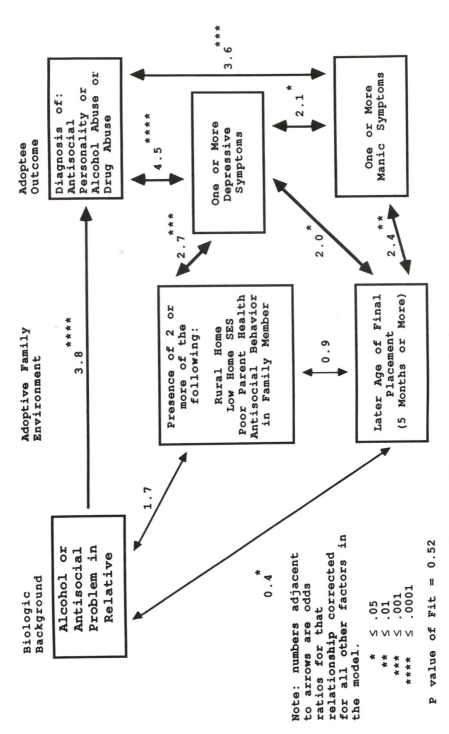

Figure 1. Genetic and environmental factors in affective symptoms in male adoptees.

biological background of alcohol or antisocial problems were lumped into one category: presence in the adoptee of antisocial personality or alcohol abuse, or drug abuse.

The final model obtained in this process is shown in Figure 1. The basic genetic relationship appears in the significant odds ratio of 3.8 ($p < .0001$) between the genetic factors and adoptee outcome of the three commonest diagnoses, antisocial personality, alcohol abuse, and drug abuse. While controlling for this gene–outcome relationship the model also shows significant relationships of depressive and manic symptoms to each other as well as to the three major outcome diagnoses. To this model consisting of the genetic factors, the outcome diagnosis, and the two types of affective symptoms we added singly the nine environmental factors listed in the methods section.

These analyses showed significant correlations between one or both types of affective symptoms and the following dichotomous environmental factors: rural adoptive home, adoptive home with lower SES, poor health reported in adoptive parent, antisocial behavior reported in an adoptive family member other than the adoptee, and late age of final adoptee placement in adoptive home (5 months or more). Of these environmental factors, the last, occurring during the adoptee's first and second year of life, appeared to be unrelated and of different quality than the first four factors. On the other hand, the first four factors appeared to be more related to each other, as evidenced by the fact that significant correlations were found between antisocial behavior in family and poor parent physical health ($p = .05$); rural home and low SES ($p < .0001$); and low SES and poor parent physical health ($p < .003$). However, none of the correlations between late age of placement and the remaining four environmental factors were significant. These findings suggested a simpler environmental model in which age of placement acted independently of rural home, low SES, poor parent health, and antisocial adoptive family member. Accordingly, age of placement was added to the model as a separate environmental factor, and the remaining factors were combined to form one factor. This was done by adding the number of these adoptive home variables present in an individual and scoring the new factor positive if an adoptee was exposed to two or more of these home conditions. The results of this analysis also appear in Figure 1 and show that the new adoptive home factor correlates with depressive symptoms. It does not correlate with later age of final placement as expected from the simple two-way correlations reported earlier. The factor of later placement does correlate significantly with both depressive and manic symptoms even when controlling for other environmental and genetic factors already in the model.

Selective placement was controlled in the log-linear model by forcing into the model relationships between the environmental factors and the genetic background. Only one of these relationships showed a marginally significant effect: late age of final placement in the adoptive home was associated with lack of antisocial or alcohol problems in the biological parents.

Determination of confounding variables

These log-linear analyses do not allow detailed examination of other factors that might be confounded with age of adoption and with the clinical symptoms of depression and mania. There are many possible reasons for late placement in the adoptive home, which could of themselves be associated with depression. For example, physical problems associated with pregnancy and birth could be a vulnerability factor in later depression, and these same factors could lead the adoption agency to place a child later. Indeed, some adoption records documented medical problems such as prematurity or possible retardation as reasons for delaying final placement until it was evident that the prospective adoptee was developing normally. Another confounding factor regarding age of placement in an adoptive home is the fact that during the 1930s, 1940s, and early 1950s agencies tended to delay final placement as a matter of policy and not necessarily because of a specific medical or social problem. In these data the correlation between age of final placement and birth year reflects this policy. The Pearson correlation is $-.33 (N = 241, p < .0001)$, indicating that earlier birth years were especially associated with later placement. This is important to take into account, since the number of reported lifetime affective symptoms is correlated with adoptee birth year: for depressive symptoms, $r = -.16 (N = 241, p < .01)$; and for manic symptoms, $r = -.17 (N = 241, p < .01)$. Thus older individuals who are more likely to report affective symptoms are also more likely to have been placed later, and this could account for the relationship found in the log-linear models between affective symptoms and later placement. Similarly, confounding with perinatal factors such as prematurity could also be important in assessing the importance of the age-adopted variable.

In order to remove the effect of confounding factors we re-analyzed the data using a multiple regression approach with the number of affective symptoms as a dependent variable. Depressive symptoms and manic symptoms were analyzed separately. The following possible confounding factors were used as independent variables: birth year; birth problems (total number of the following conditions: Apgar score >5, need for resuscitation, delivery by breech, cesarean section, or forceps delivery; length of labor; birth weight; maternal medical problems during pregnancy (total number of the following: took medications, smoked, drank alcohol, was physically ill). Other independent variables used were those in the long-linear analyses that were found to relate significantly to the affective symptoms: presence of a psychiatric diagnosis of antisocial personality, or alcohol or drug abuse; late age of placement; and total number of the following adoptive home factors: rural adoptive home, low adoptive home SES, poor adoptive parent health, and antisocial behavior in adoptive family member.

The result of forward and backward solutions of the multiple regression approach showed that the manic symptoms–late placement correlation remained significant no matter which potentially confounding factors were added to the model. This was in spite of the fact that, in the models, birth year significantly predicted manic symptoms. With depression the picture was somewhat different. Here the inclusion in a model of birth year reduced the significance of the age adopted–depression relationship to a *p* value of approximately .06. In all models the relationship of other psychiatric diagnoses to affective symptoms remained highly significant (<0.1% level). The relationship of number of environmental factors such as urban home to depression lost statistical significance at the 5% level.

Determination of gene–environment interaction

In order to detect gene–environment interaction we generated interaction terms by crossing the environmental factors that we had found in the above analyses with the genetic effects already in the model of Figure 1 and with the additional genetic factor of having a first-degree biological relative with an affective disorder. Mathematically, interaction terms were generated by multiplying the co-efficients for separate variables together for each individual and entering this new "dummy" variable into the regression model. These interaction factors were then added to the multiple regression model in which either depressive symptoms or manic symptoms was the dependent variable, and the independent variables were the main effects of the genetic or environmental factors which had been found significant in previous analyses. In addition, important confounding variables were also added (such as the adoptee birth year). Outcome diagnoses such as antisocial personality or substance abuse that correlated highly with affective symptoms were also included in the model.

The results for depressive symptoms appear in Table 3. Significant gene–environment interaction is evident between age adopted and having a biological parent with affective disorder. The direction of the interaction is for significantly higher depression scores, given the presence of both genetic and environmental effects, than would be predicted if each acted independently and additively.

The final model for manic symptoms appears in Table 4 and shows a similar significant gene–environment effect for manic symptom increase, given the presence of both genetic and environmental factors. In these

Table 3. *Multiple regression test for gene–environment interaction in adult male depressive symptoms* ($N = 241$)

Source of variation	Type III sum of squares	P
Affective illness in biological parent	10.65	.08
Birth year of adoptee	5.59	.21
Age adopted	57.49	.0001
Adult diagnosis of antisocial personality or substance abuse	168.44	.0001
Adoptive home environment	15.88	.035
Interaction (age adopted × affective illness in parent)	45.21	.0004

$R^2 = .265$

Table 4. *Multiple regression test for gene–environment interaction in adult male manic symptoms* ($N = 241$)

Source of variation	Type III sum of squares	P
Affective illness in biological parent	1.05	.34
Birth year of adoptee	2.88	.12
Age adopted	10.56	.003
Adult diagnosis of antisocial personality or substance abuse	41.79	.0001
Interaction (age adopted × affective illness in parent)	5.17	.036

$R^2 = .211$

models the main effect of age adopted on the dependent variable remains highly significant, both for manic and for depressive symptoms.

Discussion

This analysis of adoption data has shown that several environmental factors are associated with a report of lifetime depressive and manic symptoms in adult males. The correlation holds when controlling for significant relationships between genetic background and adult psychiatric diagnoses of substance abuse and antisocial personality.

The environmental effects can be divided into two types: (1) late age of placement, which occurs during the first and second year of an adoptee's life prior to final adoptive placement, and (2) a group of intercorrelated factors characterize the adoptive home and that could operate at any time after placement in that home. The first factor was found to be confounded with other variables (such as adoptee year of birth) and potentially confounded with perinatal variables. Control for confounding by a multiple regression analysis showed that the manic symptom – late age of placement correlation was essentially unaffected by inclusion of potential confounds in the model. On the other hand, the depressive symptom – late placement correlation was reduced in significance by inclusion of birth year in the models, though in the models including interaction factors, this correlation became highly significant (see Table 3). Although the depressive symptom-adoptive home environment correlation was reduced in significance from the log-linear model, it remained significant at the 5% level.

Furthermore, the analyses shown in Tables 3 and 4 indicated gene–environment interaction involving the age at final adoptive placement and a biological background of affective disorder. There was no evidence of a main effect for any of the genetic backgrounds tested (alcohol, antisocial, affective disorder) upon adult affective symptoms. The significant interaction found between affective disordered biological parent and late placement would appear to enhance the importance of the late adoptive placement.

Thus the most interesting feature of these data is confirmed: the correlation of manic symptoms and depressive symptoms in adulthood with events occurring in the first and second years of life. These early events were unconnected with the adoptive home environmental factors. The late placement variable did not appear to be correlated with potential confounds such as perinatal medical conditions. Since these infants were separated at birth (or within a few days of birth) from the biological mother, it is unlikely that adverse home care associated with a psychiatrically ill or socially crippled biological parent was a factor. What did happen to these children was a temporary placement in one or more foster homes, where they remained until their removal and final (late) placement into a permanent adoptive home. The temporary foster homes were carefully selected by the adoption agencies and thus likely delivered a high standard of care to these foster infants. These considerations lead to the conclusion that the common event in the late placement variable was most likely the change in homes from the foster care family to the adoptive family.

Thus, the relevant factor that appears to affect later life affective symptomatology in males would appear to be social disruption. This interpretation is consistent with the theoretical view of early object-relations theorists such as Bowlby (1988), Ainsworth (1985), Klein (1964) and Kohut (1971) who posit the importance of the first year of life in developing relationships with people. Disruptions of these early relationships are supposed to lead to future psychological disturbance as well as difficulties in later relationships (Bowlby, 1973, 1983). Indeed, previously reported analyses of data from females from these same adoption studies indicated that major depression was associated with earlier loss by death of adoptive parents (Cadoret et al., 1985a), an effect which has been reported from a number of other studies of depression (Lloyd, 1980).

An effect of late adoptive placement on depression in adulthood has also been reported from another adoption study. Von Knorring et al. (1982) have found that infants who stayed with the biological mother and were then adopted away after 6 months of age were more likely as adults to suffer from "neurotic depression." In the Swedish study, late placement was confounded with contact with the biological mother, so that a gene–environment interaction or stressful early life experiences such as neglect could not be ruled out. Nevertheless, at the same time, the infants were uprooted for their final adoptive placement after spending a number of months with one caretaker, and this, as in the present study, could have been the relevant event.

Recent interest in life events has focused upon remote childhood stressful experiences as a causal factor in determining the effect of later life stresses upon psychopathology (Richman & Flaherty, 1985). Remote attachment experiences and stressful life events in childhood are posited to affect external and internal social resources and social stresses, and ultimately affect psychopathology. The present findings would suggest that adoptees could be used to study the effect of early life psychosocial factors upon adult psychopathology and adult coping skills while controlling for genetic factors. The positive correlation between manic and depressive symptoms (see Figure 1) is of special interest because of their association with the antisocial personality diagnosis.

Separate analyses of affective symptoms in the 34 male adoptees diagnosed as antisocial in this sample have been carried out by L. Moreno (unpublished analyses), who found that adoptee antisocials with above-median depressive symptoms were significantly more likely to demonstrate above-median manic symptoms. Those showing increased depressive symptoms also demonstrated significantly more schizophrenic symptoms. These findings can be interpreted as consistent with the hypothesis of two types of sociopaths, the primary and secondary, as described by Karpman (1947) and Blackburn (1973). Primary sociopaths are individuals who manifest low levels of anxiety and guilt and usually engage in antisocial activity with a minimum of subjective distress. In contrast, the secondary sociopath, who demonstrates antisocial behavior similar to the primary, suffers from guilt, anxiety, depression, and other psychiatric symptoms. The importance of the early environment in sociopathy was confirmed in these data by conducting a multiple regression analysis in the 34 male sociopaths with a count of depressive symptoms as a dependent variable and the items in Table 3 as independent variables. Even with the greatly reduced number of observations, the variable of "age adopted" still predicted adult depressive symptoms at the 5% level. Unfortunately, the sample was not large enough to estimate and test the interaction of age adopted with a genetic background of affective disorder. The present findings would suggest that secondary sociopathy with its characterizing guilt, depression, and other "nervous" symptoms could have its roots in an environmental effect (Tables 3 and 4) in operation at some time during infancy.

It is interesting to speculate upon the clinical implications of the present findings. Obviously, the affective symptoms correlate highly with drug, alcohol, and personality (antisocial) problems. However, looking at the affective symptoms from a different descriptive perspective, the findings could be very relevant to the clinical types described by Akiskal under the rubric of the "subaffective spectrum," containing individuals with cyclothymic mood disorders, bipolar II disorders, and dysthymic disorders (Akiskal, 1981, 1983*a* & *b*). Relating these conditions to developmental events involving gene–environment interaction in infancy and childhood could lead to greater nosologic understanding of adult affective disorders, since this paper has demonstrated that early life events appear to affect the manifestations of psychopathology in later life.

Acknowledgment

Research was funded by NIAAA Grant No. R01 AA06159–01A2 and departmental grants from the University of Iowa.

References

Ainsworth, M. D. (1985). Attachments across the life span. *Bulletin of the New York Academy of Medicine, 61*, 592–812.

Akiskal, H. S. (1981). Subaffective disorders: Dysthymic, cyclothymic and bipolar II disorders in the borderline realm. *Psychiatric Clinics of North America, 4*, 25–46.

Akiskal, H. S. (1983*a*). Diagnosis and classification of affective disorders: New insights from clinical and laboratory approaches. *Psychiatric Developments, 1*, 123–160.

Akiskal, H. S. (1983*b*). Dysthymic disorder: Psychopathology of proposed chronic depressive subtypes. *American Journal of Psychiatry, 140*, 11–20.

Andrews, G., Tennant, C. Hewson, D. M. & Valliant, G. E. (1978). Life event stress, social support, coping style, and risk of psychological impairment. *Journal of Nervous and Mental Disease, 166*, 307–317.

Blackburn, R. (1973). An empirical classification of psychopathic personality. *British Journal of Psychiatry, 127*, 456–460.

Bowlby, J. (1973). *Attachment and loss. Vol. 2: Separation, anxiety, and anger.* London: Hogarth.

Bowlby, J. (1983). *Attachment and loss. Vol. 3: Loss: sadness and depression.* London: Hogarth.

Bowlby, J. (1988). Developmental psychiatry comes of age. *American Journal of Psychiatry, 145*, 1–10.

Brown, G., & Harris, T. (1978). *Social origins of depression: A study of psychiatric disorder in women.* New York: Free Press.

Cadoret R. J. (1986). Adoption studies. Historical and methodological critique. *Psychiatric Developments, 1*, 45–64.

Cadoret, R. J., Cain, C. (1980). Sex differences in predictors of antisocial behavior in adoptees. *Archives of General Psychiatry 37*, 1171–1175.

Cadoret, R. J., O'Gorman, T. W., Heywood, E., & Troughton, E., (1985a). Genetic and environmental factors in major depression. *Journal of Affective Disorders, 9*, 155–164.

Cadoret, R. J., O'Gorman, T. W., Heywood, E., & Troughton, E., (1986). An adoption study of gentic and environmental factors in drug abuse. *Archives of General Psychiatry, 43*, 1131–1136.

Cadoret, R. J., Troughton, E., O'Gorman, T. W., & Heywood, E. (1985b). Alcoholism and antisocial personality: inter-relationships, genetic and environmental factors. *Archives of General Psychiatry, 42*, 161–167.

Dean, A., Lin N., & Ensel, W. M. (1980). The epidemiological significance of support system in depression. In R. G. Simmons (Ed.), *Research in community and mental health* (Vol. 2). Greenwich: JAI Press.

Dixon, W. J. (1981). *BMDP statistical software*. Berkeley: University of California Press.

Eaton, W. W. (1978). Life events, social supports and psychiatric symptoms: A re-analysis of the New Haven data. *Journal of Health and Social Behvior, 19*, 230–234.

Feighner, J. P., Robins, E., Guze, S. B., Woodruff, Jr., R. A., Winokur, G. & Munoz, R. (1972). Diagnostic criteria for use in psychiatric research. *Archives of General Psychiatry, 26*, 57–63.

Husaini, B. A., Neff, J. A., Newbrough, T. R., et al. (1982). The stress-buffering role of social support and personal competence among the rural married. *Journal of Community Psychology, 10*, 409–426.

Karpman, B. (1947). Passive parasitic psychopathy: Toward the personality structure and psychogenesis of ideopathic psychopathy. *Psychoanalytic Review, 34*, 102–118.

Klein, M. (1964). *Contributions to psychoanalysis*. New York: McGraw-Hill.

Kabasa, S. C., Maddi, S. R., & Courington, S. (1981). Personality and constitution as mediators in the stress-illness relationship. *Journal of Health and Social Behavior, 22*, 368–378.

Kohut, H. (1971). *The analysis of the self*. New York: International Universities Press.

Langner, T. S., & Michael, S. T. (1969). *Life stress and mental health*. New York: Free Press.

Lloyd, C. (1980). Life events and depressive disorder reviewed. I. Events as predisposing factors. *Archives of General Psychiatry, 37*, 529–535.

Polmin, R., DeFries, J. D., & Loehlin, J. C. (1977). Genotype-environment interaction and correlation in the analysis of human behavior. *Psychological Bulletin, 84*, 309–322.

Rabkin, J. G., & Struening, E. L. (1976). Life events, stress and illness. *Science, 194*, 1013–1020.

Richman J. A., & Flaherty, J. A. (1985). Stress, coping resources and psychiatric disorders: Alternate paradigms from a life cycle perspective. *Comprehensive Psychiatry, 26*, 456–465.

Robins, L. N., Helzer, J. E., Croughan, J. L., Williams, J. B. W., & Spitzer, R. L. (1981). NIMH diagnostic interview schedule, version III. St. Louis, MO: Washington University.

Spitzer, R. L., & Endicott J. (1979). *Schedule for affective disorders and schizophrenia—Lifetime version (SADS-L)*, 3rd ed. New York: New York State Psychiatric Institute.

von Knorring, A. L., Bohman, M., & Sigvardsson, S. (1982). Early life expriences and psychiatric disorders: An adoptive study. *Acta Psychiatrica Scandinavica* 65, 283–291.

Wheaton, B. (1983). Stress, personal coping resources, and psychiatric symptoms: An investigation of interactive models. *Journal of Health and Social Behavior,* 24, 208–229.

17 Influences of early-life and recent factors on affective disorder in women: An exploration of vulnerability models

BRYAN RODGERS

There is a widespread belief that some individuals have a predisposition towards the development of affective disorder. These individuals may be identified by biological markers, personality or behavioral attributes, family history, some experience of damaging circumstances in the recent or more distant past, or socio-demographic characteristics. The relationships between these predisposing features and outcome may be described by simple statistical associations or may be the subject of more detailed considerations of underlying processes.

The notion of vulnerability has received particular attention in relation to the etiology of depression. Essentially, a vulnerable individual has a higher risk of disorder because of enhanced susceptibility to life stressors. This idea has been developed by Brown and Harris (1978a) with particular reference to the following vulnerability factors in women: early loss of mother, having three or more children, lack of employment outside the home, and lack of a confiding relationship with a husband or boyfriend. These four exogenous factors are thought to exert their influence on psychopathology through their effect on other psychological characteristics—self-esteem, in particular, although Brown et al. (1986) made clear that self-esteem is only part of a wider domain:

We see an important link between mastery of problems and feelings of self-esteem, but any factor contributing to low mastery would be relevant. Our reference to self-esteem should, at present, be seen as no more than a way of highlighting core notions concerning the self and biographical factors that have contributed to them (p. 259).

The key feature of vulnerability is that in isolation it does not increase the risk of disorder; it only does so in association with life events and long-term difficulties (collectively termed *provoking agents*). Statistically, one expects a significant interaction between vulnerability and the presence of provoking agents in a model, with rate of disorder as the dependent variable (Table 1). A similar but not identical pattern derives from the rather different perspective of Seligman (Seligman 1975; Abramson et al., 1978) in regard to the theory

314

Table 1. *Expected rates of disorder from vulnerability models*

	Not vulnerable	Vulnerable
Brown and Harris model of vulnerability		
No provoking agent	Low	Low
Provoking agent	Medium	High
Seligman model of vulnerability		
No provoking agent	Low	Low
Provoking agent	Low	High

of learned helplessness and human depression. Depression, according to Seligman and Peterson (1986):

> results from characteristics of an individual in conjunction with characteristics of the environment. Neither the attributional style (habitual ways of explaining the causes of good and bad events) nor the uncontrollable events alone result in widespread helplessness and depression; only their co-occurrence leads to depression (p. 227).

This view adds to the assertion that vulnerability does not give rise to disorder without a provoking agent that the assertion the provoking agent does not give rise to disorder in the absence of vulnerability (see Table 1). These vulnerability models contrast with the "additive burden" or "strain" model of depression (Dohrenwend & Dohrenwend, 1981; McKee & Vilhjalmsson, 1986), whereby life stressors and vulnerability have independent additive effects on outcome.

Several methodological hurdles are encountered in the attempt to assess whether these deceptively simple models are consistent with what actually takes place in the general population. The statistical techniques appropriate for data analysis have been one focus of concern. Tennant and Bebbington (1978) criticized the separate application of χ^2 tests to contingency tables representing associations between vulnerability and onset depression in those who have experienced a provoking agent and those who have not. Such calculations are (undesirably) sensitive to the number of subjects in the two subtables (Bebbington, 1980), and the approach does not provide a direct test of the interaction of vulnerability and experience of a provoking agent. Tennant and Bebbington (1978) considered log-linear techniques to be more suitable for this purpose. Whereas some investigators have followed this advice (Solomon & Bromet, 1982; Costello, 1982; Bebbington et al., 1984), others have not (Campbell et al., 1983). Even when there is agreement on the desirability of using formal methods in testing for interactions, debate continues with respect to the method of choice: whether to use a linear or one of several nonlinear functional models for the relationship with the dependent variable (Everitt & Smith, 1979; Kessler, 1983; McKee & Vilhjalmsson, 1986). In a re-analysis of Brown and Harris's (1978a) data on predictors of depression, McKee and Vilhjamsson (1986) showed that linear probability estimations yielded significant interaction effects for three of the four vulnerability factors (the exception being unemployment), whereas no significant interactions were found with a logit transformation. They emphasized that "there is no statistical test which would allow us to choose between the linear probability and the logit specifications." Indeed it is not easy to envisage any unequivocal criteria for making a decision. The view that "it may seem reasonable to regard differences in proportions of similar weight at any point between 0.0 and 1.0" (Brown, 1986) hardly constitutes a forceful argument. There is, however, a feature of the vulnerability model that is not affected by transformation of the dependent variable. As Brown (1986) states, "The effect of a vulnerability factor should be confined to those subjects exposed to a provoking agent." That is, the difference attributable to vulnerability for those not experiencing a provoking agent should not just be less than for those who have had such an experience, but should in fact be non-existent.

This discussion has centered on the more explicit and elaborate Brown and Harris model but has equal relevance to the similar Seligman model, which in addition predicts that the effect of provoking agents will be confined to subjects with a "depressive attributional style." Such predictions immediately point to further, less debated, methodological problems that concern misclassification in respect to the independent variables. It is apparent that any misclassification with respect to vulnerability would tend to dilute the expected interaction with provoking agents. The extent to which this could occur is unknown, since it must be assumed that not all vulnerability factors have yet been identified. If the factors measured constitute an imperfect proxy for the psychological characteristics that determine susceptibility (Brown's low mastery or Seligman's attributional style), then even their complete and reliable identification would not overcome this weakness. For these reasons the magnitude of any interaction effect is likely to be underestimated and, in the case of the Seligman model, would preclude the possibility of finding a low rate of disorder in the "not-vulnerable and provoking agent" quadrant. Similarly, a serious problem for the assessment of both the Seligman model and the Brown and Harris model is the misclassification of subjects according to the occurrence of provoking agents. In particular, allocation of individuals who had experienced a difficulty or life event to the "no-provoking agent" group would raise the probability of disorder in the "vulnerable and no-provoking agent" quadrant relative to that in the "no-vulnerable and no-provoking agent" quadrant.

The first problem, misclassification with respect to vulnerability, will not be elaborated further. It cannot be completely overcome in the study to be described here, and therefore the Seligman model is not adequately tested. One final point relating to this model that can be made, however, is that vulnerability may be conceived as a continuum rather than as a discrete attribute (Kessler, 1983) and, if so, the "not vulnerable" group would be replaced by a "least vulnerable" group.

The second problem, misclassification with respect to provoking agents, is important for two reasons. First, because the conservative approach in life stress research has been to focus attention on severe and independent events and difficulties (the intention being to exclude events that result from "effort after meaning" or are a consequence of illness), milder but perhaps effective experiences are ignored. Second, there are doubts as to the reliability of subjects' reports of life events (Neugebauer, 1981; Tennant et al., 1981). Misclassification in both of these ways will tend to conceal findings consistent with a vulnerability model.

The investigation about to be described examines vulnerability effects in the women of a large general population sample. Information is available on a wide variety of past and recent behavior and life circumstances which can constitute vulnerability factors and provoking agents. The opportunity for manifestation of vulnerability effects can be maximized by identifying those women who appeared free from recent life stressors. The women are part of the Medical Research Council's National Survey of Health and Development (NSHD), the 1946 British birth cohort study.

Study of vulnerability in women

Sample

The NSHD is a follow-up study of 5,362 individuals born in Britain in one week of March 1946. They were selected from a larger survey of all births during the week of March 3–9 (Joint Committee, 1948). Illegitimate and multiple births were excluded from further investigation, but all other children born to agricultural workers and men in non-manual occupations, along with a quarter of the remainder (working class children), were retained as the target population. They have been studied throughout childhood and early adulthood on many occasions, most recently in 1982–83 when the cohort was age 36. The type of information obtained at previous contacts has been outlined by Atkins et al. (1981), and a further summary of findings and publications has been provided by Wadsworth (1987).

In 1982, 3,754 survey members were traced (86.3% of those thought to be still residing in Britain), and 3,322 were successfully interviewed. Included in this interview was a shortened version of the Present State Examination

(PSE) as described by Wing et al., (1974), pertaining to the one-month period just prior to interview. The shortened PSE consists of standardized ratings of symptoms of depression, anxiety, and phobias, and it yields a total symptom score and an identification of cases which, in a population sample, are predominantly of minor affective disorder. The certainty of diagnosis is indicated by the index of definition (ID) derived by computer scoring (Wing & Sturt, 1978). The ID has a range of 1 to 8. Typically levels 1 to 4 and 5 to 8 are aggregated and the latter grouping is labeled "caseness" (e.g., Henderson et al., 1979). The conduct of these interviews and the reliability and validity of the PSE assessments obtained have been described elsewhere (Rodgers & Mann, 1986). Additional information was collected from each survey member concerning household and accommodation, health, employment, leisure activities (including exercise), the experience of recent life events, diet, and smoking habits. A short physical examination was also conducted.

The questions relating to life events, although not so elaborate as those utilized by some other investigators, provided valuable information for the present purpose. Interviewees were asked whether anything or any bad news in the previous year had really shaken or upset them or been a big disappointment to them and, if so, to describe such experiences. In addition, specific questions were asked about deaths, injuries, illnesses, divorce or separation of friends and relatives, burglaries and robberies, and other crises at work or in the family. Respondents were also asked how they reacted to such experiences.

Although information was available for the assessment of three of the Brown and Harris vulnerability factors, no indication of confiding relationships was sought. This was unfortunate since Tennant (1985) considered it to be the one of the original four that has been most often replicated. Other factors selected to examine consistency with the vulnerability model were the husband's unemployment, financial problems, housing problems, lone parenthood, their own previous divorce or separation, and divorce or separation of their parents. A further measure was a composite score obtained from childhood behavioral attributes and circumstances, which had been found predictive of adult symptomatology (Rodgers, in press). This score, derived from multiple regression analysis, called on the following information: nocturnal enuresis reported by mothers at age 6; childhood habits and behavior reported by mothers on several occasions; class attendance as indicated by high school records; measures of extraversion and neuroticism from the short Maudsley Personality Inventory (completed at age 16); reports of menstrual pain (at age 15); chronic or repeated serious illness or disability throughout childhood taken from mothers' reports, school attendance records, periodic medical examinations, and hospital inpatient records; and having two or more siblings. The composite score was calculated as follows: To a constant of 10.6,

add	36.4 for bed-wetting at age 6
add	14.1 for other behavior problems between ages 6 and 10
add	9.1 for behavior problems between ages 11 and 15
subtract	1.58 for each extraversion point (0–12)
add	2.38 for each introversion point (0–12)
add	23.9 for chronic illness/disability
subtract	0.41 for each attendance percentage point (2%–100%)
add	7.6 for menstrual pain
add	5.8 for two or more siblings

Results and discussion

Sample

Restriction to those women who had complete data from the appropriate childhood years resulted in a subsample of 1,144 women from the 1,653 who had valid PSE assessments at age 36. It was found that the 509 excluded women were rather more likely to meet the PSE criteria for caseness than the 1,144 who were included (9.4% as compared with 8.2%, not statistically significant). Those women excluded also had a slightly higher mean total PSE score (3.21 as compared with 2.97 for the others, again not statistically significant). A high nonresponse rate in the total 36-year sample has been noted in those who had experienced severe psychiatric disorders, particularly schizophrenia. Otherwise those followed up successfully appeared as much at risk of developing adult disorder as those lost to follow-up (Rodgers in press).

Recent life stressors and symptomatology

Two specific recent stressors were found to be largely unrelated to psychiatric symptoms at age 36. These were having a relative or friend go through separation or divorce and being a victim of robbery or burglary. However, a small number of individuals said they were "rather overwhelmed" by these experiences. Although they may have had an unusual susceptibility to adverse reaction, it is also possible that their experience was intrinsically more stressful than others' and would have constituted a provoking agent for anyone.

All other specific life events were associated with PSE symptoms. Most were highly significant, but the relationships with relatives' or friends' illness or injury were less pronounced. A positive response to the open-ended question concerning recent upsetting circumstances was also highly significant. In total, one or more stressors were reported by 916 of the 1,144 women (80.1%).

Other difficulties as potential vulnerability factors

In order to follow closely the design of Brown and Harris (1978a), who considered onset cases only, 158 women were excluded from these analyses who, when asked elsewhere in the interview about recurrent and chronic health problems, described themselves as suffering "nervous or emotional trouble or persistent depression" all or most of the time. The form of statistical analyses used was a linear modeling procedure (GLM of the SAS package) with total PSE score as the dependent variable. The use of this continuous measure rather than a discrete variable representing caseness was preferred on the basis of earlier work (Rodgers & Mann, 1986). The procedure first tests the significance of the main effects of the vulnerability factor and provoking agent and then tests their interaction.

Having three or more children did not appear to act as a vulnerability factor. It did not achieve significance either in interaction with the occurrence of a provoking agent, or as a main effect. Brown and Harris (1986) have recently reported a similar negative finding and attributed this to the changing social milieu. Loss of mother at an early age was also a poor predictor of adult disorder. Death of either parent in childhood showed a weak association with later symptoms, but death of mother was an uncommon event in this cohort (3.0% of girls experienced such a loss before age 18). Divorce or separation of parents had a greater impact, but in the majority of cases this resulted in separation of the survey child from the father rather than the mother. Whether such effects can be attributed to the separation per se is arguable, and the fact that parental separations appeared to carry a risk even when occurring in the late teenage and early adult years may indicate that earlier family discord was involved. Whatever the mechanism responsible, such early disruption did not act as a vulnerability factor in the recent onset of depression and, furthermore, the risk associated with divorce or separation of parents was no longer apparent when women with long-term "nervous or emotional trouble or persistent depression" were excluded from analysis.

Not having employment outside the home came closer to meeting the criteria for a vulnerability factor. Table 2 shows mean total PSE scores for women in paid employment and those not, subdivided by the experience of provoking agents. The interaction of these independent variables fell just short of statistical significance ($p<.075$), and it can be seen that symptom scores were actually lower for those not in employment when no provoking agent was reported. Brown and Harris (1978a) found the protective effect of outside employment to be restricted to women who lacked a confiding relationship with a husband or boyfriend, but it was not possible to identify such women in the present study.

There was some similarity in the pattern of results found for three variables: husband's employment, lone parenthood, and previous marital

Table 2. *Mean total PSE score by employment status and experience of provoking agents: for women*

Provoking agent experience	Paid employment outside home	No employment outside home
None	1.27 ($N = 128$)	1.07 ($N = 74$)
One or more	2.10 ($N = 496$)	2.84 ($N = 288$)

Significance of interaction: $p = 0.075$

Table 3. *Mean total PSE score by financial hardship and experience of provoking agents: for women*

Provoking agent experience	No financial hardship	Financial hardship
None	1.21 ($N = 188$)	1.07 ($N = 14$)
One or more	2.11 ($N = 674$)	4.02 ($N = 110$)

Significance of interaction: $p = 0.030$

separation or divorce. All three showed a significant association with caseness in this study and all contributed to high symptom scores, particularly in association with provoking agents. However, none of these interactions reached statistical significance. In view of the comparatively small numbers of individuals involved, these factors could not be ruled out as possible vulnerability factors on the basis of such negative results, but further evidence would be necessary. One feature which these three variables and the variable of employment status have in common is their association with financial problems. It could be that they each represent a diluted version of this factor. Certainly when financial hardship was examined directly, it produced a more striking relationship with symptomatology. Table 3 shows mean total PSE scores for those who said they had had to go without things they really needed in the past year because of financial hardship. This table follows the format used previously, being subdivided into those who reported one or more provoking agents during the previous year and those who did not. Although the number of "hard-up" women who did not report a provoking agent was small (not altogether surprising), there was still a significant interaction of hardship and experience of an event or difficulty, thus supporting the vulnerability model.

A further feature of socioeconomic status which had been expected to contribute to adult disorder yielded unanticipated results. Variables representing current lack of housing amenities and crowding in the home were not significantly associated with disorder at age 36. Home ownership was, however, with a rate of 7.1% in women living in homes owned by their immediate family as compared with 13.2% for women in privately rented homes or local authority housing. Home ownership did not act as a vulnerability factor and it was no longer implicated as a main effect when women with long-term problems were excluded from analysis.

The final potential vulnerability factor investigated in this study was the composite index of childhood behavior and personality. This was scored on an arbitrary scale, and a cut-off to define high-risk individuals was chosen which identified approximately one in six women. When women with chronic and recurrent emotional problems were excluded, the pattern of results shown in Table 4 was obtained. Although symptom scores were higher for those who had been "neurotic" children, this effect was confined to woman who reported recent provoking agents, with the interaction of the two factors significant.

Two possible vulnerability factors have been identified: one derived from recent circumstances (financial hardship) and the other from measures obtained at least 20 years earlier ("neurotic" behavior). They were then combined to minimize the effects of misclassification with respect to vulnerability. Table 5 shows the extent of the interaction of provoking agents with either vulnerability factor. Not surprisingly the significance of the interaction was greatly increased ($p<.002$) over that shown in Table 3 ($p<.030$) and Table 4 ($p<.033$). Of course, the interpretation of the significant interaction term rests on assumptions concerning the scale of measurement of disorder, and the fact that the total PSE score in the general population has a markedly skewed distribution could be problematic.[1] The most important feature of Table 5, however, is that there is no significant elevation of the PSE score associated with vulnerability in the subgroup which did not report a provoking agent.

One possible contributory factor to the pattern of results in Table 5 is that women in the "vulnerable–provoking agent" quadrant experienced greater adversity than those in the "not vulnerable–provoking agent" quadrant. The frequency of reporting many upsetting events (four or more) was indeed found to be higher in the former group. However, the interaction term remained significant both when the 96 women reporting many events were excluded from analysis and when the number of provoking events experienced was used in the analysis in place of the no provoking

Table 4. *Mean total PSE score by childhood behavior/personality and experience of provoking agents: for women*

Provoking agent experience	Low childhood behavior score	High childhood behavior score
None	1.23	0.95
	(N = 182)	(N = 20)
One or more	2.17	3.65
	(N = 674)	(N = 110)

Significance of interaction: $p = 0.33$

Table 5. *Mean total PSE score by vulnerability factors and experience of provoking agents, excluding women with long-term disorders*

Provoking agent experience	No vulnerablity factor	Vulnerability factor[a]
None	1.22	1.06
	(N = 170)	(N = 32)
One or more	1.88	3.83
	(N = 586)	(N = 198)

[a] Financial hardship or high childhood behavior score
Significance of interaction: $p = 0.002$

agent – provoking agent dichotomy. Unfortunately no similar check could be carried out to control for objective severity of events, and to control for the subjects' reported reactions to them would have been inappropriate.

Before accepting that these results support the general notion of a vulnerability model, there is one further aspect of the methodology requiring appraisal. In this study women reporting long-term emotional trouble or persistent depression were excluded from all analyses, with the intention of following the approach of Brown and Harris (1978a) as far as possible. Not all investigators have taken this step, however. Solomon and Bromet (1982), for example, included in their sample those with long-term affective disorder as well as recent onset. What would be the result if the NSHD data were treated in this fashion? Table 6 shows that when women with long-term "troubles" are included, the presence of a vulnerability factor is associated with higher symptom scores both in those without a provoking agent and in those who did experience a provoking agent, and the

Table 6. *Mean total PSE score by vulnerability factors and experience of provoking agents, including women with long-term disorders*

Provoking agent experience	No vulnerability factor	Either vulnerability factor[a]
None	1.44	3.79
	(N = 185)	(N = 43)
One or more	2.36	5.43
	(N = 656)	(N = 260)

[a] Financial hardship or high childhood behavior score
Significance of interaction: $p = 0.367$

Table 7. *Rate of caseness for women by vulnerability factors and experience of provoking agents*

Provoking agent experience	No vulnerability factor	Either vulnerability factor
None	1.2% (2/170)[a]	0.0% (0/32)[a]
	1.6% (3/185)[b]	11.6% (5/43)[b]
One or more	3.1% (18/586)[a]	12.6% (25/198)[a]
	4.7% (31/656)[b]	21.2% (55/260)[b]

[a] Excluding those with long-term disorders
[b] Including those with long-term disorders

interaction term becomes non-significant. Clearly the vulnerability model no longer holds. Essentially the same results were obtained when the influences of vulnerability and adversity were investigated with respect to the outcome of caseness. Table 7 shows the rates of caseness when those with chronic "troubles" were excluded and when they were included.

One plausible interpretation of the outcome with chronic disorders included is that it presents a false picture. Women with long-term disorders may well have experienced a provoking agent prior to the one-year period for which inquiries were made and thereby run a risk of misclassification in this respect, obscuring the vulnerability pattern in the way outlined in the introduction to this paper. In addition, long-term disorder could contribute to the occurrence of a vulnerability factor such as the experience of financial hardship, and this association may be manifested in those who had not experienced a provoking agent. The lesson to be drawn from this interpretation is that investigators should exclude long-term cases in their assessment of disorder.

There is a second plausible interpretation, however, based on a different view of what vulnerability represents. This view accepts that vulnerability can lead to disorder in the absence of a provoking agent. (Brown & Harris [1978*b*] provide for this possibility "under certain limited circumstances.") If certain vulnerable individuals have a predisposition to disorder in the absence of provoking agents, then no time period can be characterized as "safe," even one in which there is a total absence of provoking agents. The pattern of Table 6 might then typify the true state of affairs, with vulnerability and life stressors having additive effects on symptomatology, whereas the pattern of Table 5, the classic interactive vulnerability model, is seen as an artifact of having excluded from analysis those vulnerable individuals who develop disorders in the absence of life stressors. Unfortunately, it is not possible with the current data to choose between these two interpretations.

In conclusion, the findings from the NSHD demonstrate that a full appraisal of vulnerability models will require greater attention to chronic disorders. Studies up to now have been unsystematic in their inclusion or exclusion of chronic disorders, and the accompanying debate has largely ignored their theoretical significance.

Note

1 In practice a logarithmic transformation of the score had little effect on these results. This was also noted by Parry and Shapiro (1986).

References

Abramson, L. Y., Seligman, M. E. P., & Teasdale, J. D. (1978). Learned helplessness in humans: Critique and reformulation. *Journal of Abnormal Psychology, 87*, 49–74.

Atkins, E., Cherry, N., Douglas, J. W. B., Kiernan, K. E., & Wadsworth, M. E. J. (1981). The 1946 British birth cohort: An account of the origins, progress, and results of the National Survey of Health and Development. In S. A. Mednick & A. E. Baert (Eds.), *Prospective longitudinal research: An empirical basis for the primary prevention of psychosocial disorders.* London: Oxford University Press.

Bebbington, P. (1980). Causal models and logical inference in epidemiological psychiatry. *British Journal of Psychiatry, 136*, 317–325.

Bebbington, P., Sturt, E., Tennant, C., & Hurry, J. (1984). Misfortune and resilience: A community study of women. *Psychological Medicine, 14*, 347–363.

Brown, G. W. (1986). Statistical interaction and the role of social factors in the aetiology of clinical depression. *Sociology, 20*, 601–606.

Brown, G. W., & Harris, T. O. (1978*a*). *Social origins of depression: A study of psychiatric disorder in women.* London: Tavistock; New York: Free Press.

Brown, G. W., & Harris, T. O. (1978*b*). Social origins of depression: A reply. *Psychological Medicine, 8*, 577–588.

Brown, G. W., & Harris, T. O. (1986). Stressor, vulnerability and depression: A question of replication. *Psychological Medicine, 16*, 739–744.

Brown, G. W., Harris, T. O., & Bifulco, A. (1986). Long-term effects of early loss of parent. In M. Rutter, C. E. Izard, & P. B. Read (Eds.), *Depression in young people: Developmental and clinical perspectives* (pp. 251–296). New York: Guilford Press.

Campbell, E. A., Cope, S. J., & Teasdale, J. D. (1983). Social factors and affective disorder: An investigation of Brown and Harris's model. *British Journal of Psychiatry, 143*, 548–553.

Costello, C. G. (1982). Social factors associated with depression: A retrospective community study. *Psychological Medicine, 12*, 329–339.

Dohrenwend, B. S., & Dohrenwend, B. P. (1981). Life stress and illness: Formulation of the issues. In B. S. Dohrenwend & B. P. Dohrenwend (Eds.), *Stressful life events and their contexts* (pp. 1–27). New York: Prodist.

Everitt, B. S., & Smith, A. M. (1979). Interaction in contingency tables: A brief discussion of alternative definitions. *Psychological Medicine, 9*, 581–583.

Henderson, S., Duncan-Jones, P., Byrne, D. G., Scott, R., & Adcock, S. (1979). Psychiatric disorder in Canberra. *Acta Psychiatrica Scandinavica, 60*, 355–374.

Joint Committee of the Royal College of Obstetricians and Gynaecologists and the Population Investigation Committee. (1948). *Maternity in Great Britain*. London: Oxford University Press.

Kessler, R. C. (1983). Methodological issues in the study of psychosocial stress. In H. B. Kaplan (Ed.), *Psychosocial stress: Trends in theory and research*. New York: Academic Press.

McKee, D., & Vilhjalmsson, R. (1986). Life stress, vulnerability, and depression: A methodological critique of Brown et al. *Sociology, 20*, 589–599.

Neugebauer, R. (1981). The reliability of life-event reports. In B. S. Dohrenwend & B. P. Dohrenwend (Eds.), *Stressful life events and their contexts*. New York: Prodist.

Parry, G., & Shapiro, D. (1986). Social support and life events in working class women. *Archives of General Psychiatry, 43*, 315–323.

Rodgers, B. (in press). Behavior and personality in childhood as predictors of adult psychiatric disorder. *Journal of Child Psychology and Psychiatry*.

Rodgers, B., & Mann, S. A. (1986). Reliability and validity of PSE assessments by lay interviewers: A national population survey. *Psychological Medicine, 16*, 689–700.

Seligman, M. E. P. (1975). *Helplessness: On depression, development and death*. San Francisco: W. H. Freeman.

Seligman, M. E. P., & Peterson, C. (1986). A learned helplessness perspective on childhood depression: Theory and research. In M. Rutter, C. E. Izard, & P. B. Read (Eds.), *Depression in young people: Developmental and clinical perspectives* (pp. 223–249). New York: Guilford Press.

Solomon, Z., & Bromet, E. (1982). The role of social factors in affective disorder: An assessment of the vulnerability model of Brown and his colleagues, *Psychological Medicine, 12*, 123–130.

Tennant, C. (1985). Female vulnerability to depression. *Psychological Medicine, 15*, 733–737.

Tennant, C., & Bebbington, P. (1978). The social causation of depression: A critique of the work of Brown and his colleagues. *Psychological Medicine, 8*, 565–575.

Tennant, C., Bebbington, P., & Hurry, J. (1981). The role of life events in depressive illness: Is there a substantial causal relation? *Psychological Medicine, 11*, 379–389.

Wadsworth, M. E. J. (1987). Follow-up of the first British national birth cohort:

Findings from the MRC National Survey of Health and Development. *Paediatric and Perinatal Epidemiology, 1,* 95–117.

Wing, J. K., Cooper, J. E., & Sartorius, N. (1974). *The description and classification of psychiatric symptoms.* London: Cambridge University Press.

Wing, J. K., & Sturt, E. (1978). *The PSE-ID-CATEGO Systems: supplementary manual.* London: Institute of Psychiatry (Mimeo).

18   Two pathways to schizophrenia in children at risk

TYRONE D. CANNON, SARNOFF A. MEDNICK, AND JOSEF PARNAS

The high-risk method was developed in the 1950s to offset methodological weaknesses involved in studying the etiology of schizophrenia by comparing schizophrenic patients with nonschizophrenic controls (Mednick & Higgins, 1960). In the latter approach it was difficult to determine whether differences between schizophrenics and controls were related to the causes of the disorder or were merely the result of the unique life experiences of the schizophrenic. It became clear that it would be useful to examine schizophrenics premorbidly, in a prospective framework, before the lifelong concomitants of their illness could obscure potential etiological agents.

The high-risk, prospective design is attractive first because selecting children of severely schizophrenic mothers increases the yield of psychopathology. Schizophrenia has been found to occur in 10% to 16% of such individuals, as compared to 1% among the general population (Gottesman & Shields, 1982). Second, in the prospective design, assessments of premorbid experiences and functioning of these subjects are obtained systematically, uniformly, and prospectively, and are therefore free of the biases of retrospective reporting or knowledge of the subjects' eventual diagnostic status. In addition, by including a low-risk control group it is possible to examine the effects of environmental etiological agents at two levels of genetic vulnerability, thus encouraging study of gene–environment interaction effects. (A detailed statement of the rationale for high-risk research can be found in Mednick & McNeil, 1968.)

The Copenhagen high-risk project

In 1962, Mednick and Schulsinger initiated a prospective, longitudinal investigation of 207 Danish children with severely schizophrenic mothers and 104 matched controls without a family history of mental illness (Mednick & Schulsinger, 1965, 1968). Demographic characteristics of the high-risk (HR) and low-risk (LR) groups appear in Table 1. At the time of the initial assessment in 1962 the subjects had a mean age of 15.1 years and none was psychiatrically ill.

328

Table 1. *Sociodemographic characteristics of the high-risk and low-risk groups*

	High risk	Low risk
Number of cases	207	104
Boys	121	59
Girls	86	45
Mean age (in 1962)	15.1	15.1
Mean social class[a]	2.2	2.3
Mean years education	7.0	7.3
Reside in children's homes		
(5 years or more)[b]	16%	14%
Mean number of years in children's homes		
(5 years or more)[b]	9.4	8.5
Reside in rural setting[c]	26%	22%

[a] On a scale of 0 (low) to 6 (high)
[b] In matching the samples for amount of institutional rearing, we only considered experience in children's homes of 5 years' or greater duration
[c] Population of 2,500 persons or fewer

One goal of the current study is to discover early characteristics and experiences which forecast an adult diagnosis of schizophrenia. Another goal is to describe the clinical course of development of the disorder. The diverse clinical manifestations of schizophrenia suggest that etiological factors may differ among its phenomenological subtypes. Unfortunately, the many subtyping systems proposed in the history of schizophrenia research have contributed little to our understanding of causes. Recently, there has been a revival of interest in the distinction between "positive" and "negative" symptoms (Strauss et al., 1976; Crow, 1980; Andreasen & Olsen, 1982). *Positive symptoms*, which include delusions, hallucinations, formal thought disorder, and bizarre behavior, are suggestive of a state of excessive activation, or disinhibition, or both. In contrast, *negative symptoms* are thought to reflect deficits in several areas of functioning, including drive, energy level, emotionality, social and sexual relations, and attention (Andreasen, 1982).

We recognize that both the positive and negative syndromes are complex behavioral patterns which are multidetermined. In this paper we attempt to contribute to a partial understanding of some aspects of these syndromes. We present early and recent findings of the project, which suggest that there are two pathways to schizophrenia among individuals at high genetic risk, each pathway involving a distinct pattern of stressful environmental experiences, premorbid behavior disturbance, and adult symptomatology.

Five-year follow-up assessment

By 1967, when the subjects averaged age 20, 20 HR subjects out of 207 had suffered some form of psychiatric breakdown (not necessarily schizophrenia). The "sick" group was matched on a variety of characteristics (including level of adjustment in 1962) to 20 well-functioning HR subjects ("well" group) and 20 well-functioning LR subjects. Factors which differentiated the sick group from the control and the well groups included a higher incidence of pregnancy and birth complications (PBCs), loss of mother early in life to psychiatric hospitalization, psychophysiological lability in adolescence, and poorly controlled and disruptive school behavior (Mednick & Schulsinger, 1968).

The perinatal findings suggested that in order to avoid schizophrenia, a genetically vulnerable child must be born with a relatively intact brain. Mednick (1970) postulated that hippocampal damage resulting from perinatal insult may be an etiological precursor of schizophrenia.

Ten-year follow-up assessment

Eighty-five percent of the subjects were recontacted in 1972–1974 for diagnostic evaluations (Schulsinger, 1976). The procedure included two structured psychiatric interviews: the Present State Examination (PSE) (Wing et al., 1974) and the Current and Past Psychopathology Scales (CAPPS) (Endicott & Spitzer, 1972). Each interview allowed making a psychiatric diagnosis. In addition, the interviewer formed an ICD-8 (World Health Organization, 1967) clinical diagnosis on the basis of the two structured interviews and a set of additional items. Table 2 lists the frequencies of the various psychiatric diagnoses assigned to the HR and LR groups under each set of diagnostic criteria. The 13 HR subjects who received clinical diagnoses of schizophrenia also received schizophrenia diagnoses by CAPPS or PSE criteria or both. An additional 2 HR subjects who had committed suicide prior to the interview period were diagnosed schizophrenic on the basis of psychiatric hospital records (see Schulsinger, 1976, for further details of the diagnostic assessment). Relating the premorbid data bank to these diagnoses enabled us to delineate several precursors of schizophrenia.

Results and further analyses

Precursors of schizophrenia

Rearing factors. We have previously noted the association of separation from the mother in childhood with early breakdown of HR subjects

Table 2. *Frequencies of psychiatric diagnoses in the high-risk and low-risk (in parentheses) groups at 10-year follow-up*

	Interviewer (ICD-8)		CAPPS (By DIAGNO II)		PSE (By CATEGO)	
Schizophrenia	13[a]	(1)	30	(6)	10	(1)
Borderline states	71[b]	(5)	20	(1)	35	(3)
Psychopathy	5	(4)	2	(1)	4	(4)
Other personality disorders	26	(10)	3	(2)	22	(9)
Neuroses (symptoms and character)	34	(44)	31	(16)	43	(38)
Nonspecific conditions	0	(0)	43	(17)	24	(17)
No mental illness	23	(27)	44	(47)	15	(17)
Other conditions[c]	1	(0)	0	(1)	20	(2)
Total	173	(91)	173	(91)	173	(91)

[a] Two additional schizophrenics had committed suicide before the interview period, but hospital charts clearly indicated the presence of schizophrenia (with predominantly positive symptoms).

[b] These 71 individuals include 29 borderline schizophrenics (SPD), 29 schizoid personality disorders, and 13 paranoid personality disorders. Neither the CAPPS nor the PSE diagnostic systems included a category for SPD.

[c] Including affective and paranoid psychoses.

(Mednick & Schulsinger, 1968). In subsequent analyses we examined the amount of parental separation experienced by HR subjects with the diagnosis of schizophrenia, schizotypal personality disorder (DSP) or no mental illness (NMI) at the 10-year follow-up. The schizophrenics had experienced more separation from both their mothers and fathers than had the SPD or NMI groups. Since greater contact with a schizophrenic mother is unlikely to improve mental health, we reasoned that there may be some factor associated with parental absence which could account for the poor psychiatric outcomes. For many of the HR subjects, parental absence resulted in prolonged placement in a public child care institution. Table 3 shows the amount of institutional rearing experienced by the schizophrenic, SPD, and NMI groups. The schizophrenics had experienced more institutionalization during the first five years of life than had the other two groups, and significantly more than the NMI subjects. Better outcomes were obtained by HR children fortunate enough to be placed in foster homes (Walker et al., 1981). It is important to note that the effect of institutionalization is significant even with mother's age of onset (with earlier onset indicating a greater genetic loading) and amount of parental separation controlled statistically (Parnas et al., 1985). Institutionalization was associated with schizophrenia *only* in HR children; there was *no* elevation in the rate of schizophrenia among LR subjects who were matched to the HR group for amount of institutional rearing in 1962.

Table 3. *Institutional rearing during the first 5 years of life for schizophrenic, schizotypal personality disorder, and no mental illness groups*

	Schizophrenic		Schizotypal personality disorder		No mental illness	
	Mean	SD	Mean	SD	Mean	SD
Institutionalization (in months)	15.6*	23.3	10.8*†	16.5	0.6†	2.1

Note: Means with the same superscripts are not significantly different at a comparison-wise alpha level of .05.

Taken together, these results provide support for a gene–environment interaction model of schizophrenia. The level or quality of stress associated with institutional rearing is only pathogenic among individuals who share a genetic risk for schizophrenia. It is interesting to note, however, that the variance in separation and institutionalization is quite high *within* the schizophrenic group. This large variance indicates that some HR subjects who became schizophrenic had had little separation from their parents.

Birth factors. We noted previously that early signs of psychiatric breakdown were associated with severe complications during pregnancy and birth (Mednick & Schulsinger, 1968). Table 4 shows the PBC scores of the HR subjects diagnosed schizophrenic, SPD, and NMI in the 1972 assessment. The schizophrenics had suffered significantly more perinatal complications than had HR subjects with more favorable diagnostic outcomes. The SPD group, which has been shown to resemble the schizophrenics on indices of genetic liability, actually experienced fewer birth problems than did the NMIs. There were no schizophrenia outcomes among a group of LR subjects matched to the HR subjects for frequency and severity of PBCs. We interpreted these results as suggesting that perinatal disturbances may interact with genetic risk in producing the schizophrenic phenotype, and that genetically vulnerable individuals may avoid decompensation to schizophrenia by escaping serious perinatal trauma (Parnas et al., 1982). As was found for rearing factors, however, the variability in PBC scores within the schizophrenic group is large (indicating that a substantial subgroup of the schizophrenics had experienced uneventful births).

CT scan evidence. The association of schizophrenia with birth difficulties suggested the possibility that the HR subjects who became schizophrenic were those who suffered perinatal brain damage. There is a substantial

Table 4. *Pregnancy and birth complication (PBC) scores for schizophrenic, schizotypal personality disorder, and no mental illness groups*

	Schizophrenic		Schizotypal personality disorder		No mental illness	
	Mean	SD	Mean	SD	Mean	SD
PBC frequency score	1.50	1.38	0.40	0.76	0.85	1.09
PBC severity score	1.08	0.90	0.40	0.71	0.72	0.83
PBC total score	3.17	2.82	0.76	1.67	1.92	2.85

Note: On each index, the schizophrenic group scored significantly higher ($p = .02$) than the schizotypal personality disorder group (Mann-Whitney U tests).

Table 5. *Mean third-ventricle widths and ventricle–brain ratios for schizophrenic, schizotypal personality disorder, and no mental illness groups (1980 diagnoses)*

	Schizophrenic		Schizotypal personality disorder		No mental illness	
	Mean	SD	Mean	SD	Mean	SD
Third ventricle (mm)[a]	4.4[*]	2.1	2.7[†]	1.1	3.2[*,†]	0.8
Ventricle-brain ratio, %[b]	11.4[*]	6.7	5.5[†]	1.9	6.8[†]	1.9

Note: Means with the same superscripts are not significantly different at $p<.05$ (Mann-Whitney U tests).
[a] On the test contrasting the schizophrenic and NMI groups, $p<.066$.
[b] On the test contrasting the SPD and NMI groups, $p<.067$.

literature indicating that a subgroup of chronic schizophrenic patients show enlarged third and lateral ventricles on computerized tomographic (CT) brain scanning (see Shelton & Weinberger, 1986). In a pilot study conducted in 1980, we obtained CT scans on a subsample of HR subjects, including 10 schizophrenics, 10 SPDs, and 14 NMIs (Schulsinger et al., 1984). Table 5 presents the mean third-ventricle widths and ventricle–brain ratios (VBRs) of the three groups. It was found that the schizophrenics evidenced significantly larger third ventricles and VBRs than the other groups. In parallel with the results obtained for perinatal complications, the SPD group actually had smaller ventricles than the NMIs ($p = .06$). Subsequent analyses revealed that perinatal disturbances were strongly correlated with third-ventricle width and VBR measured 33 years later (Silverton et al., 1985). Birth weight accounted for 30% of the variance in VBR, while the combination of low birth weight and father's schizophrenia spectrum disorder (which was the major source of genetic variation in these HR subjects) accounted for an additional 17% (Silverton et al., 1988). We interpreted these results as suggesting that part of the genetic liability for schizophrenia consists of a heightened vulnerability of the fetal brain to perinatal insult. Once again, it is important to note the large variability in third-ventricle widths and VBRs within the schizophrenic group. Some schizophrenics evidenced narrow third ventricles and small VBRs.

Third-ventricle enlargement, autonomic nonresponding, and negative symptoms. Several findings led us to consider that perinatal brain damage may be involved in a specific pattern of abnormal development in the course of schizophrenia. First, Andreasen, et al. (1982) found that in schizophrenics with enlarged ventricles, negative symptoms were particularly prominent, whereas in narrow ventricle schizophrenics, the symptomatology was predominantly of the positive type. This result suggests that structural brain damage may, in part, underlie some aspects of the functional deficits in drive, affect, and attention observed in some schizophrenic patients (see Crow, 1980). Second, there is a parallel finding of reduced autonomic nervous system (ANS) responsiveness in a subgroup of schizophrenics. Approximately half of schizophrenics are electrodermal nonresponders, that is, they emit no or few responses in a series of habituation trials and show lower than normal resting arousal levels (see Bernstein et al., 1982; Dawson & Nuechterlein, 1984; Ohman, 1981; Spohn & Patterson, 1979). Several studies have found that schizophrenics who are ANS nonresponders show more negative symptoms than do schizophrenics who are ANS responders. In the latter, positive symptoms are more prominent (Straube, 1979; Gruzelier, 1976; Frith et al., 1979; Bartfai et al., 1983; Bernstein et al., 1981).

Since both structural brain abnormalities and electrodermal nonresponding have been linked to negative symptoms, we hypothesized that there may be specific damage to ANS excitatory brain centers indexed by enlargement of the ventricular system which causes ANS nonresponsiveness and deficits in excitatory behavior. The anterior hypothalamus, which surrounds the base of the third ventricle (Barr, 1979), is one brain area that may be involved, since a possible cause of widening of the third ventricle is atrophy of the surrounding tissue, which includes the anterior hypothalamus. Wang (1964) has demonstrated that the anterior hypothalamus is the most important excitatory center of autonomic activity in the brain. Damage to the anterior hypothalamus might be expected to reduce ANS responsiveness and, in association with genetic factors and other precursors, contribute to flat affect, anergia, and other symptoms of negative schizophrenia.

We compared the HR subjects with wide and narrow third ventricles with respect to the electrodermal data that had been collected at their first contact

18 years earlier in 1962. Enlargement of the third ventricle was associated with a marked reduction in the amplitude and frequency of electrodermal responses overall, and to orienting, conditioned, and generalization stimuli in particular. These effects remained significant even with size of the lateral cerebral ventricles (VBR) controlled statistically (Cannon et al., 1988). Apparently, it is widening of the third ventricle that is specifically related to reduced ANS responsiveness.

On the basis of these findings, we hypothesized that in HR individuals perinatal damage to the tissues surrounding the third ventricle would reduce ANS excitatory behavior, which along with genetic factors would result in a relative lack of energy, emotion, and social engagement premorbidly, and in a form of schizophrenia dominated by negative symptoms. Thus we predicted that HR individuals who were ANS nonresponders in 1962 would evidence premorbid behavior analogous to clinical negative symptoms, and that these same individuals would be at elevated risk of succumbing to schizophrenia characterized by a predominance of negative symptoms.

Schizophrenia with predominantly negative symptoms

Premorbid behavior disturbance. To test this hypothesis, we first identified ANS responders and nonresponders within the schizophrenic, SPD, and NMI groups. Subjects were classified as responders and nonresponders on the basis of the number, latency, and recovery time of responses to the eight orienting trials, five conditioned stimulus trials, and nine generalization stimulus trials in the 1962 psychophysiological examination. ANS nonresponders were those with no responses on the 22 trials or those who responded infrequently (i.e., three or fewer trials), with extremely slow latency and recovery time. We then examined relevant school behaviors to determine whether ANS nonresponder schizophrenics exhibited premorbid sings of the negative syndrome. Tables 6 and 7 list the items which we considered to represent premorbid behavioral analogs of adult negative symptoms and adult positive symptoms. These items were taken from teachers' reports of the (pre-1962) school behavior of the subjects and were completed at the same time as the 1962 electrodermal assessment. Cronbach's alpha was .76 for the negative-type behavior scale and .84 for the positive-type behavior scale.

Table 8 shows the mean adolescent negative- and positive-type behavior scores of the ANS responders and nonresponders by psychiatric diagnosis. The data shown are standard scores, where 50 represents the mean of the HR sample (with a standard deviation of 10). As can be seen from Table 8, schizophrenics who were ANS nonresponders evidenced significantly more negative-type premorbid behavior disturbance (i.e., passivity, lack of spontaneity, social unresponsiveness, isolation) than did the ANS responder

Table 6. *School report items in the negative-type premorbid behavior scale*[a]

1. Rarely takes part in spontaneous activities despite being asked to join.
2. Seldom laughs or smiles when with other children; keeps a serious, "I don't care" expression.
3. Has difficulty making friends; seems lonely and rejected by the others.
4. Seems content with isolation.
5. Is very shy, reserved, and silent.
6. Does not react when praised or encouraged by the teacher.
7. Behavior is characteristically passive.

[a] Cronbach's alpha = .76.

Table 7. *School report items in the positive-type premorbid behavior scale*[a]

1. Is easily excited and irritated with little apparent reason.
2. When excited or emotional, persists in the reaction and continues to be high-strung and distractable.
3. Often disturbs class with completely inappropriate behavior.
4. Is extremely violent and aggressive, frequently creating conflicts with classmates.
5. Presents a disciplinary problem for the teacher.

[a] Cronbach's alpha = .84.

schizophrenics. (As will be discussed, the schizophrenics who were ANS responders evidenced no elevation on the adolescent negative behavior scale.) In addition, ANS nonresponder schizophrenics were not found to evidence elevated positive-type behavior scores. These results suggest that autonomic nonresponding is associated with a pattern of premorbid behavior disturbance which is similar to the adult negative symptom complex.

Adult symptomatology. Scales of adult negative and positive symptoms were constructed by combining items from the PSE, the current symptoms portion of the CAPPS, and a set of additional items administered during the 1972 diagnostic interview. First, all items potentially relevant to the negative and positive symptom constructs were ascertained. Then, using Andreasen's criteria (Andreasen, 1982; Andreasen & Olsen, 1982), pools of candidate items were formed in four negative symptom categories (alogia, asociality–anhedonia, anergia–retardation, and flat affect) and three positive symptom categories (hallucinations, delusions, and formal thought disorder). Too few items were available to form pools for "attentional impairment" and "bizarre behavior." After defining the candidate pools of

Table 8. *Mean standard scores[a] of the HR sample on negative- and positive-type premorbid behavior scales according to their ANS reponse level and adult diagnosis*

ANS responder and nonresponder groups by diagnosis	N	Premorbid behavior scale analogs of adult symptomatolgy	
		Negative-type behavior	Positive-type behavior
Schizophrenia			
Responder	8	45.5[†]	62.5[*]
Nonresponder	7	61.6[*]	50.5[†]
Schizotypal personality			
Responder	24	50.6[†]	49.7[†]
Nonresponder	4	54.7[*,†]	47.8[†]
No mental illness			
Responder	18	46.9[†]	47.7[†]
Nonresponder	5	45.6[†]	44.4[†]

Note: Means with the same superscripts (within the negative–type behavior and positive–type behavior columns) are not significantly different at a comparison-wise alpha level of .05.
[a] The distribution of scores in the high-risk sample on each of the scales was standardized to mean = 50, SD = 10.

items on a rational basis, the procedure attempted to maximize coefficient alpha by adding or subtracting items with high or low correlations with scale totals. This method is related to other approaches to scale construction, such as factor analysis (Hennrysson, 1962), but generally produces superior results (Hase & Goldberg, 1967; Nunnally, 1967). Composite scales of negative and positive symptoms were formed by adding all items retained in the respective symptom scales.

Tables 9 and 10 list the items in the negative symptoms scales and positive symptom scales, respectively. The negative symptom scales appear highly internally consistent. Cronbach's alpha was .93 for composite negative symptoms, .84 for affective flattening, .82 for anergia-retardation, .78 for anhedonia–asociality and .78 for alogia. The positive symptom scales also have excellent reliabilities. Cronbach's alpha was .96 for composite positive symptoms, .90 for hallucinations, .92 for delusions, and .92 for thought disorder. The composition and reliabilities of these scales are comparable to those of measures designed and administered specifically for the purpose of assessing negative and positive symptoms (Andreasen, 1982).

Previous work has indicated that there is one subgroup of schizophrenics

Table 9. *Adult negative symptom scales*

Flat affect

 1. Blunted affect during interview (PSE)
 2. Unmodulated vocalizations (INT)
 3. Unmodulated facial expression (INT)
 4. Unvaried serious expression (INT)
 5. Emotionally impoverished (INT)
 6. Emotionally blunt (INT)
 7. Expressionless, "smooth" face (INT)
 8. Lowered mood (INT)
 9. Pallid contact (INT)
10. Sullenness (INT)
11. Poor facial colors (INT)

Anergia–retardation

 1. Retardation (CAPPS)
 2. Slowness and underactivity during interview (PSE)
 3. Subjective anergia and retardation (PSE)
 4. Personal neglect (PSE)
 5. Inertness (INT)
 6. Apathetic contact (INT)
 7. Passivity (INT)
 8. Lacking spontaneity (INT)
 9. Pale, indifferent, passive contact (INT)

Alogia

 1. Slow speech during interview (PSE)
 2. Undertalkative (INT)
 3. Underelaborative (INT)
 4. Underspecific (INT)
 5. Blocking (INT)

Asociality–anhedonia

 1. Leisure impairment (CAPPS)
 2. Social isolation (CAPPS)
 3. Loss of interest (PSE)
 4. Social withdrawal (PSE)
 5. Loss of libido (PSE)
 6. Loss of emotions (PSE)
 7. Social impairment due to psychosis (PSE)
 8. Lack of drive (INT)
 9. Anhedonia (INT)
10. Detachment (INT)
11. Conspicuous avoidance (INT)
12. Lacking emotional contact on examination (INT)
13. Autism (INT)
14. Sensitive and withdrawing (INT)

Note: Items are from the Current and Past Psychopathology Scales (CAPPS), Present State Examination (PSE), and clinical interview (INT) (Schulsinger, 1976).

Table 10. *Adult positive symptom scales*

Hallucinations
 1. Hallucinations (CAPPS)
 2. Auditory hallucinations (CAPPS)
 3. Visual hallucinations (CAPPS)
 4. Nonverbal auditory hallucinations (PSE)
 5. Verbal hallucinations based on mood or voice calling subject (PSE)
 6. Voices discussing subject in third person (not based on mood) (PSE)
 7. Voices speaking to subject (not based on mood) (PSE)
 8. Dissociative hallucinations (PSE)
 9. Visual hallucinations (PSE)
10. Olfactory hallucinations (PSE)
11. Other hallucinations (PSE)

Delusions
 1. Suspicion-persecution (CAPPS)
 2. Delusions (CAPPS)
 3. Thought echo or commentary (PSE)
 4. Thought withdrawal (PSE)
 5. Delusion of thoughts being read (PSE)
 6. Delusion that subject smells (PSE)
 7. Delusions of control (PSE)
 8. Delusions of reference (PSE)
 9. Delusions of misinterpretation and misidentification (PSE)
10. Delusions of persecution (PSE)
11. Delusions of grandiose abilities (PSE)
12. Religious delusions (PSE)
13. Delusional explanations of paranormal phenomena (PSE)
14. Delusional explanations in terms of physical forces (PSE)
15. Primary delusions (PSE)
16. Subculturally influenced delusions (PSE)

Formal thought disorder
 1. Speech disorganization (CAPPS)
 2. Pressure of speech during interview (PSE)
 3. Neologisms and idiosyncratic use of words or phrases during interview (PSE)
 4. Incoherence of speech during interview (PSE)
 5. Flight of ideas during interview (PSE)
 6. Illogical explanations (INT)
 7. Wanders around verbally (INT)
 8. Gives answers unrelated to questions (INT)
 9. Poor hierarchical organization of ideas (INT)
10. Shifts spontaneously in train of speech (INT)
11. Unrelated sequential thoughts (INT)
12. Impaired transitions between themes, topics, and ideas (INT)
13. Repetitious form of speech (INT)
14. Metonomy (INT)
15. Literalization of abstract meaning (INT)
16. Categorical confusion (INT)
17. Loose tangential associations (INT)

Note: Items are from the Current and Past Psychopathology Scales (CAPPS), Present State Examination (PSE), and clinical interview (INT) (Schulsinger, 1976).

who evidence negative symptoms only, and another subgroup who exhibit both positive and negative symptoms but in whom positive symptoms are relatively primary (c.f., Andreasen & Olsen, 1982; Andreasen et al., 1982; Andreasen, 1985; Crow, 1985). This pattern of symptomatic expression held for schizophrenics classified by degree of conditioned autonomic responsiveness in the 1962 assessment. Tables 11 and 12 show the mean adult negative and positive symptom scores of the ANS responders and nonresponders by psychiatric diagnosis. The data shown are standard scores, where 50 is equivalent to the HR sample mean (with SD of 10). As can be seen from Table 11, schizophrenics who were ANS nonresponders did not differ significantly from the responder schizophrenics on three of the four negative symptom scales (flat affect, anhedonia–asociality, and alogia) or on the composite negative symptoms scale. However, the nonresponder schizophrenics scored significantly higher than the responder schizophrenics and all other subgroups (which did not differ significantly from each other) on the symptom complex of anergia–retardation, particularly with respect to the symptoms of anergia, apathy, and underactivity during the interview. In addition, as can be seen from Table 12, schizophrenics who were ANS nonresponders scored significantly lower than the responder schizophrenics on each of the positive symptom scales (i.e., hallucinations, delusions, thought disorder, and composite positive symptoms).

These results suggest that all schizophrenics manifest some negative symptoms, but that the nonresponder schizophrenics are specifically characterized by a high degree of anergic-retardation symptomatology and few positive symptoms. In addition, ANS nonresponder schizophrenics premorbidly evidence exclusively negative-type and no positive-type behavior disturbance.

Etiology. What are the precursors of the type of schizophrenia characterized by low ANS responsiveness in adolescence, premorbid behavioral anergia, and adult negative symptoms? We have indicated two chief explanatory precursors of schizophrenia in individuals at high genetic risk: (1) severe disruption of the early family rearing environment, (2) periventricular atrophy secondary to complications during pregnancy and birth. We have also noted the large variance among the schizophrenic subjects on these factors. The large variance indicates that not all HR subjects who became schizophrenic had suffered severe perinatal disturbances and enlargement of the ventricular system, and not all had experienced prolonged institutional rearing during infancy and childhood. In view of the empirical relationships between third-ventricle enlargement, reduced autonomic responsiveness, and negative symptoms, we hypothesized that perinatal brain damage may be an environmental precursor only among the HR subjects who developed predominantly negative-symptom schizophrenia. We conducted a series of analyses to test this hypothesis.

Table 11. *Mean standard scores[a] of the HR sample on scales of adult negative symptoms according to their ANS response level and adult diagnosis*

ANS responder and nonresponder groups by diagnosis	N	Flat affect	Anergia	Asociality	Alogia	Composite negative symptoms
Schizophrenia						
Responder[b]	6	64.1*	50.8[†]	73.4*	53.6*[†]	65.3*[†]
Nonresponder	7	68.8*	68.8*	71.6*	60.1*	72.1*
Schizotypal personality						
Responder	24	55.9[†]	51.2[†]	55.2[†]	54.7*[†]	55.3[‡]
Nonresponder	4	59.9*[†]	52.8[†]	52.9[†]	56.9*	56.4[†‡]
No mental illness						
Responder	18	41.9[‡]	45.3[†]	41.1[‡]	46.8[†]	41.8[§]
Nonresponder	5	43.2[‡]	44.2[†]	41.4[‡]	43.2[†]	41.4[§]

Note: Means with the same superscripts (within each symptom column) are not significantly different at a comparison-wise alpha level of .05.

[a] The distribution of scores in the high-risk sample on each of the scales was standardized to mean = 50, SD = 10.

[b] No symptom scores are available for the two schizophrenics who committed suicide before the 1972 assessment. Their psychiatric records indicate that they evidenced a preponderance of positive symptoms.

Table 12. *Mean standard scores[a] of the HR sample on scales of adult positive symptoms according to their ANS response level and adult diagnosis*

ANS responder and nonresponder groups by diagnosis	N	Hallucinations	Delusions	Thought disorder	Composite positive symptoms
Schizophrenia					
Responder[b]	6	86.4*	90.3*	90.7*	94.2*
Nonresponder	7	58.1[†]	58.6[†]	54.5[†‡]	57.8[†]
Schizotypal personality					
Responder	24	52.4[†‡]	49.8[†‡]	53.3[†‡]	51.9[†‡]
Nonresponder	4	50.1[†‡]	48.5[†‡]	56.5[†]	52.1[†‡]
No mental illness					
Responder	18	47.1[‡]	47.4[‡]	44.4[‡]	45.8[‡]
Nonresponder	5	47.1[‡]	47.4[‡]	44.7[‡]	45.9[‡]

Note: Means with common superscripts (within each symptom column) are not significantly different at a comparison-wise alpha level of .05.

[a] The distribution of scores in the high-risk sample on each of the scales was standardized to mean = 50, SD = 10.

[b] No symptom scores are available for the two schizophrenics who committed suicide before the 1972 assessment. Their psychiatric records indicate that they evidenced a preponderance of positive symptoms.

We first asked whether schizophrenics who were ANS nonresponders had experienced an especially stressful family rearing environment. We compared the amount of institutional rearing during the first five years of life of the ANS responders and nonresponders within the schizophrenic, SPD, and NMI groups. Nonresponder schizophrenics had experienced the *least* institutionalization (mean = 0.08 years) of all the subgroups, significantly less than the responder schizophrenics (mean = 2.22 years) ($p < .0001$). Only one of the seven nonresponder schizophrenics had been institutionalized during childhood, compared to six of the eight responder schizophrenics. The findings for maternal separation mirrored these results. We concluded that since the nonresponder schizophrenics had experienced no more separation or institutionalization than subjects with more favorable diagnostic outcomes, disruption of the early family rearing environment is probably *not* an important etiological precursor·of schizophrenia with predominantly negative symptoms.

If separation and institutionalization are not associated with predominantly negative-symptom schizophrenia, then perhaps structural abnormalities are responsible. In a frequency analysis we found that there was a strong relationship between third-ventricle widening (measured in 1980) and electrodermal status assessed in 1962. Seven of the ten subjects with third-ventricle widths above the median were ANS nonresponders. In contrast, there was only one ANS nonresponder among the 24 subjects with narrow third ventricles ($\chi^2(1) = 17.0$, $p < .0001$, ϕ coefficient = .71).

We then considered factors which could have contributed to enlargement of the ventricular system. The best obstetrical predictor of VBR was low birth weight ($r = -60$) (Silverton et al., 1985). Low birth weight infants include many born prematurely and many who suffer complications during delivery (*Lancet*, 1984; Sostek et al., 1987). We formed a scale of complications suffered at delivery (e.g., abnormal fetal position, premature rupture of membranes, asphyxiation, uterine inertia). We then conducted a set of stepwise multiple regression analyses (maximum R-square improvement method) predicting third-ventricle width and VBR and using as possible predictor variables delivery complication score, birth weight, father schizophrenia spectrum disorder (FSPEC), and the interactions of FSPEC with the two obstetrical factors. The best single predictor of third-ventricle width was the interaction of FSPEC with delivery complication score, which accounted for 56.2% of the variance ($r = .75$). This term entered the equation first and was the only effect in the model which maintained significance after all other effects were controlled for ($p < .03$). The solution with VBR as the dependent variable also included the FSPEC–delivery complication score interaction as its only significant term ($R^2 = 49.3$, $r = .70$).

Subsequent analyses revealed that schizophrenics who were ANS nonresponders had experienced significantly more delivery complications (mean = 3.00) than the responder schizophrenics (mean = 0.57) and the other diagnosis-responder subgroups (all p's < .001). All 7 of the nonresponder schizophrenics had experienced two or more severe delivery complications. Only one of the 8 responder schizophrenics (12.5%), 5 of the 29 SPD subjects (17.2%), and 5 of the 23 NMI subjects (21.7%) had experienced a comparable number of disturbances during delivery (χ^2 = 17.4, df = 5, p < .004).

Summary. We have drawn several conclusions from our study of subjects at genetic risk:

> Schizophrenics who were ANS nonresponders did not evidence an elevated level of family disturbance.
> ANS nonresponder status is strongly related to third-ventricle widening.
> Third-ventricle widening is predicted by severe delivery complications.
> Delivery complications and third-ventricle widening are associated with negative-type premorbid behavior and later predominantly negative symptom schizophrenia.

Taken together, these results suggest that the subtype of schizophrenia characterized by predominantly negative symptoms has an etiology and developmental course which is to some extent distinct from that of schizophrenia with predominantly positive symptoms. We have suggested the following speculative framework to explain some aspects of the development of predominantly negative symptom schizophrenia.

One part of the genetic predisposition to schizophrenia may be a heightened vulnerability of the developing fetal brain to perinatal insult. A vulnerable infant may suffer peri- and intraventricular hemorrhaging or hypoxia in the course of a difficult delivery, which would not occur in a less susceptible infant. These injuries may result in necrosis of cells of the tissues surrounding the third ventricle. The extent of this damage will depend on the severity of the delivery complication(s) and the degree of genetic risk for schizophrenia. Excitatory centers of the ANS (such as the anterior hypothalamus) may be damaged. This damage to ANS excitatory centers may reduce autonomic responsiveness and, in the long run, markedly reduce capacity for emotional behavior.

As adolescents, these individuals may be chronically unresponsive to their environments. They may evidence an abnormally low level of energy and lack of interest in pleasurable activities. They may prefer isolation to the company of their peers. As these individuals enter early adulthood and are faced with the responsibilities of adult life, it may become apparent to both themselves and others that they are unskilled in meeting social and occupational demands. They may appear to their relatives and others as distant, listless, and somber. Dependent on family or the state for most basic needs, they may eventually be delivered to the care of the mental health establishment to be diagnosed as schizophrenic, with predominantly negative symptoms.

Schizophrenia with predominantly positive symptoms

We have alluded to the large variance in perinatal history and brain morphology within the schizophrenic group. The size of this variance indicates that some HR subjects who became schizophrenic had normal births and narrow third ventricles. We noted previously that subjects who evidenced narrow third ventricles in 1980 showed a relatively high level of autonomic responsiveness in the 1962 psychophysiology examination (Cannon et al., 1988). These results suggest that genetically vulnerable individuals who escape perinatal damage to ANS excitatory centers maintain a vigorous level of autonomic responsiveness.

Several studies have found that schizophrenics who show normal CT scans and normal-to-high levels of autonomic responsiveness evidence more active, positive symptomatology (e.g., gross motor excitement, assaultive behavior, florid psychosis) than schizophrenics who evidence enlarged ventricles and low levels of autonomic responsiveness (Frith et al., 1979; Gruzelier, 1976; Straube, 1979; Andreasen et al., 1982). Rubens and Lapidus (1978) found that schizophrenics who were ANS responders evidenced a reduced ability to tolerate and cope with stimulation. These results suggest that part of the basis of the positive symptom complex may be a propensity for excessive autonomic activation and/or disinhibition; i.e., a poorly regulated ANS.

Since a high degree of autonomic excitability is associated with positive symptoms in adult schizophrenics, we reasoned that there may be aspects of premorbid autonomic functioning that predict the development of positive symptom schizophrenia. Quite early in the project we noted that the average autonomic lability of the HR group was significantly elevated above that of the LR group, which suggested that poor ANS regulation may be part of the genetic predisposition to schizophrenia (Mednick & Schulsinger, 1965, 1968). However, since only some of these individuals eventually became schizophrenic, ANS lability could not by itself be sufficient to cause schizophrenia. Rather, we suggest that autonomic lability reflects an underlying vulnerability and requires environmental stressors to produce decompensation.

In view of these considerations, we hypothesized that vigorous autonomic responsiveness may render HR subjects especially vulnerable to highly stressful early rearing environments. (ANS hyperresponsiveness may also contribute directly to disruption of rearing conditions by making the HR infant difficult to manage.) This vulnerability may produce poorly controlled emotional reactions to stress experienced in school. These poorly controlled emotional reactions may be precursors of later schizophrenia with predominantly positive symptoms.

Premorbid behavior disturbance. To investigate this hypothesis, we first examined relevant school behaviors. The items in the positive-type premorbid behavior scale are shown in Table 7. They encompass distractibility, aggression, excitement, and irritability. Schizophrenics who were ANS responders evidenced significantly more such premorbid behavior disturbance than did the nonresponder schizophrenics and all other subgroups (who did not differ from each other) (see Table 8). Recall that the responder schizophrenics did not manifest signs of negative-type behavior disturbance in adolescence. Taken together, these findings suggest that a high degree of autonomic responsiveness in the premorbid state is associated with a pattern of contemporaneous behavior disturbance, which is analogous to the adult positive symptom complex.

Adult symptomatology. We noted previously that responder schizophrenics evidenced a degree of (certain) negative symptoms which was comparable to that of nonresponder schizophrenics (see Table 11). Analysis of the positive symptom scores revealed that schizophrenics who were ANS responders had developed significantly more hallucinations, delusions, thought disorder, and overall positive symptomatology at the time of diagnosis than had the nonresponder schizophrenics and all other diagnosis-responder subgroups. The extreme severity of these symptoms in the schizophrenic responders is attested to by a mean score which is at least four standard deviations above the mean of the total HR sample on each of the scales (see Table 12).

In summary, ANS responder schizophrenics differed from nonresponder schizophrenics in that they evidenced *only* positive-type behavior disturbance premorbidly and in that they later developed a form of schizophrenia in which positive symptoms were prominent, but which also included certain of the negative symptoms.

Etiology. What are the precursors of the type of schizophrenia characterized by autonomic responsiveness in adolescence, premorbid distractibility and aggressiveness, and adult positive symptoms? We have already indicated that the HR subjects who were ANS responders in 1962 showed narrow third ventricles in the 1980 CT examination, suggesting that periventricular brain damage is not a factor in the development of predominantly positive symptom schizophrenia. In addition, we have indicated that PBCs are probably not etiologically significant for the ANS responder schizophrenics, since these subjects did not differ from the SPD and NMI subgroups on these indices.

As stated above, the HR group as a whole displayed unusually high levels of autonomic responsiveness to a stressful stimulus (Mednick & Schulsinger, 1965, 1968); yet only some of these subjects eventually became schizophrenic. This fact suggests that autonomic lability by itself is not sufficient to cause schizophrenia, but that the capacity for large autonomic reactions may become etiologically significant in interaction with severely stressful environmental provoking agents, such as unstable early rearing conditions.

In view of these considerations, we hypothesized that among HR individuals who were ANS responders, the experience of severely stressful early rearing environments would lead to the development of predominantly positive symptom schizophrenia. Analysis of the family histories of the diagnosis-responder subgroups revealed that ANS responder schizophrenics had experienced significantly more shifts of home, separation from mother, and institutional rearing than nonresponder schizophrenics and all other HR subgroups. The mean amount of maternal separation during the first 5 years of life for responder schizophrenics was 2.83 years, as compared to 0.08 years for nonresponder schizophrenics, 0.91 years for SPDs and 0.05 years for NMIs. Six of the 8 responder schizophrenics had been separated from their mothers for more than 1½ years; one had been separated from her mother for one of the first 5 years, and the other (who had been reared by his father) was said by his siblings to have been a severely physically abused child. In contrast, none of the 7 nonresponder schizophrenics, 9 of the 29 SPD subjects, and none of the 23 NMI subjects had experienced a comparable amount of maternal separation ($\chi^2 = 24.9$, df $= 5$, $p = .0001$).

In summary, the ANS responder HR subjects who became schizophrenic had an extremely disrupted rearing experience.

Summary. These findings suggest the subtype of schizophrenia with predominantly positive symptomatology has an etiology and developmental course which is to some extent distinct from that of predominantly negative symptom schizophrenia. Our hypotheses concerning the development of this syndrome are summarized as follows:

The genetically vulnerable fetus who experiences an uneventful perinatal period seems to escape periventricular atrophy and damage to excitatory centers of the ANS (such as the anterior hypothalamus). One consequence of this favorable perinatal experience may be to leave the pre-existing capacity for autonomic responsiveness intact. As noted previously, part of the genetic predisposition to schizophrenia may involve a tendency for ANS hyperresponsiveness, which may permit poorly controlled emotional responses to stress.

Venables (1960), Carlsson (1987), Oke and Adams (1987), and Crosson and Hughes (1987) have suggested another (not mutually exclusive) possibility. The excessive ANS arousal and responsiveness observed in some schizophrenics may reflect poor filtering of stimulation. This inadequate filtering may produce periodic stimulus flooding. The poor filtering may be due in part to genetically programmed disruption during gestation, which affects the development of the sensory gating systems of the thalamus and other regions (Carlsson, 1987).

Individuals with this basic vulnerability may be particularly susceptible to instability in parental contact and family structure. In such individuals, the experience of a highly stressful early rearing environment may very likely produce periods of high levels of autonomic excitation and reduced inhibitory control. These children may find the ordinary school environment overstimulating. The stimulation may be expected at times to overwhelm their fragile controls, resulting in outbursts of disruptive, aggressive and poorly controlled emotional behavior. Repeated over time, the combination of a highly reactive ANS and stressful environmental experiences may lead to periods of overexcitement and poorly controlled emotional behavior. On occasion, the cycle of stress–inappropriate responses–the environment's negative reactions–and consequent additional stress may drive emotionality and arousal to intolerable levels. These excessive levels of arousal (and the possible inadequate sensory gating) may reduce the individual's ability to discriminate sensory stimuli, sometimes resulting in misidentification of sounds and sights and, in the extreme, hallucinatory experiences.

These individuals may be able to learn to avoid the stressful stimulation by directing their attention away from the stress to irrelevant or remote associations. This avoidance may produce momentary relief which may reinforce and instill the avoidance response. The clinical picture may alternate between stormy psychotic symptoms and extreme withdrawal and inaccessibility. Avoidance of social contact and stimulation may serve to reduce the likelihood of challenge to the fragile ANS controls. Successful learned avoidance may eventually lead to an increase in certain aspects of the negative symptom complex such as social avoidance and emotional withdrawal. Whereas in predominantly negative symptom schizophrenia, negative symptoms may reflect an underlying lack of normal capacity for emotional responses, in the case of predominantly positive symptom schizophrenia, some aspects of negative symptoms may reflect a learned avoidance process or secondary coping mechanism. An early, more detailed statement of this learned avoidance process can be found in Mednick, 1958. See also Venables & Wing, 1962.

Conclusion

We have identified some of the factors involved in the development of predominantly negative and predominantly positive symptom schizophrenia. These syndromes are multidetermined, however, and we are certain to have omitted important contributing factors in these analyses. Some (both negative and positive) symptoms may be genetically determined; some (both negative and positive) symptoms may result from environmental etiological agents; and other (both negative and positive) symptoms may be due to an interaction of genetic and environmental factors. One example of multiple causation of negative symptoms was observed in the negative symptoms evidenced by schizophrenics with predominantly positive symptoms. Their social avoidance and emotional blunting are unlikely to have resulted from the precursors of predominantly negative symptom schizophrenia, since they did not evidence an elevated level of delivery complications or an autonomic response deficit. Both the predominantly positive and predominantly negative symptom schizophrenics may share genetically influenced negative symptoms.

Additional work is needed to identify the symptoms (both negative and positive) which may be fundamental to schizophrenia, reflecting the genetic predisposition, and to isolate more of the possible environmental stressors which may contribute to the negative and positive subtypes.

Acknowledgments

This research was supported by a Research Scientist Award (1 K05 MH 00619-01) from the ADAMHA awarding institution (NIMH) and Grant 5 R01 MH 37692-02 to S. A. Mednick, Grant 1 R01 MH 41469 to J. Parnas, and a University of Southern California Predoctoral Merit Fellowship to T. D. Cannon.

References

Andreasen, N. C. (1982). Negative symptoms in schizophrenia: Definition and reliability. *Archives of General Psychiatry*, *39*, 784–788.

Andreasen, N. C. (1985). Positive vs. negative schizophrenia: A critical evaluation. *Schizophrenia Bulletin*, *11*, 380–389.

Andreasen, N. C., & Olsen, S. (1982). Negative vs. positive schizophrenia: Definition and validation. *Archives of General Psychiatry*, *39*, 789–794.

Andreasen, N. C., Olsen, S., Dennert, J. W., & Smith, M. R. (1982). Ventricular enlargement in schizophrenia: Relationship to positive and negative symptoms. *American Journal of Psychiatry*, *139*, 297–302.

Barr, M. L. (1979). *The human nervous system* (3rd ed.). Hagerstown, MD: Harper & Row.

Bartfai, A., Lavender, S., Edman, G., Schalling, D., & Sedvall, G. (1983). Skin conductance orienting responses in unmedicated recently admitted schizophrenic patients. *Psychophysiology*, *20*, 180–187.

Bernstein, A. S., Frith, C. D., Gruzelier, J. H., Patterson, T., Straube, E., Venables, P. H., & Zahn, T. P. (1982). An analysis of the skin conductance orienting response in samples of American, British, and German schizophrenics. *Biological Psychology*, *14*, 155–211.

Bernstein, A. S., Taylor, K. W., Starkey, P., Juni, S., Lubowsky, J., & Paley, H. (1981). Bilateral skin conductance, finger pulse volume, and EEG orienting response to tones of differing intensities in chronic schizophrenics and controls. *Journal of Nervous and Mental Disease*, *169*, 513–528.

Cannon, T. D., Fuhrmann, M., Mednick, S. A., Machon, R. A., Parnas, J., & Schulsinger, F. (1988). Third-ventricle enlargement and reduced electrodermal responsiveness. *Psychophysiology, 25,* 153–156.

Carlsson, A. (1987, April). *The role of dopamine in normal and abnormal behavior.* Paper presented at the International Congress on Schizophrenia Research, Clearwater, FL.

Crosson, B., & Hughes, C. W. (1987). Role of the thalamus in language: Is it related to schizophrenic thought disorder? *Schizophrenia Bulletin, 13,* 605–621.

Crow, T. J. (1980). Molecular pathology of schizophrenia: More than one disease process? *British Medical Journal, 280,* 1–9.

Crow, T. J. (1985). The two-syndrome concept: Origins and current status. *Schizophrenia Bulletin, 11,* 471–486.

Dawson, M. E., & Nuechterlein, K. H. (1984). Psychophysiological dysfunctions in the developmental course of schizophrenic disorders. *Schizophrenia Bulletin, 10,* 204–232.

Endicott, J., & Spitzer, R. (1972). Current and past psychopathology scales (CAPPS). *Archives of General Psychiatry, 27,* 678–687.

Frith, C. D., Stevens, M., Johnstone, E. C, & Crow, T. J. (1979). Skin conductance responsivity during acute episodes of schizophrenia as a predictor of symptomatic improvement. *Psychological Medicine, 9,* 101–106.

Gottesman, I. I., & Shields, J. (1982). *Schizophrenia: The epigenetic puzzle.* Cambridge, England: Cambridge University Press.

Gruzelier, J. H. (1976). Clinical attributes of schizophrenic skin conductance responders and nonresponders. *Psychological Medicine, 6,* 245–249.

Hase, H. D., & Goldberg, L. R. (1967). Comparative validity of different strategies of constructing personality inventory scales. *Psychological Bulletin, 67,* 231–248.

Hennrysson, S. (1962). The relation between factor loadings and biserial correlations in factor analysis. *Psychometrika, 27,* 419–424.

Ischaemia and haemorrhage in the premature brain. (1984, October). *Lancet,* 847–848.

Mednick, S. A. (1958). A learning theory approach to research in schizophrenia. *Psychological Bulletin, 55,* 316–327.

Mednick, S. A. (1970). Breakdown in individuals at high risk for schizophrenia: Possible predispositional perinatal factors. *Mental Hygiene, 54,* 50–63.

Mednick, S. A., & Higgins, S. (1960). *Current research in schizophrenia.* Ann Arbor, MI: Edwards Brothers.

Mednick, S. A., Machon, R., Huttunen, M. O., & Bonett, D. (1988). Adult schizophrenia following prenatal exposure to an influenza epidemic. *Archives of General Psychiatry, 45,* 189–192.

Mednick, S. A., & McNeil, T. (1968). Current methodology in research on the etiology of schizophrenia: Serious difficulties which suggest the use of the high-risk group method. *Psychological Bulletin, 70,* 681–693.

Mednick, S. A., & Schulsinger, F. (1965). A longitudinal study of children with a high risk for schizophrenia: A preliminary report. In S. Vandenberg (Ed.), *Methods and goals in human behavior genetics* (pp. 255–296). New York: Academic Press.

Mednick, S. A., & Schulsinger, F. (1968). Some premorbid characteristics related to breakdown in children with schizophrenic mothers. *Journal of Psychiatric Research, 6,* 267–291.

Nunnally, J. C. (1967). *Psychometric theory.* New York: McGraw-Hill.

Ohman, A. (1981). Electrodermal activity in schizophrenia: A review. *Biological Psychology, 12,* 87–145.

Oke, A. F., & Adams, R. N. (1987). Elevated thalamic dopamine: Possible link to sensory dysfunctions in schizophrenia. *Schizophrenia Bulletin, 13*, 589–604.

Parnas, J., Schulsinger, F., Teasdale, T. W., Schulsinger, H., Feldman, P. M., & Mednick, S. A. (1982). Perinatal complications and clinical outcome within the schizophrenia spectrum. *British Journal of Psychiatry, 140*, 416–420.

Parnas, J., Teasdale, T. W., & Schulsinger, H. (1985). Institutional rearing and diagnostic outcome in children of schizophrenic mothers: A prospective high-risk study. *Archives of General Psychiatry, 42*, 762–769.

Rubens, R. L., & Lapidus, L. B. (1978). Schizophrenic patterns of arousal and stimulus barrier functioning. *Journal of Abnormal Psychology, 87*, 199–211.

Schulsinger, H. (1976). A ten year follow-up of children of schizophrenic mothers. A clinical assessment. *Acta Psychiatrica Scandinavica, 53*, 371–386.

Schulsinger, F., Parnas, J., Petersen, E. T., Schulsinger, H., Teasdale, T. W., Mednick, S. A., Moller, L., & Silverton, L. (1984). Cerebral ventricular size in the offspring of schizophrenic mothers. *Archives of General Psychiatry, 41*, 602–606.

Shelton, R. C., & Weinberger, D. R. (1986). X-ray computerized tomography studies of schizophrenia: A review and synthesis. In H. A. Nasrallah & D. R. Weinberger (Eds.), *The neurology of schizophrenia* (pp. 207–250). Amsterdam: Elsevier Science.

Silverton, L., Finello, K. M., Mednick, S. A., & Schulsinger, F. (1985). Low birth weight and ventricular enlargement in a high-risk sample. *Journal of Abnormal Psychology, 94*, 405–409.

Silverton, L., Mednick, S. A., Schulsinger, F., Parnas, J., & Harrington, M. E. (1988). Genetic risk for schizophrenia, birthweight, and cerebral ventricular enlargement. *Journal of Abnormal Psychology, 97*, 496–498.

Sostek, A. M., Smith, Y. F., Katz, K. S., & Grant, E. G. (1987). Developmental outcome of preterm infants with intraventricular hemorrhage at one and two years of age. *Child Development, 58*, 779–786.

Spohn, H. E., & Patterson, T. (1979). Recent studies of psychophysiology in schizophrenia. *Schizophrenia Bulletin, 5*, 581–611.

Straube, E. R. (1979). On the meaning of electrodermal nonresponding in schizophrenia. *Journal of Nervous and Mental Disease, 167*, 601–611.

Strauss, J. S., Carpenter, W. T., & Bartko, J. J. (1976). The diagnosis and understanding of schizophrenia: II. Speculations on the processes that underlie schizophrenic symptoms and signs. *Schizophrenia Bulletin, 1*, 61–76.

Venables, P. H. (1960). The effect of auditory and visual stimulation on the skin potential responses of schizophrenics. *Brain, 83*, 77–92.

Venables, P. H., & Wing, J. K. (1962). Level of arousal and the subclassification of schizophrenia. *Archives of General Psychiatry, 7*, 114–119.

Walker, E. F., Cudeck, R., Mednick, S. A., & Schulsinger, F. (1981). Effects of parental absence and institutionalization on the development of clinical symptoms in high-risk children. *Acta Psychiatrica Scandinavica, 63*, 95–109.

Wang, G. H. (1964). *The neural control of sweating*. Madison: University of Wisconsin Press.

Wing, J. K., Cooper, J. E., & Sartorious, N. (1974). *The measurement and classification of psychiatric symptoms*. London: Cambridge University Press.

World Health Organization. (1967). *Manual of the international classification of diseases, injuries and causes of death* (8th ed.). Geneva: Author.

19 High-risk children in adolescence and young adulthood: Course of global adjustment

L. ERLENMEYER-KIMLING, BARBARA A. CORNBLATT, ANNE S. BASSETT, STEVEN O. MOLDIN, ULLA HILLDOFF-ADAMO, AND SIMONE ROBERTS

We began the New York High-Risk Project, a study of children at risk for schizophrenia or major affective disorders, more than 17 years ago (Erlenmeyer-Kimling & Cornblatt, 1987). One of the major questions that we and other investigators in high-risk research on mental disorders were asking concerned prediction of psychiatric outcomes, the search for early indicators or markers that might identify those members of the high-risk group with the greatest predisposition, or liability, to develop the disorder. At the outset, the greatest dilemma for many researchers seemed to be the choice of a pool to fish in to find predictor variables and, the pool once chosen, the hooking of exactly the right kind of fish.

In high-risk research on schizophrenia, quite a few pools have been looked into over the years (e.g., Watt et al., 1984) with some promising results from several studies suggesting that good fish are to be found in at least one, or possibly several, pools. In the New York High-Risk Project, for example, we have obtained substantial evidence that attentional and information-processing dysfunctions in childhood serve as predictors of late psychopathology in at least some children at risk for schizophrenia (e.g., Cornblatt & Erlenmeyer-Kimling, 1985; Cornblatt et al., 1989; Rutschmann et al., 1986), and recently, analyses of a totally different type of data, namely scale scores and profiles from the Minnesota Multiphasic Personality Inventory (MMPI), suggest that such data collected in adolescence may represent either another category of predictors or early signs of emerging illness (Moldin, 1987). Research by other investigative groups supports our results with respect to attentional and information-processing dysfunctions (e.g., Asarnow et al., 1978; Lifshitz et al., 1985; Nuechterlein, 1983) and suggests that neurological signs and developmental lags, too, may be predictive of later psychiatric outcome in offspring of schizophrenic parents (e.g., Fish, 1987; Marcus et al., 1985). For all of these classes of variables, however, considerably more work remains to be done to establish firmly their roles as predictors.

Unfortunately, as high-risk researchers have learned more by following their subjects over time, it has become evident that, whereas the dilemma of

351

identifying predictors has been paramount in our thinking up to now, there is an equally important dilemma and that is how to define outcome: what kind of outcome are we hoping to predict, and when in follow-up can we consider that an outcome has occurred?

When most of the high-risk studies of schizophrenia began, the main expectation was that some 10% to 15% of the offspring would develop schizophrenia later in life (e.g., Slater Cowie, 1971). When some of the contemporary research on lifetime morbidity risks in the relatives of schizophrenic probands began to show considerably lower risks than they had in earlier studies (e.g., Tsuang et al., 1980), there was concern that high-risk studies would yield too few future schizophrenics to be useful. Fortunately, though, the concept of the schizophrenia spectrum was revived to prominence by the Danish adoption studies (e.g., Kety et al., 1978), leading to the expectation that, in high-risk studies, we could still expect to find a relatively large percentage of the children of schizophrenic parents eventually showing a fairly clear manifestation of the genotype, either as definite schizophrenia or as an alternate expression in the schizophrenia spectrum. What we knew in the 1970s led some of us to think of these two conditions—schizophrenia and its milder personality variants—as being additive in a high-risk sample: some children should turn out to be schizophrenic and some, probably a higher percentage, should turn out to manifest spectrum disorders. The overall percentage expected would depend on the genetic model adopted by the investigator, but, for example, both Heston's (1970) single dominant gene model and a multiple-threshold multifactorial model (e.g., Gottesman et al., 1987; Reich et al., 1979) accommodate the idea of additivity.

There were three things that workers in high-risk research forgot to think of concerning outcome, which, after all, is the ultimate means of validating the predictive value of an indicator. The first concerns problems of co-morbidity. For example, in the New York High-Risk Project, 41% of all the subjects (53% of the offspring of schizophrenic parents, 50% of the offspring of depressed parents, and 31% of the offspring of normal parents) received more than one Axis I diagnosis on the SADS-L administered during late adolescence to early adulthood. (These figures dropped only slightly, to 35%, 47% 42%, and 26%, respectively, when the diagnosis of minor depression was removed.) On the same SADS-L interview, 19% of the subjects (27%, 22%, and 13% of the offspring of schizophrenic, depressed, and normal parents, respectively) received at least one Axis I diagnosis coupled with at least one Axis II diagnosis. On the Personality Disorder Examination (PDE, an interview for making DSM-III Axis II diagnoses) (Loranger et al., 1985) administered in young adulthood in our ongoing assessment round, the coexistence of more than one probable or definite personality disorder is very high, with, for instance, 87.5% of all subjects classified as having probable or definite schizotypal personality disorder also having at least one other probable or definite personality disorder. Co-morbidity is a relatively recent issue in psychiatric research, but it is an importnat one that pushes to the fore the question, What is the phenotype that high-risk researchers expect their variables to predict? What shall we conclude if we find disorders in the offspring of schizophrenic parents that have not been thought previously to be associated with schizophrenia, *and* what if our best early indicator variable appears to predict such disorders at least as well as it predicts schizoprenia?

The second problem that we did not recognize earlier was that the schizophrenia spectrum as it has been defined and operationalized might not be specific to schizophrenia. For example, interviews designed to elicit DSM-III and DSM-IIIR Axis II disorders reveal schizotypal personality disorder and other disorders that might be thought to complete the schizophrenia spectrum as frequently in the offspring of parents with affective disorders as in the offspring of schizophrenic parents (Squires-Wheeler & Erlenmeyer-Kimling, 1987*a*,*b*). Analogous findings on the relatives of schizophrenic and affectively ill probands are beginning to be reported by other groups (e.g., Ingraham & Kety, 1987). We are hopeful that there are characteristics specific to a schizophrenia spectrum, but the concept as it is now operationalized evidently requires reworking. It does not appear to be ready to fit into genetic models or to help serve as a validator of predictor variables.

Third, too little thought had been given in high-risk research to the problem of the course of psychiatric disorders. Investigators have been aware that the risk period for schizophrenia is long, but, because the peak is relatively early, they expected that follow-up in young adulthood would identify the majority of the subjects who would ever become cases. However, coupled with the problem of co-morbidity and appreciable uncertainty about the definition of onset, recently emphasized by Carpenter (1989), another problem is that the pathway to final outcome is often not straight. This makes it difficult to know when a high-risk subject has, indeed, reached an outcome of signifiance. The remainder of the current report will focus on the problem of the variability of the course of psychopathology in our subjects.

The New York high-risk project

In this report, we are concerned with a subset of the first (Sample A) of the two samples that comprise the New York High-Risk Project. Both samples consist of offspring of schizophrenic parents, offspring of affectively ill parents, and offspring of normal parents followed since the ages of 7 to 12. Mentally ill parents in both samples have been diagnosed or rediagnosed

Table 1. *New York High-Risk Project: Sample A total number, number with completed follow-ups, and number classified as dysfunctional*

Group	Total subjects in Sample A	Number with completed follow-up (to July 1987)	Number and percentage classified as dysfunctional		
			Hospitalized	Problems	Total
HR	63	44	10 (23%)	10 (23%)	20 (45%)
AFF	43	33	4 (12%)	4 (12%)	8 (24%)
NC	100	79	2 (2%)	6 (8%)	8 (10%)
Other	2	2	—	—	—
Total	208	158	16 (10%)	20 (13%)	36 (23%)

Abbreviations: HR = High risk, i.e., children of schizophrenic parents, AFF = children of affectively ill parents, NC = normal controls, i.e., children of normal parents, Other = children of parent with undiagnosed disorder.

with the Research Diagnostic Criteria (RDC) based on SADS-L interviews and other available materials, and analyses of parental MMPI protocols (Moldin et al., 1987) support the validity of the RDC diagnoses. (Detailed descriptions of the samples and diagnoses of the parents appear in Erlenmeyer-Kimling & Cornblatt, 1987.) Sample A, which was recruited in 1971–1972, is currently being examined for the fifth time, with interviews designed to elicit DSM-III and DSM-IIIR Axis I and Axis II diagnoses, as well as overall level of present functioning. The average age of subjects in sample A is just over 24 years.

Of the 208 children in Sample A, 159 had been examined in the ongoing round of assessments by July 1987, when we closed the data file to prepare the present report. The percentages of subjects who have been followed range from 71% to 79% across the three groups and should rise to 85% to 90% by the completion of these assessments.

As shown in Table 1, of the 159 subjects followed thus far, 36 are classified as dysfunctional, either because they have had one or more hospitalizations for psychiatric reasons or because they have received more than 6 months of treatment for serious psychiatric problems or were rated as showing impaired functioning during the ongoing clinical assessments. (Subjects were classified as showing impaired functioning if they scored 1 or 2 on the 5-point Global Adjustment Scale [GAS] as will be explained.) These 36 dysfunctional subjects are the main focus of this discussion. It should be noted, however, that because of the problems of co-morbidity, uncertainty about the true nature of the schizophrenia spectrum, and vagaries of course, we cannot say that most of these subjects are necessarily manifesting disorders that will eventually be considered their final outcomes. Some of

Table 2. *Dysfunctional subjects who have ever been psychotic*

Group	Number of dysfunctional subjects	Number and percent ever psychotic	Number and percent never psychotic
HR	20	8 (40%)	12 (60%)
AFF	8	3 (37.5%)	5 (62.5%)
NC	8	2 (25%)	6 (75%)
Total	36	13 (38%)	23 (62%)

Abbreviations: HR = High risk, i.e., children of schizophrenic parents, AFF = children of affectively ill parents, NC = normal controls, i.e., children of normal parents.

the hospitalized subjects, however, do have clear-cut, probably lifetime, diagnoses.

As Table 1 indicates, among those children of schizophrenic parents who were followed, 45% are currently classified as dysfunctional, half of them having been hospitalized. Among the children of parents with affective disorders, 24% are classified as dysfunctional, with again, half having been hospitalized. Among the children of normal parents, 10% are classified as dysfunctional, but only a fourth of these dysfunctional subjects have been hospitalized.

The difference between the high-risk and normal comparison groups with respect to the proportion of subjects classified as dysfunctional is highly significant ($\chi^2 = 19.32$, 1 df, $p < .001$). However, the difference between the group with affectively ill parents and the normal comparison group just fails to reach significance at the .05 level ($\chi^2 = 3.79$, 1 df), and the two groups with mentally ill parents also fail to show a significant difference ($\chi^2 = 3.40$, 1 df).

The third author has reviewed the lifetime histories of the 36 dysfunctional subjects, blind as to parental diagnoses, and has classified them according to whether or not they are known to have ever had a psychotic episode. Table 2 shows that a substantial percentage of the dysfunctional subjects in each group has had a psychotic episode. There are no significant differences among the three parental diagnostic groups. (However, if we used total number of subjects followed per group as a denominator rather than number of dysfunctional subjects per group, the percentage of psychotic subjects in the normal comparison group would be 2.5%, considerably lower than the figures that would be obtained in the other two groups—18% among children of schizophrenic parents and 9% among children of affectively ill parents.) Among the 13 subjects with psychotic episodes, nine are considered to be chronic, two are currently in remission, and two are improved but not in full remission. Only three of these 13 subjects have definite diagnoses of chronic schizophrenia or schizoaffective disorder with a predominantly schizophrenic-like picture, and these three are all offspring of schizophrenic parents (one has two schizophrenic parents). Eight of the remaining 10 subjects with psychotic episodes are strongly suspected to have a schizophrenic disorder according to the second author's blind review of their files; of these, three are offspring of schizophrenic parents (one also has a manic-depressive parent), three are offspring of affectively ill parents (two of these three are siblings with one ill parent and the third subject has two affectively ill parents), and two are offspring of psychiatrically normal parents. Diagnostic classification of the final two subjects with a history of psychotic episodes is unclear.

Methods

We are going to examine pathways to psychopathology by tracing the subjects' GAS scores at four points in time, from early adolescence to young adulthood. All of the GAS ratings of global adjustment have been converted to a 5-point scale, scored in the direction of mental health; that is, the higher the score the better the level of adjustment (see Cornblatt & Erlenmeyer-Kimling, 1984, for description). If the GAS scores could be compared to school grades, the following relationships would hold:

GAS score	School grade
5	A
4	B
3	C
2	D
1	F

All GAS ratings were done blind with respect to parental diagnoses and other information about the families. Sources of the GAS ratings at the four time points that we have used are described in Table 3. The 1980, 1983, and 1986–1987 GAS ratings were made when the subjects were, on the average, aged 17, 21, and 24 respectively.

The 1977, 1980, and 1983 ratings were based on cumulative information up to the time that the rating was made, whereas the 1986–1987 rating was based only on current information. Although the GAS ratings at the several time points were based on different materials collected from different informants and entailed a certain degree of subjectivity of judgment, they do give us quantitative scores of the general level of functioning for each subject that can be compared over time.

Results

Table 4 present the mean GAS scores at the four selected time points for subjects categorized as nondysfunctional or dysfunctional at the most recent

Table 3. *Global Adjustment Scale (GAS) ratings*

Time point	Description of GAS and basis on which rating was made
1977 (between rounds 2 and 3)	100-point GAS rescaled to 5 points: Ratings by child psychiatrists, based on excerpts of parent and child interviews at rounds 1 and 2 and social workers' telephone follow-up interviews with parents at intervals of 3–6 months.
1980 (approximately end of round 3)	5-point behavioral GAS: Ratings based on social workers' telephone follow-up interviews with parents at intervals of 3–6 months.
1983 (round 4)	Same as 1980
1986–87 (round 5)	7-point SCID-II Global Assessment of Personality (rescaled to 5 points): Ratings by psychologist or psychiatric social worker based on Axis I and II structured interviews and adjusted for social workers' and other current information about the subject.

Note: All ratings blind as to group.

Table 4. *GAS mean scores and standard deviations at four assessment points*

Assessment time	HR		AFF		NC	
	Non-dysfunctional	Dysfunctional	Non-dysfunctional	Dysfunctional	Non-dysfunctional	Dysfunctional
1977	3.5 ± .8	2.8 ± .9	3.8 ± 1.0	2.9 ± .6	4.2 ± .8	3.2 ± .9
1980	3.3 ± .8	2.1 ± .9	3.7 ± .8	2.5 ± 1.3	4.0 ± .5	3.1 ± 1.0
1983	3.5 ± .5	2.3 ± 1.0	3.6 ± .5	1.8 ± .5	3.9 ± .5	2.6 ± 1.1
1986–1987	3.7 ± .5	2.3 ± .7	3.9 ± .6	2.0 ± .8	4.2 ± .7	2.3 ± .9

Abbreviations: HR = High risk, i.e., children of schizophrenic parents, AFF = children of affectively ill parents, NC = normal controls, i.e., children of normal parents.

follow-up. None of the subjects had received or required treatment for psychiatric problems at the time of entering the study in 1971–1972. At that time average GAS ratings were high (nondysfunctional) for all groups and did not differ between subjects now classified as dysfunctional and subjects classified as nondysfunctional, within risk groups. By early adolescence, 5 to 6 years later, however, all subject groups showed some decline in global adjustment, with significantly lower GAS scores for the now dysfunctional subjects compared to the nondysfunctional subjects. Differences between the dysfunctional and nondysfunctional subjects in each group continued to be significant at the 1980, 1983, and 1986–1987 assessments. Thus, as a

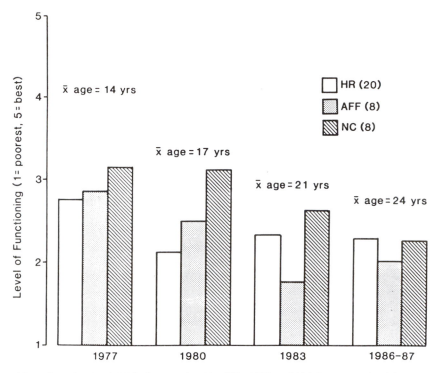

Mean Longitudinal GAS Scores for the HR, AFF and NC Dysfunctional Subjects

Figure 1. Mean longitudinal GAS scores for the children of schizophrenic (HR), affectively ill (AFF), and normal (NC) dysfunctional subjects.

group, the subjects now called dysfunctional have shown impairment in global adjustment for some time.

The mean GAS scores for the currently dysfunctional subjects at the four time points are plotted in Figure 1 for easy comparison of the parental diagnostic groups. In group-by-group comparisons at each time point, the only significant difference occurs between the children of schizophrenic parents and the children of normal parents at the 1980 time point ($p = .01$). All other differences are not significant, although the difference between children of parents with affective disorders and the children of normal parents in the 1983 ratings just misses significance.

Figure 2 offers the same type of comparison between psychotic and nonpsychotic dysfunctional subjects for the three parental diagnostic groups pooled. The subjects now classified as having had a psychotic episode had considerably lower GAS scores than the subjects classified as nonpsychotic at all assessment times, although at the first assessment the difference was not significant and at the most recent assessment, at the mean age of 24, the

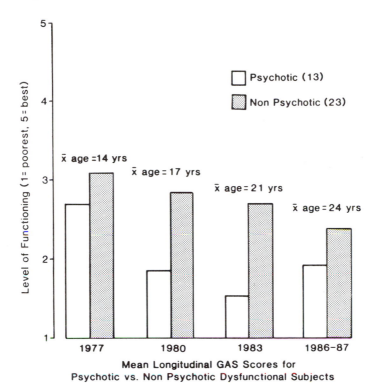

Figure 2. Mean longitudinal GAS scores for the psychotic and nonpsychotic dysfunctional subjects.

difference in GAS scores of the psychotic and nonpsychotic subjects has narrowed ($p = 0.34$) compared to the 1980 and 1983 differences ($p = .009$ and $p < .000$, respectively).

Group mean scores are not necessarily representative of individual subjects, and we were interested, therefore, in tracing the personal pathways in global adjustment followed by the dysfunctional subjects, as reflected by their GAS scores at the four time points. Examination of the individual pathways in Figure 3 for three selected subjects in each parental diagnostic group reveals considerable variability, with some subjects showing poor GAS scores from early adolescence onward, others falling from high scores and remaining at low scores, and still others showing a pattern of improvement and deterioration over time. Clearly, the task of using predictor variables to forecast future outcomes is complicated by the fact that subjects now considered to be dysfunctional have demonstrated quite variable patterns in reaching that classification.

This variability also occurs, of course, among many of the subjects in the group currently regarded as nondysfunctional. Some obtained GAS scores

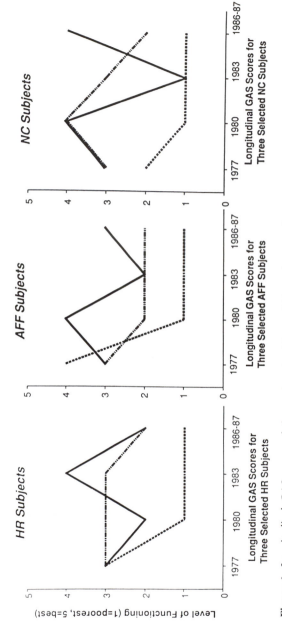

Figure 3. Longitudinal GAS scores of three selected subjects within each targeted group.

Table 5. *Frequency with which subjects obtained low (impaired) GAS scores*

Subject classification	Number of assessments with GAS scores of 3 or below (%)						Number of assessments with GAS scores of 2 or below (%)					
	0	1	2	3	4	Total	0	1	2	3	4	Total
Nondysfunctional	52 (42.6)	30 (24.6)	26 (21.3)	10 (8.2)	4 (3.3)	122 (100.0)	114 (93.4)	7 (5.7)	1 (0.8)	—	—	122 (100.0)
Dysfunctional	—	1 (2.6)	3 (8.3)	12 (33.3)	20 (55.6)	36 (100.0)	2 (5.5)	13 (36.1)	11 (30.6)	5 (13.9)	5 (13.9)	36 (100.0)
Nonpsychotic	—	1 (4.3)	2 (8.7)	9 (39.1)	11 (47.8)	23 (100.0)	2 (8.7)	9 (39.1)	9 (39.1)	3 (13.0)	—	23 (100.0)
Psychotic	—	—	1 (7.7)	3 (23.1)	9 (69.2)	13 (100.0)	—	4 (30.8)	2 (15.4)	2 (15.4)	5 (38.2)	13 (100.0)

of 3 (equivalent to a school grade of C) or even scores of 2 at one or more of the assessment points, as shown in Table 5. Although nondysfunctional subjects certainly received such scores far less frequently than did the currently dysfunctional subjects, especially those who have had psychotic episodes, many were rated as having only fair adjustment at some point, and eight of them would actually have been classified as dysfunctional on one or more occasions in the past.

Discussion

The points that we wish to emphasize about the data presented here are as follows:

> Although subjects classified as dysfunctional in their mid-20s tend, as a group, to have been assessed as showing poor adjustment since early adolescence, individual subjects have followed widely differing courses, so that there are truly both straight and devious pathways leading to their current status.
> Although subjects classified as nondysfunctional at present tend, as a group, to have received relatively good GAS scores throughout, a number of these subjects have received only fair ratings on one or more occasions, and eight subjects have received assessments of poor functioning in the past and could have been considered at those time points to be heading for poor outcomes.
> The variability among individual subjects is not confined to any one of the parental diagnostic groups, and no particular pattern of global adjustment over time describes a particular group or distinguishes between subjects who have or have not had a psychotic episode, although it is true that subjects who have had a psychotic episode by the time of the fourth assessment tend to have had low GAS scores more frequently than dysfunctional subjects without a psychotic episode.

Thus, for subjects with erratic courses, their status as dysfunctional versus nondysfunctional is very much a question of when the classification is made. We have not had an opportunity here to discuss the problems of co-morbidity and diagnostic specificity or stability, but suffice it to say that when one moves from quantitative to qualitative classification, the dilemma for high-risk research is compounded. This is the dilemma, as we have noted, of defining what constitutes "outcome" and deciding when outcome occurs. The value of candidate predictor variables cannot be established firmly until this dilemma is resolved.

The variable patterns of adjustment that we have observed in the subjects in the New York High-Risk Project, and that undoubtedly characterize other high-risk samples as well, suggest that the answers that risk research are seeking may require longer follow-up than had been anticipated. There is a positive feature of this enforced extension of follow-up in high-risk populations, however. Namely, prolonged examination of these subjects provides a rare opportunity to document through long segments of the life span both the stressors and buffers that, together with the subjects' genes, shape their evolving outcomes.

Acknowledgments

This research is supported in part by the National Institute of Mental Health grant MH 19560 and by the Department of Mental Hygiene of the State of New York. The Computer Center of the New York State Psychiatric Institute, where the data were analyzed, is supported in part by NIMH grant MH 30906. We wish to acknowledge the assistance of Ms. Karen Brumer and Ms. Marilyn Kaplan, our project social workers who diligently maintain telephone contacts with the subject families and document the information on which GAS ratings can be based. Drs. John Rainer, Michael Stone, Irving Gottesman, and Leonard Heston took part in the diagnostic assessments of the parents, to which Mr. Thomas J. Adamo, Mrs. Ulla Hilldoff Adamo, and Dr. Jean Endicott contributed also.|Drs. Clarice Kestenbaum and Hector Bird and their colleagues at St. Luke's Hospital participated in assessments of the study children in both samples and supplied the 1977 GAS ratings, as well as the 1971–1972 ratings, which are not reported here. We are grateful to Dr. Elizabeth Squires-Wheeler, who contributed to the planning of this paper and provided valuable commentary. We especially thank Ms. Marietta Bell for her assistance with the data analyses, Ms. Barbara Maminski for help with preparing the figures, and Ms. Mimi Simon and Ms. Sky Pape for typing the manuscript.

References

Asarnow, R. F., Steffy, R. A., MacCrimmon, D. J., & Cleghorn, J. M. (1978). An attentional assessment of foster children at risk for schizophrenia. In L. C. Wynne, R. L. Cromwell, & S. Matthysse (Eds.), *The nature of schizophrenia: New approaches to research and treatment* (pp. 339–358). New York: John Wiley & Sons.

Carpenter, W. T. (in press). Diagnosis of negative symptoms (deficit state) in schizophrenia. In S. Schultz & C. Tamminga (Eds.), *Schizophrenia: Scientific Progress*. New York: Oxford University Press.

Cornblatt, B. & Erlenmeyer-Kimling, L. (1984). Early attentional predictors of adolescent behavioral disturbances in children at risk for schizophrenia. In N. F. Watt, E. J. Anthony, L. C. Wynne, & J. E. Rolf (Eds.), *Children at risk for schizophrenia: A longitudinal perspective* (pp. 198–212). New York: Cambridge University Press.

Cornblatt, B., & Erlenmeyer-Kimling, L. (1985). Global attentional deviance as a marker of risk for schizophrenia: Specificity and predictive validity. *Journal of Abnormal Psychology, 94*, 470–486.

Cornblatt, B., Winters, L., & Erlenmeyer-Kimling, L. (1989). Attentional markers of schizophrenia: Evidence from the New York High-Risk Study. In S. Schultz & C. Tamminga (Eds.), *Schizophrenia: Scientific Progress*. New York: Oxford University Press.

Erlenmeyer-Kimling, L., & Cornblatt, B. (1987). The New York High-risk Project: A follow-up report. *Schizophrenia Bulletin, 13*, 451–463.

Fish, B. (1987) Infant predictors of the longitudinal course of schizophrenic development. *Schizophrenia Bulletin, 13*, 395–409.

Gottesman, I. I., McGuffin, P., & Farmer, A. E. (1987). Clinical genetics as clues to the "real" genetics of schizophrenia (A decade of modest gains while playing for time). *Schizophrenia Bulletin, 13*, 23–47.

Heston, L. L. (1970). The genetics of schizophrenia and schizoid disease. *Science, 167*, 248–256.

Ingraham, L. J., & Kety, S. S. (1987). *Schizophrenia spectrum disorders.* Poster presented at the International Congress on Schizophrenia Research, March 28–April 1, 1987.

Kety, S. S., Rosenthal, D., Wender, P. H., Schulsinger, F., & Jacobsen, B. (1978). The biologic and adoptive families of adopted individuals who became schizophrenic: Prevalence of mental illness and other characteristics. In L.C. Wynne, R. L. Cromwell, & S. Matthysse (Eds.), *The nature of schizophrenia: New approaches to research and treatment.* New York: John Wiley & Sons.

Lifshitz, M., Kugelmass, S., & Karov, M. (1985). Perceptual-motor and memory performance of high-risk children. *Schizophrenia Bulletin, 11*, 74–84.

Loranger, A. W., Susman, V. L., Oldham, J. M., & Russakoff, L. M. (1985, May 15). *PDE (Personality Disposition Examination).* White Plains, NY: The New York Hospital–Cornell Medical Center, Westchester Division.

Marcus, J., Hans, S. L., Mednick, S. A., Schulsinger, F., & Michelsen, N. (1985). Neurological dysfunctioning in offspring of schizophrenics in Israel and Denmark: A replication analysis. *Archives of General Psychiatry, 42*, 753–761.

Moldin, S. O. (1987). *Psychometric indicators of liability for schizophrenia in children at genetic risk.* Unpublished doctoral dissertation, Yeshiva University, New York.

Moldin, S. O., Gottesman, I. I. & Erlenmeyer-Kimling, L. (1987) Psychometric validation of psychiatric diagnoses in the New York High-Risk Study. *Psychiatry Research, 22*, 159–177.

Nuechterlein, K. H. (1983). Signal detection in vigilance tasks and behavioral attributes among offspring of schizophrenic mothers and among hyperactive children. *Journal of Abnormal Psychology, 92*, 4–28.

Reich, T., Rice, J., Cloninger, C. R., Wette, R., & James, J. (1979). The use of multiple thresholds and segregation analysis in analyzing the phenotypic heterogeneity of multifactorial traits. *Annals of Human Genetics, 42*, 371–390.

Rutschmann, J., Cornblatt, B., & Erlenmeyer-Kimling, L. (1986). Sustained attention in children at risk for schizophrenia: Findings with two visual continuous performance tasks in a new sample. *Journal of Abnormal Child Psychology, 14*, 365–385.

Slater, E., & Cowie, V. A. (1971). *The Genetics of Mental Disorders.* London: Oxford University Press.

Squires-Wheeler, E., & Erlenmeyer-Kimling, L. (1987a). *Axis II in children of schizophrenic parents.* Presentation at the American Psychiatric Association Symposia, Chicago, IL.

Squires-Wheeler, E., & Erlenmeyer-Kimling, L. (1987b). *Epidemiology of DSM-III-R schizotypal personality disorder.* Poster presented at the Young Investigator Program, International Congress on Schizophrenia Research, Clearwater, FL.

Tsuang, M., Winokur, G., & Crowe R. (1980). Morbidity risks of schizophrenia and affective disorders among first degree relatives of patients with schizophrenia, mania, depression and surgical conditions. *British Journal of Psychitary, 137*, 497–504.

Watt, N. F., Anthony, E. J., Wynne, L. C., & Rolf J. (Eds.). (1984). *Children at risk for schizophrenia: A longitudinal perspective.* New York: Cambridge University Press.

20 Adopted-away offspring of schizophrenics and controls: The Finnish adoptive family study of schizophrenia

PEKKA TIENARI, ILPO LAHTI, ANNELI SORRI,
MIKKO NAARALA, JUHA MORING,
MERJA KALEVA, KARL-ERIK WAHLBERG, AND
LYMAN C. WYNNE

Data from the Danish adoption studies of schizophrenia have confirmed genetic hypotheses: there were more schizophrenic and schizophrenia-related disorders in the biological relatives of schizophrenic adoptees and in the adopted-away children of schizophrenic parents than in their control groups (Kety et al., 1978; Rosenthal et al., 1971). However, environmental hypotheses and joint effects of genetic and rearing variables have been studied only to a limited extent in the Danish and American adoption studies. In a Danish study, Rosenthal et al. (1975) conducted retrospective interviews with adult offspring adoptees about "various aspects" of their past life with their rearing parents. Rank-order ratings of offspring statements about the parent-offspring relationship were correlated with rank-order ratings of offspring psychopathology manifest in the same interviews. In an American study, the functioning of adoptive parents themselves was assessed with specific categories of communication deviance (CD) by Wynne et al. (1976), who scored blindly the individual parent Rorschach protocols of Wender et al. (1986). Wynne and his colleagues found no differences in the frequency of individual CD in biological parents who had reared their schizophrenic offspring and in adoptive parents who had reared a schizophrenic; but CD in both of these parental groups was significantly more frequent than in a control group of patients who had reared normal adoptees. In later adoption studies of schizophrenia, no assessments have been reported of direct interaction or relationships between family members, evaluated either currently or prospectively.

A major goal in the Finnish adoptive family study is to evaluate both genetic and family-rearing contributions to schizophrenia and other psychopathology. We are interested in assessing to what extent genetic variables and family relationship variables jointly contribute to psychopathology of the adoptees. We would like to elucidate whether the genetic risk may be counteracted and resilience promoted by a healthy, possibly protective, family environment. We also would like to know whether the direction of effects between genetic and family–environmental factors can be clarified through a prospective, longitudinal study of adoptees at risk.

A study of adopted-away offspring of schizophrenics

Method

Selection of index cases. A nationwide sample was collected of all the women in Finland who have been hospitalized because of schizophrenia. The sample includes both the inpatient population on January 1, 1960, and later consecutive admissions for schizophrenia through 1979, making a total of 19,447 schizophrenic women. Information supplied by local civil and parish population registers showed which of these women had had babies given up for adoption.

Through these registers, 264 mothers were found who had given up 291 offspring for adoption. Of these offspring, 94 were excluded from the field study for various reasons (34 adopted by a relative, 35 adopted abroad, 24 adopted after age 4, and 1 for whom adoption could not be confirmed). After either the biological mother or the adoptive family had been contacted, 12 new cases were excluded (2 offspring had died before reaching the age of risk for schizophrenia, 1 had been adopted by a relative, 3 of the families had moved abroad when the child was still young, and 6 mothers were excluded because a personal interview did not confirm the diagnosis of schizophrenia).

A total of 185 offspring of 171 index schizophrenic women make up the final sample of index cases. These children were adopted-away offspring of schizophrenic mothers and had been placed in adoptive families with Finnish nonrelatives during their first 4 years of life.

The index cases were initially identified by a hospital diagnosis of schizophrenia (or paranoid psychosis) for the biological, adopting-away mother. Paranoid psychoses were included because we expected that the boundaries between schizophrenia and paranoid psychosis would be unclear and could be later checked. All of the hospital records were collected and copied. Two raters (both experienced psychiatrists) reviewed the records and tried to confirm the diagnosis of schizophrenia by using the diagnostic criteria that are traditional in Finland (and correspond closely to Langfeldt's criteria). Two additional raters (psychiatric residents) applied the Research Diagnostic Criteria (RDC) to the hospital records of the biological mothers. Personal interviews and tests of the biological index mothers are in progress and, to date, 94 have been interviewed. These psychiatric interviews include a modified Present State Examination (PSE) with added items that facilitate DSM-IIIR and RDC diagnoses, a 10-card Rorschach, MMPI, and information on the biological fathers. In as much detail as possible, data have been obtained on the psychiatric hospitalizations, symptoms, and personal characteristics of the biological relatives of both the biological and control parents, including formal diagnoses and information on personal eccentricities, patterns of adjustment, and major somatic illnesses.

The DSM-IIIR criteria will be applied to the hospital records and the PSE interviews of the biological parents. Using the same kind of interviews as for the biological index mothers, we have begun to interview the biological index fathers and biological control parents. We will attempt to evaluate whether the psychiatric diagnoses of the biological fathers add to the risk of the offspring. We will later use the following items in order to dimensionalize the status of the biological parents: Global Assessment Scale (GAS), duration of hospitalization/treatment, onset of illness, work and social functioning ratings, premorbid adjustment measures, MMPI measures, and Rorschach measures, especially the Thought Disorder Index and Communication Deviance.

All the interviews and tests were tape-recorded. Taping makes it possible to carry out blind ratings, reliability checks, and reclassifications by other investigators in the phase of the project that is now under way.

Selection of matched controls. The index offspring and their adoptive families have been blindly compared with matched controls, that is, adoptive families with adopted-away offspring of biological parents who have not been hospitalized because of psychosis. Pairwise matching was done outside our department by persons who were given the criteria and who independently carried out the case-by-case matching. The criteria for matching the control and index cases were as follows: the age difference between the index and control adoptees is less than one year; the age difference between the adoptive parent versus the control parent is less than 10 years; the index and control adoptees are matched for sex; the age of placement in the adoptive families must be in the same time period (less than 6 months, 6–11 months, 12–17 months, 18–23 months, 24–29 months, 30–35 months, 36–41 months, 42–47 months, and 48–59 months).

The two series were further matched with regard to social class, family residence (urban or rural), and family structure (adoptive mother and father versus only father or only mother). Social class in Finland is determined by occupation. Biological control parents have been excluded only if they have been treated for psychosis. Hence, some of the biological parents in the control series have received psychiatric help for reasons other than psychosis. The adoptive index and control series were numbered randomly so that the four psychiatrists conducting the personal interviews were blind as to whether the case in question was an index or a control family.

Assessment of adoptive families and individuals. Our clinical study has so far focused on the offspring (and their adoptive families) who were born in 1970 or earlier, in other words, on those who are now at the age of risk for schizophrenia. The adoptive index and control families have been investigated in their homes directly and intensively with procedures that usually take 2 days (14–16 hours). The family relationships are studied through family and couple interviews, as well as the Consensus Rorschach (Loveland et al., 1963) and the Interpersonal Perception Method (Laing et al., 1966). Both of the adoptive parents and the offspring are individually interviewed to assess their current psychiatric status and past history. Individual Rorschachs are given after the Consensus Rorschach. In the adoptive families, the MMPI has been given only to the adoptive offspring. An abbreviated version of the WAIS is used for screening intellectual deficiencies and gross perceptual and organic difficulties (Tienari et al., 1987*a* & *b*).

The diagnostic assessments of the adoptees and adoptive parents will eventually include application of DSM-IIIR criteria, which is also being done with the biological parents. Although few changes are being found when Finnish diagnoses of schizophrenia are compared with RDC and DSM-IIIR diagnoses, the wider range of nonschizophrenic diagnoses in the biological fathers, the adoptive parents, and the adoptees requires a more complicated comparison of Finnish and DSM-IIIR diagnoses. As of this report, the DSM-IIIR rediagnoses are still in progress.

When the collection of data from the adoptive families was begun in 1977, a classification system was used that provided the basis for the preliminary data analyses. A 6-point scale for the severity of illness was combined with qualitative diagnoses, collapsed into four diagnostic levels for this report. Level 6 (psychosis) includes schizophrenia, paranoid psychosis, and affective psychoses; these Finnish diagnoses appear to be similar to those in DSM-IIIR. Level 5 (borderline syndrome) and Level 4 (severe personality disorders) are combined in Tables 1 through 5 of this report. Further specification will be carried out with the DSM-IIIR criteria. Levels 4 and 5 together presumptively include the schizotypal and paranoid personality disorders diagnosed with criteria similar to those of DSM-IIIR, as well as what used to be called latent schizophrenia and pseudoneurotic schizophrenia. Additionally, and to be sorted out in future rediagnoses, these levels include borderline and narcissistic personality disorders and some cases of severely dysfunctional, egosyntonic "character disorders." Level 3 (neurosis) includes those disorders with moderate and mild symptoms as well as the less severe personality disorders. Levels 1 and 2 (no diagnosis) are combined and include healthy individuals and those with mild eccentricities or symptoms that fall short of meeting criteria for a mental disorder.

Family mental health ratings. The total interview material has also been used for global ratings of the mental health of the families, as obtained from interviews of entire families and parental couples. These global ratings represent clinical assessments by the research psychiatrists based upon the 2-day interviews of each adoptive family. Because of rules imposed by the adoption agency, only one investigator was permitted to visit each family. Therefore, a possible bias was present when the same person interviewed and rated first the adoptive family and later the adoptee. As a partial check on this source of bias, the four interviewers have been conducting inter-rater reliability studies from audiotapes, independently rating the conjoint family interviews. They have also developed a 33-item family rating scale that will dimensionalize the initial, more global ratings of the adoptive families. The results of these reliability studies are not yet available. For this preliminary report, data from three levels of globally rated family functioning have been obtained. These levels have been collapsed from the five levels described in more detail elsewhere (Tienari et al., 1985*a* & *b*). "Healthy" (Levels 1 and 2 combined) denotes families in which conflicts are transient or rare, psychological boundaries between the family members and between the family and the outside world are well defined, anxiety and depression are mild, and role functioning is appropriate to the stage of the family life cycle and external circumstances of the family. "Moderately disturbed" (Level 3) denotes families in which unresolved conflicts of mild or moderate severity are present, psychological boundaries are clear, and reality testing is good; but the family roles are somewhat inappropriate for the ages or capabilities of the members, as well as somewhat constricted and repetitive. "Severely disturbed" (Levels 4 and 5 combined) denotes families that either are maladaptive because of major unresolved and unacknowledged conflicts or are openly chaotic; their psychological boundaries are either rigid or unclear and stable, and family roles do not change flexibly in response to the major life events and transitions in the family life cycle.

Follow-up assessments. Telephone interviews of 221 of the adoptive families have been conducted 5 to 7 years after the initial assessment. These telephone follow-ups of adoptees have revealed one new case of schizophrenia, one bipolar manic psychosis, one paranoid psychosis, and two suicides. In these cases, the family evaluations had taken place prospectively before the onset of the adoptee's illness. We also plan to invite all the offspring to face-to-face assessments at follow-up that will include standardized interviews, retesting, and possibly videotaping.

Perliminary results

By October 1987, 298 families (index and control combined) had been contacted for field study, with data from 287 partially scored (134 index and 153 control cases). We must point out that all the results at this time are preliminary because not all families have been interviewed, and because some diagnoses and family ratings need to be confirmed with reliability checks.

Adopted-away offspring: Index versus control differences

Matched-pair data. Table 1 shows the mental health ratings of the adopted-away offspring for the 128 index cases (schizophrenic biological mothers) and their matched controls (nonschizophrenic mothers) who had been examined by October 1987. Overall, the offspring of schizophrenics are more disturbed than the offspring of controls ($p = .0278$; one-tailed sign test for matched pairs). We can see that of the 11 psychotic subjects, 10 are offspring of schizophrenics and only one was a control offspring ($\chi^2 = 7.694$, $p = .005$). One of the psychotic index offspring was given a diagnosis of manic-depressive psychosis (confirmed by a separate rater), 6 were given a diagnosis of schizophrenia, and 3, paranoid psychosis. The total percentage of severe diagnoses (psychosis, borderline syndrome, and severe personality disorders) is 28.1% (36/128) in the index group and 15.6% (20/128) in the control group ($\chi^2 = 5.851$, $p = .016$).

Sex differences. In Table 2, the data from the same 128 matched pairs are presented for males and females separately. When the sample is thus divided by sex of offspring, the overall difference between index and control offspring is no longer significant for either males or females. However, for the males, the percentage of severe and psychotic disturbances is significantly higher in the index male group (35.8%) than in the control group (15.1%) ($\chi^2 = 6.013$, $p = .014$). The difference between index and control females is not significant. The literature suggests that females become schizophrenic at a later age than do males. Hence, an index-control difference for the females may emerge as the adoptees pass more fully through the age of risk.

Taking the index adoptees separately, the males show a trend toward a higher percentage of severe disturbance (35.8%) than the females (22.7%) ($\chi^2 = 2.67$, $p = .102$); there is no such trend of difference between control males and control females.

RDC diagnoses. In calculating the preceding results, the biological index mother had had a hospital diagnosis of schizophrenia using Finnish criteria. In a review of the hospital records, these diagnoses were confirmed using RDC criteria for 88 index mothers of 93 offspring. Additionally, diagnoses are being checked for all biological mothers who are available, using PSE interviews and DSM-IIIR criteria. These results are not yet available; they will be especially important for the biological index mothers for whom the hospital records did not give sufficient information to meet specific RDC criteria for schizophrenia. Table 3 shows the results for the 93 index offspring of mothers with an RDC diagnosis of schizophrenia; 29 (31.2%) had a severe diagnosis as compared with 14 controls (15.1%) ($\chi^2 = 6.806$, $p = .0191$). Overall, the offspring of RDC schizophrenics are significantly more disturbed than the offspring of control mothers ($p = .0182$). Thus, the findings are essentially the same using Finnish diagnoses and RDC criteria with the hospital records.

Table 1. *Mental health ratings of adopted-away offspring*[a]

	Biological mothers' hospital diagnoses	
	Schizophrenic	Nonschizophrenic
	Index offspring	Control offspring
No diagnosis (Groups 1 + 2)	58	67
Neurosis (Group 3)	34	41
Borderline syndrome and severe personality disorder (Groups 4 + 5)	26	19
Psychosis (Group 6)[b]	10	1
Total	128	128

[a] 128 matched pairs at initial assessment, as of October 1987; $p = .0278$; one-tailed sign test for matched pairs, overall comparison

[b] Four additional psychotic adoptees (3 index, 1 control) have been identified as of October 1987. They are not included in this table because the matched control for one index case has not yet been studied, and 3 adoptees (2 index, 1 control) became psychotic after the initial assessment, according to changes reported in telephone follow-ups.

Table 2. *Mental health ratings of adopted-away offspring, males and females separately*[a]

	Males		Females	
	Biological mothers' diagnoses		Biological mothers' diagnoses	
	Schizophrenic	Nonschizophrenic	Schizophrenic	Nonschizophrenic
No diagnosis	22	24	36	43
Neurosis	12	21	22	20
Borderline syndrome and severe personality disorder	14	8	12	11
Psychosis	5	0	5	1
Total	53	53	75	75

[a] 128 matched pairs at initial assessment, as of October 1987; $p = .0825$ for males, $p = .1016$ for females; one-tailed sign test for matched pairs

Total sample data. When subjects are included who are in matched groups but not in matched pairs, the currently available sample expands to 134 index cases and 153 control cases, including some second controls (see Tienari et al., 1987c, for details). When telephone follow-up data are included, the adoptee outcomes as of October 1987, reveal a total of 15

Table 3. *RDC diagnoses of biological mothers and mental health ratings of their adopted-away offspring*[a]

	Biological mothers' hospital diagnoses	
	Schizophrenic	Nonschizophrenic
	Index offspring	Control offspring
No diagnosis	42	51
Neurosis	22	28
Borderline syndrome and severe personality disorder	21	13
Psychosis	8	1
Total	93	93

[a] 93 matched pairs at initial assessment, as of October 1987; $p = .0182$ one-tailed sign test for matched pairs

Table 4. *Global adoptive family ratings and adoptee diagnoses for index cases and their matched-pair controls*

	Global adoptive family ratings							
	Total N		Healthy		Neurotic		Severe	
Adoptee disturbance	Index	Control	Index	Control	Index	Control	Index	Control
Healthy	58	67	41	35	11	21	6	11
Neurotic	34	41	7	11	12	16	15	14
Borderline syndrome and severe personality disorder	26	17	2	1	6	8	18	8
Psychotic	8	1	0	0	3	0	5	1
Total	126	126	50	47	32	45	44	34

Note: In comparison to Table 1 with 128 matched pairs, this table omits two pairs in which the adoptive family ratings are not available.

psychotic adoptees, 13 index, and 2 controls, (9 identified in direct initial assessments, 3 through registers, and 3 through follow-up telephone interviews). Of the 13 index cases, 7 are schizophrenic, 4 paranoid psychotic, and 2 manic-depressive psychotic. Both of the control subjects are schizophrenic.

Age corrections. The adoptees' ages covered a wide range, up to age 61. Thus far, a total of 78 adoptees have been interviewed initially when they were under age 20. Using Weinberg's abridged method, the age-corrected

Table 5. *Adoptees with one or both severely disturbed adoptive parents*

| | Parental mental health ratings | | | |
	Severely disturbed parent and spouse, no diagnosis	Severely disturbed parent and neurotic spouse	Severely distrubed parent and severely disturbed spouse	Total
No diagnosis	13	20	3	36
Neurotic	7	13	12	32
Borderline syndrome and severe personality disorder	2	10	15	27
Psychotic	1	0	3	4
Total	23	43	33	99

Note: At initial assessments as of October 1987: index and control adoptive families combined; only those 99 couples are included in which one or both parents are severely disturbed. $\chi^2 = 21.779$, df $= 6$, $p = .0013$

morbid risk figure for the schizophrenia subgroup is 10.77% among the index cases and 2.58% among the controls (4.17:1) in the total sample of 284 cases thus far studied. The risk figure in the index group is 16.92% for schizophrenia and paranoid psychosis combined, and 3.08% for manic-depressive psychosis.

According to Strömgren's (1938) calculations, the morbid risk figures are the following: for schizophrenia in the index group, 9.46% ; in the control group, 2.38% (3.97:1). The combined figure for schizophrenia plus paranoid psychosis in the index group was 14.87%; no paranoid or manic-depressive psychotics were in the control group.

Clinical adoptive family assessments

Global adoptive family ratings. If we look at the relation between the global mental health ratings of the adoptive families and the diagnostic ratings of the offspring, we see that in healthy-rearing families the adoptees have little serious mental illness *whether or not their biological mothers were schizophrenic* (see Table 4). In contrast to the healthy-rearing families, the adoptees have much more disturbance when the index or control adoptive-rearing families are disturbed, but more so in the index cases than in the control cases.

Individual adoptive parent ratings. In addition to making global family ratings, the adoptive family interviewers made individual diagnostic assessments of the adoptive parents. Wynne et al. (1977) had found that one healthy parent (as rated on tests) could seemingly compensate for the hypothesized impact of a disturbed spouse, so that offspring were much less disturbed when only one parent was disturbed.

In the Finnish sample, the clinical ratings of the adoptive-rearing parents appear to confirm Wynne et al.'s finding obtained with biological parents who also were rearing parents. When the individual ratings of the adoptive parents are considered in pairs, we found that when one of the adoptive parents (index and control cases combined) had been considered healthy and the other disturbed, the offspring had significantly more healthy ratings compared to the offspring of both parents rated as disturbed (see Table 5).

Test ratings of adoptive families.   An important methodological difficulty with the preceding clinical ratings of the adoptive families is that the same interviewer assessed the adoptive families to make global family ratings, individual parent ratings, and adoptee ratings. To check on the halo effect or bias that may have resulted, independently rated tests have been obtained for both the adoptive parents and adoptees.

MMPI adoptee ratings.   The MMPI ratings were assessed blindly by a psychologist who was not aware of either the clinical data for the biological adoptive parents or the mental health ratings of the adoptees. The MMPI ratings of the offspring were significantly correlated ($p<.001$) with clinical ratings made of them independently (Tienari et al., 1985*b*). The paranoia and schizophrenia scale ratings of the MMPI correlated highly significantly with the clinical ratings of the offspring. Furthermore, the offspring classified as "severely disturbed" in their MMPIs had been reared significantly more often in adoptive families clinically rated as severely disturbed ($p<.002$), thus confirming the relationship found between the clinical ratings of the adoptees and the clinical ratings of the adoptive families (Tienari et al., 1985*b*).

Rorschach adoptee ratings.   The individual Rorschach protocols ($N = 529$) have also been scored blindly with psychopathology ratings by five psychologists after a training and reliability check period. The weighted kappa reliability varied between different pairs of psychologists: from 0.529 ($p<.001$) to 0.710 ($p<.001$). These global psychopathology Rorschach ratings of the offspring correlated highly significantly with the clinical ratings made of them independently.

Further assessments along these lines will be carried out using other MMPI scoring procedures, as well as individual Rorschach assessments of communication deviance and thought disorder, in order to assess the individual characteristics of adopted-away offspring separately, insofar as possible, from the family system evaluation.

Beavers-Timberlawn family ratings. As another check on the independence of obtained ratings, we used the Beavers-Timberlawn Family Rating Scales (Lewis et al., 1976) on Couple Rorschach audiotapes (and separately on Family Rorschach audiotapes). A psychiatrist who had had no clinical contact with the families made these ratings of functioning by listening only to the audiotaped discussion of the adoptive parents as they were trying to reach agreement on the Rorschach percepts. Her ratings of the Couple Rorschach tests correspond significantly (p=.0019) to the clinical family ratings made by the psychiatrists (Tienari et al., 1985b). Furthermore, the Couple Rorschah ratings were significantly correlated (p = .002) with the clinical ratings of the adoptees (Tienari et al., 1985b).

Note that the offspring are not present in the Couple Rorschach sessions, so that their behavior does not bias these consensus Rorschach ratings. Also, the interviewer does not participate in the Couple Rorschach interaction. Taking the component Beavers-Timberlawn scales separately, Couple Rorschach ratings of family closeness, empathy, overt power relationships, and parental coalitions all correlated significantly (p<.05 or better) with the individual adoptee mental health ratings (Tienari et al., 1985b, 1987b, 1987d).

Logistic regression analysis. We have used mathematical models for studying the joint effects of genotype (G) and environment (E) on the liability to psychiatric illness, as described by Kendler and Eaves (1986). These methods test models in which the probability of illness in adoptees is a function of liability to illness. We have carried out several logistic regression analyses using different illness cut-off points for the dependent variable, which have been rated in six levels of psychopathology for the adoptees. Table 6 gives the results with a logistic regression model using the forward selection procedure to predict the two most serious levels of disorder (Levels 5 + 6, borderline syndrome + psychotic), versus the other levels (1–4, two levels of healthy, neurotic, and severe personality disorders). The independent genetic variable was indexed by schizophrenic versus nonschizophrenic status of the biological mother. The independent environmental variable was indexed by three levels of global adoptive family ratings: healthy, neurotic, and severely disturbed. In Table 6, if the p value of the improvement χ^2 is small, this means that a variable that has been included in the model gives more information (i.e., improves the model). In this model, the environmental variable, the genetic variable, and the interaction effect all significantly improve the model. When age, as an additional independent variable, was trichotomized (<20, 20–29, >29), the improvement was not significant (p = .629). In other analyses, we also included individual psychopathology ratings of the adoptive parents, but these were set aside by the computer program when global family ratings were included.

Table 6. *Logistic regression model (forward selection procedure): Prediction of serious disorders (borderline syndrome & psychosis) versus other disorders in adoptees*[a]

Step no.	Term entered	df	Logistical likelihood	Improvement χ^2	p-value	Goodness of fit χ^2	p-value
0			−93.635			60.075	0.000
1	Family global rating (E)	1	−73.523	40.223	0.000	19.852	0.227
2	Genetic variable (G)	1	−70.632	5.783	0.016	14.068	0.520
3	(E × G)	1	−68.210	4.844	0.028	9.224	0.816

[a] $N = 284$, 131 index cases, and 153 controls; 255 healthy, neurotic, and severe personality disorder offspring (Groups 1–4); 29 borderline or psychotic (Groups 5 and 6).

Discussion

Study modifications

If given an opportunity to replicate the study, we would broaden the sample to include all the biological mothers with a hospital diagnosis of functional psychosis. The concepts of psychiatric diagnoses have been modified since 1967–1968, when this study was planned. It would have been useful to include affective psychoses in order to check more specifically for the possible genetic risk for schizophrenia versus affective psychoses, as well as the possible differences in family rearing patterns.

Practical considerations made it necessary for us to investigate the families and their members in their homes. It was not realistic to invite these nonpatient families to a laboratory or a hospital. The number of refusals would probably have been high, which would have resulted in a sample bias, because the families with more psychopathology would have been more likely to refuse. Also, as we expected, valuable information on both verbal and nonverbal behavior of the family members has been obtained during these home visits, and the home visit has also improved the quality of our contact with the families.

There was, however, an administrative requirement that no more than one investigator be allowed to visit each family. Thus, the interviewer had to conduct all the interviews and tests of individual family members, the parents, and the family as a whole. But this meant that the same interviewer had to meet and rate both the parents and the adoptee. As a partial corrective to the possible bias ("halo effect"), we collected tape-recorded interview and test data that could be rated independently by other investigators. We also believed that multiple measures obtained from different procedures were superior to single measures in minimizing bias. Nevertheless, because of the possibility that the experimental procedures might be skewed in the home setting, we sought additional, independent test measures such as the MMPI and Rorschach.

These blind, independent ratings of the adoptees and adoptive parents provide preliminary data suggesting that the potential bias of the clinical raters who saw both the family and adoptee does not substantially influence the $G \times E$ interaction that has been observed.

Joint effects of genetic and environmental factors

The statistical interaction between the genetic and family environmental factors can be interpreted in several ways. It is possible that the genetic factors are specific and necessary and interact with nonspecific environmental factors. Another possibility is that the genetic factors are nonspecific and contribute to vulnerability to schizophrenia as well as to a wider variety of psychopathologies. Genetically transmitted vulnerability, to be expected in only a portion of those at risk, may be a necessary precondition for schizophrenia, but a disturbing rearing environment may also be significant in transforming the vulnerability into clinically overt schizophrenia. Being reared in a healthy family may also be a protective factor for a child at risk. Finally, there is the possibility that the genetic vulnerability of the offspring manifests itself in a way that includes dysfunction in the adoptive family.

Kendler and Eaves (1986) presented three major models for the joint effects of genes and environment on the liability to psychiatric illness: additive effects of the genotype and the environment; genetic control of sensitivity to the environment, which also can be described as environmental control of gene expression; and genetic control of exposure to the environment. These alternatives will be considered in a prospective study, now under way, in which a subsample of the adoptive families is studied prior to the onset of illness in the offspring. If the multiplicative, joint effects of genetic and environmental variables continue to be demonstrated in the prospective study, and if the issue of interviewer bias can be surmounted, the findings will lend support to the second model of Kendler and Eaves, that of genetic control of sensitivity to the environment.

The question of the direction of effects between adoptive parents and adoptees must remain open, but it should be reconsidered as soon as prospective data are available. This issue can be expressed as a question of whether the illness in the adoptees induces dysfunction in the adoptive parents, or whether parental dysfunction contributes to pathology in the adoptees, and parental healthy functioning promotes health in the adoptees despite the genetic risk associated with illness in a biological parent.

Developmental theorists generally believe that such effects become bidirectional over time, regardless of their origins. Nevertheless, the Finnish program will be the first attempt in schizophrenia research to combine the direct adoptive family strategy and the risk research strategy in order to study adoptive families and adoptees prospectively, beginning prior to the onset of illness in the offspring.

Acknowledgment

Supported by NIMH grant 5-R01-MH 39663-02 and by the Finnish Medical Research Council. Presented of Life History Research meeting, St. Louis, October 14, 1987.

References

Kendler, K. S., & Eaves, L. J. (1986). Models for the joint effects of genotype and environment on liability to psychiatric illness. *American Journal of Psychiatry, 143*, 279–298.

Kety, S. S., Rosenthal, D., Wender, P., Schulsinger, F., & Jacobson, B. (1978). The biologic and adoptive families of adopted individuals who became schizophrenic: Prevalence of mental illness and other characteristics. In L. C. Wynne, R. L. Cromwell, & S. Matthysse (Eds.), *The nature of schizophrenia: New approaches to research and treatment.* New York: John Wiley & Sons.

Laing, R. D., Philipson, H., & Lee, A. E. (1966). *Interpersonal perception: A theory and a method of research.* London: Tavistock.

Lewis, J. M., Beavers, W. R., Gossett, J. T., & Phillips, V. A. (1976). *No single thread: Psychological health in family systems.* New York: Brunner/Mazel.

Loveland, N. T., Wynne, L. C., & Singer, M. T. (1963). The family Rorschach: A method for studying family interaction. *Family Process, 2*, 187–215.

Rosenthal, D., Wender, P. H., Kety, S. S., Welner, J., & Schulsinger, F. (1971). The adopted-away offspring of schizophrenics. *American Journal of Psychiatry, 128*, 307–311.

Rosenthal, D., Wender, P. H., Kety S. S., Schulsinger, F., Welner, J., & Rieder, R. O. (1975). Parent-child relationships and psychopathological disorder in the child. *Archives of General Psychiatry, 32*, 466–476.

Strömgren, E. (1938). Beitrage zur psychiatrischen Erblehre. *Acta Psychiatrica (Kbh)*, supplement 19.

Tienari, P. Lathi, I., Sorri, A., Naarala, M. Morning, J., Wahlberg, K.-E., & Wynne, L. C. (1987a). The Finnish adoptive family study of schizophrenia. *Journal of Psychiatric Research, 21*, 437–445.

Tienari, P., Lahti, I., Sorri, A., Naarala, M., Wahlberg, K.-E., Rönkkö, T., Moring J., & Wynne, L. C. (1987b). The Finnish adoptive family study of schizophrenia: Possible joint effects of vulnerability and family interaction. In K. Hahlweg & M. J. Goldstein (Eds.), *Understanding major mental disorder: The contribution of family interaction research.* New York: Family Process Press.

Tienari, P., Sorri, A., Lahti, I., Naarala, M., Wahlberg, K.-E., Moring, J., Pohjola, J., & Wynne, L. C., (1987c). Genetic and psychosocial factors in schizophrenia: The Finnish adoptive family study. *Schizophrenia Bulletin, 13,* 477–484.

Tienari, P., Sorri, A., Lahti, I., Naarala, M., Wahlberg, K.-E., Rönkkö, T., Moring, J., & Pohjola, J., (1987*d*). Family environment and the etiology of schizophrenia: Implications from the Finnish adoptive family study of schizophrenia. In H. Stierlin, F. B. Simon, & G. Schmidt (Eds.), *Familiar realities: The Heidelberg conference.* New York: Brunner/Mazel.

Tienari, P., Sorri, A., Lahti, I, Naarala, M., Wahlberg, K.-E., Pohjola, J., & Moring, J. (1985*a*), Interaction of genetic and psychosocial factors in schizophrenia. *Acta Psychiatrica Scandinavica, 71,* (319), 19–30.

Tienari, P., Sorri, A., Lahti, I, Naarala, M., Wahlberg, K.-E., Rönkkö, T., Pohjola, J., & Moring, J. (1985*b*). The Finnish adoptive family study of schizophrenia. *Yale Journal of Biology and Medicine, 58,* 227–237.

Wender, P. H., Rosenthal, D., & Kety, S. S. (1968). A psychiatric assessment of the adoptive parents of schizophrenics. In D. Rosenthal & S. S. Kety (Eds.), *The transmission of schizophrenia.* Oxford: Pergamon.

Wynne, L. C., Singer, M. T., Bartko, J. J., & Toohey, M. L. (1977). Schizophrenics and their families: Research on parental communication. In J. M. Tanner (Ed.), *Developments in psychiatric research.* London: Hodder & Stoughton.

Wynne, L. C., Singer, M. T., & Toohey, M. L. (1976). Communication of the adoptive parents of schizophrenics. In J. Jørstad & E. Ugelstad (Eds.), *Schizophrenia 75: Psychotherapy, family studies, research.* Oslo: Universitetsforlaget.

Index

Numbers in italics refer to figures and tables.